# Shakespeare Left and Right

# Shakespeare Left and Right

EDITED BY IVO KAMPS



ROUTLEDGE NEW YORK AND LONDON

Published in 1991 by

Routledge
An imprint of Routledge, Chapman and Hall, Inc.
29 West 35th Street
New York, NY 10001

Published in Great Britain by

Routledge
11 New Fetter Lane
London EC4P 4EE



Printed in the United States of America



**Library of Congress Cataloging-in-Publication Data**

Shakespeare left and right / [edited by] Ivo Kamps.
p. cm.
Includes bibliographical references.
ISBN 0-415-90375-0.—ISBN 0-415-90376-9 (pbk.)
1. Shakespeare, William, 1564–1616—Criticism and interpretation—History—20th century. 2. Shakespeare, William 1564–1616—Political and social views. 3. Political plays, English—History and criticism. 4. Social problems in literature. I. Kamps, Ivo.
PR2970.S52 1991
822.3′3—dc20 91-22707
CIP

**British Library of Congress data also available.**

. . . for the eye sees not itself
But by reflection, by some other things.

—*Julius Caesar*

# Contents

Acknowledgments ix

1. Introduction: Ideology and Its Discontents
*Ivo Kamps* 1

Part I. Critique and/or Ideology

2. Ideological Criticism and Pluralism
*Richard Levin* 15

3. The Myth of Neutrality, Again?
*Gayle Greene* 23

4. Where Does Ideology Hang Out?
*Michael D. Bristol* 31

5. MLA Response to Levin, Greene, and Bristol
*Victoria Kahn* 45

6. Reply to Michael Bristol and Gayle Greene
*Richard Levin* 47

7. Straw Women and Whipping Girls: The (Sexual) Politics of Critical Self-Fashioning
*Carol Cook* 61

8. Against "Ideology"
*Edward Pechter* 79

9. Ordinary People and Academic Critics: A Response to Richard Levin
*Gerald Graff* 99

10. Commentary: "You've Got a Lot of Nerve"
*Michael Sprinker* 115

Part II. Ideology and Critical Practice

11. Character and Ideology in Shakespeare
*Joseph A. Porter* 131

12. Violence and Gender Ideology in *Coriolanus* and *Macbeth*
*Marilyn L. Williamson* 147

13. "A Woman's War": A Feminist Reading of *Richard II*
*Graham Holderness* 167

14. *Julius Caesar*, Allan Bloom, and the Value of Pedagogical Pluralism
*Darryl J. Gless* 185

15. Transfer of Title in *Love's Labor's Lost*: Language, Individualism, Gender
*Katharine Eisaman Maus* 205

16. On the Continuity of the *Henriad*: A Critique of Some Literary and Theatrical Approaches
*Harry Berger, Jr.* 225

17. "The King Hath Many Marching in His Coats," or, What Did You Do During the War, Daddy?
*David Scott Kastan* 241

18. A Tale of Two Branaghs: *Henry* V, Ideology, and the Mekong Agincourt
*Chris Fitter* 259

19. Commentary: "In the Destructive Element Immersed"
*Lawrence Danson* 277

20. Afterword: Poetics from the Barrel of a Gun?
*Linda Woodbridge* 285

Bibliography 299

Index 325

Contributors 333

# Acknowledgments

The first four papers printed after the "Introduction" in this volume were initially presented at a Special Session of the Modern Language Association on "The Role of Ideology in the Criticism and Metacriticism of Shakespeare" held in Washington, D.C. in 1989. A portion of Richard Levin's "Ideological Criticism and Pluralism" is also included in a book tentatively entitled *Professing Shakespeare Now*, edited by Robert Merrix and Nicholas Ranson, forthcoming from the Edwin Mellen Press. Sections of Graham Holderness's essay were included earlier in his contribution to *Critical Essays on "Richard II,"* edited by Bryan Loughrey and Linda Cookson (Harlow: Longman, 1989), and in "Der Widerspenstigen Zahmung: Eine Art Historie," *Shakespeare Jahrbuch* (1988). I wish to thank the editors and publishers of these publications for their permission to reprint these materials here.

Diana Fuss was extremely helpful in getting this project off the ground in the first place. Without her I doubt there would have been a *Shakespeare Left and Right*. In the course of the incubation period required to produce a collection like this one, I no doubt incurred more debts than I can here record or remember. But I would like to mention and thank Tom Roche and Robert Mack who offered encouragement and advice over many a lunch. Looking back on how I came to be editor of a collection of this kind, I realize I owe an enormous debt to Mary Ann Klein, Joe Messina, and especially Mowbray Allan, who first introduced me to the joys and hazards of a good academic debate. To acknowledge a recent and most notable debt, I should mention four contributors to this collection who were also my teachers in graduate school: Lawrence Danson and Victoria Kahn at Princeton, and Richard Levin and Michael Sprinker at Stony Brook. I feel quite fortunate to have studied with four such eminent and fundamentally different scholars, but I'm also slightly astonished to have been able to bring them "together" in one book.

I should also wish to thank William Germano, who had enough faith in this project to give a book contract to a novice editor. At the University of Mississippi, Sara Selby skillfully crafted and re-crafted the bibliography. Carel Kamps was a great help in putting the index together. A special thanks goes to Carla Sommerstein and the production staff at Routledge. Ms. Sommerstein's diligence and professionalism made the production of this volume a truly pleasant and instructive experience for its editor.

I owe a life-long debt to my Dutch mate, economist Guus Ankum, with whom the debate over Left and Right continues.

As always the most irreplaceable contribution was made by Deborah and Malcolm, who put things in the proper perspective.

# 1

# Introduction: Ideology and its Discontents

**Ivo Kamps**

> As the rhythmic words subside/ My Common Ground invites you in/ or do you prefer to wait outside/ Or is it true/ The Common Ground for me is without you . . . Oh is it true/ There's no Ground Common enough for me and you.

Are recent methods of literary scholarship causing literature and art in general to be displaced by politics? The question implies a fundamental opposition between them—an opposition which is real and permanent to many traditionalists but which is deeply ideological to many feminist, Marxist, and new historicist readers of Shakespeare.[1] Put simply, the prevailing sentiment on the Right is that Shakespeare transcends his historical moment—he is not for an age but for all time—because his genius allowed him to capture what is most true, universal, and enduring about human nature. A recent wave of counter-criticism, however, has focused close attention on the various ways in which the playwright's texts participate in, are subversive of, or reflect on Renaissance institutional practice and ideologies designed to oppress and control the people. Both these approaches to Shakespeare are ideological, and both are, for different reasons and to different degrees (discussed in detail in this volume), prone to disguising their ideological content. Traditional criticism, in particular, is ordinarily aligned with the dominant culture and contains little or no impetus in its politics or method for self-critique.[2] In addition to a greater self-awareness, a large contingent of Marxist, cultural materialist, and feminist critics consider it a crucial part of their mission not only to reinterpret Shakespeare but also to expose the conservative ideologies which quietly shape the orthodox readings of the plays.[3]

During the last decade, the literary criticism of the Left has matured to the extent that it has come to represent a powerful and viable alternative to the old historicism and New Criticism which have dominated English departments for the better portion of this century.[4] Whereas a radical approach to literature might have presented traditionalists with an unpleasant anomaly in the not too distant past, today there is a feeling of deep apprehension among many of them that the Left will soon control English departments, the curriculum, and the professional journals and university presses—an apprehension manifesting itself in the call to rescue the traditional canon of Western Civilization from being dislodged from anthologies and course syllabi by the literatures of women, minorities, and ideologues.

Although Richard Levin would robustly reject the suggestion that he is anxious about the inroads made by the Left in the academy,[5] he nonetheless has taken it upon himself to critique a variety of its methodological and ideological assumptions. *Shakespeare Left and Right* grew out of a Special Session of the Modern Language Association on the Role of Ideology in Shakespeare studies, held in Washington, D.C., in December 1989. I proposed the Session to the MLA organizers for a very specific reason: to facilitate in a public forum the continuation of a rather heated if not bitter exchange in *PMLA*'s Forum over the publication of Richard Levin's "Feminist Thematics and Shakespearean Tragedy." A letter to the editor, cosigned by 24 scholars, denounced Levin's essay as a paternalistic, reductive, "tired, muddled, unsophisticated" piece unworthy of publication in *PMLA* (Adelman et al. 77–78). At the close of his Forum Reply to his 24 detractors, Levin registered his dismay at what he perceived as a lack of substance concerning the charges brought against him. He expressed the hope to engage his critics at some point "into a real discussion of the issues" (79) he had tried to raise, so that some kind of consensus might be attained. I felt that such a discussion—the record of which is printed in part one of this volume—should take place for at least three reasons.

First, with the publication of "Feminist Thematics" in the profession's supposed flagship journal, Richard Levin touched (perhaps inadvertently) on matters of tremendous significance to critics on the Left and the Right. For reasons explored in detail in this collection, Levin's essay and the Forum letter brought to the fore urgent questions about censorship, oppression, discrimination, and reverse discrimination—all of which have a direct bearing on the national debate over politics and art. For anyone like myself who believes that the aesthetic and the ideological are necessarily intertwined in literature and literary criticism, a controversy which makes this alliance explicit is of intrinsic interest. Second, like many others, I was deeply intrigued to learn what the "real discussion" Levin had alluded to would sound like, if indeed the opposing voices in this debate could come to some kind of shared understanding as to what in fact the salient "issues" are.

Third, a vigorous public exchange between advocates of established and new critical approaches is in itself an infrequent and exciting phenomenon, and therefore worthy of further consideration. While critical innovation is always indebted to already institutionalized modes of critical discourse, it is also true that new critical movements almost invariably carve themselves a place in the academy at the expense of established approaches. New approaches, driven by an assortment of professional and ideological factors, routinely seize upon elements in traditional approaches (considered no longer compelling) for the specific purpose of replacing or displacing them. Names like *New* Criticism, *new* historicism, *post*-structuralism, and *de*construction signal an unmistakable effort to supersede and displace that which came before. Given a view of the university which emphasizes tenure and career, there is, of course, nothing surprising about this. What is surprising is that established scholars in the later stages of their careers rarely defend themselves in print against these efforts to displace them, to render them largely obsolete.[6] Richard Levin is one of the most vocal exceptions to this rule.[7] Publishing his views in such prominent journals as *PMLA*, *Textual Practice*, *Modern Philology*, and *New Literary History*, he may be the only representative of a generation of scholars of the Renaissance drama trained in the 1950s who is trying not only to hold his critical ground but who has also launched an admonishing and systematic offensive against the new critical schools.

Levin's effort is, needless to say, provocative and also potentially useful to Shakespeare studies for a number of reasons. It presents feminist, neo-Marxist, and new historicist criticism with a challenge, one which would ideally help these approaches strengthen their interpretative methods. Second, Levin's work indirectly gives us a complex but instructive picture of the mind set of a segment of the profession by appealing, according to Carol Cook, to an "audience of traditional literary scholars who have felt displaced and bypassed by the rapid movement of literary theory into new difficult areas." Levin may well wish to distance himself from some of the reactionary voices that are speaking out in his defense, but, as Cook argues, it is too late for that now: these voices have been encouraged to speak by "the appeal of Levin's essay and the 'us against the feminist hordes' mentality it endorses." Finally, Levin's work is useful simply because he *reads* and *engages* the new criticisms in the pages of some of our profession's most prestigious journals. Speaking for a group of feminist critics, who first emerged during the late 1970s and early 1980s, Gayle Greene laments the fact that "older colleagues don't read us," and that "contemporaries and younger colleagues . . . either ignore us . . . or attempt to climb to the top on our bodies."[8] Greene cares little for the way Levin reads feminist criticism of Shakespeare, but, as she noted in a verbal aside that day in Washington, *at least* Levin reads us.

The MLA Session papers by Levin, Greene, Michael D. Bristol, and respondent Victoria Kahn, and the subsequent labors of Gerald Graff, Edward Pechter, Carol Cook, and Michael Sprinker certainly do not produce the consensus Levin is in search of, but they do help to clarify some of the local tensions and, more importantly, the larger issues at stake in the Levin controversy.[9] Taken as a whole, the essays in part one resolve some of the specific points of friction between Levin and his detractors, but they also aim to take up broader issues suggested by this debate: how—if at all—do critics communicate with each other? what is the role played by ideology in such communications? and what are the possibilities for a critique of ideology (something which both Levin and his Marxist and feminist detractors hold out for).

If the contributors to part one are primarily concerned with theory and ideology, the essays in part two of this book seek to make visible the ideology or value systems implicitly present in literary criticism of the plays and/or in the plays themselves. For example, in his essay on *Julius Caesar*, Darryl J. Gless reflects on the "processes of reading which have helped make Allan Bloom a popular cultural commentator, and helped him make Shakespeare father to his own patterns of blindness and bias." Joseph A. Porter explores the role of ideology in the construction and development of the term "character" in Shakespeare studies by looking at what "character" meant to Samuel Johnson, Maurice Morgann, S. T. Coleridge, William Hazlitt and more recent critics. Harry Berger, Jr., in turn, critiques a number of critical approaches (including those generated by the Left) to the *Henriad*, shows where they are reductive, and proceeds to construct a complex new "rhizomatic" model of reading designed specifically for the *Henriad*. In his essay on *1 Henry IV*, David Scott Kastan takes issue with Stephen Greenblatt's theory of containment and the idea that the theater merely produces and legitimizes "the ideology of royal power." Following a recent trend among historicist critics to hold out for "a space for the resistance to power,"[10] Kastan points out that "the labile and unlegitimated representations of the popular theater prevent the drama, regardless of any overt political intentions . . . from simply reproducing the dominant ideology." He then goes on to examine the subversive impact of the subplot on the representation of monarchal authority in the play. Chris Fitter mounts a polemical attack against Kenneth Branagh's film of *Henry V*, which he argues "immorally" resanctifies an Anglophone imperialism which Shakespeare's play demystifies.

In a conscious effort to include the important work done in gender studies which, as Gayle Greene has noted, is often allotted only limited space in revisionary anthologies on the Renaissance, part two of this book also presents four essays with an explicitly feminist orientation. In addition to Gless's reconsideration of Portia's profound impact on Brutus and *Julius Caesar* as a whole, Graham Holderness retrieves from *Richard II* "vestigial traces of femininity"; while Katharine Eisaman Maus demonstrates that *Love's Labor's Lost*'s linguistic issues, frequently discussed in a supposedly neutral context, are in fact "inseparable from [the play's] generic, comic concern with sexual politics and with the construction of a gendered identity in a social context." Marilyn L. Williamson explores the surplus of violence produced when gender ideology is intruded upon by political ideology in *Coriolanus* and *Macbeth*.

In our society, ideology is something of a dirty word. It's a word politicians (and literary critics) use to discredit and to dismiss their otherwise "distinguished" opponents. In the public arena of contemporary American politics, ideology seems primarily associated with voices of the extreme Left or Right. Conceivably, this is the historical residue of potent anti-Nazi and cold war propaganda machines. Notwithstanding the fact that the old apparatus has momentarily stalled, the term ideology still generally connotes political extremism and an anti-democratic agenda. The availability of the term therefore offers an instant opportunity to smear anyone willing to use it against a political adversary (regardless of the adversary's actual politics). Ideology deserves a better fate, not least because it is a far more subtle and sophisticated concept, but also because it offers a powerful analytical tool capable of exposing the political agenda of those who distort its meaning.

Louis Althusser argues with cogency that "those who are in ideology believe themselves by definition outside ideology" (175). His point is that none of us, regardless of our race, gender, class or education, is in a position to transcend social, economic, and institutional constraints placed on us in the historical moment. We may be capable of rising above some of the forces that constitute our context, but not all. In trying to articulate the delicate balance between human autonomy and wholesale determinism, Marx declared that "men make their own history but not under conditions of their own choosing" (*Eighteenth Brumaire* 15). For Althusser, the economic and social "conditions" under which we make our choices always remain mystified to a significant degree. But this is only in part due to the presence of ideology as a recognizable and definable body of doctrine or "false consciousness" put to work by a powerful elite for the purpose of oppressing the members of the lower strata of the society. Althusser's "ideology" is also an inescapable mode of cognition, a mode which finds expression in the "imaginary relationship of individuals to their real conditions of existence" (162). However, since we do not experience this "relationship" as imaginary, it becomes clear that ideology, in a sense, is not "false consciousness," but consciousness itself. The cognitive view, which holds any specific embodiment of ideology to be illusory (alluding to reality without corresponding to that reality), has a history prior to Althusser's powerful articulation of it. We find the idea implanted in what Voloshinov described in the 1920s as a group or society's "lived," "most fundamental" and inarticulable "social evaluations." And Jonathan Dollimore has recently argued that Montaigne's conception of custom, defined "as embedded in social practices, institutions and rituals," already shares crucial features of "ideology" (*Radical Tragedy* 18). As Michael Sprinker has noted, on the whole, "the impact of Althusserianism in the United States has never been especially great" (*Imaginary Relations* 2), but the recent predilection in the academy for a politically self-conscious criticism, combined with the powerful promise of new interpretive strategies afforded by a conception of ideology as partially invisible or silent (to be recouped by the critic), has granted the broader definition of ideology tremendous currency in Renaissance literary studies.

This is not to suggest that the more orthodox view of ideology as a definable body of doctrine has disappeared from the political arena or the academy. On the contrary, if anything the Reagan-Bush era has helped to foster an unequivocal reaffirmation of the position that it is always the "other" who is ideological. For instance, a television commercial for the reelection of North Carolina Senator Jesse Helms in 1990 labeled Helms's Democratic opponent as a champion of "liberal values" while ascribing to the Senator, *by contrast*, "North Carolina values." In the ad, "liberal" clearly stands for a political ideology, while Helms attempts to equate himself with the fundamental identity and values of the state. That North Carolina is a state deeply divided on a wide range of political/ideological issues—a division which precisely calls the state's identity into question—is of course overlooked. Helms's effort to transcend actual political conditions may appear all too transparent and feeble, but Althusser's observation about our inhabitation of ideology (despite our conviction that we are outside of it) does raise some serious epistemological dilemmas. How, if we are all *in* ideology, is it possible to offer an objective critique of even so simplistic an example as the Helms commercial—let alone the work of a sophisticated literary critic or a Renaissance playwright?

If we are all in ideology, then it would only be reasonable to assume that every critique of ideology is itself necessarily ideological. Every critique would require its own critique, and so on, producing an infinite regress of critiques without any hope for non-ideological knowledge. Bristol and Sprinker press for a scientific approach to ideology, while Richard Levin suggests that we can only resolve the present epistemological dilemma by appealing to objectivism, pluralism, and rationalism. In Levin's view, we gain objective knowledge of a text by defining knowledge within the parameters of the particular critical approach that gathers it. If one proceeds in this way, Levin maintains, "various approaches can attain such knowledge in their own terms, since they are not 'intervening' to 'produce' different objects but are only different ways of viewing the object." Reason, which Levin holds to be "neutral," is called on to perform a critique of a given approach, for instance, by reproving it "for being inconsistent with the postulates of that approach." For Levin, reason thus promotes meaningful communication between critics of different methodological and political persuasions without running the risk of reducing literary criticism into an argument about politics. Most of Levin's co-contributors share a desire for better communications, but Greene, Bristol, Kahn, and Pechter all seem to agree that an appeal to "neutral reason" serves, in the words of Gerald Graff, only "to reproduce the circularity in which the [present] controversy has been trapped," insofar as it ignores the complex matrix of socio-historical and ideological circumstances which shape, guide, and press "reason" into service. Victoria Kahn, who agrees with Levin that there is no "univocal" connection *per se* between a critic's politics and her critical practice, insists that this hardly dissociates critical method from ideology, "precisely because, as Bristol and Greene argue, ideology is not simply a consciously held position." "To recognize this tie is not to reduce art to politics [as Levin would have it]," but rather to acknowledge that texts, regardless of their intended purpose, necessarily contain sets of ideological values. It is for this reason that Gayle Greene exhorts "all critics [to] acknowledge the ideological and political and gendered bases of their judgments."

But this does not remove the epistemological barrier to a non-ideological critique. In fact, Edward Pechter posits (after scrutinizing the efforts of several neo-Marxist critics) that such a critique is simply "unattainable." He further urges that we jettison the term ideology altogether because if "everything is ideology" then "nothing is ideology": "ideology is a positive term without a difference."

By no means do I wish to minimize the logical force and cogency which inform Pechter's stance "against ideology," but I should note here that elimination of the term ideology would mean erasure of the very term that has made a *new* kind of political criticism possible. It is precisely the tendency of much literary criticism (on both the Left and Right) to present itself as non-ideological or apolitical that makes the availability of the most sophisticated notion of ideology as an analytical tool so useful and necessary. Not, as Althusser would have it, so that we can "interpret" and "discover the reality of the world behind

[the] imaginary representation of that world" (162), but to "interpret" the "representation" in such a way that the social and political values that shape and inform it become visible, intelligible, and articulable.

What we must do, it seems to me, is to give up the demand that a critique of ideology be objective in any absolute sense. Such a demand is itself already profoundly ideological (not objective or impartial) and establishes an arbitrary hierarchy of knowledge that seeks to silence or dominate alternative modes of inquiry.[11] A critique of ideology that acknowledges its positional status is not free from implying the existence of a hierarchy of knowledge (on the contrary, I think that on some level we all value certain ways of reading over others), but it makes that hierarchy an overt and therefore political feature of the critical debate. The *un*conscious dimension of ideology—a dimension which suggests that no critic can ever tell the whole story—is only a relative hindrance here to the execution of a successful critique. As we are shaped by and respond to our ever changing social, economic, and ideological circumstances, we change our values and critical methods and thereby facilitate the exposure of hitherto invisible (or unconscious) ideologies in texts. Such new exposures, needless to say, do not produce unmediated truth. However, "the point is not," in the words of Graff, "that there is no truth but that truth is never politically neutral . . . ."

Yet there has been a chorus of voices objecting to the (Left's) politicization of literature. In *The Death of Literature*, for example, Alvin Kernan laments that the new critical approaches strip literature of "positive value" and "social usefulness," and empty it "out in the service of social and political causes that are considered more important then the texts themselves" (212, 213). If we wish literature to survive, Kernan maintains, critics should cease viewing it as "the instrument of oppression, furthering imperialism and colonialism, establishing male hegemony, suppressing any movement towards freedom from authority" (213). I empathize with the author's serious qualms about using literature as an ideological whipping boy. Nonetheless, I would argue that in our particular historical moment there is definite "positive value" in exposing and resisting political, racial, or gender-based oppression if and when we encounter it in literary texts, as well as in our own readings or in those of others.

The chances that a new reading of a Shakespeare play will noticeably affect our world are negligible. And yet there is clear value in literary interpretation, particularly in the classroom, because it offers us a chance to try to provide students with some type of antidote to the lack of encouragement for independent thought offered by political and educational institutions, as well as by the media. In his *Necessary Illusions*, a seminal study of the North American media, eminent linguist and political scientist Noam Chomsky submits compelling evidence that the media, despite frequent charges of subversiveness against it, induce "conformity" by reducing the "general public . . . to its traditional apathy and obedience," and by driving it "from the arena of political debate and action" (10, 3). In practically every segment of our culture, there is a tendency to limit severely "the range of opinion permitted expression" (12); the result is an insidiously manufactured social consensus. In this volume, Michael Bristol argues against Levin's call for pluralism—in which all approaches are "seen as equally valid"—precisely because it would "*block* any social consensus at the point where it might ensue in social action." Bristol's observations appear to contradict Chomsky's. However, Chomsky's "engineering of consent" and Bristol's pacifying pluralism essentially amount to the same thing: they describe a society in which moderate differences are allowed to exist, but within which there is no opportunity for true opposition. As a society with a tradition of anti-intellectualism, we are not inclined to self-scrutiny. For most of our students, it is simply easier to be a traditionalist than a radical, or even a skeptic. It's more natural to belong than to question. Indeed, a Budweiser television commercial, geared toward young people nation-wide (including those attending colleges and universities), takes the prohibition on critical debate to its most extreme form in its current slogan: "Why ask why?"—the suggestion being that a six-pack is a preferable alternative to pondering life's questions. In combatting this state of affairs, we aren't—or at least I'm not—talking about revolution but about "a course of intellectual self-defense" (Chomsky viii). I utterly agree with Victoria Kahn that we simply can't give up on "the possibility of persuasion and critique"; if we do the rest will indeed be silence.

When, for example, in *Julius Caesar* Brutus pleads with the plebeians to be absolved of the assassination because it was committed on behalf of Rome—"Who is here so vile that will not love his country?" (3.1.32–33)[12]—it could be productive to urge students to note a parallel to another Republican party which, enthralled by last winter's military victory, sought to translate the success of Patriot missiles into popular support by equating uncritical support of the war against Iraq with being a good American. "Who is here so vile that will not love his country?" And one could further stress a crucial difference between the two situations. While the politically naive Brutus allows rival Mark Antony to speak beside the bleeding body of Caesar, our administration, during the period of the military build-up, made a concerted effort to limit the political debate about the pending war. It is unquestionably disturbing to see that a simplistic equation between patriotism and support for the war can be so effective, and that the government of a democratic nation seeks to curb public debate; but it is outright frightening that during the period of post-war euphoria it became an un-American act even to *suggest* a fuller discussion of the politics and attitudes that drove us over the brink of war.[13]

Notwithstanding the serious objections that have been raised against using literary interpretation in the classroom to promote increased social and political awareness,[14] the university and the works of Shakespeare are in some sense the ideal site on which to conduct such a critique. Since Shakespeare, as the central pillar of the literary establishment, is still by far the most frequently taught English author, critiques of his works and his commentators reach a proportionally large audience. What's more, the still popular notion of literature as somehow transcending immediate social and political circumstances, and its confinement to the classroom, have largely left the question of what is to be done with literature to those who teach it (see Kernan, *Death* 11-31). University professors are often considered to be living in their "own little world." Hence, teachers and critics of literature in general (but feminists, Marxists, new historicists, psychoanalytic critics, and deconstructionists in particular) resemble the Renaissance dramatists themselves, who practiced their craft outside the London city limits, in the relative safety of the geographical and social margin, and outside the immediate control of the city fathers. Moreover, like the dramatists whose marginal status did not prevent royal patronage or a full pit, teachers of literature too enjoy a measure of state and private support and are able to reach a significant segment of our population in the classroom. We may be far removed from the centers of political power, but we are in a powerful position.

For the present editor, the overall aim of *Shakespeare Left and Right* is less to elevate the political Left over the Right (or vice versa), or to emphasize the importance of a leftist critique of neo-conservative and/or liberal humanist critics who disguise the ideological nature of their enterprise (or vice versa), than to demonstrate the operation of ideology in literary and critical texts and to demonstrate how different modes of analysis can locate and explore those ideologies. To do otherwise is to further the anti-participatory trend in our democratic system: the number of voters declines steadily, political incumbents are reelected at astonishingly high rates, and sometimes even run unopposed, despite the public's overwhelming dissatisfaction with the budget debacle of November 1990. A primary goal in teaching my Shakespeare course, therefore, is to try to make sure that students do not accept unthinkingly any reading of Shakespeare—Left or Right. The test of a shrewd analysis is not whether it produces the truth, but whether it can recognize what is at stake in adopting one system of representation over another.

To those conservatives who must insist that literature is by nature apolitical and that only the Left politicizes literature, I can only say that although the current historical tide does not indicate this, perhaps the day will come when feminists or Marxists will control political institutions and dominate the media and educational system. If it does, and if the new power were to utilize the state apparatus successfully for the rationalization, naturalization, and legitimization of their ideological program, then the Right might well wish to abandon its current notion of "neutral" reason (because the new ideology would successfully have claimed a new "neutral" reason for itself) and dust off Althusser's conception of ideology in order to assail the new hegemony.

## NOTES

1. For a cogent humanistic overview of the relationship between aesthetics and ideology, see Kernan, "Ideology as Aesthetics" (*Death of Literature* 11–31); for a full-scale consideration of the question from a Marxist point of view, see Eagleton, *The Ideology of the Aesthetic*.

2. It should be said that the Left shows a greater willingness to scrutinize its critical and political premises, except perhaps when such scrutiny comes from the Right. Although this charge is commonly brought against the Right, it cannot be denied that the Left also disguises its politics. In the "Introduction" to his excellent *Alternative Shakespeares*, for example, editor John Drakakis suggests with misplaced confidence that the contributors to his volume are in a position to examine the record "disinterestedly" (25).

3. See, for example, Francis Barker and Peter Hulme; Bristol, *Shakespeare's America*; Jacqueline Rose; Dollimore and Sinfield, "History and Ideology."

4. See Walter Cohen, "Political Criticism."

5. Indeed, Levin suggests that feminism has allowed for new critical insights and is probably here to stay and "have a permanent effect on the field," while Marxism, given the collapse of the East Block countries, will probably disappear from English departments (this volume).

6. Several other Renaissance scholars of Levin's generation were invited to contribute to part one of the present volume, but all of them declined. More than a dozen scholars with a feminist orientation declined to contribute for a variety of reasons, including constraints of time and previous commitments, but also, for some of them, because of a conscious decision not to lend credence to Levin's arguments by engaging them (a sentiment shared, to a degree, by some who did contribute, i.e. Sprinker and Woodbridge).

7. See the bibliography.

8. All quotations in the introduction are from essays printed in this volume, unless noted otherwise.

9. The essays in part one of this volume relate to each other in a way that is not self-evident. Levin's "Ideological Criticism and Pluralism" was written first and distributed to the other panelists, including respondent Victoria Kahn, some time before the MLA session took place. After the session, Levin was given the papers by Bristol, Greene, and Kahn, on which he based his "Reply to Michael Bristol and Gayle Greene." All the other contributors to part one, with the exception of Edward Pechter (who finished his contribution to the debate before Levin completed

his second essay) had the opportunity to read the Special Session papers, as well as Levin's second contribution. Only Carol Cook and Michael Sprinker were in a position to comment on all the materials included in part one.

10. See, for example, Annabel Patterson 13–31; Dollimore's "Introduction" to *Political Shakespeare*; and John Turner's "Introduction" to Holderness, Potter, and Turner.

11. See, for example, Edward Pechter, who contends that Levin's objective critique and neutral reason are geared toward a "restoration of consensus" which serves Levin's politics and which is wholly undesirable to feminist critics such as Gayle Greene.

12. *The Complete Works*, ed. David Bevington.

13. With this example, I don't mean to suggest that only Republican administrations are guilty of such stifling tactics; nor do I of course believe that discussions of Shakespeare should be limited to or even primarily consist of the drawing of parallels to contemporary events.

14. For an astute rehearsal of some of the difficulties involved in and a practical solution to using the classroom as something other than a complex extension of the state apparatus, see Margaret Ferguson's "Afterword" to *Shakespeare Reproduced*.

# I

# Critique and/or Ideology

# 2

# Ideological Criticism and Pluralism

Richard Levin

I want to thank Mr. Kamps and the Program Committee for this opportunity to fulfill the hope I expressed in the *PMLA* Forum that I might "enter into a real discussion" with some of the signers of the letter I was answering. By a real discussion I mean one that centers on a specific issue and tries to reach some kind of agreement about it, or at least to clarify and narrow the area of disagreement, and not to score points against an enemy. I should explain, however, that I do not see this opportunity as a continuation of my reply to their letter, which I think is a dead end. Instead I will draw on some statements in their letter that raise a more general issue which seems to underlie our disagreement—the issue of the role of ideology in criticism. Of course the term ideology has several meanings, but I will be using it to refer to a consciously held set of political beliefs, and I will focus on its role in what are now the most important forms of ideological criticism in this sense: feminism and the new Marxism, or cultural materialism, which is why my respondents [Gayle Greene and Michael Bristol] have been selected from these two groups.

Let me begin with a statement in their Forum letter that objected to my critique of some feminist readings of Shakespeare because I failed "to understand the serious concerns about inequality and injustice that have engendered feminist analyses of literature." What they were saying is that I did not accept feminist political ideology. I replied that I did accept it, but that this did not affect my judgment of those feminist readings, since a just cause cannot justify interpretive faults. But suppose I did not accept this ideology—would that disqualify me from judging feminist readings? Are we to say that only feminists can criticize feminist readings, and only Marxists can criticize Marxist readings? And would it follow that feminists can criticize only feminist readings, and Marxists can criticize only Marxist readings, and that we all must be confined to discussing readings that reflect our own ideology?

I think this dilemma points to the most basic problem posed by the role of ideology in criticism, and I would like to see how we got into it and then suggest a way out. It seems clear that we got into it by rejecting certain beliefs which until recently were generally accepted. The most important of these is the belief that one can attain objective knowledge of a literary text. The new Marxists reject this as a fallacy of the formalist approach—mainly the New Criticism—and of the liberal humanist ideology that is supposed to sponsor it. They maintain that interpretations are always determined by the interpreter's ideology and so are never objective. Thus they tell us that "all reading [is] an intervention and a production rather than a simple decoding" of the text, that it "is not a process of recognition but work to produce meaning," that it is not "the uncovering of 'what is already there,' " that objectivity is a "spurious notion," and that any appeal to it is "hubristic objectivism."[1] Some feminists share this view. I want to emphasize that I will not be generalizing about feminists, who are much more diverse than the new Marxists. Even that Forum letter, although it had twenty-four signers, obviously was not written by all of them, and I know they did not all agree with everything in it. But it represents the views of some feminists, and it says, "we forthrightly acknowledge the partiality of our own interpretations," which means that they too subscribe to the doctrine that interpretation is determined by the interpreter's ideology.

When we turn to their actual practice, however, we find that neither the new Marxists nor the feminists really believe this. The Marxists' inconsistency can be seen in one of their favorite projects, the attack on textual unity, which they regard as another formalist fallacy. Catherine Belsey says that formalists sought a way of "smoothing out" or "censoring" the play of ideological "contradictions" which, she insists, "in reality constitutes the literary text" (*Critical Practice* 109, 128). And I have collected many more statements of the same sort that I do not have time to read now.[2] They all claim that textual unity is a fraud perpetrated by formalism, which can only mean that the disunity—i.e., those ideological contradictions—must really be in the text prior to any critical "intervention," which of course is "hubristic objectivism." And the inconsistency of some feminists can be seen in that Forum letter itself, for soon after forthrightly acknowledging the partiality of feminist interpretations, it asserts a number of things about Shakespeare's tragedies—that they "repeatedly and poignantly ask what it is to 'be a man,' that the heroes often fantasize 'a very serious provocation by a woman' when there is none, that self-knowledge, catharsis, and the restoration of order are vexed in many" of them, etc.—which are supposed to be objective facts, independent of the feminists' ideological partiality. Indeed the letter claims that these assertions are based on "detailed analyses of the specific actions of particular heroes" in the plays.

Despite this inconsistency between their anti-objectivist theory and their practice, however, I think the theory itself contains a germ of truth, because what we see in a text is in part determined by the perspective we bring to bear on it. And to indicate this role of perspective I would like to resurrect the useful little word *qua*. If we return to the question of unity, for example, and ask whether any given text *really* is unified, the answer must be that there is no answer, since it depends on how one looks at it—in this case, on whether one looks at it *qua* artistic product, which is the formalist approach. And I want to digress here to present a brief defense of formalism, since there is a widespread impression that it has been refuted. Let me state first that I am not now and never have been a New Critic. I was trained in the Chicago Aristotelian school, which had some bitter quarrels with the New Criticism. But we did share what I would call the basic formalist perspective, which views a literary text as something intentionally produced by an author to evoke a meaningful, pleasurable response in an audience. Many new Marxists and some feminists claim this perspective is no longer tenable since Barthes, Foucault, and others have invalidated the assumptions on which it rests, such as the belief in a unified author who intends a response, which is now supposed to be another formalist fallacy.[3] But most ordinary people do view literary works in this way, as products intentionally designed to give them pleasure. I suspect it is even how Marxists and feminists view them when they are not laboring in their vocation (as Falstaff puts it), but if I am wrong I hope my respondents will explain why, in terms of their own approaches, anyone other than a professional critic would want to see a play or read a novel. The formalist approach can explain this, since it coincides with the actual experience of most audiences, and so I think its conception of a literary work cannot be invalidated, regardless of the latest French discoveries. It will always be valid, though it may slip in and out of fashion in the academy. And in terms of this approach it makes sense to treat unity as an intended goal of authors, and thus as a working hypothesis in interpreting their works.

It is essential to add, however, that this is not the only valid way of looking at literary works and hence at textual unity. For the work itself cannot tell us how we should regard it, which is why we need the term *qua*. Any work, in addition to being a product intended by an author for an audience, is also inevitably a product of its society and of the psyche of its author, and so can be viewed *qua* either of these perspectives. And from this it follows that what we call the historical and the psychological approaches—which include, but are not limited to, Marxism and Freudianism—also have their own validity (and I think most feminist critics would fall under one of these categories). And from their perspectives the concept of unity takes on meanings very different from the formalist concept (thus Marxists are talking about ideological unity, as the quotation from Belsey indicated), so their answer to the question of whether any given work is unified could always be negative. This also can account for some of the other disagreements I referred to. Is the author or what is now called the "subject" *really* unified? The answer again is that it depends on our perspective. *Qua* atomic structures, we are not unified; we are just a concourse of particles with no clear boundaries. But *qua* biological structures we do have unity; when I return to my seat I will not leave an arm here at the podium. And in poetics, if authors are viewed from the formalist approach, *qua* enactors of an artistic intention, they can be highly unified, while from another approach that views authors *qua* sites of social conflict, they may never be unified or even relevant, as Barthes's doctrine of The Death of the Author proclaims. So this *qua* gives us the basis for critical pluralism.

Although I said this perspectivism or pluralism represents the germ of truth in the anti-objectivist position, it is actually very different, since it does not deny the possibility of objective knowledge of the text. On the contrary, it affirms that the various approaches can attain such knowledge in their own terms, since they are not "intervening" to "produce" different objects but are only different ways of viewing the object, and so do not really contradict each other. Thus the interpretations of any approach can be objectively true or false. And unlike the anti-objectivist position, pluralism does not posit a necessary connection between these approaches and political ideologies. Many people now insist that there is a connection—that if you are a formalist you must then be an essentialist and a phallogocentrist and a reactionary liberal humanist and all the other nasty -ists, which line up on one side, while all the nice -ists are on the opposite side.[4] It sounds neat and simple, but it simply is not true, since formalist readings can come from Marxists and feminists; in fact the feminist readings I discussed in my *PMLA* article were formalist. (My point here has also been made by Gerald Graff ["Pseudo-Politics" 150–53] and Stanley Fish [Forum Reply 220]—it is one of the few things they agree on.) And since pluralists do not posit this political connection, they have no need to claim that one approach is superior to others. They are all seen as equally valid. Therefore pluralism enables us to live together and talk to each other because we can understand and respect our different approaches. To adapt the immortal words with which Touchstone ends his account of quarreling, "Your *qua* is the only peacemaker; much virtue in *qua*."

Many new Marxists, however, also reject pluralism, which to them is another formalist fallacy.[5] And the reason they are against it is that, unlike Touchstone, they are not seeking peace but victory. They do not want Marxism to be regarded as one among several valid approaches; they want it to be the *only* valid approach, as can be seen in their frequent references to it as "scientific" (which means all other approaches are unscientific), and in the last chapter of Terry Eagleton's *Literary Theory*, which argues for this claim. And they view pluralism as a devious strategy to domesticate their approach, like the "co-opting" and "repressive tolerance" we heard about in the 1960s. What they demand instead is that we engage them in a "struggle for meaning"[6] in the interpretation of literature, a struggle they expect to win. But they never explain how they will win it. Unless they intend to force us into submission—poetics comes from the barrel of a gun?—they will have to persuade us. But how can they persuade us that their interpretation of a text is better than ours, when they insist that objective knowledge of the text is "spurious," and that all interpretations of it are "interventions" determined by the interpreter's ideology? For this means there could be no appeal to any factual evidence within the text in a struggle with non-Marxists, and so it is hard to see how non-Marxists could ever be persuaded by a Marxist interpretation. Presumably they would first have to be converted to Marxist ideology, on political rather than poetic grounds. This seems to be Eagleton's position when he says that the disagreement between two readings based on different approaches is really "a distinction between different forms of politics. . . . There is no way of settling the question of which politics is preferable in literary critical terms. You simply have to argue about politics" (*Literary Theory* 209). And we have already seen some feminists taking this position in the Forum letter, when they made acceptance of their politics a prerequisite for judging feminist analyses of literature.

That puts us in the dilemma described at the outset, where each approach is confined to its own hermeneutically sealed-off discursive space, and adherents of different approaches can only discourse with each other about the politics of their respective ideologies. But the way out has already been indicated—it is by rejecting the rejection of objectivism and pluralism. If we believe one can attain objective knowledge of a text, then it is possible to criticize an interpretation even though it comes from an approach different from ours; for instance, we can fault it for distorting the text. And if we believe there are several valid approaches, then it is possible to criticize an interpretation from another approach in its own terms; for instance, we can fault it for being inconsistent with the postulates of that approach. Moreover, the belief in these two "fallacies" enables not only negative judgments of interpretations derived from other approaches but also positive ones. Thus we can praise an interpretation based on a different approach because it has taught us something new about the text. I think we have all had this experience; but it is only possible when we believe that something is objectively there in the text to be learned, and that our approach is not the only valid way of learning it. If I am wrong, however, if objectivism and pluralism really are fallacies, and interpretations and judgments of interpretations really are determined by political ideology, then our journals and conferences such as this should stop discussing literature or criticism and instead sponsor debates about politics—about the relative merits, say, of capitalism and socialism. Then, when enough people have been converted to the right political position, pluralism can be suppressed in favor of monism, which is its only alternative, and all of us will have to practice the same form of ideological criticism.

Of course even this scenario assumes that rival ideologists in their attempt to persuade can invoke rational standards that are themselves not ideological. But many new Marxists also reject this idea as another humanist fallacy. And so do some feminists in what I thought was the most depressing part of their Forum letter, where they attack my appeal to "evidence that compelled the assent of all rational people, regardless of their gender or ideology." They even attack the Enlightenment for its faith in rationality. But in their arguments against my article they must be appealing to a neutral reason. For example, they try to show that I contradicted myself. I do not think they succeed, but their effort assumes that self-contradiction is bad, which is a rational standard. And they object to the publication of my article because others are more "cogent," which makes cogency a criterion independent of ideology. But if I am wrong on this too, if we cannot invoke reason, then even attempts at political persuasion are futile, and every dispute about politics or poetics or anything else really would have to be settled from the barrel of a gun. The alternative that I am offering to this is a peace treaty based on the three principles of objectivism, pluralism, and rationalism. It certainly will not eliminate all our disagreements, which I do not think is possible or even desirable. But it should clarify and narrow these disagreements, and give us the ground rules for entering into a productive discussion about them.

## NOTES

1. Barker 15; Belsey, *Critical Practice* 138; Evans 137; Howard, "Recent Studies" 340; McLuskie, "Patriarchal Bard" 91.

2. See my quotations from Barker and Hulme 196–98; Dollimore, *Radical Tragedy* 60, 67–68; Eagleton, *Literary Theory* 80–81; Evans 249, 254; Holderness, *Shakespeare's History* 159; Howard, "New Historicism" 30; and Stallybrass, "Rethinking Text" 100–01, in Levin, "Cultural Materialist."

3. See, e.g., Belsey, *Critical Practice* 3; Moi 4; and the articles by Barthes ("Death") and Foucault in the bibliography.

4. Thus Moi asserts that the formalist approach is "inherently reactionary" (10), although her own approach denies the existence of inherent qualities. See also the quotations collected in Graff, "Pseudo-Politics" 145–46.

5. See Barker 48; Barker and Hulme 193; Bristol, "Lenten Butchery" 220–21 and *Shakespeare's America* 169; Drakakis 17, 25; Eagleton, *Literary Theory* 50, 198–99; Evans 98, 198, 245; Holderness, *Shakespeare's History* 160; and Rooney.

6. Barker and Hulme 193, 205; Belsey, "Literature" 19, 21; Paul Brown 69; Holderness, *Shakespeare's History* 149; McLuskie, "Patriarchal Bard" 95.

# 3

## The Myth of Neutrality, Again?

**Gayle Greene**

First, about ideology. Mr. Levin suggests that ideology "has several meanings," but that he'll use it to refer to "a consciously held set of political beliefs." I don't think he gets to do this: ideology has a specific meaning, a meaning derived from Althusser ("Ideology and Ideological State Apparatuses") and Gramsci (*Prison Notebooks*) and elaborated by Catherine Belsey and Rosalind Coward and John Ellis—and it is not a "consciously held belief," "not an optional extra, deliberately adopted by self-conscious individuals . . . but the very condition of our experience of the world, unconscious precisely in that it is unquestioned, taken for granted" (Belsey, *Critical Practice* 5). It is that system of beliefs and assumptions, unconscious, unexamined, invisible, by which we imagine and represent the world, that pervades every aspect of our thought and defines our imaginative horizons—"a kind of vast membrane enveloping everything," a "skin" that "encloses us like a net or like closed eyelids" (Cixous 145).

To understand ideology as unconscious is quite different from viewing it as a consciously-held belief that can be put on and put off at will. It implies that we are ideological whether we like it or not—whether we know it or not, whether we admit it or not. Thus even Mr. Levin is ideological, and ideological in ways that have little to do with whether he belongs to his local chapter of NOW; he is every bit as much the prisoner of beliefs and dogmas, of cultural assumptions, as we—feminists—are. But since ideology is always somebody else's, never one's own—as Althusser says, "the accusation of being in ideology only applies to others, never to oneself"(175)—feminists and Marxists, who hold opinions that are not generally accepted, get called "ideological" (and "political," "partisan," "polemical," and lots of other things) whereas those approaches which are more traditional, closer to what is familiar (Aristotelians, New Critics, formalists) get to pass as "neutral" and objective. Thus Marxists and feminists do "ideological criticism" whereas Richard Levin does not. This is an assumption underlying Levin's *PMLA* article and his MLA paper (it's there in his very title, "Ideological Criticism"—as though some criticism is "ideological" but his is not). Though it seems rather late in the day to have to point out that all critical positions are ideological—this understanding of ideology has been one of feminism's underlying principles from the beginning—it seems to need repeating.

This means that, yes, "interpretations and judgments of literature really are determined by political ideology" (Levin, this volume). The notion of a common "reader" or audience that Levin implies when he refers to "most ordinary people," "most audiences," a reader who reads according to a principle of "sense" (this volume) (and he has always been a "he"), has been, like the notion of universals itself, an idea which did not survive the onslaughts of feminist and Marxist and post-structuralist critiques in the past fifteen years. A fundamental premise of feminist scholarship is that the perspective assumed to be "universal" that has dominated knowledge, shaping its paradigms and methods, has actually been male and culture-bound. I find it astonishing that this needs repeating.

The standards of reason and rationality, sense and common sense, the notion of "objectivity" that Mr. Levin laments we feminists do not share with him, have been similarly called into question. Levin suggests that we grant that there is objective knowledge of a text, something objectively there in the text, but that we also grant pluralism—that there are several valid approaches: then it will be "possible to criticize an interpretation even though it comes from an approach different from ours" (this volume). Similarly, he concludes his *PMLA* piece with an appeal to "evidence that compels the assent of all rational people, regardless of their gender or ideology" ("Feminist Thematics" 136). The response, signed by twenty-four feminists, which was published in *PMLA* a few issues later, singled out this phrase, noting that what passes for rationality at a particular historical moment may look like irrationality at another, that affirmations of shared attributes often mask oppression based on unexplored assumptions of hierarchical difference (Adelman et al. 78). Levin in turn singled this out as "the most depressing part" of our letter and lamented that feminists had lost faith in the Enlightenment.

I think that this talk about objectivity betrays a kind of nostalgia for a simpler past when the world seemed knowable and manageable. Yes, feminists are suspicious of a standard which has brought the planet to its present disastrous condition, of that "reason" which has arrogated to itself so much power, the control not only of women but of as much of the world's resources and population as it has been able to grab. So was Shakespeare—his villains use reason to mask the most appalling irrationality—and he rightly identified such rationality with the new order, the "brave new world" he saw on the horizon, the Enlightenment, perhaps, whose spirit of protestantism and capitalism, he suspected, did not bode well.

It's time that all critics acknowledge the ideological and political and gendered bases of their judgments. I read and write as I do because I am white, female, middle-class, middle-aged and have lived through the feminist revolution; I can do no other. But to admit to this, to recognize our own partiality, does not mean that we cannot make judgments or take positions, that we throw everything up for grabs: in fact it makes us better readers because it makes us aware of the existence of other possible perspectives. Isn't this what irony means? that old New Critical virtue? (Much virtue in irony.) Some readings do remain better than others; there are what Robert Scholes calls "readings that are more or less rich, strategies that are more or less appropriate" (144–45). I believe in supporting assertions by reference to the text, but since I also believe that human ingenuity can prove anything—look at the "unity" that biblical exegesis discovered in biblical texts—I am suspicious of whatever "unity" I find; though I do enjoy the process of discovery, I do not reify my discoveries or detach them from myself as a reader. Nor does acknowledging the partiality and limitations of all positions lead to a relativism that justifies evasion of political positions—though it might and has in some instances (any position can lead to any other position if you push hard enough), it does not for feminists.

I am a feminist and a formalist; I believe in the partiality of all positions and I believe that I know truth from error when it comes to taking positions. I live amidst contradictions and so does everyone else, even those who believe they are "objective." Perhaps this is another way of saying that I embrace "pluralism," in which case I might be agreeing with Levin on this point, in his call for pluralism; but this is hardly an original position for a feminist; it's a position that feminist critics have often taken—since 1980 when Annette Kolodny described "our task" as "a playful pluralism, responsible to the possibilities of multiple critical schools and methods, but captive of none" (161). Once again, this discussion gives me a strong sense of *déjà vu*.

No, I do not think that we should turn our literary journals over to debates about politics, or at least not all of them, though in some cases this might represent an improvement over what currently gets discussed in them. But, as it's often said, arguments about politics never settle anything, and this is because underlying political positions are emotional positions which are not rational or susceptible to change by reason: which is not to say that people cannot change, but that it takes something more than rational argument to change them—it takes experience and a change in consciousness, values, and vision. (And if you want evidence that opinions about literature are ultimately political, just look at how tenaciously they are held.) Therefore I write this knowing full well that I will not change Mr. Levin's mind and he will not change mine; and everyone will leave this room believing what they believed when they walked in. But I think I understand my biases and emotional investments; I wonder if Mr. Levin recognizes his. One of the most telling moments in his *PMLA* article is at the end, when he accuses feminists of debasing tragic heroes "to a level beyond the reach of tragic sympathy" for pointing out their misogyny (135), of having "little sense of compassion" for them (131). The basis of this criticism seems to be that we're insufficiently compassionate, insufficiently nurturing: bad mothers. Levin is not the only one to have responded to feminists this way: many feminist scholars have encountered precisely this response from our male mentors and colleagues, men with strong unexamined investments in these tragic heroes who confuse our critiques of them with critiques of *them*.

In revealing that a category as apparently "natural" as gender is socially constructed, feminism critiques the most fundamental assumptions of Western epistemology, and at our most radical, we make common cause with Marxist and certain kinds of post-structuralist critiques. But Levin seems oblivious of these larger issues: this is what we meant when we said in our response that he failed "to understand the serious concerns . . . that have engendered feminist analyses of literature." What I found the "most depressing" aspect of Levin's paper—if we're going to outdo one another's depressions—was that Levin mounted an attack on a large and complex body of criticism without understanding its wider cultural and theoretical implications. Like a New Critic doing close readings, he read our articles as isolated texts, without attending to how they fit into the matrix of social change and critical debates of the last fifteen years, or to the theoretical issues behind those debates—and for this he gets published in *PMLA*. When we respond that this is "muddled" and "unsophisticated," we get called name-callers.

But what really interests me is the politics of this whole discussion—why we are talking about this now; why Levin's article was taken sufficiently seriously to get into *PMLA* and to warrant an MLA session, when it strikes me, as it did the other signers of that feminist response, as theoretically naive about its own premises and the implications of the position it tackles. I want to shift the focus slightly and deconstruct the terms of this discussion, and ask what it is about the cultural moment that brings us here to discuss these issues. I'd like to address the politics of the publication of this essay, Levin's response to our response, and responses to that response. For academic discussion, even about aesthetic standards and the unity of texts, does not take place in empty space; it takes place in institutions that have social and political contexts.

In his response to our response, Levin draws attention to a widespread feeling on the part of "many of my correspondents" that "*PMLA* is now controlled by the feminist and other new approaches"; "the fact that it is publishing a steady stream of feminist articles is not enough, in their view; they also want to deny publication to any criticism of them that they disapprove of" (79). He tars Marxists with the same brush, describing them as "not seeking peace but victory," of wanting Marxism to be the only valid approach—"Poetics comes from the barrel of a gun?" (6).

From where I sit as a feminist it does not look to me as if I control *PMLA* or much of anything else in the profession. In the late seventies when I and my coeditors were asked to submit names of readers for our anthology *The Woman's Part: Feminist Criticism of Shakespeare*, we had difficulty coming up with the names of two senior Shakespeareans who would not trash the idea of a feminist reading of Shakespeare; what we encountered again and again was the response I have described—that we were desecrating something sacred ("How dare we call Othello hysterical!"). When by the early 1980s our book was published and we'd achieved some recognition and were working together with the pleasure and excitement of a just cause, we had become sufficiently threatening to be characterized by a former friend of mine as "the Shakespeare mafia"; a group of women working together—we had become a "mafia." I was interested to hear that the term "the black mafia" was applied to a comparable group of revisionist critics in Afro-American studies. I also heard that MLA letter signed by twenty-four feminists referred to as a "gang-bang."

Such terms and metaphors reveal anxiety about something. We are perceived as viragoes, amazon women wielding their meat axes, or whatever amazons wield; we are taking over the academy. This will be good news to those feminists—and that's most of us—who have not exactly been elated by what's going on in feminist scholarship and feminism today, who have, in fact, been appalled by the virulence of the backlash our efforts have inspired. Here's how much women have taken over the academy: A 1987 *New York Times* article ("Women Gain Little in Academic Jobs," 23 July 1987) suggests that two decades of affirmative action have made little difference in higher education: "Women who teach in colleges still suffer from discrimination" and "in nearly all institutions surveyed"—these were University of California institutions—"faculty women are paid less than men, rise through the academic ranks more slowly and receive tenure at lower rates than men." A Luce Foundation study in 1986 concluded that "although women make up more than one-half of the undergraduate population and are earning one-third of all doctorates, they hold only 12 percent of tenured faculty positions" ("Luce Fund Offering Aid to Scholarly Women," *New York Times*, 31 Jan. 1987).

What's the view like from the feminist scholar? I personally do not see much cause for complacency. If you really want to know, I feel beset from all sides. Older colleagues don't read us; most simply ignore us, hoping that if they wait it out we'll eventually go away. Our contemporaries and younger colleagues, eager to make a space for themselves, either ignore us, writing as though feminist criticism had never happened, or attempt to climb to the top on our bodies, having exposed us as theoretically "soft," anachronistic, vulgarly empiricist, naively Anglo-American—whatever: the factions that split feminist scholarship at the moment are not encouraging. Meanwhile, professional prestige has shifted to critical theory—"real theory" as opposed to feminist theory. (In my own department my course in feminist critical theory was denied equal credit with critical theory as "the senior seminar.") And now our students are telling us the battles have all been won—although these same younger women will in all likelihood have the pleasure of reexperiencing for themselves what my generation thought we'd put behind us—the illegal abortion.

A look at the space given to feminist criticism in revisionary anthologies on the Renaissance shows a similar process of erasure: a 1985 anthology has one essay on feminist criticism of Shakespeare, which attacks American feminist criticism for being reductive and essentialist (McLuskie, "Patriarchal Bard") a 1986 collection has one essay with the word "feminist" in the title, although there are a few essays on gender-related subjects (Ferguson et al.); a 1987 collection has no "feminist" essays and two gender-related essays (Howard and O'Connor). Feminist criticism has been absorbed, assimilated, usurped, by new historicists' discussions of politics, power, colonialism, the court, class, ideology—all of which have bearing on gender but, more often than not, are not brought to bear on gender.

Is it a coincidence that this is the time that *PMLA*—the most prestigious and regarded by many as the best journal in our profession—just happens to publish this attack on feminist criticism? It is not my paranoia to imagine that a feminist essay would have been subjected to far more rigorous scrutiny as to the theoretical implications of its positions, would have been required to inform itself more carefully about whatever position it was critiquing. Is it a coincidence that Mr. Levin strikes the chord that he does in those responses to our response in subsequent issues of *PMLA* which characterize our positions as "thinly disguised religious fervor or totalitarianism," as we "ganged up to attack him" (excuse me: who attacked whom?); accusing us of "inaccuracy and meanness," of "glittering generalities" and "name calling" of "a distinguished scholar" whose "trenchant critique" was "wonderfully informative as well as shrewdly deflating," "precisely the type of analysis *PMLA* should host" (Weitzman; Birnbaum 357–58). The old boys rally round; it's no surprise that there are a lot of little Levins out there. But what is frightening is how much rage is out there—about feminist criticism, feminist academics, feminism, women in the academy.

What does the state of women in the academy have to do with the question of objectivity and unity in a text? It has everything to do with the fact that we are having this discussion. The fact that feminists are being discredited, erased, has everything to do with the backlash our achievements, such as they are, have provoked. The issues raised in this discussion seem strangely anachronistic until we realize that they are actually in keeping with the times. As we move boldly forward into the 1950s, we turn again to questions of aesthetic standards as though feminism hadn't occurred, as though Marxist and feminist approaches had taught us nothing about the way aesthetics and interpretive judgments are shaped by gender, history, culture, and institutions.

I'm afraid this brings us back to the point with which Levin concludes his *PMLA* article. Levin tells us that "this 'feminist' conception of masculinity"—that men are unconscious misogynists—"is just as much a distortion of real life as it is of the tragedies" (136). Why then, he asks, do we feminists accept this conception of masculinity? He concludes that we "want to believe it," and we want to believe it because "it neatly turns the table on the Freudian theory of penis envy" (136). It's hard to know who's envying whom for what in this dizzying set of assertions, but let me assure you that we do *not* want to believe it—what woman would want to believe it? Most of us can hardly believe it but are made to understand on a daily basis how little a woman needs to accomplish in order to provoke fear and rage, how terrified men are, how hysterical they are, about women making inroads into the professions—as this whole exchange indicates.

# 4

# Where Does Ideology Hang Out?

Michael D. Bristol

At the beginning of the 1990s, at least in the United States, cultural debates have become highly visible items on the public agenda. The discussion of such issues as flag-burning, the exhibition of sexually explicit photographs by Robert Mapplethorpe, and the arrest by municipal authorities of 2 Live Crew for its sexually explicit performances has been characterized by the extreme rancor of its rhetoric as well as by its sense of urgency and threat. A similar sense of urgency and menace is also present in the discussion of broader and more "philosophical" cultural topics such as the closing of the American mind, threats to the legacy of Western Values, and the general decline of cultural literacy (Bloom, *Closing*; Bennett, "Lost Generation," "To Reclaim"). Like the sex-and-censorship debates, the canon-and-curriculum debates seem to be something more than routine hassles between liberal and conservative interpretations of American cultural hegemony.

That disputes over the literary and cultural curriculum should have become matters of widespread public concern is perhaps only a symptom of a certain American predilection for scandal and sensation, which seem to be the only socially acceptable forms in which intellectual questions can be brought to the attention of a wide audience. It is also possible, however, given the acrimonious tone of these disputes, that there are increasing strains and potential instabilities within the social consensus, tensions that the apparatus of ideological production is no longer able to manage or regulate. Fear about this latent instability within the social/cultural consensus seems to be one of the motives behind the recent and ongoing neo-conservative cultural offensive, which, in its more lucid moments, appears to recognize the possibility that deep and enduring cultural antagonisms could indeed destabilize or even permanently derange our present system of economic and social arrangements. The neo-conservative diagnosis of the underlying conditions responsible for this increasingly manifest antagonism is far less cogent, however, and the proposed remedy in the form of a national curriculum or program of universal cultural literacy seems in the end absolutely fantastical (Balch and London; Bennett, "Lost Generation").

In light of the importance of his plays as an institution of acculturation and socialization in the United States, it is not surprising that Shakespeare should have emerged as one of the important sites of controversy in this increasingly exacerbated cultural policy debate, not only in professional journals, but in mass-circulation publications as well (Bristol, *Shakespeare's America*). News about Shakespeare, of course, makes the *New York Times* more or less regularly, usually in connection with fast-breaking stories about the authorship controversy, the discovery of new manuscripts, or the recent excavation of the foundations of the Rose Theater. It is only in the past several years, however, that coverage of Shakespeare has had strongly political and ideological implications.

Recent journalistic coverage of cultural policy debates on literature in general and on Shakespeare in particular has focused on the role of ideology in recent scholarship. In what is surely one of the more bizarre examples of such journalistic "contributions" to the cultural policy debate, Marvin Hunt relates that participants in a recent Folger Institute seminar on "New Directions in Shakespeare Criticism," led by ideologically motivated critics, were engaged in plotting revolution in the basement of the Folger Library. Hunt may well have intended his description of Shakespeare scholars plotting revolution as a joke, although his estrangement from the activities of the Institute Seminar is very clearly evident. Hunt evidently wants both to ridicule the radical scholars he encountered for their hypocritical, self-serving vanity and to denounce them as a serious cultural threat. For the primarily neo-conservative readership he addresses in the *Spectator* the possibility of an ideological appropriation of Shakespeare in the interests of a revolutionary conspiracy would hardly be viewed as a joking matter, even if the radical scholars have no realistic chance of success with their social agenda. Shakespeare after all is construed within this cultural milieu as a privileged embodiment of Western Values and as a fundamental element in the substantive curriculum of Western Culture. On this view, correct interpretation of the plays is a matter of national interest.

Shakespeare has been recruited in the service of an American cultural policy at least since the time of the First World War. The very existence of the Folger Shakespeare Memorial Library is intended as a way to sustain the link between Shakespeare studies and the advancement of United States cultural policy. Broadly speaking his plays are viewed as the embodiment of "priceless values" that place his writing beyond ideology. Ironically this doctrine of affirmative culture is itself an ideological position that has formed a durable background consensus within American cultural policy debates. Two important strains within that debate emerge at about the same time. A "neo-conservative" cultural thematics in respect of Shakespeare is first articulated by Charles Mills Gayley in *Shakespeare and the Founders of Liberty in America*, first published in 1917. This text is linked to the wider cultural-political thematics of Wilsonian reform. The neo-conservative discourse remains in circulation through the end of the Second World War, and it is frequently connected with ideas of a "Southern *risorgimento*" (Craig). The alternative to this view is articulated in an influential and frequently reprinted lecture by George Lyman Kittredge, entitled simply *Shakespere* [sic]. In this lecture the expressive autonomy of the private subject displaces the neo-conservative notion of socio-cultural discipline as the primary cultural value sedimented in Shakespeare's plays. At the end of the Second World War this alternative cultural thematics is linked up with the ideology of "advanced liberalism" as it emerges in the postwar decades. Influential studies such as Northrop Frye's *A Natural Perspective* and C. L. Barber's *Shakespeare's Festive Comedy* emphasize a broadly ecumenical and pluralistic system of meaning in Shakespeare, in which repression and social discipline are kept in the background.

Since the cultural policy debate about Shakespeare has gone public, reaching out to the wider constituency of literary intellectuals through *PMLA* as well as to a wider intelligentsia through the *New York Times*, the *New York Review of Books*, the *Spectator*, etc., Richard Levin has emerged as the self-appointed representative of a certain intellectual and cultural community. Although it is likely that not all members of Levin's natural constituency would choose him as their spokesman, nevertheless, to judge from correspondence elicited by his recent *PMLA* article on feminist Shakespeare criticism, many do see him as their champion. In any case Levin has become an active and even an obstreperous controversialist, both in the professional media and in mass circulation publications—a role I believe to be an extremely important one. For this reason I sincerely wish that he had used the occasion of the MLA panel discussion for which the present essay was originally written to articulate his own theoretical position more explicitly.

Richard Levin has given us, over a period of many years now, a sustained and comprehensive series of normative satires of the individual follies and vices of many different scholars and of many different types of scholarship (*New Readings*; "Leaking Relativisim"; "Feminist Thematics"; "Bashing"). However, the normative horizon within which that satire is grounded remains unarticulated and under-theorized. These exposés and denunciations—they cannot really be called critiques—at times seem to have an epistemic bent in the way they echo certain ideas that have been prominent within the philosophy of science, notably those of Karl Popper in his *Conjectures and Refutations* (see also Harriet Hawkins). At other times these writings sound more like those of a lapsed or fallen liberal reiterating themes set out by Daniel Bell in his *The End of Ideology* (1961). In the discussion that followed the MLA panel discussion, Levin emphatically declared himself to be a liberal in the sense of a civil-libertarian, affiliated with such organizations as ACLU and NOW. However, that discussion failed to clarify the relationship between Levin's version of advanced liberalism and his current polemic against what he has characterized as ideological criticism in the field of Shakespeare studies.

There is no doubt as to the utility of a discussion of the issues, as Levin proposes in his essay, assuming we can agree on what the issues that need discussing are. However, Levin's paper, because of its deeply equivocal character, does not really give me assurance that a discussion is what is really wanted here. To begin with, Levin's reference to feminism and Marxism as "the most important forms of ideological criticism" seems to imply that there are forms of criticism in which ideology has no role. As a self-proclaimed liberal, Levin does not claim to have personally transcended ideology in his view of the world. However, he does claim that his own ideological bias plays no role in his scholarly and critical writing. It seems to me, however, that we are owed an explanation of exactly how Levin's criticism or any criticism for that matter escapes contamination by ideology. Here the more basic difficulty emerges, which is the "definition" of ideology as "a consciously held set of political beliefs." Does this statement mean that if political beliefs are not consciously held they don't count as ideology? What about the situation where beliefs are consciously held, but are construed by the believer as something other than political ones? Finally, what about those situations where political beliefs are consciously held but not openly expressed because they are held with the conviction that they are founded in common sense and therefore do not require discussion? Since all of these are situations that I would regard as central to any consideration of the problem of ideology, it is hard for me to see exactly how to engage with the agenda set out for this session.

Despite these very serious reservations, however, I believe it might be possible for us to have the discussion that Levin says he wants, and, in light of that possibility, I would like to try to set out my own view of the problem of ideology and its critique. It is probably fair to say that my view is a Marxist one in the sense that many of my own most important ideas have their ancestry in the writings of Karl Marx, though I do not claim to "represent" what is, after all, a complex, conflicted, and still developing ensemble of theory and practice. Ideology is certainly a term with a wide range of divergent meanings, and for the purposes of this discussion I want to exclude certain usages in order to make it clear just what it is that a critique of ideology is attempting to do (Barth; Lichtheim). In my discussion of the problem, I am not very much concerned with what I would like to call substantive ideology, that is, with any ideology that can be designated as a conveniently named "ism." This usage is what Raymond Geuss has called "ideology in a positive sense." In this usage, ideology is something to be created as a programmatic set of themes and interpretations useful in the organization of a social group or political movement. This is pretty clearly what Lenin had in view when he set out his program for a working class ideology in *What Is to Be Done?* It is this same usage that is operative in Bell's *The End of Ideology*, where the notion of ideology is explicitly linked to programmatic movements of a revolutionary type. Richard Levin appears to adopt this usage as well, though it is not entirely clear whether or not his "consciously held political beliefs" are linked to the idea of revolutionary change, as they are in Bell's account. Daniel Bell had his own theory as to why ideology in this sense had come to an end, and in fact it might be worth discussing neo-conservative theories of culture if that is what Levin is here to represent.

Ideological criticism in the sense of interpretations motivated by an ideology of a substantive and programmatic kind is not very likely to have *any* positive role in criticism if criticism is predicated on the criterion of a "contribution to knowledge" as in other kinds of research. On the other hand, such ideological criticism could have overriding strategic importance to anyone whose primary affiliation is with the militant phase of a particular social movement. There is a serious issue here, which concerns the status of "knowledge" *vis-à-vis* ideology. To what extent is knowledge independent of historically determinate social interests? The controversy out of which this session emerges has not really addressed this question in a useful way, mainly because it has proceeded as what Peter Burger has called mutually opposed dogmatic critiques. Specifically, one side maintains an extreme and unexamined form of the position that knowledge is absolutely independent of social determination, while the other side maintains that knowledge can be reduced without remainder to the social determinations that produce it.

In addition to the usage that defines ideology as a substantive political agenda, I want to exclude the obverse sense in which ideology means simply any more or less systematic and widely held world view. You have your ideology, I have my ideology: I'm OK., you're O.K. To refer to cultural difference or to the fact that people often disagree by describing such differences and disagreements as ideologies evacuates the critical force of this important concept. I take the position that ideology is a mode of cognition that needs to be compared and strongly contrasted both with knowledge (or even truth, if you like) *and* with malicious deception. In other words ideology is a type of distorted communication that nevertheless has a functional equivalence to truth. Typically the ideological exposés elaborated both by traditional humanism and by cultural materialism have for the most part focused on the mistakes inherent in the symbolic systems they analyze. Such exposés usually do not explain why false beliefs appear plausible to their adherents. Nor do they give any indication how ideological convictions can be in contradiction to social reality and at the same time enable the groups who possess these convictions to function adequately within that social reality.

The concept of ideology as I understand it is derived from two closely related ideas, both of which have their origins in certain writings of Marx. The first of these is the notion of false consciousness as set out in *The German Ideology*. The second is the critique of religion as expressed in the *Critique of Hegel's Philosophy of Right* and more fully elaborated in the basic tenets of Emile Durkheim's "sociology of religion."

The concept of false consciousness emerges as early as 1845, and it is based on the observation that the "ruling *material* force of society, is at the same time its ruling *intellectual* force. . . . The ruling ideas are nothing more than the ideal expression of the dominant material relationships . . ." (Marx, *German* 136). Marx notes three possible relationships *vis-à-vis* dominant ideas that might be possible within a given society. First, there are certain members of the dominant class whose main task is the creation and elaboration of that class's legitimating fictions. Second, there is the larger fraction of the ruling class whose relationship to these legitimating fictions is mainly passive and receptive. Finally, there are the members of the non-ruling classes who adopt the dominant ideas notwithstanding that these ideas do not express their class interest. Strictly speaking the notion of false consciousness refers only to this third relationship. However, there is a more developed sense of false consciousness that emerges out of Marx's analysis of revolutionary change.

In the context of large-scale historical change, new configurations of power emerge as dominant, together with a new set of legitimating fictions. This new conceptual vocabulary takes on an appearance of universality, in contrast to the legitimations of declining ruling groups.

> Each new class which puts itself in the place of one ruling before it is compelled . . . to represent its interest as the common interest of all the members of society. . . . It has to give ideas the form of universality, and represent them as the only rational, universally valid ones. . . . It can do this because, to start with, its interest really is more connected with the common interest of all other non-ruling classes. . . . Its victory, therefore,

> benefits also many individuals of the other classes which are not winning a dominant position. (Marx, *German* 138)

In this analysis, the concept of false consciousness encompasses both the idea of active dissimulation and the idea of delusion. What is false about false consciousness here specifically is its abstract universality organized around an equally abstract category familiarly known as Man. Although this idea is developed in terms of the general case in which any dominant class misrepresents its particular interest as the interest of the whole society, it is clear that Marx and Engels have in mind the unique example of what they call the bourgeoisie. False consciousness or false universality is actually a phenomenon that emerges in the specific historical struggle to overthrow the *ancien régime* of landed wealth and aristocratic privilege.

Before we abandon this fundamentalist interpretation of false consciousness in favor of the more sophisticated variants set out, e.g., in Gramsci or in Raymond Williams and his followers, it is perhaps worthwhile to consider the possibility that false consciousness is a historically recent and essentially contemporaneous phenomenon. In this view it would be important to note that earlier dominant classes had their own legitimating fictions, but that these fictions were based not on an abstract and universal category of Man, but rather on the idea of hierarchically differentiated estates or conditions, as in the ladder of degree, etc. Furthermore, social stability did not arise primarily from any of these legitimating fictions. Instead, as Robert Weimann points out, dominance was maintained partly through kinship and dynastic loyalties, partly by the use of force against social transgression ("Towards").

The narrow interpretation of ideology would have certain consequences for our understanding of Shakespeare. To begin with, it would mean that the much-derided Elizabethan World Picture was *not* an ideology in the modern sense, but rather a traditional world view fostered by the landed aristocracy and articulated as a highly differentiated system of duties and obligations. At the time Shakespeare was writing, the class-bound character of this world view was already apparent, as was the decadence of the great feudal classes whose interest it expressed. Insofar as they exceeded the horizons of this traditional world picture, the plays would have been *diagnostic* of ideology as a socially emergent phenomenon in early modern England. The belated "discovery" of "the Great Shakespeare" in Germany and the United States in the early part of the nineteenth century would in fact be an act of incorporation of Shakespeare's *oeuvre* into the larger ensemble of ideological practices as these were constitutive of bourgeois consciousness and its "false" projections as universal values (or Western Values, as in the nineteenth and twentieth century Imperialist variant of that consciousness). Shakespeare "takes hold" in a historically unprecedented way in this new social environment, and it becomes possible for Americans to recognize in Shakespeare a "founding father" of their Republic. This (mis-)recognition is based on an interpretation of Shakespeare's plays within the normative horizon defined by such "universal" social principles as the doctrine of liberty under the law and individual autonomy.

To the extent that Shakespeare's plays are said to represent something called "The Human Condition" or, in Emerson's phrase, "the interests of general humanity," they are linked to Engels's conception of false consciousness. Shakespeare has a more complex ideological function within contemporary society, however, in that he is seen not only as the affirmation of "Man," i.e., of bourgeois ideology in its universalistic form, but also as a kind of therapeutic relief from bourgeois ideology in its crass and oppressive manifestation as the tyranny of the price system and of GNP (Walter Cohen; Don Wayne). This "transcendence" of ideology is itself an ideological phenomenon best explained by way of Marx's critique of religion.

Durkheim characterized Marxism not as a philosophy, but as a "cry of pain." This is certainly related to the Marxist refusal of all religious and cultural palliative therapies. The refusal is expressed in Marx's notorious, though often misquoted, discussion of religion.

> The wretchedness of religions is at once an expression of and a protest against real wretchedness. Religion is the sigh of the oppressed creature, the heart of a heartless world and the soul of soulless conditions. It is the opium of the people. (Marx, *Critique* 131)

It is important to stress here that Marx does not simply denounce religion as a mere palliative and still less as a malicious deception. Opiates do, after all, alleviate pain. Religion is regarded as a contradictory phenomenon, in which a powerful truth (the perception of social injustice and the desire for redress) is united with an equally powerful untruth (God exists and He will redeem all injustice in some other world). In other words, the ideological is what makes possible the integration of functional and dysfunctional elements within social reality (Burger). For our purposes as literary scholars we would need to be concerned with the integration of aesthetic with anaesthetic functions within the sphere of cultural production.

For Marx, religion was a means for stabilizing socially dysfunctional inequalities by the practice of mass deception. For Durkheim, however, the forms of religious belief, despite their evidently fantastical character, could never be entirely a matter of simple mass delusion.

> A human institution cannot rest upon an error and a lie. . . . If it were not founded in the nature of things, it would have encountered in the facts a resistance over which it could not have triumphed. (Durkheim 464–65)

Durkheim's analysis of religion as a "human institution" stipulates the objective cogency of the doctrines and the ritual practices of the believers. These beliefs and practices do indeed represent a fundamental set of truths about the world, although this truth is not expressed in the self-understanding of the members of the religious community. On the contrary, for Durkheim, religious doctrines are a misrecognition of the actual ensemble of the social relations. The sacred is a disguised but nevertheless effective transformation of the secular order necessary for the solidarity of its members. This solidarity is sustained, not through an equilibrium achieved by individuals pursuing their own rational self-interest, but by an irrational though affectively binding displacement of the structure of social relations into an imaginary ensemble of myths and symbolic practices.

Is it possible that the general protocol of our present system of relations with Shakespeare is a misrecognition of our own situation-bound existence? It is certainly true that the idealizing of Shakespeare's authority has a quasi-religious character. This is true whether we are talking about submission to that authority as in a hermeneutics of reconstitution, or about more recent apostasies and indecisions as in various post-structuralist orientations. I have argued in another context that Shakespeare, at least in the United States, is a kind of inner *sanctum* of ideological practice, and that this position is consolidated through institutionally mandated oscillations between the production of variant forms of false consciousness (partial interest for general interest) and the production of variant forms of misrecognition (culture for nature) (*Shakespeare's America*).

As a Marxist I would be committed to the possibility that Shakespeare's plays still hold in reserve something of their originary diagnostic or heuristic value. This is the position suggested by Brecht:

> There is a lot in these works that is dead, distorted and empty. This can continue to be printed; for all we know it may be shamming dead, and it may anyway explain other aspects of this past period. I would . . . sooner draw your attention to the . . . living elements still to be found in such works at apparently dead junctures. (63)

The works may be only "shamming dead," but the "living elements" may be difficult to recover because the contemporary positioning of Shakespeare within the apparatus of ideological production is extremely complex. If there is indeed emancipatory potentiality sedimented in this textual material, it cannot be realized through purely substantive revision of Shakespeare's meanings. It is not enough to say forbidden things about Shakespeare.

Ideology is an ensemble of discursive practices or, to put it another way, it is a complex system of figurations or tropes (Wofford 11–17). These figurations typically misrepresent the part for the whole (false consciousness) or culture for nature (*méconaissance*). The possibility exists for movement between one type of figuration and another without ever exceeding the horizons of the dominant system; this gloomy state of affairs has been recognized in a number of contemporary accounts of ideology. Althusser, for example, describes ideology as the "imaginary relationship of individuals to their real conditions of existence" (162). This has been an extremely controversial formulation for Marxists and for non-Marxists alike, and I do not propose to enter into the polemic here, or to consider such questions as whether Althusser really understood Lacan's concept of the imaginary, whether that concept made any sense in the first place, or whether the doctrine of "ideological blindness" is the best way to read Althusser. For the purposes of this discussion, it is important to stipulate that the overcoming of ideology or the possibility of its critique can never be as simple as the "demystification" or "subversion" of a substantive thematic content. The reason for this stipulation is that ideology as an institution is never reducible to a single substantive content or even to a single system of figurations, although ideology does make use of substantive themes, images, and even philosophical ideas.

Ideology is perhaps best thought of as a two-tiered apparatus consisting of the possible set of substantive ideologies together with the higher order discursive and institutional mediations that keep these conflicting interpretations in some sort of more or less stable equilibrium. Under these conditions, false universality takes on the form of appearance of a false multiplicity. It would follow from this that the ideological apparatus is not defined by its ability to produce consensus, but, on the contrary, by its ability to produce a fragmented set of endlessly divided variants of false consciousness along lines of race, gender, and social class (Bourdieu 200; John Thompson 63). Domination, or if you prefer, social stability, would be effectuated not through a "dominant ideology" but rather through the production and the valorization of cultural heterogeneity or the ecumenical multiplication of divergent points of view. The decisive effect of ideology then is actually to *block* any social consensus at the point where it might ensue in social action. Ideology is a kind of open secret or practical consensus with respect to the determinate class-consciousness that constitutes the normative horizon for all classes (Bourdieu 152 ff). This analysis is not "good news" for advocates of postmodern discourses, since it equates "alterity" and the politics of pure difference with ideology. On the other hand, it is not good news for partisans of any movement for greater social justice, in that ideology, like weather, is something everyone can complain about but no one can see how to change.

The critique of ideology is linked to the possibility of its transcendence, and here again it is useful to consider widely circulated statements to the effect that such transcendence is already achieved in the writings of Shakespeare. The argument that the writings of Shakespeare lie "beyond ideology" is not wrong so much as it is meaningless. Only someone who knows exactly what, if anything, lies "beyond ideology"—that is, a subject fully emancipated from his or her own ideological overdetermination—would be in a position to say whether or not Shakespeare is in fact located there. The *desire* to transcend ideology, however, is anything but meaningless, and in this perspective the possibility of linking Shakespeare with a critique of ideology would depend not on achieving some sort of ultimate transcendence, but on the articulation of some sort of counterfactual or oppositional norms for the interrogation of actually existing conditions.

Richard Levin's proposals are an attempt to articulate a set of norms for a possible critique of ideology, or at least for the adjudication of competing ideological claims. From the understanding of ideology that I have outlined in the preceding discussion, however, these proposals appear extremely equivocal and, in the time remaining, I want to look at this agenda in somewhat closer details. Levin wants a *rapprochement*, and he suggests that the way towards that is through the three principles outlined in his talk, viz., objective meanings, pluralism, and rationalism (sic.).

The notion of an "objective meaning" seems to be almost a kind of oxymoron, in that for many of us the idea of meaning is by definition subjective in the sense that it inheres in inter-subjective relations. In these terms "objective meaning" would be a meaning that is invariant in all possible contexts of reception. There are all sorts of philosophical problems with this, mainly having to do with describing the conditions of possibility for the existence of such historically invariant meaning. Assuming such a meaning actually existed, there would still be a problem about how anyone could recognize an invariant meaning even if it jumped up and bit them, and about why such a meaning would be binding on every readership. I would be less interested in hearing a discussion of these philosophical problems, however, than I would in having a clarification of the relationship between the concept of "objective" meaning privileged in this paper and the concept of "established" meaning privileged in Levin's 1979 book, *New Readings vs. Old Plays*. (And by the way, it would be extremely interesting to know how these concepts relate to Harriet Hawkins's category of the "obvious" meaning as set out in her *The Devil's Party*.) Are "objective" meaning and "established" meaning synonymous or has Levin shifted his ground over the last ten years? More important, are these proposals motivated primarily by a wish for consensus and deep common accord (as in, e.g., Gadamer), or by a concern for the pursuit of knowledge within a binding framework of rationality or discursive ethics (as in, e.g., Habermas, *Communication*).

The doctrine of pluralism has been discussed here, and more exhaustively in much recent theoretical writing. Two points seem to me to require clarification in Levin's paper. First, the doctrine of pluralism seems to contradict both the idea of an "established" meaning and its present surrogate, the "objective" meaning. Is an objective meaning binding or is it not, and if it is binding, what meaning can we attach to pluralism here? Second, exactly what manner of pluralism does Levin have in view here? Is this a type of framework relativism, or wishy-washy pluralism, in which everyone is permitted to play whatever language game they feel comfortable with? Or is this the idea of interpretive communities, or supply-side pluralism, in which the importance of ideas is a reflection of the influence of those who hold them or of their impact on opinion polls?

Finally, it would be extremely useful to have a full clarification of what is meant by rationalism here. In the ongoing polemic between postmodern philosophies of dispersal, alterity, or the politics of pure difference (Paris) and the latter-day champions of Enlightenment rationality reconceived as an ethics of discourse (Frankfurt), Levin seems to line up on the side of Frankfurt. Since my own views are derived from this position, I should probably see Levin as a possible ally. Unhappily, I do not find his paper to be at all reassuring as to the realization of any such possible alliance. The idea of alliance is related to the possibility of social action in accordance with a set of specific social goals; these goals might entail sweeping changes in the social relations of production and of reproduction or they might entail an organized resistance to such change (as in the current neo-conservative cultural offensive). In any case, such action would presumably be founded on rational deliberation and the achievement of consensus. In my reading of the current proposals set out by Levin, however, the real agenda here seems to be an administrative protocol for scholarship that would serve primarily to optimize the ideological functioning of intellectual cadres as outlined in the preceding discussion. There is a strategic vacillation here between the doctrine of one truth (objective meaning) and many truths (pluralism) mediated by *neutral* canons of rationality and discursive etiquette designed to guarantee that the issue of a coordinated research agenda can never be settled and therefore that decisive arguments can never emerge.

In this paper I have followed Brecht's injunction to return to the classics, (i.e., the Marxist classics, and the early ones at that). For Marx, the disappearance of ideology was linked to the final abolition of class society and the achievement of revolutionary emancipation under communism. There is something quixotic and even paradoxical in the effort to criticize ideology from within a normative horizon that only exists as an indefinitely extended and imaginary future. Marxist thinkers recognize this difficulty and attempt to overcome it by a strategy which typically posits such a future horizon but refuses to talk about its substantive social content. This is a difficult stance to maintain, and right now it is even more difficult than in the relatively recent past. In light of the enormous resources currently allocated to ideological production of the kind outlined in the preceding discussion, the possibility of a "complete exit from the present order of life" has taken on an increasing urgency. This is a very big problem, but our little parochial piece of that problem is what we call "Shakespeare."

In our social and cultural dispensation dominated by the activities of market exchange, even priceless cultural objects can be assigned a market value. Certainly Shakespeare has not eluded appropriation by the price system. Scholarship has typically deployed its resources as a strategic resistance to such appropriation. The problem with this position is that the "real world" of market exchange does not recognize anything that falls outside the general audit of profit and loss. Priceless values are, in the understanding of the "real world," indistinguishable from worthless values.

The critique of ideology that I am proposing here has to begin with an attempt to determine just what question is posed for us by the dispensation of political economy, by the price system, and by the cultural division of labor that has brought us all here to this discussion. That division of labor is what accounts for the "differences" between those of us who are labeled as Marxists or feminists, and the more invidious differences between those who must accept such labels and those who do not. The possibility of alliance is not going to be realized by means of a purely formal and value-neutral reason that doesn't know what it wants to talk about. On the other hand, the *discussion* of alliance can begin with a search for a common or a coordinated research agenda not within a framework of a god-like Reason, but within a struggle for reasonable conditions.

# 5

# MLA Response to Levin, Greene, and Bristol

Victoria Kahn

You're heard Richard Levin defend objectivity and pluralism; Michael Bristol say they're incompatible (since while some standard of rationality is necessary for a critique of ideology, pluralism is itself an ideology which is at odds with the project of critique); and Gayle Greene reject objectivity but espouse pluralism. In thinking about this debate I found it useful to return to Levin's original article and in particular to his distinction between thematic and genre criticism, between a reading of the tragedies in terms of theme or in terms of dramatic action. A purely thematic reading is of course something we criticize our students for—the implication being that such analysis is too paraphrastic, insufficiently contextual, that it doesn't take account of how themes are rendered dramatically. This is what we call bad thematic criticism. But once we acknowledge the truism that to say what a text means is inseparable from how it means, it's hard to see how good thematic and dramatic criticism can be separated. It would be just as hard, that is, to describe the dramatic action of a play without having any sense of its themes as vice versa. There is another sense in which all criticism or commentary is ultimately thematic or—as Northrop Frye said long ago—allegorical in that it comments on and renders explicit the meaning of a given text. And this meaning, as Bristol and Greene argue, will inevitably be determined by the assumptions (explicit or implicit), education, and interests of a particular reader. It is important to see, however, that good thematic criticism is no more extrinsic to a text than genre criticism, which reads a given text in terms of the forerunners in the genre but must also in every case see how a given text renders, transforms and comments on the conventions of that genre. Curiously, then, Levin's privileging of dramatic action is either inexplicable on his own terms (i.e., it can't account for how one knows what the dramatic action is) or it runs the risk of perpetuating a kind of extrinsic criticism which is precisely what he condemns feminist readings of Shakespeare for.

## Victoria Kahn

I agree with Levin that modes of literary criticism are not strictly identifiable with political positions, i.e., that there is no *univocal* relationship between rhetoric and ideology in a text. In fact, I would go further and argue that there is no univocal relationship between the ideological position a literary critic espouses in his or her critical work and the ideological position one occupies in life (precisely because, as Bristol and Greene argue, ideology is not simply a consciously held position). I would also insist with Bristol and Greene, however, that with respect to any given text there will be a tie or ties between formal features and ideology. To recognize this tie is not to reduce art to politics as Levin claims. That would be to ignore aesthetic mediation and to read thematically in the way that Levin condemns. It would in short mean isolating theme from context, politics from the formal dimension of representation. Levin's formulation of his objections to some feminist critics is based on this distinction—that, I suppose, is precisely why he objects to them. One wonders why Levin bothers to take issue with this sort of criticism (granting for a moment his description of it) when he admits there are other far more compelling strains of feminist criticism of Shakespeare. His argument would have been more interesting if he had addressed the sort of reading he mentions approvingly but only briefly in the *PMLA* article: a reading which brackets the question of intention and determines what a play's "gender assumptions really are by deriving them inductively from the play itself, and then proceed [ing], again inductively, to see if they could derive valid generalizations about the assumptions of the tragedies as a genre" ("Feminist Thematics" 134), and it would have been more interesting if he had acknowledged and discussed the assumptions behind his own brand of dramatic criticism, as Greene and Bristol have already suggested.

In conclusion I want to express my substantive agreement with Bristol and Greene—especially the latter's account of why we are here in the first place. I want to take issue, however, with Greene's assertion that, like Levin, she is in favor of pluralism. I think her position is far closer to Bristol's, with its claim for the possibility of a *critique* of ideology. Similarly I think she does her argument a disservice—actually misrepresents it—when she claims that political positions are emotional positions. This amounts to accepting the false alternative between objective reason and irrationality; it amounts to giving up the possibility of persuasion and critique which are precisely what we want to preserve, and which she and Bristol both assume in participating in the current debate.

# 6

# Reply to Michael Bristol and Gayle Greene

Richard Levin

I am afraid that I must begin by expressing my disappointment at the two responses to my paper. I had proposed a kind of peace treaty, based on pluralism, objectivism, and rationalism, that I thought would enable practitioners of the various critical approaches to engage in productive arguments and to learn from each other. My respondents were of course under no obligation to accept the terms of this proposal; but if they did not I hoped they would give us some alternative that might attain the same end. So far as I can see, they are not interested in this because they seem to be too busy beating my plowshares into swords in order to continue and even heighten hostilities, though they go about it in different ways.

The main portion of Michael Bristol's response is an account of different conceptions of ideology that makes some interesting points, although I do not understand their relevance to my proposal. That relevance emerges only at the end of the account when he presents his own conception of a "higher order" of ideology that turns out to be pluralism itself, which is seen as a strategy to produce the "appearance of a false multiplicity," "endlessly divided variants of false consciousness," "cultural heterogeneity," and a "multiplication of divergent points of view" in order to "block" what he calls a "consensus" or "alliance." But this seems to be just a refurbished version of the old doctrine of "repressive tolerance" that I referred to in my paper, which held that the acceptance of diversity is a trick designed to maintain the oppressive status quo, or, in Orwellian terms, that Freedom Is Slavery.

His idea of a "consensus" or "alliance" is presumably meant to refute, by presenting a third possibility, my contention that the only alternative to pluralism is coercive monism. But he never explains what it is or how my pluralism is supposed to block it. If he is talking about literary criticism and advocating an alliance to promote a greater understanding and appreciation of Shakespeare, then I would like to join it. I thought I was proposing such an alliance, which, I argued, should be pluralistic because many different approaches can contribute to this goal. Even if he wants to build an alliance around one approach (as implied in his references to "a co-ordinated research agenda"), I do not understand why pluralism would block this. Indeed if it is to be a voluntary consensus, based on what he calls "rational deliberation," then it can only occur under pluralism because such deliberation requires a free choice among competing approaches. Moreover, even when it is formed it will still have to deal with these other approaches (since he cannot hope for unanimity) and thus must either accept them as legitimate, which is pluralism, or suppress them, which is coercive monism. I do not see any third alternative, and so I think he should have told us whether he regards his approach as the only legitimate one or as only one among several legitimate approaches.

It seems clear, however, that his real interest is not in criticism but in politics, where his "primary affiliation" lies, since he says that pluralism blocks consensus "at the point where it might ensue in social action" and that "the idea of alliance is related to the possibility of social action." But in the political sphere the argument for pluralism applies with even greater force. Our democracy is based on pluralism, on the existence of different parties and interests that are allowed to compete in the public arena. And this pluralism has certainly not blocked the formation of alliances leading to social action. In recent years, for instance, we have seen major improvements in the situation of blacks and women, brought about through alliances and an evolving consensus that were enabled by our pluralistic system. For Bristol these actions apparently do not count, perhaps because they involve only the first two terms of his triad of "race, gender, and social class," whereas for Marxists (at least the orthodox ones) everything depends on class. According to their theory, class oppression is the real cause of race and gender oppression, which will end when—and only when—the capitalist class system is replaced by a classless socialist society.[1] Any improvements short of that, therefore, are mere band-aids or window dressing, which presumably is why Bristol wants "sweeping changes in the social relations of production and of reproduction." One cannot be sure of this, however, because he never tells us what kind of "social action" or "sweeping changes" he favors, and even though he says this action requires "specific social goals," he never identifies them. This reticence is typical of the new Marxist critics, who regularly end their books and essays with a call for political action without explaining the nature of this action or its goal.[2] Bristol is very atypical in admitting that the goal is "imaginary" and has no substantive content that can be discussed. But this admission, while commendable, negates his entire case against political pluralism, which he based on the contention that it blocked the attainment of this goal. It also negates his case against critical pluralism since that depends on the same contention and the same mysterious goal.

His political argument seems to be directed primarily at the liberal position. In fact he tries to erase it by implying that the only alternative to those "sweeping changes in . . . social relations" must be "organized resistance to such change," which leaves out the liberals, somewhere between his two extremes, who value the freedom and diversity promoted by our pluralist democracy and work for reforms (such as those noted above) within this system, instead of trying to overthrow it for the sake of an undiscussible and, I believe, unattainable utopia. (His polarizing strategy here reminds me of the Communists' old claim that they were the only alternative to fascism, which the Fascists simply reversed.) And at one point he accuses me of being a "lapsed or fallen liberal" (although at other points I seem to be a "neo-conservative"). I am a liberal, neither lapsed nor fallen. That is my ideology (in the sense of a consciously held set of political beliefs), the one attacked as "the L-word" by right-wingers here, and as "bourgeois liberalism" by the Communist troops in Tiananmen Square, and as "liberal humanism" by the cultural materialists, and as "secular humanism" by our religious fundamentalists. I am proud of my liberal ideology and of the enemies it has earned among the anti-liberal forces on the Left and the Right, and I rejoice to see it emerging now in parts of the world that were subjected to Marxist rule.

Because Bristol is silent about these developments, his political argument takes on an air of eerie unreality. Although he makes the usual Marxist obeisance to historical specificity, one could never guess from the content of his paper that it was presented at the time when we were watching in many countries the collapse of Marxism as a political and economic system, and movements toward political pluralism and a market economy. (In fact his second paragraph suggests that we may instead be watching the collapse of what he elsewhere calls "late capitalism."[3]) Since he dislikes both pluralism and the market, we can assume that he opposes these movements;[4] but then we would like to know whether he favors "social action" to crush them and restore the Marxist regimes or some other option (which, one hopes, does not rely on that undiscussible goal). I think he was obliged to tell us this, if he wants to base his attack on pluralism upon political grounds.

While I do not believe he has made a successful case against pluralism, he has succeeded in another sense in that he has made me meet him in the political arena, thereby confirming what I thought was a *reductio ad absurdum* of the tendency of the ideological approaches, which would force us to "stop discussing literature or criticism and instead sponsor debates about politics." I still insist, however, that this is irrelevant to my original argument, since, I repeat, there is no necessary connection between any critical approach and any political position. Critics from all parts of the political spectrum practice all the basic approaches, and one does not even have to be a political liberal to accept critical pluralism.

Bristol's comments on the other two planks of my peace platform are much briefer. He criticizes "the notion of an 'objective meaning,' " but I never used that phrase; I defined objectivism as "the belief that one can attain objective knowledge of a literary text," and I think he should share this belief. Since he refers to "social reality" and characterizes some ideas about it as "true" and others as "false" or "fictions" or "misrecognitions," he must believe in the possibility of objective knowledge of the external world (it is hard to see how he could be a Marxist if he did not), and this should include literary texts: for example, does he not think it is objectively true that they contain those "ideological contradictions" I referred to? His main criticism, however, is aimed at what he sees as a contradiction between my objectivism and my pluralism—or as he puts it, "between the doctrine of one truth (objective meaning) and many truths (pluralism)." But that is precisely the problem I tried to resolve by the concept of *qua*, which he never mentions. I argued that this concept enables us to distinguish different approaches to a text, within each of which interpretations "can be objectively true or false," so that there is no doctrine of one truth and yet there still is truth. This in fact was the basis of my pluralism. My argument here may be wrong—it is probably oversimplified—but I think he should have addressed it before accusing me of contradiction.

I do not understand why he objects to rationalism, my third plank, since his views on the role of reason seem rather close to my own. He approves of "rational deliberation" and his paper consists of carefully constructed arguments that clearly are based on reason and are meant to appeal to the reason of his audience. And even though we disagree on many substantive issues, we seem to agree, for the most part, on how one goes about proving or disproving a proposition, on what constitutes a logical difficulty (such as contradiction), and so on, and therefore we presumably share a sense of, and reliance upon, rationality. Yet at the end he attacks me for invoking a "god-like Reason" that "doesn't know what it wants to talk about." Of course reason cannot know what it wants to talk about; only people can know that (thus I wanted to talk about criticism, while he wanted to talk about politics but not about his political goals). And the reason (lower case) that I invoked is not at all "god-like"; it is all too human-like and therefore fallible and vulnerable to the pressures of emotion and biases related to race, gender, class and many other factors, which we must continually look out for. But it is still the best instrument we have for dealing with the world and with each other.

I would not want to end my response to Bristol without commenting on his charge that I am "the self-appointed representative" of a certain community. I have never claimed or attempted to represent anyone else. I also thought that in our critical activity we were all self-appointed and did not need any authorization; but if I am wrong he should have told us who appointed him to do what he does. Does he prefer the situation that obtained in those collapsing Marxist regimes, where no one was self-appointed (except the rulers) and critics did what they were told, or is he thinking of the future establishment of his "consensus" that would assign critics their tasks?

Gayle Greene begins by objecting to my definition of ideology because it "has a specific meaning . . . derived from Althusser." But he was not speaking from Mount Sinai and there is no single correct definition of such terms, so we are free to choose from among the current meanings, as long as we make ourselves clear. I chose one that is often used today by many people, including Marxists, as Bristol notes. In fact most Marxist regimes have an official in charge of "ideology," which must refer to a consciously held set of political beliefs.[5] She does not seem to be aware, moreover, that her Althusserian definition raises some major problems. If everyone is supposed to be the "prisoner" of this ideology, why do we disagree on so many basic issues, including the assumptions of the ideology itself? And if this ideology is supposed to be "unconscious," how do we know about it? She says this "ideology is always somebody else's, never one's own," which would mean that if we admit we are ideological (as she does), then we are not ideological, which sounds like an ideological contradiction to me.

Her next objection, to my designating certain critical approaches as "ideological," follows from her belief that the term has only one true meaning and disappears once we recognize that two definitions are involved. According to her definition all approaches are ideological (though this definition requires that they all have the same ideology), while according to mine the term applies only to approaches that are consciously produced from, and meant to serve, a political creed. (This has nothing to do with my attitude toward that creed, as she claims; I accept feminism but not Marxism, yet I consider both approaches ideological.) But even if I adopted her definition and called all approaches ideological, this would not affect my argument. I would just have to find another term to designate those approaches consciously produced from a political creed,[6] which I wanted to discuss separately because I thought they were significantly different from the others in the threat they pose to pluralism.

Greene then objects to my statement that "most ordinary people" or "most audiences" view literary works as pleasurable, since this universalizes them and treats them as male. But I did not posit a universal here, and am well aware that people go to literature for various and often mixed motives; I was only arguing that the common denominator, for most of them, was the expectation of pleasure. (I assumed they were people in our society, but I certainly did not assume they were men, unless she wants to deny that women enjoy literature.) If I was wrong she could easily show this, not by going back to that tired old argument about universals, but by taking up my invitation (which Bristol also declines) to explain why, in terms of her own approach, "anyone other than a professional critic would want to see a play or read a novel."

The middle portion of her response deals primarily with the Forum letter (Adelman et al.), which, as I said in my opening remarks, is a dead end. It leads her to repeat the arguments in the letter and me to repeat my answers to them, making it harder for us to move forward. And it locks her into a defensive posture that prevents her from acknowledging any of the letter's logical and rhetorical flaws, which were obvious to many readers. (One of them accused me of writing the letter myself since it makes the signers look so bad and so makes me look pretty good.) Fortunately for my purposes, however, the three parts of the letter that she focuses on are related to the three planks of my peace treaty.

On the issue of rationalism, she defends and even amplifies the letter's attack upon reason and the Enlightenment, precipitated by my call for a scientific study of human development based on "evidence that compelled the assent of all rational people, regardless of their gender or ideology." First she relativizes reason by repeating the point made in the letter that the concept has been applied differently in different historical periods, to which I can only repeat my reply that this has happened to many such concepts (including the values invoked by the letter), but does not prevent us from using them. Then in an about-face she reifies reason as a monster who has "arrogated" power, tried to "grab" resources and people, and "brought the planet to its present disastrous condition."[7] Of course it would make just as much (or as little) sense to credit reason with the good things that happened on the planet, such as the movements for sexual equality, the abolition of slavery, and Jewish emancipation, which all came from the Enlightenment. But it is absurd to treat reason as an agent; indeed it is very like the hypostatization of a "god-like Reason" that Bristol imputes to me, except that Greene's is a satan-like Reason. Then she co-opts Shakespeare by claiming that "his villains use reason to mask the most appalling irrationality." Yet she could not call it irrational unless she had a concept of true rationality by which to judge it—a concept that must transcend gender and history, since Shakespeare shares it, and that now turns out to be a positive standard for her and for him. And she ends by having him oppose the Enlightenment, Protestantism, and capitalism. Now I think it can be argued that some of his plays denigrate the kind of individualism and acquisitiveness that came to be associated with capitalism, but this denigration is based on an endorsement of feudal values.[8] There is a similar tendency to idealize feudalism in Marxist thought—in the opening of *The Communist Manifesto,* for example, which indicts the bourgeoisie for drowning chivalrous sentiment in the icy waters of egotistical calculation, etc. And since Greene's alliance with Shakespeare also implies this attitude, she would seem to be guilty of the "nostalgia" that she accuses me of.

She returns to the attack on reason later with the assertion that our debate will not change anyone's mind because deeply held beliefs "are not rational or susceptible to change by reason." If she means they are not *wholly* rational and cannot be changed by reason *alone,* then I agree, although she is wrong to limit them to politics (as in her argument that views about literature must be "ultimately political" because they are held "tenaciously") since they are found in many other areas, such as religion—in fact we often call a change in any deeply held belief a "conversion." And even though such conversions are not brought about by reason alone, it often plays a significant role in them, as we learn, for instance, in accounts from former Freudians or Marxists explaining how they came to see the light. But I did not think we were talking about conversion here. The main point of my plea for pluralism was that it allows critics to debate productively *without* the need to convert everyone to their own approach. And I certainly was not arguing for political conversions. I have no wish to convert Greene from her feminism, which I share, and I do not even want to convert Bristol from his Marxism, which I do not share. Soon the only surviving Marxists in the world may be holding out in the faculties of capitalist universities, and I think we should try to preserve some there, like any other endangered species.

Greene also raises the issue of rationalism at the very end when she turns to my discussion of theories of human development that triggered the letter's attack on reason. She says that feminists accept Nancy Chodorow's theory of masculinity, even though they "do *not* want to believe it," because they are "made to" by the fact of male rage. Although she does not seem to realize it, she is proceeding here exactly as I recommended, by judging these theories on the basis of the evidence rather than her own wishes or interests as a woman and a feminist. I think she is wrong in this case, however; the fact of male rage (of which more later) does not prove the Chodorow theory, since there are other ways to account for it, as Chodorow herself now recognizes (*Feminism* 1, 5–6, 15). But Greene's argument shows that she really does believe such questions should be settled by "evidence that compelled the assent of all rational people, regardless of their gender or ideology."

On the issue of objectivism, she simply replicates the confusion I noted in the Forum letter, which acknowledged the partiality of feminists' readings and then presented their readings of Shakespeare as objective facts. Thus she tells us, on the one hand, that interpretations of literature "really are determined by political ideology," that we must admit their "ideological and political and gendered bases," and that she reads and writes as she does because she is "white, female, middle-class, middle-aged and . . . lived through the feminist revolution"; but, on the other hand, that this does not lead to "relativism," that "some readings do remain better than others" since they are more "appropriate" (to the text, presumably, rather than to her ideology), and that she "know[s] truth from error." Nor does she see any need to reconcile these two positions, being content to "live amidst contradictions." I think that her problem here (shared by many other feminist and Marxist critics) has been created in large part by the genetic fallacy, which claims that our views of the world are caused by our race, gender, class, and similar factors, and that they therefore must be judged on the basis of those causes. But both of these claims are false. Our views may often be influenced by such factors, but are not necessarily determined by them. If they were, there would be no male feminists or female anti-feminists, no bourgeois radicals or proletarian reactionaries, and the millions of people who meet Greene's five specifications would all read and write as she does. Moreover, even if our views were caused by these factors, it does not follow that they must be judged on that basis. This is obvious in the "hard" sciences: the fact that some physicist's theory was generated by his personal or political bias, for instance, would be wholly irrelevant to its evaluation, which would be based on objective, neutral criteria shared by other physicists. (I am not referring to some absolute objectivity or neutrality, if they exist, but to the standards of the discipline itself, which are independent of the biases of individual physicists.) Otherwise we would end up with a white, female, middle-class, middle-aged, feminist physics; a yellow, male, working-class, old-aged, liberal physics; a black, female, upper-class, youthful, conservative physics; and so on and on.[9]

Although the objective criteria may be more difficult to apply, the same principle should operate in the "soft" sciences and, I am arguing, in literary criticism, with my *qua* proviso (about which Greene is as silent as Bristol).

This can be shown by returning to my *PMLA* article ("Feminist Thematics"). The readings I dealt with there were all formalist and I criticized them *qua* that approach, trying to prove, for instance, that some of them ignored parts of the text that did not fit their thesis. I may have been wrong in any given case, of course; but the way to refute me would be, not by a genetic argument claiming that my motivation was sexist (even if that were true), but by an objective demonstration that the part in question really was not ignored in the reading or really did fit its thesis. It is significant that neither the Forum letter nor Greene's paper attempts to do this, and that what she calls "one of the most telling" examples of error in my article is cast in the genetic mode. She says that I objected to the critics' lack of compassion for the tragic hero because of my sexist assumption that as women they should have been more "nurturing." But my objection had nothing to do with the gender of the critics (who in fact were not all women); it is the same point I made in *New Readings* against the older ironic critics of Shakespeare, most of whom were men (85–102, 114–25). It would be interesting to see how she could account for my motivation in that book, where the great majority of the people I criticized shared not only my gender but also my race, class, and politics. If I was not criticizing them on objective grounds, then what was the real basis of my arguments?

She affirms her "embrace" of pluralism, the third plank in my platform, but it is a limited embrace since she is committed to defending the letter's objection to the publication of my article, which is not a very pluralistic stance. She repeats the charge in the letter that my article should have been denied publication because I failed to understand the feminist cause,[10] to which I can only repeat, once more, that I did understand and support this cause, but that a just cause cannot justify interpretive faults. As I already explained, I was judging the essays there as interpretations of Shakespeare, which is what they claimed to be, but she insists that this was unfair since they must be judged in terms of the "larger issues" of feminism. And Marxists often make the same complaint that those who criticize their readings of literature are ignoring (or opposing) their just political cause. (The difference of course is that feminists really have one.) This defensive move from criticism to politics is one of the major tendencies distinguishing what I call the ideological approaches from all the others. The older historical critics and the old New Critics may have been ideological in Greene's sense of the term; but when I attacked their readings they did not mount an ideological defense, in the name of liberal humanism or any other cause. Unlike them, the Marxists and feminists seem to claim a special privilege for their approaches, on political grounds, that grants immunity from the kind of scrutiny to which other approaches are subjected and so would amount to a denial of pluralism, since it would in effect mean that only feminists can criticize feminist readings and only Marxists can criticize Marxist readings. I raised this point at the beginning of my paper, but neither Greene nor Bristol responded to it.

Her second objection to the decision of the *PMLA* Editorial Board is also political, but focuses on what she calls "the politics of the publication of this essay." Now *PMLA*, as I noted, has published a steady stream of feminist readings, but that apparently was not political. Yet when it publishes one lonely critique of some products of this approach, that suddenly becomes political because it is connected to male rage against feminists and to the injustices women still suffer on our faculties. I would certainly agree that there is a lot of male rage out there, which I encountered in some of the letters I received when my article appeared. There is also a lot of geriatric rage, felt by older men and women in the profession reacting against all the new approaches. All I can say is that I do not feel this rage and never appealed to it. And I certainly agree that there is sexual discrimination in faculty pay and promotions, for I contributed to a successful suit brought by women teachers at my university to rectify this. But what does that have to do with the publication of my article? Is she saying that no criticism of feminist readings should be published until all the rage and injustice have been eliminated? But that would be again to privilege this approach on political grounds and thus to disembrace pluralism. And she carries this argument over to the later letters in the Forum responding to our exchange, by dismissing them as further expressions of male rage, anxiety, or hysteria. Of course such feelings could have generated some of the letters (though she might have mentioned that one comes from a woman college president); but that does not constitute a refutation of their statements, which would be the genetic fallacy again.[11] She cannot entertain the possibility that any of their statements might be right, because she cannot entertain the possibility that there was anything wrong with the letter she signed, or that there was anything right in my article that this letter opposed. She has polarized the field into a battle between "us" and "them," with all the truth and virtue on "our" side and all the error and vice on "theirs." I think this is a general tendency of the ideological approaches, and the underlying cause of their threat to pluralism and their creation of an atmosphere that prevents "us" and "them" from talking to and learning from each other.[12] That is why I presented my peace treaty, which she seems to treat as a declaration of war. But I am not her enemy, and my pluralism extends to her even if hers does not extend to me.

The final part of her paper focuses on the present status of feminist criticism and attempts to refute my claim that this approach has achieved victory. Here

I think we are both right, depending on how one defines the arena. In the prestigious arena I am right, as can easily be demonstrated from the programs of the latest *MLA* conventions and other major conferences, the book ads, and the articles in our leading journals, including *PMLA*. But this is only a small sector of the profession. There is also a vast hinterland (which in academia is not a geographic designation) full of people who resist feminism and the other new approaches, producing most of that "rage" and "backlash," or who may not even be affected by them. In this arena she is right, but it is not the one that counts in the long run. However, she also tries to disprove the feminists' victory in the prestigious arena by contrasting the excitement of the late 1970s, when they were all working together against the establishment, with their situation now, when they are split into factions and are taken for granted, absorbed, or usurped by younger colleagues who "attempt to climb to the top on our bodies." But her account of their early difficulties in finding a publisher for *The Woman's Part* really shows how far and how fast they have advanced, when compared to the ease with which feminist anthologies are published today, so here she is arguing against herself.[13] And her other complaints are also evidence of their victory. Young colleagues try to climb on their bodies because they are on top, where those colleagues want to be, just as they themselves climbed on the bodies of the New Critics when they were on top, who in turn climbed on the bodies of the historical critics. She wants the process to stop with her group, but that is not how it works. And it is because feminists are now on top that they can afford to disagree, and other critics can take their work for granted and move on to the fields to which prestige has shifted. Those are the fruits of victory. Greene seems to want the excitement and solidarity of permanent struggle upward and the satisfaction of total and permanent success, but she could never have both and now cannot have either. That does not mean, however, that the feminist victory has "taught us nothing" and will have no lasting consequences.

It would require much more confidence than I possess to try to predict the directions that criticism will take in the future. About all we can be reasonably sure of is that it will continue to change, and that in a few years most of the work that now claims to stand at the cutting edge will look as quaintly old-fashioned as the New Criticism seems to us today. Some Marxists will probably linger on for a while, still waiting for the imminent collapse of "late capitalism" from its "irreconcilable contradictions,"[14] but it is hard to see how they will recruit our students, who are smart enough to realize that this is the era of late communism. Freudianism will also probably linger on in various permutations (such as Chodorow's) before finally giving up the ghost; a newer new historicism will probably replace the present one; and so on. Some of these approaches, I suspect, will disappear without leaving much behind, except as material for future dissertations on the strange history of criticism. But this is not true of feminism, which seems to be the only one of the new approaches that is certain to have a permanent effect on the field, because it has permanently raised our consciousness of the importance of gender and gender-bias in literature and literary criticism. The approach itself may slip out of fashion, but I cannot believe we will ever return to the time when critics (male or course) could argue that the theme of various Shakespearean plays was "What is man?" without ever asking themselves whether they were talking about half or all of humanity, or when they could assert with impunity that Lucrece "subconsciously" wants to be raped, or that Desdemona "shrinks from the reality of the whore within her, the potential whore which exists within all women," or that "the prime sources of disaster in Shakespeare's plays are to be found in women who neurotically forget their biological role (like Lady Macbeth) or their social tact (like Desdemona and Cordelia), or who attempt to seize physical supremacy from the male (like Queen Margaret or Cleopatra)."[15] We all know better than that now because of the work of feminist criticism, and for this we are all in its debt.

## NOTES

1. Thus Moi says that opposition to "patriarchy and sexism . . . necessarily also entails" opposition to capitalism (10), and Greene that "sexism and the values of patriarchy are inherent in capitalism" since their "root is economic" ("Feminist" 41–42). This attempt to blame sexism on capitalism is an example of the Marxist propensity for deducing facts from theory; the facts are that sexism long preceded capitalism and also thrives under communism.

2. See Barker 116; Barker and Hulme 205; Belsey, "Literature" 26; Bristol, "Lenten Butchery" 220–21; Dollimore, *Radical Tragedy* 271; Dollimore and Sinfield, *Political Shakespeare* viii; Eagleton, *Literary Theory* 210, 217; Evans 263–64; Holderness, *Shakespeare's History* 226; Jameson, "Science" 301–302; Moi 10–11; and the end of Walter Cohen's essay (38–39), where he details at length the alliances that "leftist professors of literature" should seek with students, high-school teachers, media people, etc., and then adds in his last sentence that the purpose of all this is "social change," with no hint of what change he has in mind.

3. *Shakespeare's America* 211. This presumably is the belief—or hope—behind his references to those "strains" and "tensions" that the ISAs are "no longer able to manage" and that could "permanently derange our present system." In *Shakespeare's America* he presents the same argument, again citing my work (along with Cavell's and Greenblatt's) as evidence of "very deep rifts" in our society (209). For many years now Marxists have seized on such signs of conflict to justify their predictions of the imminent collapse of capitalism from its own "irreconcilable contradictions" (see n. 14), while the absence of conflict in Marxist lands was supposed to prove their stability.

4. He detours near the end to attack the market system for treating the "priceless values"

of art as "worthless values," which is another example of the Marxist deduction of facts from theory. In fact the arts are flourishing in America, partly because of infusions of money from capitalists, who are not aware that they are paying for worthless values. And artists themselves do not seem to be aware of their plight in a market economy, judging from the number who emigrate from socialist to capitalist societies as compared with the number proceeding in the other direction.

5. Many subjects of these regimes had *two* ideologies in this sense—the official Marxist one that they parroted in their indoctrination courses and when government informers might be present, and a very different one that they actually believed and that often approximated my "lapsed or fallen" liberalism.

6. Practitioners of those approaches sometimes call them "committed" or "informed," implying that critics using the other approaches are simply unaware of their own ideology (which is usually supposed to be liberal humanism).

7. This sounds like the standard Marxist indictment of capitalism, which she equates with reason, even though Marxists usually claim it is communism that is really rational or "scientific." In view of that claim, I wonder if she would expand her account of reason's criminal career to include the horrors of Stalin's purges, Mao's Cultural Revolution, and Pol Pot's holocaust.

8. Delany's essay presents a good case for that view. In "Bashing" (81–83) I discuss this tendency to idealize the past (I call it "edenism"), which has led both reactionaries and radicals to attack capitalism as worse than feudalism. Greene indulges in it when she says that capitalism "reduces" people to "objects for exploitation" ("Feminist" 39, 41). She never explains what they were reduced *from*, but it must be from the Good Old Days of serfdom.

9. The USSR had a Marxist science of genetics, promoted by Lysenko on ideological grounds (with no pluralistic dissent permitted), but it has not survived.

10. She also repeats the letter's charge that my article should have been rejected because it is "unsophisticated," which assumes that sophistication is a neutral, objective standard. Unfortunately neither the letter nor her paper inspires confidence that she is a better judge of it than the *PMLA* Editorial Board. Later she complains, with no sense of the irony, that young feminists now levy this same charge against her own group ("naively Anglo-American").

11. I discuss this tactic for refuting opponents by attributing anxiety to them (which the Forum letter also employed against me) in "Panic."

12. This point is made more eloquently in Ellis, "Radical" 8 and Mueller 29–30. I agree with Graff's criticism (*Professing* ch. 15) of the all too common "departmental" pluralism that simply avoids conflict by leaving teachers alone to do their own thing (though this is still preferable to monism since at least the students are exposed to various approaches); but that is not a necessary consequence of pluralism, which also makes it possible for practitioners of different approaches to engage in productive arguments, as I tried to show, by abandoning the claim that their approach is right and the others are wrong.

13. She also argues against her claims here when she says at the outset that some feminist principles are now so well established that it is "rather late in the day to have to point [this] out," and is "astonishing that this needs repeating," so that my failure to adopt them proves my ignorance or naiveté.

14. Jameson now denies that Marxism is a predictive science ("Science" 290), which would surprise Marx himself and all his followers who thought the laws of economic determinism gave

them the key to the future; but it is easy to understand Jameson's disclaimer because none of Marx's predictions has come true.

15. Battenhouse, *Tragedy* 16; Rice 219; Richmond 71. I criticize some of these sexist interpretations in *New Readings* 99, and the "What is man?" theme in 21–22, 56. The Forum letter also claims that the tragedies often "ask what it is to 'be a man,' " but it is clearly referring to males.

# 7

# Straw Women and Whipping Girls: The (Sexual) Politics of Critical Self-Fashioning

Carol Cook

To enter into a critical debate is to take up a position and to position others—allies, competitors, objects of attack. Whether we acknowledge it or not, we are constantly engaged, as critics and theorists, in a certain intellectual imaginary, a certain matrix of specularities, identifications, repudiations, motivated by investments that go beyond a disinterested search for truth.[1] This, I would suggest, is unavoidable. What interests me here is the way that feminist criticism has been positioned in recent essays on the subject of Shakespeare studies.

Critics of feminist critics of Shakespeare often begin by acknowledging a certain diversity within feminist scholarship, but tend quickly to target a group of books dating from the early 1980s—the first body of work on Shakespeare to emerge as conspicuously feminist in the United States. This body of work includes Juliet Dusinberre's *Shakespeare and the Nature of Women*, Lenz, Greene, and Neely's collection, *The Woman's Part*, Irene Dash's *Wooing, Wedding, and Power*, Marilyn French's *Shakespeare's Division of Experience*, Coppélia Kahn's *Man's Estate*, and Linda Bamber's *Comic Women, Tragic Men*. Thus, Richard Levin's "Feminist Thematics and Shakespearean Tragedy" refers to "the quantity and diversity" of feminist work on Shakespeare, but chooses to focus on "one major trend of the movement in this country" (125), the "trend" characterized by *The Woman's Part*, Kahn, French, and others whose work belongs to the early 1980s. Kathleen McLuskie, coming at the subject from quite a different direction, asserts at the beginning of her essay, "The Patriarchal Bard," that "feminist criticism can only be defined by the multiplicity of critical practices engaged in by feminists," but is primarily concerned with the ahistoricism and theoretical weaknesses of "the mimetic essentialist model of feminist criticism" of Bamber, French, Kahn, and Dusinberre. Jonathan Goldberg, in a post-structuralist critique, does not make the gesture of remarking on the diversity of feminist criticism but immediately zeroes in on his target, "a body of [feminist] criticism that ignores . . . complexities of genre, and that seems intent upon straitlacing the Shakespearean text into rigidities of form and meaning" ("Inscriptions" 117). This "body of criticism" is represented in Goldberg's essay only by Linda Bamber and by Carolyn Heilbrun's review of Bamber's book. Goldberg does, in effect, acknowledge other feminist criticisms by the inclusion of an epigraph from Jane Gallop and by a later reference to Luce Irigaray, whose psychoanalytic feminism will be enlisted in Goldberg's argument in opposition to Bamber.

When feminist criticism of Shakespeare is the subject, these are the usual suspects who are rounded up. There are other suspects who could be rounded up—that is, there are, as Levin and McLuskie acknowledge, other feminists writing about Shakespeare now.[2] The targeting of this particular group has to do, I believe, with their awkward position in the middle of something. In order to understand what defines these feminist critics as a group (despite methodological differences among them), it is useful to contextualize their work in a chronology of recent criticism.[3] Dusinberre's book was published in 1975, *The Woman's Part* and the books by Bamber, French, Dash and Kahn were all published between 1980 and 1982. The impetus behind this body of work was the women's movement of the 1960s and 1970s, a movement that brought women academics to reconsider the subjects of their scholarship and teaching in light of a new feminist politics. The group of American feminists who first began to publish on issues of gender in Shakespeare had mostly received their professional training at a time just prior to the emergence of theory (post-structuralism and cultural materialism) in American departments of literature. This meant that the feminist books of the early 1980s did not build their readings of plays on rigorously developed theoretical positions. Their strategies and focus tend to be "humanist," that is, concerned with character, with ethical and psychological meanings, viewed in light of feminist concerns about sexual difference instead of in the "universal" terms previously claimed by Shakespeare criticism.[4]

Hence, these feminist critics rebelled against their academic fathers by daring to politicize discussions of the most sacred of secular writers but made the foray into political criticism without the carefully armored theoretical positions that have now become the rule in academic criticism. The result is the feeling Gayle Greene expresses of being "beset from all sides":

> Older colleagues don't read us; most simply ignore us, hoping that if they wait it out we'll eventually go away. Our contemporaries and younger col-

> leagues, eager to make a space for themselves, either ignore us, writing as though feminist criticism had never happened, or attempt to climb to the top on our bodies, having exposed us as theoretically "soft," anachronistic, vulgarly empiricist, naively Anglo-American—whatever. . . . (this volume)

It is not my purpose here to defend feminist critics, nor to examine—at least in detail—the substance of the disagreements between this group of feminist critics and their antagonists on the Right and Left. Rather, I wish to examine what is unspoken in these attacks, in the tacit politics signalled by strategy and style. My own position in this conflicted territory is equivocal. I am a feminist critic of Shakespeare whose work was partly made possible by those who published feminist criticism in the early 1980s when I was working on my dissertation. At the same time, I suppose I must be included in that group, cited by Gayle Greene, who have found this inaugural feminist work on Shakespeare theoretically unsatisfactory. Nonetheless, I am concerned by a tendency that I see in current discussions of Shakespeare criticism to make feminist criticism the straw woman, to hypostasize a field of criticism that is internally divided and still developing, fixing it as a specular image of the Other to be repudiated. In my readings of essays by Richard Levin and Jonathan Goldberg, I will suggest that the representation of feminist criticism serves to underwrite a certain representation of the critic's self, facilitating an identification with a chosen audience through aggression directed at the feminist target in what Gayatri Spivak has called "the scramble for legitimacy in the house of theory" ("Feminism and Deconstruction" 218).

In two recent *PMLA* essays, "Feminist Thematics and Shakespearean Tragedy" and "The Poetics and Politics of Bardicide," Richard Levin takes on feminist criticism. The first essay deals primarily with those feminists discussed above as "humanist"; the second deals with feminist psychoanalytic critics and with cultural materialists (some of whom are feminists), whose critical practices, different as they are in some respects, are linked in their explicitly political analysis of literature and in their rejection of the intentionalist understanding of meaning. Levin styles himself something of a contemporary Swift, conducting his critiques of feminist criticism in a satiric vein. His method relies as much on tone and self-presentation as it does on critical analysis, for the rhetorical effect of Levin's essays is not to engage the reader in a genuine analysis of the feminist work under discussion. Rather, Levin appeals to a particular audience, an audience of traditional literary scholars who have felt displaced and bypassed by the rapid movement of literary theory into new and difficult areas. Thus, the "Bardicide" essay opens with an implicit definition of the audience to whom it is meant to appeal:

> Anyone who has tried to keep up with the ensemble of new critical discourses currently circulating around and recirculating Shakespeare's dramatic texts must have noticed that a curious thing has happened to Shakespeare himself. Any trace of his responsibility for what goes on in these texts is being systematically occluded, and even his name, if it appears at all, is often placed under erasure by quotation marks, so that uninitiated readers might think they have inadvertently transgressed onto some anti-Stratfordian discursive space. (491)

Here Levin appeals sympathetically to those "uninitiated readers" who have tried (effortfully, futilely, it is implied) to "keep up with" the extravagances of contemporary criticism. Toward the end of the essay Levin will appeal again to "the uninitiated reader who was trying to follow the reasoning of these critics" as described and summarized by Levin himself. This audience of the "uninitiated," we gather by implication, is a happy few, a band of reasonable men, innocently curious, disinterested, but certainly bewildered by those tendentious feminists and obfuscating Marxists. Levin enlists his audience's confidence that he has taken it upon himself to master the peculiar language of these theorists, since he sprinkles his opening sentences with words intended to imply that he has penetrated the strange rites of the "initiated," words like "discourse," "trace," "text," "under erasure," "transgressed," and "discursive space"—a ventriloquizing appropriation of critical language characteristic of Levin's satiric strategy.

Levin's satiric persona is not unlike Swift's Gulliver—sometimes the bemused rationalist, sometimes wide-eyed and wondering in the face of the inexplicable practices of those he purports to analyze. Thus, in "Feminist Thematics" he takes the first tack, suggesting ironically that according to feminist critics "the characters themselves [in Shakespeare's tragedies] are unaware of the real cause of their misfortunes . . . which seems a pity, for if they only knew they might have given us some great last words" (127), words which Levin then goes on to invent for us to great comic effect. In "Bardicide," Levin sometimes takes the direct satiric stance, but at other times plays the *ingénu*, the reasonable man engaged in an open-minded attempt to achieve a rational understanding of the irrational. Thus, in discussing critical arguments about displacement in Shakespeare's plays, Levin writes "I did not note any difference between the Marxist and the neo-Freudian treatments of this strategy" (495), in a tone intended to suggest sincere interest. He presents himself as genuinely seeking an understanding of these "new critical discourses," but baffled in his attempts by the peculiar resistance of these critics to reason. In "Feminist Thematics" Levin begins by complimenting feminists (could we say gallantly?) for their "intelligent and dedicated" efforts, and later suggests that feminist critics "are moving . . . in the right direction, *toward* a promising line of inquiry for feminist critics into the *actual* nature of the gender assumptions in these plays," which, however, would "mean holding in abeyance . . . their own attitudes toward gender . . ." (134, my emphasis). In "Bardicide," he introduces his attack on non-intentionalist criticisms by saying "The examples were not selected on the basis of their approaches, but most of the first type that I found come from the Marxist cultural materialists and the feminists associated with them, and most of the second from critics employing a feminist revision of Freud that I call neo-Freudian" (491). In both essays, Levin seems anxious to mark out his position as apolitical, disinterested, in fact sympathetic to feminists (if only they could discard their unfortunate prejudices). He did not choose to attack feminists in "Feminist Thematics" because they are feminists, but because they are thematists. He didn't choose his targets in "Bardicide" on political grounds, but they just happened to be leftists.

Levin's critical satire depends, as satire must, on presenting the objects of his attack as excessive, extravagant, eccentric when measured against the rational norm evident in the satirist's voice or implied position. Naturally, the success of this strategy depends, to an extent that Levin would perhaps be reluctant to acknowledge, on caricature. He needs to present a large number of different critics as unified in their positions, as all making the same moves, the same arguments, the same mistakes. He creates a false unity in order to unify the antagonism against it. In "Feminist Thematics" he cites a number of different critics as examples of the same approach, labeling as "thematic" the work of some feminist critics whose methodology could be characterized as humanist or formalist (Novy) but also that of feminists whose approach is psychoanalytic. He includes among the thematic critics Madelon Gohlke (Sprengnether), whose essay in *The Woman's Part* advocates what is clearly a non-thematic kind of reading, a "reading on the margins of discourse." At one point Levin (belatedly) acknowledges that Gohlke isn't exactly doing thematic criticism (130) but his attack on her defines her by that model.

In "Bardicide," Levin is dealing with two critical modes which he correctly characterizes as differentiated in certain respects but allied in others, allowing him, once again, to create a unified object of attack—"new critical discourses." His characterization of both feminist psychoanalytic and cultural materialist critics consistently betrays a certain ignorance about the premises and theoretical underpinnings of these critical discourses. For example, he constructs a category he calls "neo-Freudian," which is made to include the work of critics drawing upon object relations theory (Kahn), new historicists (Montrose), and those influenced by Lacan (myself), to all of whom Levin ascribes the idea of a "feminine or maternal 'subtext,' " an idea that approximates certain aspects of Coppélia Kahn's work (but also misrepresents it, insofar as this idea is rendered meaningless in this decontextualized state) but does not reflect the ideas of others identified by Levin as "neo-Freudians."

"The Poetics and Politics of Bardicide" is such a tangle of misinformation and disinformation that it would require more time and patience than I have here to address its confusions. I will single out then only its primary satiric device as one example of its method. Levin argues that once feminist and materialist critics dispense with the idea of an author's intention as that which produces and controls meaning, the author function is merely ascribed to "the play itself or, as they usually prefer to call it, the text" (492). The bulk of the essay then consists of a list, in escalating order of absurdity, of the "Good Moves and Bad Moves" that "these critics" allegedly ascribe to "the text": "the text has a project," "the text displaces," "the text conceals," "the text offers scapegoats," etc., and most preciously, "the text gets nervous." This is highly comic, of course, but the comedy has a further rhetorical effect: the laughter elicited by this apparent exposé of critical absurdity tends to pre-empt a closer examination of how the satiric target has been constructed.

If we make that examination, though, we might recognize that Levin offers countless examples, quoting from a remarkably wide and varied group of critics, but it is notable that in almost none of these quotations does the word "text" appear. Levin supplies the word "text" and then quotes brief bits of sentences containing the desired buzz words—"scapegoat," "displaces," etc. This is because the critics Levin quotes do not, for the most part, talk about the text as he is suggesting they do. Although Levin ascribes to all of the critics discussed in his article a "preference" for the word "text" over "play," he does not offer any account of what the word "text" has come to signify in current critical discourses or how it might differ from "play." In fact, the word "text" is most notably associated with post-structuralist criticism, and hence with only some—not all—feminist psychoanalytic criticism. Cultural materialists do not especially tend to refer to the "text" but more often to "plays" since their concern is with theater as a social institution and not with "reading" in the post-structuralist sense. Levin cites, under the heading "the text has a project," Dollimore and Sinfield's essay on *Henry V*. The word "text" does not appear in that essay, and the authors talk about the *play* in ways precisely contrary to what Levin implies: rather than reify and hypostasize the play, assigning it a unified *agency*, they read it as a site of ideological conflict.

The point I wish to make here is that while Levin presents himself as interested in understanding those he criticizes, in subjecting feminist work, for example, to a scrutiny which would actually be cleansing and clarifying, thus helping feminist critics to advance their cause, he has not bothered to do the work that would be required to engage in such a critique. He consistently ascribes to his targets ideas which they do not hold, defines disagreements about central issues by misrepresenting basic premises (choosing, for example, in "Ideological Criticism and Pluralism" to define "ideology" as "consciously held ideas" without justifying that definition in light of the extensive *disagreement* and debate among leftist critics about what ideology is), and creates a unified target of attack out of an internally divided, if politically allied, group of critics (while insisting that politics are not the issue). The effect of this misrecognition and homogenization of feminists and other ideological critics through satire, whatever Levin's intentions, is to elicit a kind of vengeful glee and venting of spleen from those who, I suspect, may in the past have grumbled among themselves but not openly attacked feminist critics.

Levin would, I'm sure, object to the idea that he directs his remarks to an audience implicitly defined as male. What leads me to this conclusion is both that the traditional critics included in the "uninitiated" are overwhelmingly apt to be tenured professors of a generation older than the feminists under attack—a generation that includes (as do those after it) very few tenured women—and that Levin creates a sense of solidarity with his audience by suggesting that men have been systematically victimized by feminists. In "Feminine Thematics," he refers to Shakespeare's male characters as "victims" of feminist reading (129) and accuses feminists of "a sexist stereotyping of the [male] protagonist" of Shakespearean tragedy (131). This accusation gathers steam until, near the end of the essay, Levin charges feminists with an unfairness to all men: "I think we would have to say, finally, that this 'feminist' conception of masculinity is just as much a distortion of real life as it is of the tragedies" (136). In "The Poetics and Politics of Bardicide," as the title suggests, Shakespeare himself is the victim, since the theoretical issue of the death of the author, as articulated by Barthes and Foucault, is here treated as an instance of political assassination.

That this tactic strikes a chord with readers of *PMLA* is suggested by the letters to the *PMLA* Forum that appeared after a group of feminists responded angrily to Levin's article. Clearly there was aggression on both sides in this dispute, but the letters, which appeared in the May 1989 issue—all from men—impute aggression only to the feminists who are accused of having "ganged up to attack" Levin, and of "religious fervor," "totalitarianism," "faddist methods" (Weitzman), of "meanness" and of "insult[ing] a distinguished scholar," in "personal attacks" (Purdy), and of "propaganda" (Birnbaum). In contrast, Levin is characterized in these letters as "temperate—yes, rational and courageous" (Weitzman) and as a "victim" whose "reasoned reply" might not be heard above the clamor of his attackers. In this scenario, feminists appear as shrill, irrational harpies whose brute force must be resisted by the "principles" of scholarship (Purdy). This is a scenario familiar to feminists, who have repeatedly been characterized in precisely these ways. Is it fair to tax Levin with the language of these letters, which is not, of course, his own? It does seem to me that the letters tell us something about the appeal of Levin's essay itself and the "us against the feminist hordes" mentality that it endorses.

In Levin's writing, feminist criticism becomes the whipping girl on whom a collective aggression is vented. Insofar as the attack on feminist criticism energizes and facilitates an identification among men, it may be seen to occupy the position of "woman" in the scenario Luce Irigaray calls "hom(m)osexualité," where women serve to mediate relations among men.[5] This aggression may be ugly in itself, but what is more insidious is its disingenuousness, its unreserved claims to disinterested principles and a higher truth. The rhetorical strategies Levin employs preclude any reflexivity, leaving his own investments unexamined.[6] If, in the face of feminism's diversity, I could point to one shared principle, it might be the principle of reflexivity. To articulate a position from which one speaks, acknowledging the provisional and partial nature of one's discourse, is to risk a certain vulnerability. Not to do so is to shield oneself in claims to mastery that ultimately, in another register, may be more vulnerable still.

Jonathan Goldberg comes at feminist criticism from a very different place in his essay "Shakespearean Inscriptions: The Voicing of Power." Goldberg speaks the language of theory, of deconstruction and Lacanian psychoanalysis, as well as the language of historicism. He addresses himself to an audience clearly distinguished from Levin's—an audience of the theoretically "initiated," as is signaled by his citations of Gayatri Spivak, Roland Barthes, Luce Irigaray, and especially Jacques Lacan ("for he has been behind this text throughout and perhaps should be named now, allowed the flourish of his signature," Goldberg interjects toward the end—131). The authority of French theory is enlisted against an American feminism charged with "blindness" and "rigidity" (117).

Goldberg raises objections to "a body of criticism" which is represented in his essay by a single book, Linda Bamber's *Comic Women, Tragic Men*. Like Levin, Goldberg disavows any antagonism to feminism itself ("My argument is not with feminism . . . " 117), but (also like Levin) he sees in *some* feminism a threat: "Bamber's work . . . is in *danger* of being hailed as the forefront of a new approach to Shakespeare" (117, my emphasis). The threat that Goldberg sees is not the one that Levin sees—not politics itself—but rather a limiting essentialism by which "feminists like Bamber reimpose the prescriptions that must be seen through and must be read beyond for a genuine feminist discourse to arise" (118). Goldberg objects to Bamber, then, in the interests of a "genuine feminist discourse."

Specifically, Goldberg objects to Bamber's undertheorized account of both gender and genre, an account that tends to treat gender and generic categories as stable and definitive, that "allows for little traffic between the kinds, and . . . denies the play and energy that . . . characterize the multiplicity of the Shakespearean text," assuming "a male/female opposition and a notion of character that lacks historical support" (117). I concur with Goldberg's point that "an informed common sense" cannot substitute for more carefully worked out methodological and theoretical positions and that some of the early feminist criticism of Shakespeare, including Bamber's, exemplifies precisely these weaknesses.[7] My concern here is not to examine these weaknesses, however, but to consider the way that Bamber, and the feminist criticism she is made to represent, are being positioned in Goldberg's essay.

Judged on the substance of its argument, Goldberg's essay would emerge above Bamber's book as the more theoretically sophisticated and arguably the more radical critical statement in that it contests the traditional humanist understanding of subjectivity and gender that defines Bamber's analysis. His style itself operates as a kind of sign in the essay, implicitly representing certain claims. Although the essay begins in the expository manner of conventional criticism, it occasionally shifts as the argument develops into (what have become) mannerisms familiar to readers of deconstruction—the breaking of syntax, the self-conscious play with punctuation, the quasi-cryptic or oracular mode that has become a kind of code in academic writing:

> Who (or what) speaks in the voice that articulates (it)self?
> Who, especially, speaks when I do? . . . Who is in question.
> Speaking is in question. (118–19)

This style, visibly modeled on the verbal play of Derrida, Lacan, and other French theorists whose analysis demands a constant attention to the level of the signifier, signals as well a certain politics—a refusal of totalizing discourse, a reflexiveness that marks the writer's place on the side of the "not all," even of the feminine.[8] Both the argument and the style of Goldberg's essay mark out a political position by repudiating essentialist humanist feminism in favor of a deconstructive (by implication, more radical) understanding of gender, "a genuine feminist discourse."

If we look at how Goldberg defines himself in opposition to the feminist criticism represented by Bamber, however, the politics of his discourse appear more ambiguous. Looked at in its performative aspect, his essay appears to make a deconstructive attack on feminist essentialism that threatens to *elide* sexual difference in a way that would disable any genuinely political discussion of gender. Ironically, Goldberg makes this gesture by his strategic invocations of Jane Gallop and Luce Irigaray. Clearly their authority is enlisted in Goldberg's essay partly to bolster his attack on Bamber from the grounds of "a genuine feminist discourse." The psychoanalytic feminist theorists are brought in as ammunition, but also to signify Goldberg's alignment with some version of a feminist analysis of gender. Since Gallop and Irigaray are among the most incisive of thinkers on the subject of the politics of sex, it is curious that Goldberg's quotations from their work tend to erase sexual difference.[9] His essay begins with two epigraphs, one from Gallop and one from Montaigne:

> The penis is what men have and women do not; the phallus is the attribute of power which never men nor women have.
>
> (Jane Gallop, *The Daughter's Seduction*)

> Les masles et femelles sont jettez en mesme moule.
>
> (Montaigne, *Sur des vers de Virgile*)

Standing thus together on the page, the epigraphs appear to constitute a kind of equivalence, both asserting a certain sameness underlying conventional assumptions about difference. Gallop's Lacanian point about the phallus is the psychoanalytic argument against essentialism: the penis is not the phallus. Inscribed in the order of language, both men and women take up positions of castration in relation to the phallus, which is the attribute of neither sex. The point introduced by the epigraphs is central to the argument Goldberg proceeds to make about gender and voice in Shakespeare. He objects to the argument that "women in Shakespeare lack the autonomy of a voice, and are barred from discourse or limited and placed by male discourse," pointing out that "no one—neither men nor women in Shakespeare—has such autonomy or power" (119).

Goldberg locates the inadequacy of humanist feminist criticism, by implication at least, in its failure to distinguish the imaginary from the symbolic. In its essentialist understanding of gender and its primary focus on character, this feminist criticism has been "blind" to what, for Goldberg, is the central issue: "The generation of character from text, the effacement of voice, or the submission of voice (silence *or* speech) to serve the generic design that limits text. . . ." (130). This submission of voice to what generates it is the condition of men and women in Shakespeare (and Goldberg suggests, in the world)—the condition of sameness that underlies or overrides difference. He demonstrates the point with reference to the Portias of *The Merchant of Venice* and *Julius Caesar*. In *The Merchant of Venice*, Portia disguises herself as a man and assumes the voice of the law when she goes to court as Balthazar to settle the case of the merchant and the Jew. Goldberg argues that "Portia has a voice *within* the law; not that it constricts and denies her, not that she must submit to the father, but that she *becomes* the father precisely because the law is not the father's and not exclusively a male territory" (120–21). If voice is not gendered masculine, neither is silence essentially feminine. Of the Portia in *Julius Caesar*, Goldberg argues that "early in the play Portia has a voice, demanding from Brutus that he acknowledge the equality of their partnership by revealing to her the distraction that so palpably divides him from himself" (128). Brutus is the silent one, refusing at first to speak in answer to Portia's demand. Once he does speak, however, both speech and silence are divided: Portia is admitted to Brutus's self-divided interiority when he shares his secret with her. "After this scene, Portia can only speak with two voices. . . . One with Brutus, she is two" (129). Her suicide by swallowing fire stops her voice, "yet Portia's silence is not a result of her exclusion from the world where men destroy themselves and each other. Rather, it marks her participation" (128).

Goldberg's analysis offers clear advantages over a too easy thematizing and essentializing of (masculine) speech and (feminine) silence.[10] Insofar as humanist feminist criticism has treated Shakespeare's characters as men and women, it has misrecognized the critical problem central to its enterprise, the problem of the relation of gender to discourse, to representation, to the symbolic.[11] But can Goldberg's analysis be said to lay the groundwork for "a genuine feminist discourse"? If men and women occupy essentially the same position (in relation to the symbolic) or if difference is, at least, so fluid and complex as to render irrelevant the reductive binarism of masculine and feminine, what work is there for "a genuine feminist discourse" to do? Is feminism to be subsumed into deconstruction so that gender can no longer be a subject of analysis (except to dismiss the subject as illusory)?

While Goldberg correctly identifies some of the conceptual problems that limit humanist feminist criticism, his readings of Shakespeare, and even of feminist theory, tend to erase sexual difference as a critical issue. To return to Goldberg's use of the Gallop epigraph, I would suggest that the strategic function it is made to serve belies, in a sense, the political implications of Gallop's larger discussion of gender. Immediately following the sentence Goldberg excerpts, about the phallus being the attribute of neither sex, Gallop writes: "But as long as the attribute of power is a phallus which refers to and can be confused (in the imaginary register?) with a penis, this confusion will support a structure in which it seems reasonable that men have power and women do not" (97). Goldberg might not disagree with this, but wishes to direct attention away from the imaginary, where such confusions occur, to focus on the symbolic, where a different truth is inscribed, and away from essentialist feminism to theory. Feminism lacks what theory has. But as Gallop herself points out, this mastery of feminism by post-structuralist theory ends up reinscribing a certain sexual politics: "The phallus is the attribute (always necessarily veiled) of the powerful. . . . Perhaps the word 'phallus' is also an attribute of power, belonging to the masters, the theoreticians" (96). Furthermore, Gallop suggests, the insistence on an absolute distinction between the penis and the phallus does not acknowledge the implication of the phallic signifier (or the theory of it) in the social order: "Certainly the signifier 'phallus' functions in distinction from 'penis,' but it must also always refer to 'penis.' Lacanians seem repeatedly to try to clear up that distinction as if it could be done once and for all. . . . The question of whether one can separate 'phallus' from 'penis' rejoins the question of whether one can separate psychoanalysis from politics" (96–97).

Thus, while Goldberg calls upon Gallop's authority as a feminist theorist to counter the humanist feminism of critics like Bamber, Gallop's own discussion of penis and phallus might be said to complicate the position Goldberg means her to cement. While Gallop would not collapse the distinction between "penis" and "phallus," between the biological and the symbolic, she suggests that to make the distinction absolute, "polarized . . . into an opposition" (97), would be to effect a questionable separation of theory from politics.

Goldberg's argument about Portia's masquerade as a lawyer might illustrate just such an evasion. In arguing that "Portia has a voice within the law . . . because the law is not the father's and not exclusively a male territory," Goldberg gives the word "law" a double valence. It refers to the laws enforced by courts but also the Law of the symbolic order ("The law Portia enacts knows no kind; it is the law of genre"). The Law that knows no kind, it is implied, supersedes the law that privileges one sex over the other. In a footnote, Goldberg acknowledges "Legally, it is true, women in Renaissance England were bound and powerless except in very special circumstances . . . . Yet Renaissance legal theory is full of holes, and attempts to place women in the law ran into all sorts of difficulties. . . . Within the most conservative discourses of the Renaissance, contradictions are rampant . . . " (135). Again, Goldberg makes an important point in countering "modern readings of patriarchy as a simple dualistic hierarchy of the sexes operating with an all-embracing, hegemonic power" (135). Ahistorical, formalist accounts of gender that *simply* align masculinity with power misrepresent a far more complex social reality. But in this argument the acknowledged sexism of the Renaissance legal system is treated parenthetically, the emphasis falling on the contradictions and slippages that undermine monolithic institutions so that the recognition of such slippages seems to *obviate* the point about sexism. In making the theoretical point about slippage, Goldberg's essay also performs a certain slippage, whereby the issue of sexism is displaced. My point here is not to reject Goldberg's argument, for his more complex recasting of the issues of gender and power is crucial to a more adequately historicized feminist critique—or would be, except that in its *performance*, this argument tends to suspend the discussion of sexism as a historical reality in favor of a discussion of its theoretical contradictions.

This competitive silencing of feminism emerges definitively in the closing paragraph of the essay where Goldberg writes: "Perhaps—just perhaps—the reason we cannot find Shakespeare reflecting his culture's supposed patriarchalism and sexism is that the culture represented on stage *is* the culture off-stage" (134). The culture, on-stage and off, is full of contradictions, slippages, differences ever in motion, so that the rigid binarism and monolithic thinking Goldberg ascribes to feminists is belied by a more fluid social reality (" 'The world' is . . . a larger and more complex item than Heilbrun inagines," he writes patronizingly of Carolyn Heilbrun—118). But what is the meaning and especially what is the rhetorical effect of the word "supposed" in Goldberg's sentence? *Supposed* patriarchalism and sexism? When feminists *suppose* these things, are they imagining them? To say that patriarchalism is inhabited by contradictions is one thing, but to suggest that the contradictions render it illusory is another.

Goldberg portrays feminist criticism as taking up a specular relation to English Renaissance culture, hypostasizing it into a rigid unity to be repudiated as sexist. Feminism, this suggests, is entangled in an imaginary relation to what it purports to analyze. Theory tends to privilege the symbolic (which is aligned with the father) over the imaginary (associated with the mother and the maternal dyad). In a recent essay on the recurrence of the imaginary in critical theory, Cynthia Chase elucidates a certain irony attendant on this implicit hierarchy, for theorists' antagonism to the imaginary produces a replication of it: the theorist enters into an imaginary relation to the imaginary, as it were, identifying whatever theoretical position is aligned with the imaginary as an antagonist to be repudiated.[12] In "Shakespearean Inscriptions," Goldberg takes it upon himself to speak for "a genuine feminist discourse" against the essentialist feminism that cannot extricate itself from the imaginary. Feminist criticism serves his argument as the straw woman to be knocked down in a display of theoretical mastery. But Goldberg's wish to position himself on the side of a "genuine feminist criticism" is called into question both by the depoliticizing tendency of the substance of his argument, and equally by the politics *enacted* by his argument, where feminism takes the fall for theory. This aggressive scapegoating of feminism serves, as it does in Levin's essays, to invite an identification between the critic and his like-minded audience in their repudiation of feminism. Levin appeals to traditional critics, Goldberg to post-structuralist theorists, over "a body of criticism" that politicizes gender.[13]

The point of this essay is not, of course, that feminist criticism is above scrutiny or that it should not be subject to the kinds of questions both Levin and Goldberg raise about it. While Levin's account of feminism is insufficiently informed and precise to be useful (since his real interest is ridicule and not analysis), Goldberg raises crucial theoretical questions about gender, representation, and history that help to elucidate problems he very correctly identifies in humanist feminism. In its performative aspect, however, Goldberg's essay resembles Levin's in using feminist criticism to construct specularities and identifications in an imaginary register within theory itself.

Critical discourse cannot be understood simply as a discourse *about* politics, whether implicitly or explicitly, centrally or incidentally (much less can it be understood as a discourse *not* about politics). Critical discourse also *is* a politics, enacting a struggle for power in the academy and in intellectual circles. When this power struggle entails the targeting of feminism, if only of "a version of feminism," perhaps it is time to examine criticism's political unconscious.

## NOTES

1. Teresa Brennan discusses the way identifications and antagonisms of this sort have arisen within feminist theory itself in her introduction to *Between Psychoanalysis and Feminism*.

2. Since the mid-1980s, the emphasis in Shakespeare criticism generally has shifted toward new historicist and cultural materialist analyses, and the concerns of feminist criticism have been largely subsumed within these historicist modes of analysis. One could perhaps mark the shift toward historicizing gender issues with the publication in 1983 of Lisa Jardine's *Still Harping on Daughters: Women and Drama in the Age of Shakespeare*, the introduction to which sounds a rather sharp attack on American feminist critics for their ahistorical modes of interpretation. The

move to historicize the sexual politics in/of Shakespeare's plays has also been made by Linda Woodbridge (*Women and the English Renaissance*), Kathleen McLuskie ("The Patriarchal Bard"), Karen Newman (" 'And Wash the Ethiop White' "), Catherine Belsey ("Disrupting Sexual Difference"), and others. As new historicism and cultural materialism absorb the issue of gender, it becomes increasingly difficult to decide what to call "feminist" criticism. In some historicist analyses that discuss gender issues, for example Louis Montrose's essay on *A Midsummer Night's Dream* (" 'Shaping Fantasies' ") or Jean Howard's on *Much Ado About Nothing* ("Renaissance Antitheatricality"), the issue of sexual inequality is not necessarily a primary focus or motivation (which is not to say, however, that such analyses don't contribute to the project of feminist criticism).

There has been less conspicuous feminist work on Shakespeare that one could label post-structuralist, though some of the historicist critics have been influenced by post-structuralist theory. This seems to me to be an unfortunate gap in feminist Shakespeare criticism. Coming to Shakespeare through deconstruction and structuralist/post-structuralist psychoanalysis is one way to complicate and refine the theoretical premises of feminist criticism of the plays and poems, and can complement the less specifically textual and theoretical historical treatment of gender issues. Since the problem of gender is inevitably also a problem of signification, representation, and subjectivity, post-structuralist theory can help to move the discussion of sexual politics in Shakespeare beyond the humanist focus on the psychology of characters that has defined a great deal of feminist work.

3. Walter Cohen offers quite an even-handed, partly historical account of feminist criticism in "Political Criticism of Shakespeare."

4. Even this generalization is something of a distortion, though, as it blurs distinctions among those critics who treat the plays as rather transparently referential and those more concerned with strategies of representation, those whose methodology is formalist and those who draw upon psychoanalysis. Irene Dash, for example, tends to treat Shakespeare's female characters as *women*: "Today, Shakespeare's women characters have a relevance and vitality. They offer insights into women's perceptions of themselves in a patriarchal world . . . " (6) Madelon Gohlke, on the other hand, stands out among the contributors to *The Woman's Part* in drawing upon post-structuralism, reading "on the margins of discourse," calling attention to the sexual politics of representation. Some of these feminist critics, like Bamber and French, use what we could describe as "formalist" methodology, relying on attention to textual patterns and what Goldberg calls "an informed common sense" (117); others, like Coppélia Kahn and Janet Adelman, draw upon a version of psychoanalytic theory informed by ego psychology and object relations theory. The feminist Shakespeare criticism of the early 1980s did not (unfortunately, in my view) draw upon a more post-structuralist reading of Freud or on the work of Lacan and French feminist psychoanalysts.

5. See "Women on the Market," in *This Sex Which is Not One* 170–91.

6. Levin does, of course, outline at least by implication a certain *critical* position from which he speaks—the position that texts have knowable objective meanings, that meaning is produced and controlled by authorial intention, etc. What I mean by "investments" is what motivates this position at a less purely rational level.

7. Bamber's introduction displays the theoretical problems she encounters in attempting to define gender, as she seems to adopt both essentialist and non-essentialist positions without confronting their contradictions, and often refers to men and women in ways that assume gender to be a given, an unproblematic and *a priori* matter of kind.

Bamber initially seems to blur the distinction between essentialism and a non-essentialist definition of gender: "For my purposes the crucial quality of the feminine is simple difference; the feminine here is that which exists on the other side of a barrier, the barrier of sexual differentiation" (4). If this defines gender difference as purely relational, not a matter of differences inscribed in nature, it reinscribes essentialism in its notion of the "barrier of sexual differentiation," a barrier not precisely defined but evidently fixed. The biologism of Bamber's essentialism returns in her notion of the "gender perspective" of writers: "gender perspective . . . seems to me, first of all, inevitable. Men must write as men and women as women" (5).

8. See Diana Fuss on Derrida's and Lacan's styles as attempts to "speak (as) woman" (12).

9. Goldberg invokes Irigaray at a moment when he wishes to contest an essentialist reading of *The Merchant of Venice* that would simply construe Portia's "career [as the lawyer Balthazar] as her inscription in the patriarchal order" (124). "Rather," Goldberg suggests, "let us read it otherwise." To read it otherwise is to recognize that "the return of the letter doubles back upon itself, revealing the duplicity in the text, revealing, in Irigaray's terms, the sex which is not one" (125). To set up Irigaray over and against essentialism, though, is to avoid her own complex negotiations between essentialist and anti-essentialist theoretical positions, a negotiation Diana Fuss characterizes as the "double gesture" of Irigaray's feminism (68). In other words, Goldberg is enlisting Irigaray to underwrite a theoretical understanding of "reading" that would seem to suspend the political problem of "the patriarchal order," but this theoretical move involves a certain political gesture which Irigaray's work would not, in fact, endorse.

10. It might be pointed out here, however, that this thematic treatment of speech and silence is not attributed in Goldberg's essay to anyone in particular. This is the argument he wishes to contest as the pretext for his own deconstruction of speech and silence, but evidently he could not locate precisely these ideas in Bamber's book. He therefore shifts his ground, turning from Bamber to a more vaguely defined target: "In arguments of the sort that I am calling into question, it is said that women in Shakespeare lack autonomy of voice . . . " (119). The generality here ("arguments of the sort I am calling into question") and the evasiveness of the passive construction (by whom is it said?) suggest that Goldberg is constructing an imaginary opponent, a feminist straw woman whose errors will authorize his corrective argument.

11. This tendency to treat characters as people emerges, for example, in the introductions to Irene Dash's *Wooing, Wedding, and Power* and Lenz, Greene and Neely's *The Woman's Part*. Dash offers Shakespeare's female characters as role models for women, locating in them a feminine subjectivity: "They offer insights into women's perceptions of themselves in a patriarchal world" (6). Lenz, Greene, and Neely describe the project of the contributors to their volume in a way that also invites women to identify with and intercede for Shakespeare's women: "The critics in this volume liberate Shakespeare's women from the stereotypes to which they have too often been confined" (4). This language of "liberation" suggests that there are women in Shakespeare's plays who, "confined" by the misrepresentations of sexist critics, have gone unrecognized. There is a sense in which this is true: sexist critics *have* sometimes read Shakespeare's female characters in accordance with sexist stereotypes. But Shakespeare's female characters are also at times constituted by or as stereotypes—stereotypes that may be understood to be endorsed or called into question depending on how one reads the politics of the plays. Feminist criticism has to shift its attention from the psychology of character to the politics of representation in order to address these (from my point of view) more fundamental questions. For two rather different feminist attempts to counter this treatment of female characters, see Lisa Jardine's *Still Harping on Daughters* and my essay on *Troilus and Cressida*, "Unbodied Figures of Desire."

12. In "The Witty Butcher's Wife: Freud, Lacan, and the Conversion of Resistance to Theory," Chase pursues the implications of de Man's argument in "The Resistance to Theory" that resistance to "theory" (understood as "a resistance to *language*, or to the rhetorical nature of language") recurs within the theoretical enterprise itself when language is taken to operate as a code rather than as rhetoric. Chase points out that Lacan's distinction between the imaginary and symbolic registers has sometimes been treated as a kind of code or binary opposition. She counters this tendency, arguing that "*Lacan's* thinking on identification tends in two different directions. One is the diagnosis of a delusive moment of identification at specific points in an unfolding process, an entry into language that resembles a developmental process, though it consists rather in the phases of a dialectic. The other direction of Lacan's thinking is the vision of the mirror-stage as the permanent predicament of beings that speak." Chase emphasizes that "both these directions are in some sense indispensable. Without the first, the pinpointing of moments of delusive identification, one wouldn't get the precise analysis of the nature of the illusion involved. But without the second—if Lacan were only to describe the specular moment of identification as an error to be surpassed—he would repeat the error of the delusive identification of language as a code, in prescribing an emergence *out of* and *beyond* a distorting specularity" (1003–4). Goldberg's attack on humanist feminism identifies it as the kind of resistance to theory at issue in Chase's article, but Goldberg does not give enough play to the irreducibility of the imaginary in the construction of his attack on feminism.

13. I would hope that it is clear that I do not see feminism and deconstruction as incompatible enterprises, any more than feminism and psychoanalysis are. For a searching exploration of the relations of feminism and deconstruction see Gayatri Spivak's "Displacement and the Discourse of Woman" and "Feminism and Deconstruction Again: Negotiating with Unacknowledged Masculinism." Diana Fuss's lucid study of the argument between essentialist and anti-essentialist feminism, *Essentially Speaking: Feminism, Nature, and Difference*, also explores this relation.

# 8

# Against "Ideology"

**Edward Pechter**

One of the most powerful moments in Ivo Kamps's MLA session on Ideology in Shakespeare Criticism occurred near the end of Gayle Greene's paper. In response to Richard Levin's remark about the success of feminist criticism, Greene said, "From where I sit as a feminist it does not look to me as if I control *PMLA* or much of anything else in the profession" (this volume). Upon this Greene recounted the familiar but no less depressing statistics of women's position and pay in the academic work force, the rage of the patriarchal Right against her work, and the contemptuous dismissal of the same work by the neo-materialist feminist Left. Since Greene writes in a beautifully direct way, readers can pick up from the printed text how frustrated she feels at the increasing marginalization of her work by both Left and Right.

A similarly moving moment came a few minutes later when Richard Levin rose to respond to the criticism lavished upon his work by the other panelists. He had a lot to choose from, but oddly enough he focused on an apparently incidental remark of Michael Bristol's, that Levin's writings sometimes "sound . . . like those of a lapsed or fallen liberal" (this volume). Not so, Levin assured us; his Liberal faith he kept. He was still "that L-word," proud of being, even in these days of the Bush presidency, a card-carrying member of the ACLU. Unlike Greene's, Levin's frustration never found its way into the printed record; you had to be there to feel it. This is one among many differences between them, yet what struck me then, and lives in my memory still, is their similarity. For Levin too sees himself pincered between a neo-conservative Right and a neo-materialist Left. "If you really want to know, I feel beset from all sides." It was Greene who said this (this volume), but it might as well have been Levin.

This similarity doesn't bear much scrutiny. Since the positions of Greene and Levin are supposed to constitute the field, they can't both represent themselves as the besieged victims of a dominant majority. One of them must be wrong, one of them must *be* the dominant. In retrospect it would be easy enough to decide who was right (though we wouldn't all come to the same conclusion), or even to analyze why the sense that they're both right was an illusion of the moment. Conference papers always include a theatrical element which tends to blunt analytical response, and all elements of the theatrical last only a moment, dying in the cradle where they lie. But the flip side of this transience is the particular immediacy of the moment: "In Dramatic composition, the *Impression* is the *Fact*" (Morgann, 1970, 4). I want to stick to the impression. Let's say that Gayle Greene and Richard Levin are, with all their differences, both right, and further that they speak for all of us, with all our differences, Shakespeareans or otherwise, Left, Right, or wherever. This starting point leaves me with two questions to consider here. How can it be that we all feel beset from all sides? And what should we be doing about it?

Kamps organized his session around two concepts, ideology and Shakespeare criticism. Since I've written too recently on disputes peculiar to Shakespeare criticism to have any new bright ideas ("Teaching Differences"), it's ideology in general I'll be concentrating on here. Or rather, "ideology," the term as it is used in current critical practice. The distinction is important because, for reasons I hope to make clear, ideology is something you can be neither for nor against, since you're in it and it's in you. "Ideology," though, the term as variously deployed in current critical arguments, is a different matter, and it's this "ideology" I'm against. In announcing my opposition, though, I have to acknowledge at the outset that the term has a wide and bewildering range of often contradictory meanings. I'll be talking about this problem, but for the moment it should be enough to stand proudly with Groucho Marx as Professor Wagstaff, breaking into song in *Horse Feathers* upon his inauguration as President of Huxley College: "Whatever it is, I'm against it."

We can begin with Robert Alter's argument in a recent book called *The Pleasures of Reading in an Ideological Age*. In "looking at literature with the apparatus of different systems of abstract thought" (10), Alter tells us, we have lost touch with a "passionate engagement in literary works" and the "deep pleasure in the experience of reading." This situation "is distressing" because such abstract "discussion in the second degree" has "come to displace the discussion of literature itself." Hence, "one can read article after article, hear lecture after lecture, in which no literary work is ever quoted, and no real reading experience is registered" (11). The practitioners of this abstract criticism are so given to "ideological tendentiousness," Alter says, that they "might be better off teaching sociology or history, psychology or political science" (13).

Alter's argument is based on several unexamined and (as I think) indefensible assumptions. One is in the phrase "literature itself," which Alter seems to take as a natural phenomenon of the real world. He nowhere confronts the various current arguments about literature as historically determined and socially constructed. He merely asserts its existence as a stable and self-sustaining category of being, and thus winds up assuming what he is obliged to demonstrate. The "deep pleasure" of "real reading experience" rests upon similarly problematic assumptions. If reading were truly such an innocent and instinctive activity with pleasures so immediately accessible, why do we have literature professors or literary critics? Alter never answers this question; he never even asks it, though it hangs like a cloud over the discussion right through to the very end of his book.[1] Maybe he doesn't really believe his own claims about the immediately pleasant accessibility of literature. If so, why remind us that the critical practice of those tendentious ideologues currently invading literature departments "requires neither a special liking for literature nor an ability to discriminate between derivative and original, second-rate and first-rate writers" (13)? When did the natural instinct for reading professionalize itself into "a *special* liking?" When did passionate experience turn into the abstract business of discriminating between the great and the near-great?

Alter's argument is based on a set of distinctions that don't stand up to analysis. For instance, he complains about the "ideological coerciveness" of a "neo-Marxist" critic like Terry Eagleton "in proposing that a curricular move be made from literature to 'discourse studies,' " but what is Alter himself if not ideologically coercive in proposing that we decontaminate literature departments of neo-Marxists by banishing them into the sociological wilderness? Alter claims to speak for real pleasure against ideological abstraction, but as Barthes points out (*Pleasure* 22), the distinction between textual pleasure and political tendentiousness is itself a familiar, conventional, public construct, appropriable according to one's interests; in other words, an ideological distinction. Alter lines up behind common sense against special interests, but as Catherine Belsey points out (*Critical Practice* 1–36), common sense, like literature itself, seems to be a floating category of various meaning (that is, a category capable of serving different special interests), whose least and perhaps only common denominator is the claim to be a transcendent signified, to mean the same uncontestable and non-ideological thing no matter who's using it.

In short, though Alter thinks he's distinguishing between ideology and something ontologically prior, some instinct inherent in nature and common sense, he's distinguishing rather between two kinds of ideology, one he likes and is used to, one he doesn't and isn't. Moreover, this claim to be above ideology has the effect, whether intentional or not, of disguising ideological interest (from the author maybe even more than from his audience); and as any neo-Marxist (and many of us who aren't) will tell you, disguised ideology is one good working definition of ideology at its best.

Despite their differences in intelligence, interest, and generosity, the points I've made about Alter apply to Richard Levin as well. Levin's argument too seems to depend upon unscrutinized and highly problematic assumptions. In "Ideological Criticism and Pluralism," he excludes ideological critics because their presence seems to disallow the possibility of negotiated settlement. But why is it that the only "real discussion" (like Alter's "*real* reading experience," the adjective has a strong evaluative implication) is one that "tries to reach some kind of agreement" (this volume)? The same question can be asked of another recent essay of Levin's, "The Problem of 'Context' in Interpretation." After granting that interpretation requires the establishment of a context, Levin tries to solve the problem of determining which context is appropriate by limiting the differences to those critics who share an intentionalist assumption. His reason is that "the nonintentionalist critic is completely free to choose any context he pleases" (89). Even if Levin's contention here were right, his argument is still going in circles around the same unacknowledged and apparently unacknowledgeable central assumption—namely, that agreement is self-evidently the goal of critical activity. For a lot of non-intentionalists, those who see a repressive censorship and exclusion at work in both psychological and political domains, agreement is not a good thing. Since it is the opening of critical activity to such non-intentionalist assumptions that has effectively created the problem, Levin's exclusion of the non-intentionalists doesn't solve the problem so much as beg the question. If we can limit the discussion to people who agree with us we'd eliminate disagreement: if we had bacon we'd have bacon and eggs—if we had eggs. But suppose, instead of bacon and eggs, that we want *cervelles au beurre noir* or *matzoh brei*. Suppose we aren't even hungry. If (but only if) agreement is an absolute value, then exclusion is necessary; but if the inclusion of new and different voices is the goal, then disagreement may be necessary. Levin seems unable to stand outside the belief that agreement is a good thing; he assumes what is at issue. And this is where coercion comes in, another similarity with Alter. Levin complains about the coerciveness of ideological critics, but for those who do stand outside the belief that agreement is a good thing, it's Levin, with his inaugurating gesture of exclusion, whose intention looks coercive, like "enforced submission—poetics from the barrel of a gun" (this volume).

The chief similarity between Levin and Alter is in their desire to contrast themselves to ideological critics; like Alter the distinction Levin makes is rather between the ideology he likes and the ideology he doesn't. In the move to exclude, in tolerating a restricted difference, the kind that can be articulated, negotiated and resolved, Levin is following the familiar lines of pluralism. Pluralism allows for a limited and gradual change; it therefore serves the interests of those who want both to contain and to enlarge the area of legitimate exchange, to distribute the limited goods available more widely yet within definite boundaries. Pluralism will seem good or bad depending on where you stand. To some it's bad for its containment and restriction; to others good for its distributive largesse; to yet others it may seem like a good trade-off between contradictory goods. But whether you like it or not, it's hard to see how it can be characterized in contrast to an ideological position.

So much for the Right and the unattainable desire for the transcendence of ideology. If we waffle now to the Left, what we find is the unattainable desire for the critique of ideology, which turns out to be pretty much the same thing.

Consider Francis Barker and Peter Hulme's argument about "alternative criticism" (192–94) in their essay on *The Tempest*. Starting from the position that all texts are "installed in a field of struggle," Barker-Hulme try to determine the best way of "combating the dominant orthodoxies" in order "to displace" them. With combat, struggle, and displacement, we've been moved to a position diametrically opposed to Levin's negotiation and reconciliation. Such language makes it clear that negotiation is not (*pace* Levin) a universally shared or self-evident good. But it works the other way around as well; someone inhabiting Levin's position would wonder why struggle is installed as a desideratum, a question for which Barker-Hulme either do not or cannot provide a direct answer.

Perhaps, though, they provide an implicit answer in the main argument they make about alternative criticism, that it shouldn't invest too heavily in original meaning. The trouble with original meaning, they tell us, is that it's irretrievable with any certainty. As a consequence, any argument about it is likely to be

> wholly dissolved into an indeterminate miscellany [and] the only option becomes the voluntaristic ascription to the text of meanings and articulations derived simply from one's own ideological preferences . . . a procedure only too vulnerable to pluralistic incorporation, a recipe for peaceful coexistence with the dominant readings, not for a contestation. . . .

Such contestation "can only occur if two positions attempt to occupy the same space," so Barker-Hulme exhort us to shift attention away from indeterminate historical questions and over to the "critique of the dominant readings of a text" as they exist in the present. The dominant contemporary orthodoxy can be seen and challenged for what it is; it thus provides a purchase for authentic critique, or what Barker-Hulme call "a *properly* political" criticism, in which the "different readings struggle with each other on the site of the text, and all that can count, however provisionally, as knowledge of a text, is achieved through this discursive conflict."

But why assume that the contemporary dominant is any easier to determine than original meaning or critical history? What allows Barker-Hulme to believe they have direct access to it—the contemporary dominant *as in itself it really is*—unmediated by their own interpretive interests? Such questions arise when you consider that their text chosen to illustrate contemporary orthodoxy, Kermode's New Arden "Introduction," was thirty-four years old at the time of Barker-Hulme's publication, and written by a critic who, it may sometimes seem, has done nothing *but* change during the course of his career.[2] Even more problematic is their definition of the critical views which are said to constitute the dominant orthodoxy. Though "no adequate reading" of *The Tempest* "could afford not to comprehend *both* the anxiety [of irresolution] and the drive to closure it necessitates," it is just "these aspects of the play's 'rich complexity,' " Barker-Hulme tell us, that

> have been signally ignored by European and North American critics, who have tended to listen exclusively to Prospero's voice: after all, he speaks their language. It has been left to those who have suffered colonial usurpation to discover and map the traces of that complexity by reading in full measure Caliban's refractory place in both Prospero's play and *The Tempest*. (204)

But despite this claim, there were plenty of humanist critics around prior to Barker-Hulme who were able to recognize and respond to just such subversive energies in the play. In the Pelican "Introduction" (published almost exactly halfway between Kermode and Barker-Hulme), Anne Barton emphasizes at length how the play works against the resolving gestures of conventional closure (40–44). And the claim that the dominant version of the play is uttered by or within Prospero's voice simply ignores the very substantial body of non-alternative interpretation during the past twenty-five years which has made a nasty Prospero into such a regular feature of Shakespearean interpretation both academic and theatrical—arguably even the *dominant* feature.[3]

To reverse a memorably tendentious phrase from Stephen Greenblatt's High Functionalist period, Barker-Hulme can be described as transgression producing authority (the dominant orthodoxy) as a way of extending its own (counter-hegemonic) legitimacy. From this perspective, Barker-Hulme's entire rationale for concentrating the struggle in contemporary criticism disappears. Stick to the current stuff, they tell us, and the argument won't be "wholly dissolved into an indeterminate miscellany"; but this move merely displaces the problem of indeterminacy onto the very question (what *is* the current stuff?) that was supposed to eliminate it—and thus turns out to be a horizontal rather than vertical move. Let's get beyond "simply . . . one's own ideological preferences," they urge us, to provide a ground from which to critique ideology; but what I'm suggesting is that, since Barker-Hulme's understanding of the dominant orthodoxy is perforce derived in fundamental ways from the interests they bring to the question, it cannot satisfy their desire to ground the critique of ideology because it is itself ideologically constituted.

In *Criticism and Ideology*, Terry Eagleton provides a clear statement of the strong claim for Left critique:

> Historical materialism stands or falls by the claim that it is not only not an ideology, but that it contains a scientific theory of the genesis, structure and decline of ideologies. It situates itself, in short, outside the terrain of competing "long perspectives," in order to theorise the conditions of their very possibility. (16–17)

There are many similarities here to the claims on the Right for the transcendence of ideology. In both there's a category of genuine being (*real* reading experience, literature *itself*, conditions of *very* possibility) that can be discerned objectively (that is, either *rationally* or *scientifically*) from a disinterested position (either above *political interests* or outside the *terrain of competing long perspectives*). Both positions rest in self-validating assumptions vulnerable to attack from anyone inhabiting a different set of assumptions. At this point, though, a difference emerges. For while Right transcendence is more or less internally consistent, Left critique seems to stand in a contradictory relation to its own instituting assumption, that of materialism itself. Once you invert Hegel and thereby arrive at the belief that ideas in consciousness are derived from the particular social relations in a given situation, then the ideological nature of all knowledge—its specificity, that is, to a particular position or set of interests—seems to follow as the night the day. How can Eagleton claim to situate historical materialism outside of history when it is precisely the situatedness in history that historical materialism is all about?

The answer is in the maxim Greene quotes (this volume) from Althusser, that "the accusation of being in ideology only applies to others, never to oneself" (175). Althusser thought this was "well known," and the point has indeed become something of a commonplace these days,[4] but it's not a new discovery. The extraordinary inconsistency was already old when Mannheim noted it fifty years ago in *Ideology and Utopia*. "It might have been expected that long ago Marxism would have formulated in a more theoretical way the fundamental findings . . . concerning the relationship between human thought and the conditions of existence *in general*," adding that the situatedness of thought "was perceived only in the thought of the opponent" (277). Again the same conclusion: once you accept the materialist argument about determination you cannot make any claim for "universal validity." Since (I'm now quoting Kenneth Burke's commentary on Mannheim), any " 'unmasking' of an ideology's limitations is itself made from a limited point of view" (198), then "the edges are so knocked off the Marxist definition of ideology that Marxism too becomes analyzable as an ideology" (199).

The remarkable thing is that, despite its relative familiarity and long pedigree, this same inconsistency continues to underwrite (and undermine) the project of left critique. Catherine Belsey is a case in point. As Greene notes (this volume), *Critical Practice* begins with the claim "that ideology is not an optional extra, adopted by self-conscious individuals . . . , but the very condition of our experience of the world, *un*conscious precisely in that it is unquestioned, taken for granted" (5). By the last chapter, however, Belsey wants us to engage in "a scientific criticism [which] recognizes in the text not 'knowledge' but ideology itself in all its inconsistency and partiality" (128).[5] But how can we achieve a scientific mastery of the "conditions of our experience"? Since these conditions are the ones within which we live and move and have our being, they are identical to what in a different system of thought, Augustinian Christianity, is called God (the object of ultimate ideological concern, so to speak), and as Renaissance Neoplatonists never tired of pointing out, you can't know God, at least not in the sense of specular ("scientific") knowledge; any such knowledge would require us to get outside of that which we are inside of, or indeed, that which is inside of us.[6] Donne plays with the problem in "Negative Love," making a commonplace connection between the impossibility of knowing God and the impossibility of knowing the self. The point is relevant to Belsey and other cultural materialists in the sense that any such commitment to "the scientific knowledge of ideology itself" serves willy-nilly to reinstall the sovereign subject of humanism (self-sustaining, self-knowing), which it has been the virtue of so much materialist work to call into question.

A whole book intervenes between these two statements from *Critical Practice*, and while nothing in the middle solves the problem of inconsistency, the sheer distance tends to make it less conspicuous. But critique doesn't shy away from conspicuous inconsistency. In Barker-Hulme, less than a page intervenes between an assertion about "the rootedness of texts in the contingency of history" and the authors' claim that they can themselves attain to a critical position beyond that of "ideological preference"—in other words, produce a text not rooted in the contingency of history. Sometimes these inconsistencies exist within a single paragraph, as in Michael Bristol's *Shakespeare's America*. Bristol starts from the materialist premise that "neither Shakespeare nor institutional practice stands outside historical and social determination" (4), which in turn constitutes an "acknowledgment" that any "researcher" is necessarily "position[ed] within a culture already constituted by Shakespeare." Nonetheless, Bristol proposes to undertake "a critique," that is, "an attempt at emigration from that cultural ground." But this leads back to the Belsey question, how can you get out of where you are, except to yet another "position within a culture already constituted by Shakespeare?" Unlike Eagleton, Bristol doesn't solve the problem by fiat. "It is clear," he admits, "that such emigration can scarcely expect to locate a frontier, let alone cross it," but if that's so, then emigration is what it cannot be. The emigration from history is an impossible voyage; the "critique of ideology" (the word falls predictably into place in a moment—see *Shakespeare's America* 8) is a self-contradictory concept.

Nonetheless, this isn't the conclusion Bristol reaches. Instead, he exits from the same brief paragraph that initiated and sustained a convincing argument against the possibility of critique by concluding that he intends to do just what he has shown that neither he nor anybody else is capable of doing: "In undertaking a critique of Shakespeare then, I necessarily proceed on the understanding that I am implicated in and defined by the very institutional reality I propose to analyze" (4). Bristol is, of course, aware of the contradiction. In fact, the awareness is his main point, the subject of the independent clause, and his strong implication is that the awareness is somehow empowering, as though understanding the impossibility of the undertaking makes the undertaking possible. But such "anti-foundationalist theory hope," to use Stanley Fish's term,[7] remains an empty gesture; it can never be translated into productive action, for any first step that might be imagined up and out of the institutionally and historically determined space (emigration as elevation) turns out to be, like Barker-Hulme's definition of dominant orthodoxy, just another horizontal move. And this brings us back finally to the basic similarity between Left critique and Right transcendence: they are doomed to fail by virtue of the same constraint—namely (to sum up the argument that I have been making here), that horizontal moves are the only kind we can make.

At this point we can return to the questions I asked at the beginning. The first of these, how can it be that we all feel beset from all sides? may seem now like the wrong question. Better to ask, how can we not? To be sure, there was a time when we didn't, a real historical time within memory when academic criticism, and not just about Shakespeare, seemed to proceed out of a consensus. Whether this consensus was good or bad, real or illusory, is subject to debate; in fact, it *is* the debate, or at least one version of the debate that led to (and leads from) the MLA Session on Ideology in Shakespeare. My point is that the "ideological preferences" that now divide us also serve us to define the space that is divided. If you're committed to reconciliation and negotiation, the current scene may well look as though it has been taken over by tendentious ideologues; if you're committed to radical change, then it will look as though the neo-cons are blooming, in control at the helms, or at best that the forces for change are being co-opted into meaningless tokenism. In this context it is not only possible but perfectly reasonable that all players feel like underdogs, and every position like a minority beset from all sides.

This leads to the second question, what is to be done? Bristol and Greene suggest that the first thing to do is define "ideology" properly, but even in the unlikely event they could resolve their own differences, this wouldn't constitute an argument to change Levin's mind. After all, Daniel Bell, *fons et origo* of Levin's definition, has just reissued *The End of Ideology* with a new Afterword saying that he had the term right in the first place. In the absence of a consensus around a lexical norm, the assertion of such a norm will seem just that, an assertion, with no authority beyond those who share the asserter's beliefs. The proper meaning of ideology cannot decide the conflict since it is itself the subject of the conflict—a "keyword" (Williams), an "essentially contested concept" (Gallie).

There's another option apparently open to us here: jettisoning the term altogether. I think this is a good idea. In arguing that everything is ideology (i.e., that all knowledge is bound to be historically situated, positioned in a particular set of social interests, and therefore contestable from a different position and set of interests), I have also been arguing that nothing is ideology. The term has too many meanings, because it has no meaning. Any and everything that might serve to give it meaning, all those contrasting binary captives (ideology versus true consciousness, science, the Godlike capability of reason, real social relations [unmisrecognized], what really happens [undistorted], etc.)—these contrasting categories are all nowhere to be found. (Or rather, we find them in too many different places, depending on the different positions from which we see them, which adds up to the same thing.) To turn Saussure around: ideology is a positive term without a difference.

Some years ago Raymond Williams suggested we'd be better off dropping ideology from the critical lexicon (*Marxism and Literature* 55–71); but people didn't listen to him, and they're certainly not going to listen to me. Some will simply refuse, preferring to unmask the ideology hidden behind the suggestion we stop using ideology. Even those who may wish to buy into my argument won't be able to, because the world—read "History," if you like—won't let them. As Marx said near the beginning of *The Eighteenth Brumaire* (15), we may be free to make our own history, but not totally free, not in circumstances of our own choosing. The inevitability of "ideology" in our critical lexicon these days is one of these circumstances, part of the historical weight from which there is no escape.

It's a weight that would be hard to overestimate. The standard histories of the term usually start with Destutt de Tracy around the French Revolution, but the assumptions that generate the controversial appropriations of the term on the contemporary scene have a much deeper past. Plato invented the concept of ideology, though his term for it was ("untethered") opinion, to which he contrasted ("stable") knowledge.[8] Most of the arguments on the Right for the transcendence of ideology can be traced back more or less directly to this dualism in Plato. But the critique of ideology on the Left has a long pedigree as well, even the particular strain identified earlier. Anti-foundationalist theory hope is not a postmodern discovery. The idea is central to the Frankfurt critical theorists, for whom the knowledge of cultural determination is frequently represented as the basis for critical detachment. Even Mannheim, with his insistence upon the specificity of all knowledge to a contingent context of interests, couldn't resist the same temptation. He backed away from the resolute relativism of his argument and rechristened it "relationism." In relationism, relativism has become conscious of itself, and this self-consciousness somehow allows for a move in the direction of a substantial scientific foundation, called the sociology of knowledge, upon which a progressive hope could be built. But high modernism, in either the Mannheim or Frankfurt version, is still too recent to serve as a *terminus ab quo* for anti-foundationalist theory hope. We have to go back to early modernism, for as Victoria Kahn has shown in a brilliant recent essay, the idea that the self-conscious acknowledgment of ideological interest somehow empowers the critique of ideology reenacts a central argument of Renaissance humanism. And we can go back further still, once again to Plato, where the admission of ignorance serves as the base from which genuine critical knowledge is possible.

What can account for the perennial hardiness of ideology, and of those more or less interchangeable dualisms—being/seeming, nature/culture, essence/accident—upon which the concept depends? Obviously the question is much too big for me to take on.[9] Still, a couple of matters deserve emphasis, since they are precisely the matters emphasized by those who are committed to the concept of ideology, whether from the Right or the Left, both of which claim that its abandonment would have terribly disabling consequences.

On the Right the consequences take the form of chaos come again. Unless we have some non-ideological grounds to regulate critical activity—authorial intention, the text itself, *consensus gentium*, tradition defined as a more or less consistent body of thought—then it's anything goes, a situation without any sense of purpose or direction. But this fear is groundless. The abandonment of, say, the text itself doesn't mean that we have no way to direct critical activity, only that the way associated with the text itself (with this presumed alternative to ideology which is itself an ideology) no longer carries authority. If there's anything clear about criticism during the last fifteen years or so, it's that there *has* been purpose and direction to, among other things: the introduction of gender and social position and political power as relevant considerations in the production and reception of texts; the opening up of disciplinary boundaries; and the move away from literature itself to discourse studies. This transformation has been the result not of a free-for-all, but rather of a widespread effort to transfer attention to a new and different set of concerns. Such transfers are always problematic even when they don't constitute an actual paradigm shift in Kuhn's sense. But they don't leave us without a set of rules to decide matters, simply with a new set of rules, or caught between contradictory sets of rules. Hence Gayle Greene can assure Levin and the rest of us that "I believe in supporting assertions by reference to the text" (this volume). She doesn't of course mean the same thing by the text as Levin does, but the point is that she isn't at a loss for evidence, or for ways of presenting evidence. All she has lost (she may well think it good riddance) is the particular set of beliefs and assumptions underlying Levin's sense of what constitutes real evidence and the proper way to present it.[10]

The Left, too, is anxious about the disappearance of ideology from critical analysis. Again the problem is deregulation, for if ideology disappears, then the category of the non-ideological goes as well. But where the Right sees a threat to stable order, the Left sees a threat to meaningful change. "If 'all is permitted,' " Michael Bristol warns (sounding uncannily like Levin's "free to choose any context he pleases"), "then there are no grounds for maintaining that the overthrow of the humanistic dispensation constitutes any kind of progress, social, intellectual, or otherwise" (*Shakespeare's America* 117). But again this anxiety is unnecessary. The absence of non-ideological grounds from which to argue for social change doesn't mean that such arguments can't be made. To say critique is impossible doesn't mean criticism is impossible. Critique (emigration) is impossible because there's nowhere to go that isn't inside of history and society, but since the social history within which we are situated is itself full of variety, not to say contradiction, there are lots of importantly different positions to be occupied. Bristol therefore can (and does) rise from the pathos of his emigration paragraph to write a brilliantly interesting book of just the kind he wants, one highly critical of "more affirmative types of scholarship" (4), though the book itself remains socio-historically determined and ideologically constituted—and eminently contestable.

Part of the anxiety on the Left seems to be rhetorical and strategic: it's a worry that anti-foundationalists lack authority. Who's going to believe a constructivist? In some situations, to be sure, essentialism may be persuasive, but this is not because of essentialism, but because of the situation. For instance, a strategic essentialism might be persuasive if you are talking to an essentialist (it would constitute an effective *ethos*, in the old terminology). But there are other situations in which a constructivist argument would look better—maybe, say, if you are appealing to a pragmatist to cut her fee for a lecture. There are also some situations in which neither constructivism nor essentialism will work. Richard Rorty says that "irrationalists who tell us to think with our blood cannot be rebutted by better arguments about the nature of thought, or knowledge, or logic" (*Consequences* 172), but neither will they be persuaded (Rorty would acknowledge as much) by claims for the value of keeping the conversation going.[11] There are lots of things that help make an argument persuasive: who's talking, how, and to whom (a mere three categories but they admit of a virtually unlimited number of variables); and the incalculable and unpredictable category of luck as well (*un coup de dés jamais n'abolira le hasard*). But all such determining factors work because of their specific fit to a varied and variable situation, and not because of the arguer's general theory of knowledge.

It may be that the worry here is less about convincing others and more about sustaining our own convictions. In the absence of a non-ideological category of truth, how can we even believe ourselves? And how, without such belief, can we avoid a paralysis of the will? Shakespeareans will recognize this as the *Hamlet* (or maybe *Troilus*) problem, and like *Hamlet*, it has been appropriated all across the political spectrum. On the lunatic Right, the putative abandonment of purpose and value dooms the young to wander aimlessly through the streets, souls without longing, listening to Guns N' Roses on their Walkmans. At the center, "framework relativism" means that we're condemned to a mushy formalism. On the Left, the problem is functionalism, and its consequence is the erosion of authentic resistance and oppositional agency.[12] But all of these anxieties are also misplaced, and for the same reason as earlier: beliefs are not logically dependent upon or necessarily produced by epistemological theories. Knowing that all knowledge is positional doesn't prevent you from being securely positioned in your knowledge. To quote Rorty who, if he didn't exactly put this argument on the map, seems to be the main creator of the current map on which to put it: "a belief can still regulate action, can still be thought worth dying for, among people who are quite aware that this belief is caused by nothing deeper than contingent historical circumstances."[13]

To see how this works, we can juxtapose two passages, one from M. H. Abrams explaining why he won't accept Jonathan Culler's suggestion to retitle his book *The Mire and the Swamp*, the other from Raymond Williams explaining why he's a socialist:

> What I have said does not constitute a knockout argument, far less the demonstration of an absolute foundation, for my standpoint. I believe, in fact, that this matter of the choice of the primitives for intellectual discourse is beyond all demonstrative argument except—and the exception is of high consequence—the pragmatic argument of the profitability for our understanding in choosing one set of intellectual premises over another. What I have said, then, is really an announcement of where I take my stand—a stand on certain primitives to be used in our explanative discourse about human talking, doing, and making. Which amounts to the confession that, despite immersion in the deconstructive element of our time, I remain an unreconstructed humanist. (174)

> There is of course the difficulty that domination and subordination, as effective descriptions of cultural formation, will, by many, be refused; that the alternative language of cooperative shaping, of common contribution, which the traditional concept of 'culture' so notably expressed, will be found preferable. In this fundamental choice there is no alternative, from any socialist position, to recognition and emphasis of the massive historical and immediate experience of class domination and subordination, in all their different forms. This becomes, very quickly, a matter of specific experience and argument. (*Marxism* 112)

There's a world of difference between Abrams's unreconstructed humanism and Williams's cultural materialism. They disagree, for instance, about whether social conflict or cooperative shaping constitutes the better position to assume from which to analyze and evaluate the world—a disagreement that corresponds quite closely to Levin's negotiation and Barker-Hulme's contestation from which we began. In addition, the differences between them would include a wide variety of beliefs ("opinions" might be used here, or "ideological preferences" as well): maybe what we teach, and how, and abortion law, and the designated hitter rule, and who knows what (for these beliefs aren't specified or predictable)? But in one area, causally unrelated to and logically independent of these different beliefs, Abrams and Williams are saying the same thing—namely that the beliefs themselves don't rest on any more secure (read "non-ideological") basis than that of an assumed position: don't rest, *and don't have to*.

Thus Abrams acknowledges he can't disprove Culler's retitling argument. Williams knows there's no logical way to convince humanists to become socialists, since what is involved in such "preferences" is not "choice" in the Miltonic sense ("reason also is choice"), but the contingencies of history ("immediate" and "specific experience")—not refutation but "refusal." Both Abrams and Williams know as well that their own positions are no more securely grounded in principle than those of their antagonists, but this knowledge doesn't prevent them from continuing to believe what they believe. They stick to their guns and go on advocating their positions. Williams's word at the end is "argument," and in this context he can hardly mean logical demonstration. He means rhetoric, with its inevitably agonistic and contestatory ambience, the same ambience of Abrams's "knockout argument." *Winning isn't the main thing, it's the only thing*. Winning, though, is impossible. In giving up foundations in favor of pragmatic profitability, Abrams hasn't exchanged closure at one end (origin) for closure at the other (consequences). According to Rorty (whose terms Abrams must expect us to recognize here), the pragmatist argument ends up by not ending up; it just keeps the conversation going. The same is true of Williams's history. "In most description and analysis," Williams tells us, "culture and society are expressed in an habitual past tense. The strongest barrier to the recognition of human cultural activity is this immediate and regular conversion of experience into finished products" (*Marxism* 128). *It's not over till it's over*; what Abrams and Williams both add to this is that it's never over. The game goes on, and there's no way out of the game, but this doesn't prevent you from continuing to play and playing to win.

Abrams-Williams enable us to answer the second of the two questions I raised at the beginning: What is to be done? Nothing is to be done; or at least nothing special. There are two reasons for this: *one*, nothing can be done (there's nothing outside of ideology), and, *two*, nothing special needs to be done (accepting *one* doesn't inhibit our ability to believe what we believe and to advocate the actions that we understand to follow from these beliefs).

Is there a down side to this situation? Maybe. It creates some messy pedagogical inconveniences (about which I have written elsewhere in "Teaching Differ-

anti-foundationalist theory hope throughout *Doing What Comes Naturally* (see index) as well as in his essay on new historicism, "Commentary: The Young and the Restless."

8. The distinction is of course formative and made frequently. One good example, from which I have quoted those epithets, comes near the end of the *Meno* (97[e]–98[a]; 381–82).

9. It's sometimes argued that the endurance of these dualisms proves they're right, or satisfy some essential human need. The counterargument to this is to claim that their installation at the time of Plato was a matter of contingent choice (Rorty, *Philosophy* 155–64); that they have survived, as lots of cultural values do, largely because of inertia (we're used to them; they're famous on account of being well known [Barbara Herrnstein Smith 47–53]); and finally that the same history which has entrenched the concept of ideology also includes, as a kind of poor brother or (better) weak sister, a long tradition of anti-foundationalist thought, going back to the sophists who antedated Plato, and Ovid (in contrast to Vergil), and rhetoric (in contrast to dialectic or logic). Lanham's *Motives of Eloquence* is the great recent account of this counter-tradition. The gist of Lanham is conveniently available in two Fish versions (*Doing* 471–502; and "Rhetoric").

10. Levin himself seems to have come closer to this position in his most recent *PMLA* piece. Though he again focuses his attack upon the contemporary abandonment of authorial intention, the problem is now not anarchy but repressiveness: "The rejection of The Author Function . . . creates a hermeneutic vacuum that must be filled . . . what fills the vacuum is a universal law—the Law of Concealed-but-Revealed Ideological Contradiction. . . . The Death of the Author, then, has left these critics not more but less free—certainly less free than a comparable group of formalist-humanists trying to interpret Shakespeare's intended meaning" ("Bardicide" 502). Levin seems more convincing here than earlier, though of course there's plenty of room to disagree with his understanding of how current criticism determines meaning, as well as with his implied definition of freedom and the value he places upon it ("*certainly* less free?").

Miltonists are experiencing similar difficulties about changing evidentiary protocols. I refer to the controversy surrounding Leah Marcus's attempt to interpret *Comus* with reference to the judicial process, presided over by the Earl of Bridgewater, of a rape case dating from around the time Milton composed the poem. Since no good evidence exists, even inferentially, to believe Milton knew about the case, Marcus's argument entirely abandons authorial intention, but this doesn't leave her without evidence to marshal for her conclusions. On the contrary, her essay is (characteristically) filled with the meticulous accumulation of detail derived from laborious research into primary documents. It's just that the evidence and the evidentiary rules are determined by a different set of assumptions, unspecified but probably along the lines of those I suggested earlier, that issues of gender and power are the most important ones to keep in mind in determining interpretive conclusions.

11. Jonathan Dollimore, who has written with characteristic astuteness about this problem, remarks that a homophobic response to a constructivist argument might be aversion therapy, and to an essentialist argument enforced sterilization or worse ("Shakespeare" 478–79; see also Dollimore and Sinfield, "Culture" 94–96).

12. The lunatic Right can be left namelessly beneath contempt. The center can be represented by Paisley Livingston, who argues that scientific realism, as an antidote to framework relativism, allows us to anchor critical activity in a socio-historical context. But in fact the move to historicization can be (and has often been) made independently of a realist epistemology, and this move hasn't in any case solved the problem of indeterminacy; it has simply situated it in a different position.

For the Left I am thinking of Paul Smith's brilliant book, *Discerning the Subject*. Smith begins with a vigorous rebuttal of Althusserian functionalism, locating the weak spot not in constructivism, but in totalization: it's one thing for Althusser to say that we are all interpellated as subjects, another for him to claim that the interpellation is performed under the direction of a unified cultural mechanism. Having emphasized the variety and contradictions within our situation, Smith is in a position to concede that all action is ideologically constituted without conceding anything at all. But Smith argues against such a conclusion, affirming instead that we can allow for "the possibility (indeed, the actuality) of resistance to ideological pressure" (xxxv). How? By "positing a constitutive non-unity in the subject," Smith claims he can "point toward a category of agency" (22–23), adding that "the place of that resistance has, then, to be glimpsed somewhere in the interstices of the subject-positions which are offered in any social formation" (25). All this leads to the triumphant conclusion "that ideological interpellations may *fail* to produce 'a subject' or even a firm subject-position. Rather, what is produced by ideological interpellation is contradiction, and through a recognition of the contradictory and dialectical elements of subjectivity it may be possible to think a concept of the agent" (37).

But how do we recognize subjective contradictions except through the knowledge and understanding derived from our various histories? What then enables us to claim that such recognition *is not itself ideologically determined?* or that the spaces between ideological apparatuses in disunified formations and the spaces between ideological interpellations in the divided subject *are not themselves ideologically filled?* Smith is willing to concede that we can play only the hand we've been dealt, but he refuses to concede that even knowing when to hold and fold 'em, and knowing when to fight and run belong to us only as derivatives from the same cultural dispensation that dealt us the hand in the first place. As Rorty says, "socialization, and thus historical circumstance, goes all the way down—. . . there is nothing 'beneath' socialization or prior to history which is definatory of the human" (*Contingency* xiii). And if it's culture all the way down, then it's ideology all the way up, and all across the board, including those gaps and interstices which Smith has invested with such hope for authentic oppositional agency.

Again, though, this investment isn't necessary. Once you can establish the variety and contradictions in culture, you've taken care of functionalism anyway, and you don't need to fall back to any interstitial subject position to be able to claim what you want: namely, that change is possible (indeed, necessary), and that our actions contribute to such change (though not in masterfully predictable ways). Why, then, does Smith cling against his own better knowledge to concepts, however chastened and reduced, of subjective sovereignty and non-ideological truth? My guess is that he can't finally escape from the historical nightmare I mentioned earlier, and its apparent demands precisely to transcend ideology by pulling ourselves up by our own bootstraps.

13. *Contingency* 189. Cf. *Contingency* 44–54, and "one would have to be odd to change one's politics because one had become convinced, for example, that a coherence theory of truth was preferable to a correspondence theory" (182–83). In addition to items by Fish cited earlier, I want to emphasize a particularly generous-minded and wide-ranging advocacy of this position from the Left by Howard Horwitz.

# 9

# Ordinary People and Academic Critics: A Response to Richard Levin

Gerald Graff

Richard Levin's critique of feminist interpretations of Shakespeare expresses widely shared misgivings not just about feminist criticism but about certain tendencies of academic criticism. These misgivings come across clearly in Levin's statement of his critical credo:

> I am not now and never have been a New Critic. I was trained in the Chicago Aristotelian school, which had some bitter quarrels with the New Criticism. But we did share what I would call the basic formalist perspective, which views a literary text as something intentionally produced by an author to evoke a meaningful, pleasurable response in an audience. Many new Marxists and some feminists claim this perspective is no longer tenable since Barthes, Foucault, and others, have invalidated the assumptions on which it rests. . . . But most ordinary people do view literary works in this way, as products intentionally designed to give them pleasure. I suspect it is even how Marxists and feminists view them when they are not laboring in their vocation (as Falstaff puts it), but if I am wrong I hope my respondents will explain why, in terms of their own approaches, anyone other than a professional critic would want to see a play or read a novel. The formalist approach can explain this, since it coincides with the actual experience of most audiences, and so I think its conception of a literary work cannot be invalidated, regardless of the latest French discoveries. It will always be valid, though it may slip in and out of fashion in the academy. (This volume)

Let's start with Levin's caustic observation that only "a professional critic" would "want to see a play or read a novel" as something other than a product "intentionally designed to give . . . pleasure." The target here is not just feminist criticism but "professional" criticism, that is, academic criticism, or that species of academic criticism that fails to "coincide" with the "actual experience" of "ordinary people."

Of course Levin is himself a professional academic and would no doubt distinguish between valid forms of academic criticism—ones that respect the intentions of authors and the responses of ordinary readers—and those that force texts and responses into a methodological straightjacket in order to generate fashionable new readings. Here, however, there are contradictions. At the end of his final "Reply" to his critics, Levin commends feminism as "the only one of the new approaches that is certain to have a permanent effect, . . . because it has permanently raised our consciousness of the importance of gender and gender-bias in literature and literary criticism" (this volume). I find it hard to square this acknowledgment of the permanent importance of gender issues with Levin's argument throughout these papers and in the long passage I have just quoted, which I take to be that feminist critics have intruded these issues into literature and criticism in disregard of the responses of the ordinary reader. If Levin thinks feminist criticism has permanent value, why does he associate it in the passage with professional fads that "slip in and out of fashion"? Granted, Levin exempts some types of feminist criticism from his critique, but I don't think this removes the problem.

## Transforming the Ordinary

It is worth looking closely at the role played in Levin's argument by the contrast between ordinary reading and methodologically-driven academic reading. Levin acknowledges that no interpreter is free of methodology, for, as he puts it, "the work itself cannot tell us how we should regard it . . . " and he acknowledges that many valid methodologies are possible (this volume). On the other hand, there are apparently good and bad methodologies, methodologies that respect the responses of ordinary readers and ones that disregard or violate those responses. Levin's quarrel is presumably not with academic methodological reading as such, but with the kind that deviates from ordinary reading and presumably fails to account for it.

Despite this qualification, Levin's argument cannot help appealing to those many in our culture (including many academics) who have never forgiven the university for professionalizing literary studies—people who still harbor doubts that literature should have ever become an academic subject at all. As these people see it, the result of the professionalization of literary study in universities has been to take literature away from the "common reader" (including the undergraduate student) and to turn it into the special province of a self-replicating guild whose methods and technical jargons are in fact designed to keep the lay reader out.[1]

In this view, academic criticism is seen as narcissistic, competitive, and subject to the vicissitudes of fashion, while "ordinary" reading (and the academic criticism that takes its cues from it) is seen as healthy-minded, unconcerned with the pedantries of interpretive conflict, and ultimately enduring though it may go temporarily out of fashion.[2] Whereas narrowly professional critics are partisan, self-interested, and concerned chiefly with the competition of the academic marketplace, critics who speak for the ordinary reader presumably stand outside the competitive academic fashion-parade and thus "can never be invalidated." Though Levin hypothetically grants validity to feminism, Marxism, and other "ideological" criticisms in their own sphere, his characterization of these schools fits a familiar betrayal narrative in which academic professionals are blamed for having stolen literature from common readers.

It is here, in his elevation of ordinary over narrowly professional reading that Levin, despite his disclaimer, does speak for a wider community and not just for himself (this volume). And it is here that Levin's argument seems to me ideologically suspect in at least one of the senses of "ideology" used by Levin's opponents in this exchange. It is a partisan argument that represents itself as transcending partisanship and politics and operating only on the level of neutral rationality. In appealing to "the actual experience" of ordinary readers, Levin claims to speak for all readers—even feminists and Marxists in those moments when they are being "ordinary" rather than "professional"—while he actually speaks for a certain faction in the current culture war. The implication is that whereas professional critics are "political," factional, and self-interested, critics who identify themselves with the "ordinary" reader have no politics or interests because their interests are everyone's interests.

Suppose we grant that "the actual experience of most audiences" of Shakespeare has been experience of works designed "to evoke a meaningful, pleasurable response," even though one would want to know a lot more about what lies behind this description.[3] What then follows? Unless we assume that whatever is is right, the fact that audiences can be shown to have actually responded in a certain way does not mean that audiences *ought* to respond that way. What interests Marxist, feminists, and other "ideology critics" (as I will call them for lack of a better term) is not just how the members of a culture ordinarily *do* read and respond to art, but the possibility of changing how they read and respond, including their construction of what counts as ordinary reading. This is why these critics often describe their practice as one of reading texts "against the grain" of conventional readings and why they see the very concept of the "ordinary" reader as an ideological construction that makes heterodox values seem eccentric or pathological.

So even if Levin could show that Shakespeare's contemporaries or his later audiences were as unconcerned with themes of gender as Levin supposes they were, such a demonstration would be irrelevant to the project of feminists and other ideology critics, which is precisely to ask why a mode of reading that is *not* concerned with those themes should be considered the "ordinary" and thus normative one—a mode that is "always . . . valid." Why is it that a reading that thinks nothing of the fact that Lady Macbeth has to "unsex" herself in order to qualify to commit murder has been considered the ordinary way of reading *Macbeth?* What does it mean that critics who see such questions as pertinent for literary study are seen as "political" (and therefore unliterary), while critics who regard those questions as extraneous are thought not to be doing anything political? Why is reading a literary text as "something intentionally produced by an author to evoke a meaningful, pleasurable response" considered more normal (and more literary) than a reading that reflects on the assumptions about gender that make this literary pleasure possible?

It is the culturally constructed nature of these supposedly ordinary, normal, natural ways of reading that ideology critics hope to make readers (including students) critically aware of. Once readers recognize that what passes for ordinary reading is not normal or natural but shaped by cultural attitudes toward gender, they may read Lady Macbeth's "unsex me here" speech in a new way. Once they recognize that the very distinction between what is "literary" and what is "political" has not always been drawn the way our culture now draws it, they may interpret not only literature but the rest of their experience differently. Even if it were true that "most audiences" have "ordinarily" read literature in a certain way, that would be beside the point here because the claim is that they should read differently.

In this respect, the aim of ideology criticism resembles that of the forms of theatrical defamiliarization developed by Bertolt Brecht and numerous artists and directors in Brecht's wake. The point is to disrupt, shock, or otherwise "problematize" the audience's unreflective "actual experience" in order to provoke it into critical self-reflection. From this standpoint, academic ideology criticism is just as concerned with the common reader as with the academic critical fashion parade—which again is why the characterization of that criticism as if it were narcissistic and merely concerned with fashion has ideological consequences. Such a characterization warns students, in effect: "Be careful not to become politically reflective readers—you don't want to look like fashion-mongering professors, do you?"

The same stakes can be seen in Levin's attack on thematic criticism, an extension of his critique of "thematism" a decade ago in *New Readings vs. Old Plays*. For Levin feminism, Marxism, and other ideology criticisms are versions of the thematic fixation, and the thematic fixation for him is one of the marks of the narrowly "professional" kind of academic critic. The distinction between thematic reading (professional) and non-thematic reading (ordinary) further reinforces the ideologically suspect characterization of certain forms of academic reading as prone to factionalism, self-interest, and politics in a way that ordinary reading supposedly is not.

The suggestion is that thematic reading has arisen to serve the self-interested need of academics to validate their specialized methodologies. The ordinary reader, taking her cues from the work or the author's intentions, presumably gets at literary meaning the old fashioned way—she *earns* it. Academic critics, by contrast, stack the deck in the house's favor by generating their "themes" not from the works they study but from their critical methodologies. These theme-generating methodologies—Marxism, Freudianism, deconstructionism, new historicism, feminism—give academic critics an unfair advantage over lay readers by telling them what any literary work means before they read it.

R. S. Crane, the leading figure of the Chicago school, called this procedure "the high priori road," knowing *a priori*, or in advance, what a work means because your methodology tells you so. Crane's analysis of apriorism made him and his colleagues shrewd critics of both the New Critical and the old historical schools of the 1940s and 1950s, and their critiques still apply to the critical schools of today.[4] But Crane did not deal with the apriorism that can seep into the outlook of the enemies of apriorism themselves, especially when that outlook is assumed to be wired into the "actual experience" of audiences—experiences, that is, that are viewed *a priori* as normal and normative.

In fact, what Crane called the high priori road was not too far from what current critics call "ideology." In pointing out the ideological nature of appeals to ordinary reading and common sense, current ideology criticism can be described as an attempt at a more rigorous critique of apriorism than the one Crane mounted—more rigorous because more alert to the impossibility of simply deciding not to let *a priori* presuppositions influence one's literary interpretations. It is this alertness to apriorism that leads current literary theorists to insist that critics and teachers are not free of "theories" just because they are not interested in examining them.[5]

GERALD GRAFF

## What Is Shakespeare "About"?

Levin's critique of feminist Shakespeare critics seems to me most convincing in those places where he questions their specific identifications of patriarchal and counter-patriarchal moments in the plays. To examine literary works as we increasingly do today for their moments of social "subversion" and "containment," there needs to be not only some flexibility in the judgments of what counts as subversion and containment, but also a close attention to the often shifting historical and textual contexts in which these effects operate. The temptation is to substitute a more facile procedure in which a critic scans literary works for textual features that have been defined in advance as subversive or "hegemonic," masculinist or anti-masculinist, and assigns political plus and minus points accordingly. In other words, it is one thing to ask feminist questions about the functioning of gender in a work, and another to answer those questions persuasively.

My sense, however, is that what bothers Levin about feminist Shakespeare critics is not the answers they give to feminist questions about literature but the fact that they ask such questions about literature at all.[6] What bothers Levin, to put it in the terms he uses, is that the questions feminists ask are prompted not by the "ordinary" audience's "actual experience" of Shakespeare but by a professional methodology, in this case one that also happens to be a political agenda. In other words, Levin's declared commitment to methodological pluralism is contradicted by the privileged status he accords to the "ordinary" reading.

As Levin puts it, the trouble with certain feminist critics is that they write as if "the plays are about the role of gender in the individual and in society" ("Feminist Thematics" 126). As Levin surely knows, "about" is one of the most treacherous words in modern literary criticism. It was a treacherous word when the New Critics stirred up fierce polemics by arguing that poems were not "about" extraliterary states of affairs, and it is treacherous today when even fiercer battles rage over the extent to which culture and the academic disciplines are unavoidably "about" politics. A lot hinges on what it means to say something is "about" something else.

This "about claim" is one that Levin habitually attributes to his feminist targets. At the start of "Feminist Thematics and Shakespearean Tragedy," Levin states that "probably the best way to begin the investigation is to ask what these critics think the tragedies are—or what they are *about*, which amounts to the same thing . . . " (125). Levin says that the critics he discusses all agree "that the plays are not really *about* the particular characters who appear there but *about* some general idea [gender] and, consequently, that they are not primarily dramatizations of actions but explorations of or commentaries on or inquiries into or critiques of that idea, which the characters and actions subserve" (126). Levin adds that feminists "have the obligation of proving that the play really is intended to be *about* their theme" (133; italics mine in all cases).

In summing up the claim of certain feminist critics as the proposition that Shakespeare's plays are "about the role of gender," Levin has these critics saying two things: (1) that gender is what Shakespeare consciously *intended* his plays to be about; (2) that gender is *the only thing* the plays are intended to be about. Let's take these attributions up in this order.

1. In Levin's words, when feminists claim that a play "is 'exploring' or 'commenting on' the central theme," this "implies a conscious purpose. An unintended exploration seems self-contradictory." If one recalls Levin's complaint that contemporary critics too habitually *dismiss* literary intentions, one may find it strange that he should rebuke feminists for being would-be intentionalists on Shakespeare. But it is only if feminist critics incur "the obligation of proving that the play really is intended to be *about* their theme" that they become vulnerable to Levin's charges.

So far as I can see, however, in none of the statements quoted by Levin does any feminist critic say or imply that a particular Shakespeare play or the plays in general "are *about* the role of gender in the individual and society" in the sense of intentional, "conscious purpose" stipulated by Levin. What the critics do say is that a given play is "a critique" of patriarchal attitudes (Coppélia Kahn); "a radical critique" of some of society's most cherished notions of gender (Gayle Greene); "a stud[y] of" the complexities of marriage (Irene Dash). They say that a play "treats" jealousy as part of a pathological male animus (Edward Snow) or that it "portrays 'the dialectic of gender conflict' " (Harry Berger, Jr.); or that it "contains a fierce war between gender concepts of manhood and womanhood . . ." (Robert Kimbrough); or that it "may be viewed as a vast commentary" on the absurdity of masculine consciousness (Madelon Gohlke).

Why should saying that Shakespeare "explored" or "commented on" issues of gender be thought equivalent to saying that Shakespeare had the "conscious purpose" of writing "about" gender? These ideas are not equivalent, it seems to me, if what we mean by an interpretation of an author's conscious purpose is one that the author himself would have recognized as such—which seems to me a fair criterion for classifying an interpretation as "intentionalist." An interpretation concerned with conscious purpose, that is, would be one that uses a descriptive vocabulary that the author could be imagined using or at least recognizing as his or her own.

The phrases Levin quotes from feminist critics clearly do say that issues of gender are *present* in Shakespeare's plays, but they do not suggest that Shakespeare himself would have been aware of that presence or would have described it in a feminist vocabulary. To argue that a play "comments on" concerns of gender is not the same as saying that it comments in the same vocabulary in which feminists or other later critics comment on those concerns. No feminist makes such an intentionalist "about claim," or at least no feminist *needs* to do so in order to analyze the functioning of gender in a play.

To be sure, there is a loose sense in which every interpretation claims to say what a text is "about," but in a way that hedges on the question of whether the author would have recognized or used the critic's terms of "aboutness." In fact it is to circumvent the ambiguities about such questions that arise in an increasingly contentious critical climate that critics have increasingly resorted to prudent equivocations like "the work suggests," "deals with," "treats," and so forth, expressions conventionally recognized as making weaker intentionalist claims than "is about" or "says." (The habit of saying "the work suggests" instead of "the author suggests" is another such equivocation.) The same concern prompts teachers to recommend such circumlocutions to students, correcting "*The Sonnets* are about Shakespeare's sex life" to "*The Sonnets* suggest certain attitudes toward sex." The term "theme" in fact is another of these useful equivocations that is conventionally understood as suspending the question whether the theme is an intended one or not. The question can be waived because it is assumed that a pattern can be said to be present in a text without a judgment being ventured as to whether it is intended or not.

The feminist readings singled out by Levin operate not by simply ignoring the intentions of literary texts, I think (though some feminist theorists may disagree with me on this), but by redescribing those intentions. Such redescriptions offer themselves neither as a doubling replication of the author's intentions nor as something simply "imposed" by the critic's methodology either. The pattern described is assumed to be present in the text and its intentions, but made visible as such only by the critical vocabulary in which it is redescribed. In this respect, feminist interpretations of Shakespeare are present-centered without renouncing their claim to illuminate the past: they seek not to impose present concerns on the past but to illuminate the past by redescribing it in terms the past was not aware of. It is not a question of turning Shakespeare into a feminist or an anti-feminist but of showing that some of his concerns were those we now redescribe in feminist terms.

But what about treating a Shakespearean play as a "critique" of patriarchal attitudes—doesn't this at least make a strong claim about Shakespeare's intention and one that cannot be sustained? Levin says "it seems more reasonable to conclude that the tragedies are not criticizing their own gender assumptions but just assuming them, along with other conditions underlying the dramatized action, which is their real subject. This does not mean that *we* cannot criticize those assumptions; it only means that we should separate our activity from Shakespeare's" ("Feminist Thematics" 134).

But again I see nothing anomalous about a work's being said to "criticize" certain assumptions without its author intending it to. One thinks of numerous works in which the implications of the narrative, say, or of certain figures of speech, operate as implicit criticisms of the text's or author's primary beliefs. (Derrida and de Man argue with some plausibility that this cannot *fail* to happen.) Blake and Shelley had a point when they said that Milton was of the Devil's party without knowing it—that the action of *Paradise Lost* functioned as an implicit critique of the Christian theology the work was intended to justify. In the same way it seems legitimate to see *Macbeth* as a critique of the way ambition has been gendered as male in Western society even though, again, Shakespeare presumably would not have been aware of that implication or capable of describing it in a feminist register.

The choice Levin offers between a work's criticizing gender assumptions or "just assuming" them ignores the possibility of contradictions between a work's assumptions. It is just such contradictions that feminist and other ideology critics have in mind, I think, in reading literary works as "criticisms" of their own assumptions—which is one of the things it means to read "against the grain." In this sense, the feminist critics treated by Levin not only do "separate" their "activity from Shakespeare's," contrary to Levin's charge that they don't, but their project would make no sense if they did not make that separation. The idea of reading a text against the grain is intelligible only on the assumption of a difference between the critic's interpretive vocabulary and the "grain" being read against. Levin says there are signs that some feminists are "in fact moving in this direction"—that of recognizing the difference between their own vocabularies and the authors they write about—"though they may not always be clear about it" ("Feminist Thematics" 134). It would be more accurate to say that feminist critics do not need to "move" in this direction because it is the one they have taken all along.[7]

2. The "about claim" that Levin attributes to feminist critics not only turns them into naive intentionalists, it also has them discounting everything in literature besides gender. Take the remark I quoted above that the critics Levin discusses all agree "that the plays are not really *about* the particular characters who appear there but *about* some general idea [gender] and, consequently,

that they are not primarily dramatizations of actions but explorations of or commentaries on or inquiries into or critiques of that idea, which the characters and actions subserve" (126).

Again, the aboutness is in the eye of the beholder. So far as I can see, at least, no critic quoted by Levin comes close to saying that Shakespeare's plays "are not really about the particular characters who appear there." Again we are given a bogus either/or choice—either a play is about characters and actions or it is about gender. Again, no feminist needs to make such a choice since an analysis of how gender functions in a work does not require it. It does not invalidate a feminist interpretation if a work deals with other issues besides gender, or if it explores issues of gender in the process of doing other things such as presenting characters and dramatizing actions.[8]

"About," then, is a polemical forced card in this dispute. It enables Levin to attribute to feminist critics a stronger, more intentionalist, more exclusive, and therefore more vulnerable "about claim" than they make or need to make in order to justify their interpretations.

## Ideology

The questions raised by Levin about the compatibility of "ideological criticism" with notions of objectivity, rational debate, and what Levin calls "neutral reason" (this volume) have a long history in Marxist theory and an even longer one in philosophy. Obviously the chances of useful debate over these questions depend on whether words like "ideology" and "objectivity" are being used in roughly similar senses by opposing parties. This seems to me not to be the case here.

Levin's definition of "ideology" as "a consciously held set of political beliefs" could hardly be further from the definition invoked by Gayle Greene (quoting Belsey, Coward, and Ellis), in which "ideology" denotes "not an optional extra, deliberately adopted by self-conscious individuals . . . but the very condition of our experience of the world, unconscious precisely in that it is unquestioned, taken for granted" (this volume). Levin, as he insists, is free to choose any definition he likes (this volume), but the disparity is not promising for the rational debate that Levin says he wants to facilitate. In so far as this is the key issue—is ideology a freely chosen "optional extra" or "a condition of our experience of the world"?—the debate never gets off the ground.

Perhaps Levin believes he has disposed of the opposing definition of ideology once he has charged it with self-contradiction. He says that when feminists and other ideology critics assume that all thought is ideological they necessarily trap themselves in a double bind: if you say all statements are ideological, then your own statements must be ideological and you have discredited yourself. The Liar's Paradox blocks the door of the ideology critic's den, leaving no way out. How, for example, can Catherine Belsey deny that interpretations can ever uncover "something there" in a text and then go on to speak of contradictions that "in reality" constitute the text (Levin, this volume)? I too find it hard to see how Belsey can have it both ways, but then not all ideology critics are as careless as Belsey on this point. There has been much debate within their ranks over the extent to which using "ideological" in the sense of "a condition of our experience of the world" amounts to surrendering all claims of truth and validity.[9]

Levin says that when Greene and others "insist that objective knowledge of the text is 'spurious,' and that all interpretations of it are 'interventions' determined by the interpreter's ideology, . . . *this means* there could be no appeal to any factual evidence within the text in a struggle with non-Marxists, and so it is hard to see how non-Marxists could ever be persuaded by a Marxist interpretation" (this volume; my italics). But does the one thing mean the other, or is Levin again putting words in the mouth of an opponent? Greene herself disavows the equation of ideological criticism with skepticism. She says that to reject Levin's "notion of 'objectivity' " and to admit "the ideological and gendered basis" of critical judgment "does not mean that we cannot make judgments or take positions, that we throw everything up for grabs" (this volume).

Greene doesn't explain how she can have things both ways, and it is possible that she, like Belsey, simply contradicts herself. On the other hand, Greene seems to me to be making an important point: there is a sense in which interpretations *are* "interventions" in the situations they purport to be describing from outside. There ought to be a way of making this point—that interpretations are actions, not just reflections—without throwing truth out the window. Reason, Greene argues, operates not "in an empty space" but in situations already constituted by a residue of non-rational traditions and political determinations. Before debate starts certain positions have been included and excluded and certain agendas have been selected from all the possible ones. These selective determinations can be rationalized, but the rationalizing process takes place in a setting that can't itself be exhaustively rationalized (or, as we now say, "totalized"). This I take to be Greene's point when she complains that Levin "read our articles as isolated texts," abstracted from "the politics of this whole discussion," including such questions as "why we are talking about this now . . ." (this volume).

Greene's point is that it is easy for a dominant group to experience its beliefs as neutral because it doesn't feel the consequences of those beliefs the same way a subordinate group does. Men have had the luxury to think of gender-free readings of literature as exercises of neutral reason—or as properly literary reading, uncontaminated by alien politics—because in their situation gender has not needed to be an issue. What is experienced as neutral and apolitical are those political features of one's environment that seem satisfactory as they are. What is all right as it is is experienced as "unmarked" and therefore neutral and normative.

It is this consideration of the context in which inquiry and discussion takes place, I think, that Greene and other ideology critics have in mind when they say that objectivity is "spurious." The point is not that there is no truth but that truth is never politically neutral, that it is always open to criticism from another perspective that asks why *this* truth is being selected for emphasis rather than that one, or what ends a particular truth is being used to support, or why this question was selected for investigation in the first place. In this sense, what the current critique of objectivity questions is not the possibility of truth but the possibility of the decontextualized notion of truth implied by appeals like Levin's to "neutral reason."

A case in point would be my own earlier reference to Levin's distinction between ordinary and professional reading as "ideologically suspect." What I meant to challenge was not the truth of the distinction—there is certainly a difference between "lay" and "academic" modes of reading—but the way the distinction functions in the arguments of Levin and others who use it to imply that it is only the Left in the current culture war that has a politics or that has "politicized" literature. The question was not whether a valid distinction can be made between academic and nonacademic reading, but why the distinction was being used in the way Levin used it.

It is true that it is difficult to historicize and politically situate concepts like rationality and truth without compromising one's own claims in the process. But it is also possible to see this effort not as a debunking or destroying of rationality but as an attempt to extend the scope of rationality—to widen rationality's sense of its own conditions of possibility. Nobody so far as I know has accused the speech-act philosopher J. L. Austin of irrationalism, but when Austin pointed out in *How to Do Things with Words* that "constative" assertions simultaneously operate as "performatives" that commit actions in the world, he was making a point similar to the one Greene is making about the "interventionist" and "situated" nature of interpretations. That interpretations of texts are doing things while purporting only to be describing them from the outside forces us to complicate our account of interpretive rationality.

The fact that rational debate takes place within historical and material conditions both accounts for the possibility of such debate and renders its status unstable, though the degree of the instability is always hard to determine. The current academic generation is struggling to move from a model of knowledge as an affair of detached observation to one in which the observer acknowledges responsibility as a participant—which means also acknowledging the difficulty of observing one's own observation and of judging one's participation from an authoritative viewpoint. If truth is not invalidated by such a project, it does become divided and problematized by the effort to take its own conditions of possibility into account and to acknowledge its own vulnerability to criticism.

Levin shows little interest in such complications or struggles. For him, if there is no appeal to a commonly shared neutral reason, then debate becomes impossible. Levin thinks that the existence of such a neutral reason is demonstrated by the existence of commonly shared information and reasoning practices (like the law of non-contradiction) which are shared by both the Left and the Right. He says that in their arguments against his article his critics "must be appealing to a neutral reason," since, for example, they try to show that he contradicted himself. "Their effort assumes that self-contradiction is bad, which is a rational standard" (this volume). But the existence of shared assumptions, facts, and standards between two or more hostile parties does not establish the neutrality of those shared assumptions, something which can always be challenged from some other position. The law of non-contradiction is not neutrally established just because both Marxists and non-Marxists take it for granted. At most, what has been established is a local and contingent basis on which argument for the moment can take place.

This local and contingent basis, it seems to me, is the only one we have or ever can have for dealing with disputes like the one between Levin and his critics. Attempts to find "the way out," as Levin calls it (this volume), by invoking "neutral reason" only reproduce the circularity in which the controversy has been trapped. Historicists can always point out that such appeals to neutral reason are always already situated in history and politics, and rationalists can always retort that historicists are always already forced to use rational arguments in order to formulate their historicism. Rather than look for a way out, I think we can only try to keep our arguments responsive to the social circumstances in which they must "intervene," while acknowledging that these circumstances are such that we will never see them from the outside. Therefore our arguments will always be prone to forms of blindness and non-neutrality that others will point out. This, I take it, is what feminists and other ideology critics, new historicists, and deconstructionists have been saying all along.

## NOTES

1. This hostility toward the very existence of academic criticism finds its most unrestrained expression not in the articles lamenting the death of common readers at the hands of academics, but in the responses to such articles in letters columns. Here is a specimen that recently appeared in the *New Republic* in response to an article by Irving Howe entitled "The Treason of the Critics":

> Has the common reader ever taken much interest in, or derived much benefit from, the academic community? I don't think so. . . . Our concern should be directed [not toward the common reader, but] toward the souls of the academics and literati themselves, who, as a result of social and professional pressures, have lost touch with the inner impulses that drew them to the world of books in the first place. (Toren, 6, 41)

2. See Lawrence Lipking. Lipking's article, a qualified defense of the academic intensification of the "competitive" aspect of literary interpretation, attracted its own set of letters to the editor objecting to Lipking's failure to be denunciatory enough about academic criticism. More recently, Hilton Kramer has sternly rebuked a *New Yorker* essay on T. S. Eliot by Cynthia Ozick for its failure to go beyond a merely lukewarm condemnation of the decline of literary studies since Eliot's day.

3. Long before any battles erupted over "Shakespeare Left and Right," scholars questioned the validity of appealing in the way Levin does to an imagined "Elizabethan audience" in order to justify interpretations of Shakespeare. Some of the more trenchant criticism of this tactic came out of Levin's own Chicago school. See Moody A. Prior.

4. See my favorable treatment of Crane's critique of "the high priori road" in *Professing Literature: An Institutional History* 233–40. I also make favorable reference to Levin's application of the critique in *New Readings vs. Old Plays*. I would now emphasize the blind spot of Crane's argument (as I have done in this response), in view of the tendency to single out theory-oriented critics for blame, as if "common sense" criticism were not also vulnerable to apriorism. See n. 5.

5. I failed to notice the anti-aprioristic aspect of post-structuralism in *Literature Against Itself: Literary Ideas in Modern Society*, *Professing Literature*, and elsewhere. So, I think, does Frederick Crews in *Skeptical Engagements*, which mounts the charge of apriorism against "grand theory" but fails to consider the "problematizing" impulse of recent theory itself. (See especially chapter 9, "The Grand Academy of Theory.") The same holds for ill-informed critiques like that of John Ellis, *Against Deconstruction*. It is not that post-structuralist interpretations are never prone to apriorism, but that they are no more logically prone to it than traditional interpretations. Then, too, the most searching thinking on the problem has come from post-structuralist theorists, most notably Derrida, not from their detractors.

6. It is feminist questions *per se* that bother many critics of feminist criticism. Denis Donoghue is the most candid about it:

> Was Jane Austen opposed to marriage? Did she dislike children? What did she think of motherhood? Did Shakespeare restrict women to a narrow range of emotions? Did Yeats patronize Maude Gonne and other women? These are wretched questions, even if they are excused as marking a primitive stage in the development of a more interesting feminist criticism. (34)

The questions listed by Donoghue are not the only ones feminist critics ask, nor necessarily the most interesting ones. But what it is that is "wretched" about these questions escapes me.

7. I would therefore make a different point from Victoria Kahn, who wonders why Levin "bothers to take issue" with the kind of feminist criticism he deals with, since "he admits there are other far more compelling strains of feminist criticism of Shakespeare." Levin's argument "would have been more interesting," she says, "if he had addressed the sort of reading he mentions approvingly but only briefly in the *PMLA* article: a reading which brackets the question of intention and determines what a play's 'gender assumptions really are by deriving them inductively from the play itself' " (this volume). I claim that the critics Levin treats *do* bracket "the question of intention."

The reading of literary works as a site of contradiction and thus of self-critique is too often confused with a debunking of literature. But at least since the New Critics the exposure of contradictions in literature has been a way of revealing its richness as much as of debunking it. To me, Levin's criticism of feminism becomes more interesting and even more admirable when it contradicts itself than when it is consistent.

8. Levin here dusts off his earlier charge in *New Readings vs. Old Plays* against the supposed exclusivity of thematics critics, who in playing a game of "my theme can lick your theme" allegedly ignore other elements in the work besides their pet theme. But a work can do other things in the process of having a theme or themes. Finally, Levin's case against "thematism" comes down to the argument that the original audience of the work did not read it thematically. To which one can only reply: (1) how do we know?; (2) so what?

9. The philosopher Mary Hesse, writing of the sociology of science, has called this the "strong" version of the ideology thesis. See *Revolutions and Reconstructions in the Philosophy of Science* 29–60. Terry Eagleton discusses the problems of a too categorical use of the concept of "ideology" in "Ideology and Scholarship."

those highly illiberal voices that have leapt to his defense; but as both Cook and Victoria Kahn observe, his attacks on Marxist and feminist Shakespeare criticism have given these people license to say publicly what they might otherwise have kept to themselves. It is therefore disingenuous for him now to say that he really wants us all to be friends (or at least colleagues), rather like Fielding, at the end of Forster's *Passage to India*, wondering why Aziz can't just put the whole imperial past (and present) separating them behind him. Or perhaps better, like Wilhelm II saying after the Battle of Verdun, "Das hab' ich nicht gewollt."

It pains me to have to take up the cudgels against Levin, but I can do aught else. His recent work, as far as I can tell, has been utterly pernicious in its effects, whatever his intentions in the matter. Surely this entire debate and its after-shocks must illustrate to him, if nothing else, the exceedingly tenuous hold exercised by authorial intention over interpretation. Would that it were otherwise, that we could all just be reasonable, fair-minded, objective. Too much water has passed under the bridge in this controversy for any such happy outcome. One side or the other is going to win out. The only real question, as the old union organizing song has it, is: Which side are you on?

*There are no truths outside the Gates of Eden*

The crucial theoretical issue at stake in all the papers that comprise this section of *Shakespeare Left and Right* is the relationship between ideology and knowledge production. The puzzle, which each of the papers recognizes but which only Levin, Kahn, and Graff try to solve, concerns the possibility of making true statements about literary texts while acknowledging, with varying degrees of seriousness, the obvious fact that all interpreters are conditioned by the circumstances of their birth, training, and current social status (among other things); hence, that the statements they make about literature are in some sense (how much is of course controversial) determined by the ideological position these circumstances impose on them. Levin is surely correct to criticize the view that ideology goes all the way down for being either self-contradictory or self-defeating.[1] But he is just as surely wrong to arrogate a privileged epistemological position to formalism (formalism is as liable to produce erring descriptions as any other method) and to appeal to ordinary readers' experience and to an unspecified standard of universal rationality as unimpeachable criteria by which interpretations may be judged licit or illicit. Kahn and Graff both make this point well, so I may dispense with demonstrating it in detail here.

Let us grant, then, what even Levin admits: that knowledge and ideology cannot be neatly segregated into separate, hermetically sealed epistemological jars. What follows? Probably not as much as Greene and Bristol believe, but certainly more than Levin concedes. *Pace* Greene and Bristol, I think it is possible to hold conscious commitments to particular ideologies and to understand in a fairly explicit way why one would hold such commitments at all. Hence, while I fundamentally agree with their generally Althusserian conception of ideology, I also think that Levin's stipulative definition of this concept is not wholly without merit. The term surely can encompass both "a consciously held set of political beliefs" (Levin, this volume) and "that system of beliefs and assumptions, unconscious, unexamined, invisible, by which we imagine and represent the world" (Greene, this volume). I would add that while I suspect Greene's definition of ideology captures more of one's customary experience of the world—about which most of us are thoroughly mystified much of the time—Levin's reminds us that, on occasion, we are capable of learning more about and in principle mastering small corners of our ideological universe. That much rationality and that much capacity for knowledge we must all grant each other if any progress toward human emancipation is to be achieved. Perhaps it never will be, but then, as a political friend of mine is fond of observing, "liquor is quicker."

At this point I wish to impose on the reader's patience by indulging in a bit of personal history, the sole purpose of which is to make plain (some portion of) my own ideological commitments, specifically those that bear on my sympathies toward Marxist criticism, as well as my more distant relations with feminist theory. I apologize for the length of this Gramscian inventory of my own intellectual and material traces. The details are important, and I shall advert to them at various points later on.

*You've gone to the finest school all right, Miss Lonely,*
*But you know you only used to get juiced in it.*

Like the overwhelming majority of United States citizens, I hail from an immigrant working-class background. My great-grandparents all came to this country in the second half of the nineteenth century, principally for economic reasons, to set up as farmers and artisans in a nation still demographically affected by the million lives lost during the Civil War. As far as my limited lore about these people extends, they all prospered and were able to bequeath to their children, my grandparents and great uncles and aunts, a somewhat improved position on the ladder of economic success. But as I expect would have been typical for people of their class at this period (the first three decades of this century), there was no dramatic change in their children's vocational aspirations; almost without exception, my grandparents' generation plied the same trades as their parents had. None attended a college or university; many did not graduate from high school. The women mostly kept house and raised children. A few worked outside the home, but most earned extra cash by putting out labor—my maternal grandmother, for instance, took in sewing until she was well into her sixties.

The trauma of the 1930s, which marked my grandparents deeply, called to a halt my family's cheerful participation in the American dream, as the farms went bust, the houses were seized by banks, and everyone scrambled to find such work as was meagerly available. All survived to raise much smaller families than their parents and to instill in their children the virtues of hard work and thrift that economic adversity characteristically imposes. My parents' generation, reared during the Depression, reached adulthood as the postwar boom was just commencing. Some of my younger aunts and uncles benefited from higher education's expansion to attend university. But the striking thing about my parents and their siblings is not only that they were absolutely better off than their parents; they also migrated out of the working-class occupations to which they were immediately heir into professions and businesses. With some differences in timing, all prospered in some measure, enough so that they could afford to send their sons and daughters to college, albeit in my case the necessity to perform manual labor from the age of fourteen to twenty-two still obtained.

When I went to university, a scion of lower middle-class parents who had more or less consciously turned their backs on their working-class origins (ethnicity had already disappeared in my grandparents' generation), I had every intention to continue my family's forward march into a highly paid profession—the law, as it happens. But that was the late 1960s, and a number of things intervened. Most notable to me at the time was the student anti-war movement, in which I was a desultory participant. One bit of fallout from the student agitations was an enormous flight from educational programs that led directly into "the system." I switched my major from politics to literature and ultimately to philosophy, believing that doing so would protect me from the contaminations of business, law, government service and all the other *verboten* professions in the period.

At the same time, however, because I attended a private university with more than its share of economically and educationally privileged undergraduates—it had been little more than a country club for denizens of Chicago's North Shore a decade earlier when my uncle had gone there on a football scholarship—I was thoroughly inured to the idea that the culture I was fast acquiring (being a young man from the provinces, I was under the illusion that I had none before) was linked in some intimate way with a status and self-confidence that I manifestly lacked and fervently desired. While it was not cool in those days to be in a fraternity, at least not among the numerous bright kids from backgrounds like my own who were my friends, I nonetheless dated sorority girls and tried to impress the hell out of them by referring to Nietzsche and quoting, inevitably, Shakespeare. I wanted—desperately—to be let into the club and believed that by acquiring sufficient cultural capital I might get in without having to pay the customary price of earning a handsome income from more or less dubious pursuits.

Entering graduate school in 1972, I moved a bit further upscale, educationally speaking, a fact driven home when I realized that fully one-third of my entering class in English were offspring of millionaires, while many of the rest were sons and daughters of doctors, lawyers, and other folks sufficiently well-heeled to foot their children's tuition, room and board bills at this very fancy place. I hated graduate school, be it said, and I got out as rapidly as seemed decent, but not without having acquired a further patina of ruling-class manners and tastes.

Not long after settling into my first teaching position, I came upon a book that explained to me for the first time why my graduate training had been so distasteful and helped me to rethink my position as a literature teacher along lines that enabled me to diminish my increasing alienation from my students and also to alleviate an already nagging sense of having become a traitor to my class. I resisted Richard Ohmann's *English in America* at first, because it told a story about my training and profession that my own investment in being what I then was prevented my recognizing as my own. But in the end I was persuaded that he was right about the class ideological project of modern literary study, and that this latter was a significant source of my current and past discomfort with my job and myself.

I no longer recall the further punctual circumstances of this conversion experience—and unlike most autobiographers, I don't want to invent some for dramatic purposes—but within a year or so of reading Ohmann's book, I had not only declared my Marxist affiliation, I was beginning to read and teach the Marxist texts that have remained a staple of my own intellectual diet ever since. Ohmann had taught me how literary study in the postwar period was in complicity with all those corporate goons and privileged snobs whom I'd loved to hate in high school and college; Marx and Engels, later Althusser, Gramsci, and Lenin provided me with the theoretical armature undergirding Ohmann's analysis. From that day to this, I've never stopped being a Marxist, nor has it ever occurred to me, all the surprising events in world communism over the past few years notwithstanding, that I ought to. The reason for my deep, perhaps at times dogmatic, commitment to Marxist theory and method is almost certainly the link Marxism establishes between my own youthful experience of the world, which was for the most part a working-class experience, and the discipline I work in, which frequently irritates and depresses me but which I continue to profess and limitedly honor. I can do so with a modicum of good conscience because Marxism teaches, among other things, that the sons and daughters of the working class can benefit from education, that indeed without it they are significantly handicapped in their ongoing struggle with the bourgeoisie and its hired underlings.

*When I think back on all the crap I learned in high school,*
*It's a wonder I can think at all.*
*And though my lack of education hasn't hurt me none,*
*I can read the writing on the wall.*

So much for true confessions. What has all this to do with my topic: the relationship between ideology and knowledge? My own case illustrates, for me quite dramatically, the intimate entanglement of ideology (and the socio-historical forces that are its ultimate cause) with, if the phrase be allowed by those who have a different understanding of Marxism from my own, scientific theory. Moreover, it should not be difficult for readers to fill in the numerous blanks I've left in the particular cultural ideology that shaped my experience of higher education, for I have every reason to believe that mine was, in this regard, utterly typical of humanities students from the immediate postwar period until quite recently. In sum, I would almost certainly not have become the kind of Marxist I am absent my own class formation, but the truth or falsehood of Marxist theory in no way depends upon my or anyone else's ideological investment in it. Though it should be added that without serious, ongoing commitment to the theory among a broad range of intellectuals, it will almost certainly cease to play the central role it has come to occupy in recent literary study. A true theory may languish for want of expositors, as Galilean mechanics did prior to Newton, or as Darwinian evolutionary theory might have done had Huxley not been so skilled a debater. What Marxism requires—what it will always require—is people willing to carry on the class struggle in theory. Perhaps a majority of them will necessarily come from working-class backgrounds, but if not, not. Marxist theory was born of a couple of bourgeois class traitors and has frequently been sustained by others of similar provenance. The value of a scientific theory cannot be measured by the class, race, gender or ethnic origins of its proponents. On this point at least, Levin and I agree.

Where I strenuously disagree with him is in his equation of the crisis in Eastern Europe and the Soviet Union with the defeat of historical materialist theory. The incapacity of the centrally planned economies to compete with capitalism militarily and economically at the same time demonstrates nothing with respect to Marxism as a scientific theory. Levin thinks that the apparent triumph of capitalism in the current conjuncture puts paid to Marxist crisis theory, which holds that capitalism will ultimately perish due to its internal contradictions. Such was never Marx's unequivocal view, but let's grant for the moment Levin's claim that it was and entertain the possibility that, if you will, history has proven Marx wrong. At the moment of writing, the United States economy is spiralling into recession, with no one able to predict its depth or its shock-effect on the global economy. We'll just have to wait and see how capitalism does over the "longue-durée." It took the better part of a millennium for feudalism to be defeated across Europe; capitalism may just do as well, though surely one may be allowed to hope and desire otherwise. As Althusser was fond of saying, "l'avenir dure longtemps."

*Mostly you go your way and I'll go mine.*

I am constrained to disagree slightly with Gerald Graff, whose critical evaluation of Levin I otherwise find entirely admirable and wholly persuasive. Graff ends his paper with the following injunction: "We can only try to keep our arguments responsive to the social circumstances in which they must 'intervene,' while acknowledging that these circumstances are such that we will never see them from the outside and therefore our arguments will always be prone to forms of blindness and non-neutrality that others will point out" (this volume). It's the "never" I object to here. Graff has, in my view, bent the stick too far in the direction of social construction, coming perilously close to the Fish-Rorty line that, as I've already observed, asserts, in effect, we can only know what we already know. Graff himself is exhibit A that such is not the case, nowhere more strikingly than in the present paper, where he acknowledges his earlier misconstrual of post-structuralism in *Literature Against Itself* (27–28 n. 6). Scientific theories and more local hypotheses are always subject to revision, but it does not follow from this well-recognized truism in the empirical sciences that all our theories are absolutely constrained by the ideological circumstances of their production. Nor, as is characteristi-

## Michael Sprinker

*The movie wasn't so hot;*
*It didn't have much of a plot.*

I don't know what sorts of "ordinary people" Dick Levin has been talking to in recent years, but I doubt he's queried many folks like my own family about why they read books or see plays. I've encountered precious few people outside of literature departments, of any class, race, or gender, who thought that authors created their works "as products intentionally designed to give them [i.e., presumably, the audience] pleasure" (this volume). Surely Levin can't think this either, since it involves the manifest absurdity, for example, that Shakespeare had Levin himself—or someone very like him—in mind when writing his plays. Perhaps Shakespeare wrote his plays to give someone pleasure—Elizabeth, Essex, the groundlings, though probably not any of London's newly arrived plebeian masses—but not everyone who saw the plays performed in the Globe or at court can have found them equally pleasurable, or for precisely the same reasons. And notoriously from the end of the seventeenth century lots of people found a great many things to dislike in them, to the point that they felt obliged to alter the existing texts in significant ways.

As far as I'm aware, the only members of my extended family—including all those now deceased—who have ever regularly read books are my younger sister and myself, both college-educated; none of us, myself included, is a regular playgoer. Movies, television, and popular music are our aesthetic forms. Over the years, we've had desultory conversations about such matters, and what seems clear to me is that all of us, without exception, tend to respond ideologically to what we watch and listen to, and that the pleasures we derive from these artifacts depend upon a bewildering range of determinative circumstances and prejudices forming our different taste cultures. Nor are these distinct cultures entirely static.

Country music, a white working-class art form that dominates the air waves outside large urban centers, never held much appeal for me, though it certainly did (and does) for a majority of the people with whom I grew up. I've come to appreciate at least some of it over the years, but it continues to strike me as ideologically regressive in most ways. As someone once remarked, any country and western song that does not mention trucks, mamma, getting drunk, prison, trains, falling in love, and the pouring rain doesn't authentically represent the genre. Doubtless I'm revealing another among the numerous markers of my class traitorship, a form of snobbery that I began to acquire in high school, cultivated at university and in graduate school, and gradually became aware of once I'd recognized how thoroughly high bourgeois culture had recruited me to its ranks. I expect I'll be struggling with these contradictions the rest of my life.

Why am I telling you this? Merely to point to a highly suspect appeal to the popular that Levin has tried to enlist on the side of formalist criticism. His rhetorical intent would seem to be to convict all of us professional critics of ignoring (possibly to the point of feeling contemptuous towards) the experience of ordinary folks, making us ashamed of our elitist prejudices. But the ordinary people of my own acquaintance not only don't share Levin's interpretive biases, they don't move in anything like the cultural sphere that privileges Shakespeare, Milton, Balzac, Dickens, Virginia Woolf (name your favorite canonical author) and gives points for being able to quote lines, describe scenes, and recount the plots these authors constructed. Only those trained to value and perform these skilled, somewhat technical tasks characteristically read texts in the way Levin ascribes to ordinary people, and while I'm quite willing to grant that most literature professors are ordinary in most respects, their interpretive habits and their taste culture almost certainly diverge from the norm. If you don't believe, just ask Jesse Helms about the difference between his constituents' artistic tastes and the pointy-heads who tried to defend Robert Mapplethorpe's photography in the name of art; he'll give you an earful.

> *You say you've lost your faith, that that's not where it's at,*
> *You had no faith to lose, and you know it.*

I'm told that Levin once went through a Marxist phase. Hard to believe, I know, but possibly true, given his age. Lots of people took on faint pink tones in the 1930s and 1940s, especially intellectuals. Of course, many other people—some few were intellectuals—evinced rather stronger commitments to Marxism in the same period. But North American Marxism virtually died out in the academy (and in the unions, the media, and the culture at large) with the onset of the cold war. A high price was paid locally and globally for establishing American hegemony. It's a legacy that we hardly need to reclaim, since it continues to operate in subtle and overt ways every day.

Just scan, for example, Levin's "Reply to Michael Bristol and Gayle Greene." It is littered with the clichés of cold war liberalism, the cheap sneers at "the evil empire" and its supposed dogmas that have been a staple of justifications for nearly every nasty imperial adventure on which the United States has embarked from Korea to Vietnam to Chile to Grenada to Nicaragua and El Salvador. The latest episode in the Persian Gulf, deprived of this standard ideological ballast, did not fare so well in the public opinion polls early on. Before the bombing commenced, only the phoney "nuclear threat" gambit struck a responsive chord in many breasts—perhaps because it was one of the pillars of cold war anti-communism as well.

Levin can scarcely contain his glee as he recites the tired litanies learned from capitalist ideologues proclaiming actually existing socialism (never the happiest of designations) dead, the free market triumphant. "We've won, we've won," is the universal shout from Wall Street to the Bundesbank, to which chorus Levin joins in with his professorial *basso profundo*: "Soon the only surviving Marxists in the world may be holding out in the faculties of capitalist universities," adding, just to show he's not utterly vindictive, "and I think we should try to preserve some there, like any other endangered species." Put us all in cages for a curious public to ogle? I suppose we should be grateful he isn't recommending the creation of reservations or bantustans, one historically sanctioned method capitalists have employed to control unruly populations unfortunate enough to occupy territory the capitalists coveted. At least we've been warned.

*Maybe I made you mad,*
*Something I might have said.*
*Please just forget the past,*
*The future looks bright ahead.*

Once a war has begun, it matters little who fired the first shot. We're in it now, so let's get on with the business of winning—or losing, which latter I feel is unlikely, given the present balance of forces. Since, on Levin's account, it's the special dispensation of ideological critics like myself to purvey propaganda, I'll close with a frankly partisan speech that may rally more of the masses to our cause. Its basic message will be simple enough: back a winner.

Lyndon Johnson once opined that the Vietnam War would be won in the hearts and minds of the Vietnamese people. He was right, of course, even if he was wrong about who would have the greatest appeal to the majority of those hearts and minds and about the best methods for securing their loyalty. Perhaps he believed that "bombing them back into the Stone Age" would earn their respect. And perhaps Levin feels that the best way to bring us all to the negotiating table is to bludgeon us collectively in print, smear us with nasty screeds, shower us with ridicule, then say it was all in the spirit of inquiry and that we oughtn't to have taken it personally. As Don Corleone was wont to observe, it's only business. Well I don't take it personally, but then I wasn't being individually rapped on the knuckles with the schoolmaster's cane. Dare I hope that Levin won't take this personally either?

My honest conviction is that we ideological critics—a badge of honor we should not shrink from proudly displaying—should stop wasting our time in this way. Important intellectual work needs to be done, and we should simply get on with it, instead of expending our overtaxed resources in these local skirmishes. We represent a quite numerous group in the literary academy, if nowhere near the majority projected in the paranoid fantasies of right-wing pundits like Roger Kimball and Allan Bloom. Our books garner an increasing proportion of major publishers' lists, and we get our share of shelf space in the bookstores (in all the ones I frequent, at any event). In sum, I think we're on the way to winning, and I suspect that the reaction of our self-professed non-ideological colleagues testifies to this fact. They're threatened and scared—by us, by our students, and, I think it's only fitting to add, by their own senescence. Time, among other inexorable natural determinants of human life, really is on our side.

The best way to answer Richard Levin's challenge is not to pick up the gauntlet he's thrown down, but to do the work we've been doing, to do more of it, to do it better, to sustain each other in the ways we all do when we read each other's books, assign them to our students, and disseminate the knowledge we have produced through the growing number of channels available to us. Let them have *PMLA*, if they want it. We've got *Cultural Critique*, *Signs*, *Feminist Studies*, *South Atlantic Quarterly*, *Feminist Review*, *Tulsa Studies*, *diacritics*, *boundary 2*, *Representations*, *MLN*, *Critical Inquiry*, and *Public Culture* (just to name some of the selections from my personal Top Forty). If they band together and try to close us out at Harvard, Yale, Princeton (pick your favorite boring university press list), we'll go to Routledge or Verso or Blackwell's or to the more with-it university presses like Minnesota. If they fail to promote us, so what? To modify the old Groucho Marx story slightly, would you want to be a member of any club that would have them as members? If we do the work, we'll get jobs, we'll have students, we'll survive to fight another day. But we have to continue doing the work, our work, dictated by our sense of what are the important questions to ask of literary texts.

When the United States finally removed its forces from South Vietnam and called a halt to its genocidal air war against the North, it took some time for the North Vietnamese and the Viet Cong to recuperate and regroup for the final push to overthrow the Thieu-Ky regime. Giap and his generals reckoned it would take two years or more of difficult fighting; in fact it took less than eight weeks, as most of the Army of the Republic of Vietnam fled or surrendered without a struggle. The *ancien régime* has been committing some of its heavy artillery during the past several years, to no visible effect that I can discern. Let them waste all their ammunition. One day soon we'll just seize the guns and melt them all down for scrap.

## NOTE

1. I have urged much the same point elsewhere, adding the extra fillip that such a view is also vacuous, since it asserts no more than that one can only know what one knows; see Sprinker, "Knowing." It should be said in passing that the current "anti-foundationalist" vogue in some quarters relies on a highly skewed, when it is not simply ignorant, account of recent philosophy of science; see, most prominently for recent literary theory, Fish, *Doing*, which provides the authority for Pechter's discussion of the ineluctability of ideology included in this collection. *Pace* Fish, Pechter, *et alia*, no necessary contradiction is entailed in affirming both the obvious fact that knowledge arises in history (and is therefore socially determined to some degree) and the claim that scientific knowledge is cognitively autonomous in relation to the conditions of its socio-historical production. There is no point to pressing the issue here; for those who remain skeptical but are interested in hearing the arguments, Bhaskar's *Realist Theory*, *Scientific Realism*, and *Reclaiming Reality* provide the best point of departure.

# II

# Ideology and Critical Practice

11

# Character and Ideology in Shakespeare

Joseph A. Porter

Routine as my title may look, it needs a word of explanation. First, "Shakespeare" here almost means "Shakespeare study," since I address questions of character and ideology primarily as they affect interpretive commentary on the plays.[1] Then, the conjunction "Character and Ideology" may be less innocent than it seems, as a glance at the index of "Descriptive Terms" in the most recent annual *Shakespeare Quarterly* bibliography could suggest. While *ideology* heads a fair handful of entries there, *character* is conspicuously absent. On the other hand, *characterization* does appear, and indeed heads the second-largest list, more than seven times larger than the one for *ideology*.[2] The discrepancies suggest that "character and ideology" names a substantial and relatively unexplored territory in Shakespeare study.

This essay attempts some reconnaissance and speculation, with attention mainly to what seems the sleeper of the two terms, character. Ideology in contrast must serve as something of a given, a vantage point for the survey. The operative notion of ideology is more or less standard.[3]

It would be wrong to attribute the absence of *character* in the *SQ* index to a quirk of nomenclature, and to suppose *characterization* a synonym, since items gathered under the latter typically concern particular characters—Shakespeare's devices for creating them, actors' for playing them, and similarly concrete specifics. One might therefore wonder whether sometime before 1988 Shakespeareans en masse heeded the various proscriptions against the general term that have appeared over the past two decades or so in structuralist, Marxist, deconstructionist, metatheatrical, and other critical discourse. But such is not the case either. Since 1988, as in the immediately preceding decades, character proves a viable, and sometimes important, term in Shakespeare study of many sorts.

In *Imaginary Audition*, Harry Berger, Jr., has frequent recourse to the notion of character as he develops a text-centered analytic of Shakespeare that takes generic exigencies into account more fully than have most practitioners of the sort of armchair criticism castigated by Richard Levin and other proponents of what Berger calls the "new histrionicism." Berger argues, for instance, "against the flourishing industry of character judgment—against critics who spend time worrying whether characters are good or bad . . .—on the grounds that what a character thinks of himself, how he judges himself, is more interesting than what I think of him or how I judge him" (163–64).[4] Berger's project repeatedly entails characterological discriminations, as between "the character's perspective and the reader's" (145). He draws some of these distinctions from, or in response to, other recent Shakespeare study that itself handles character, as when he responds to the distinction drawn by Stephen Booth between "characters as fictive persons . . . and characters as theatrical commodities" (58) who may please an audience or not. In response to Bert O. States' *Great Reckonings*, Berger elaborates on "the boundary between actor and character" (98). Such discriminations show the concept of character to be viable and indeed vital for Berger.[5]

In *Action to the Word*, David Young attends more to the plays as spatial entities, a bit after the fashion of G. Wilson Knight. Nevertheless, Young too relies steadily on the concept of character. It springs to hand, sometimes in ways that recall Berger, as when Young begins his treatment of dilation in *Hamlet* "by noting that the characters themselves are often aware of the dilations that surround them" (20). Young's account of a speech of Edgar as Poor Tom—"it harps on the private thoughts . . . of the imaginary character in a way that resonates with a sense of what he was like in his inmost self. We begin to forget that Tom is an invented character. . . ." (90–91)—displays a concern with the phenomenology of theatrical character, a subject I return to below.[6]

In *Young Shakespeare*, Russell Fraser has still another fish to fry, but here too the notion of character proves serviceable, as with the contrast between Marlowe and the young Shakespeare: "[Marlowe] Not capable himself of flesh-and-blood character—mysterious, he might have thought it, possibly boring—he has no characters, only gigantic cartoons . . . agreeing with the makers of the morality that character is nothing. . . . [By contrast,] Shakespeare's plays, rising from character, are replete with intention" (151). A certain peremptoriness in the familiar contrast—Shakespeare, unlike Marlowe, able to give scope to character—shows how unassailably unproblematic the concept of character is for Fraser.

In *Shakespeare's America*, Michael D. Bristol addresses ideology more than do the previous commentators, as he discusses "the formation of an implicit cultural policy in and through the practice of Shakespeare scholarship," and "connects literary analysis as it pertains to Shakespeare with . . . ideology" (8). While Bristol does not concern himself much with such textual specifics as particular characters, the concept of character arises repeatedly in his study. Bristol treats the "consideration of character and motivation . . . the discussion of individual characters" (65) by Furness and other members of the Shakespeare Society of Philadelphia, the importance of character for Kittredge (131, 136), and the emphasis on "the development of character" (73) at Folger's alma mater Amherst. A remark such as "Shakespeare's originality is closely tied to *the* [emphasis added] primary affirmative theme of much American, and also British, criticism: the analysis and celebration of individuality and of the values of expressive autonomy as these are revealed both in the various characters and in the poetic textures of the plays" (123) reveals some of the ideological weight the concept of character bears for Bristol. He notes key emphases on character not only in Shakespeare study with conservative "ideological horizons" (145) but also in a Bolshevist essay on Shakespeare's characters (144–45).

One further example from the past two years of the continued importance of the notion of character in Shakespeare study is Derek Cohen's *Shakespearean Motives*, a work listed in the 1988 *SQ* bibliography and one that might have justified the inclusion of the missing term *character* in its subject index. As Cohen notes, "The variety of approaches to the plays studied in this book will not, I hope, obscure my central interest in characterization. . . . I have found myself constantly drawn back to the question of how what happens in the plays . . . is interesting to me chiefly in what it tells about Shakespeare's characters" (9). While Cohen's interest throughout is primarily in particular characters and characterizations, the self-consciousness of that interest raises into prominence the very conceptual category of character, as in the remarks just quoted.[7]

Five books from the past two years provide the merest taste of the currency of character in Shakespeare study, but the sample will have to suffice. Should it seem over-generous, one need only recall reports of the death of character, or its no-show in the *SQ* bibliography. This seemingly contradictory evidence makes character, everywhere and nowhere, itself look ideological, unstable, and ripe for historicization and theorization.[8]

As we know, the pre-Shakespearean story of character stretches a long way back. Some of its earliest recoverable stages show in the etymology that leads from the Indo-European *gher-*, to scrape, scratch, through Greek *χαρακτήρ*, "instrument for marking or graving, impress, stamp, distinctive mark, distinctive nature" (Oxford English Dictionary), the latter already manifesting a Janus-facedness that bedevils the concept down to the present: "impress, stamp," i.e., imposed from without, vs. "nature," i.e., congenital—with "distinctive mark" sliding either way.

The OED's earliest, "literal," sense of the word," "a distinctive mark impressed, engraved, or otherwise formed; a brand, stamp," seems to resolve the contradiction in favor of imposition. However, the brand's distinctiveness and legibility continue to embroil the concept in the logic of representation, and among OED's early "figurative senses" are "a distinctive mark, evidence, or token; a feature, trait, characteristic," and "the aggregate of the distinctive features of any thing; essential peculiarity; nature, style; sort, kind, description." Also early in English, as in other European languages, the word acquires its meaning of a graphic symbol used in writing or in printing. Here too controversy has raged and continues to rage about questions of the innate, natural, or primary vs. the imposed, artificial, or secondary.[9]

The OED does not associate the word with the cluster of meanings most in view here until well after Shakespeare. The meaning

> 17a. A personality invested with distinctive attributes and qualities, by a novelist or dramatist; also, the personality or "part" assumed by an actor on the stage

is cited first from 1664, and the meaning

> 16a. A person regarded in the abstract as the possessor of specified qualities; a personage, a personality

first from 1749. Of course one might hold that such concepts were available to Shakespeare, associated with other signifiers including *person*, and one might find such meanings emerging in certain Shakespearean usages of *character*, such as that listed in OED, sv 10 from *Twelfth Night*, "I will believe thou hast a mind that suits / With this thy fair and outward character." In any case, before we slip past Shakespeare into Shakespeare study, two observations are in order.

First, I stay with the umbrella term "character"—rather than any more obvious synonym from Shakespeare such as "person," or any such derivative as "personage"—because of the term's currency in Shakespeare study. The same rationale guides my preference for "character" over such later rough synonyms as "individual" and "subject."[10]

The second observation takes longer. As even this glance at OED entries shows, Shakespeare writes out of a linguistic and cultural moment in which that link between conceptual and verbal maps I indicate by *character* seems more unstable than in the moments of most commentators on Shakespeare, at least before the very recent past. The volatility of *character* in Shakespeare's moment shows both lexically and conceptually. It shows lexically in the gap we find in lieu of the term used in most Shakespeare study (a gap echoed in the last *SQ* bibliography index), and in the momentary hiatus of the meaning "distinctive nature," which appears before in Greek and after in English, and perhaps even in the "fictitious" (OED sv) spelling with *h*, a character that intrudes into the word in sixteenth-century English.

The conceptual volatility of *character* in Shakespeare's moment shows in still other ways. Recently, in *Idea of the Renaissance*, William Kerrigan and Gordon Braden have elaborated on Burckhardt's use of the meaning marked roughly by "individual" to determine the Renaissance moment itself, and they like others before and after Burckhardt speculate about how nascent Renaissance individualism figures in drama's flowering in England (and France and Spain) and in Italy's lack of drama.[11] Joel Fineman, *Perjured Eye* (1986), locates the origin of modern poetic subjectivity—the individual-effect, one might say—precisely in Shakespeare's sonnets.[12] This lexical and conceptual volatility of *character* in Shakespeare's moment, then, bears keeping in mind here, because it seems to facilitate later ideologizing of the term, and also because we, now finding our way past modernism, may ourselves be arriving at a newly privileged vantage through that intervening ideology into a moment of high characterological volatility.

In my student years, in the twilight of the New Criticism and the glimmerings of the dawn of the present day, a commonplace of Shakespeare study was that serious character study begins with Morgann on Falstaff and ends with Bradley. Before Morgann, Shakespearean characterology appears in passing comments about particular roles and actors, and in editions and adaptations.[13] That century and a half of *ad hoc*, scattered, or ephemeral characterology, with its associated ideology, now looks increasingly interesting and accessible, with our newer tools of investigation, and it seems clear that, with more time and space than I have here, one could perform valuable unpacking and aerating of the ideology of character in treatments of Shakespeare by Dryden, Pope, Theobald, and Johnson, as well as by less prominent figures. Let me sketch, for instance, a treatment of the most famous landmark before Morgann, with some ideological issues involved, some directions that seem unprofitable, and some ways out and forward.

In the *Preface to Shakespeare* (1765), Johnson opens his inquiry into Shakespeare's excellence with the remarks on "general nature," specifically that "in the writings of other poets a character is too often an individual; in those of Shakespeare it is commonly a species" (62), and he proceeds quickly to the related claims that "characters thus ample and general were not easily discriminated and preserved, yet perhaps no poet ever kept his personages more distinct from each other" (64) and that "if he preserves the essential character, [he] is not very careful of distinctions superinduced and adventitious" (65).

Never mind that some interpretation seems required if these remarks are to jibe: we may decline any such gambit because Johnson's essentializing of human nature and valorizing of the general over the particular may now look ideological, precisely because those assumptions are no longer given, universal, and unconscious. Nor does it seem likely that in the foreseeable future any amount of further adjustment of Johnson's opposition of "general" vs. "individual"—adjustment of the sort tried sporadically from almost immediately after the publication of the *Preface* down to G. F. Parker's *Johnson's Shakespeare* (1989)—is likely to cure the barrenness of the topic.

However, another strain of Johnson's characterology, one Parker isolates as the question of our identification with Shakespeare's characters, seems more interesting, despite some of its still more conspicuous ideology. If we set aside the sexism of "Shakespeare has no heroes; his scenes are occupied only by men, who act and speak as the reader thinks that he should himself have spoken or acted on the same occasion" (65), the remark exhibits intriguing homologies with what we call reader-response discourse, not least because of the priority Johnson here as generally gives to character as an effect, not of performance, but rather of the reading of the play. In other respects too the issue of priorities of the written versus the spoken is on the agenda for Shakespeare study.[14] Furthermore the remark tantalizes with its aporia: what could it mean for a reader and a written character to be "on the same occasion"?

Similarly, in "Shakespeare must have looked upon mankind with perspicacity, in the highest degree curious and attentive. Other writers borrow their characters from preceding writers . . . " (88), if we disregard what seems empty doctrinal falsehood—the claim that Shakespeare borrows less from predecessors than other writers—we are left with the faintly repellent attentiveness Johnson attributes to Shakespeare, a differentia that accords with enough useful current views to seem valid.[15]

Near as is the provenance of Morgann's *Essay on Falstaff* (1777) to that of Johnson—the two commentators were in fact acquainted—Morgann generally, and specifically with respect to character and ideology, differs notably.[16] While the Johnson might fall equally well under several headings in the SQ index of descriptive terms, the obvious choice for the Morgann would presumably be "characterization," and the absent "character" would also serve since, although Morgann concentrates on a single character, he does so with repeated theoretical generalizations, and at a length that itself amounts to staking theoretical claims about the value and legitimacy of characterology.

Morgann almost always represents character spatially, with one or another figure (as they now look), reifying with breathtaking eighteenth-century matter-of-factness. For instance, he articulates and hierarchicalizes in "all the parts of *Falstaff*'s Character . . . the leading quality of *Falstaff*'s character" (151). He relies on a similarly Aristotelian anatomy of character and a more insistent figure in "Courage and Ability are first principles of Character . . . they are the pillars on which he [Falstaff] stands firm in spight of all his vices and disgraces . . ." (207–208). Such ways of talking about character are apt to look curious now—at once ideological and harmless, and also rather less Shakespearean than other figurations of Morgann's.[17]

Morgann avails himself of a different spatial figure, one more prominent in Shakespeare and also in the etymological history of *character*, in his opposition between views of "the external character of *Falstaff*" (208) and Falstaff seen "*from within*" (210). Here, while one may note ideology, perhaps most in the spatialization itself, one may also choose to discount it in the interests of genre theory. For this particular version of the appearance-reality chestnut seems of particular interest in current Shakespeare study as it bears on questions of the exigencies of the genre of drama. So too, at least sporadically, for Morgann in his essay on Falstaff's "Dramatic Character."

When Morgann employs his notion of wholeness of character, the figure is sometimes spatial—"there is a certain roundness and integrity in the forms of *Shakespeare*" (167n)—and sometimes less immediately so, as in the mention of "the circumstances and condition of his [Falstaff's] whole life and character" (162). The notion, in any case, matters for Morgann, enough for him to use it repeatedly, even in the near-paradox of "he is a character made up by *Shakespeare* wholly of incongruities" (200). In our English these locutions, "whole character," "wholly made up," would look weakly hyperbolical, but they seem for Morgann rather to embody strong doctrine about the character of real as well as fictional people: whatever character is, however composed, it has a distinct coherence, as much as does a person's body.

Not that the whole character need always be apparent. Indeed a virtual corollary of Morgann's notion of character as a spatially extended entity is the hiddenness of some parts: "Those characters in *Shakespeare*, which are seen only in part, are yet capable of being unfolded. . . . [Shakespeare] boldly makes a character act and speak from those parts . . . which are *inferred* only, and not distinctly shrewn" (168n). Presumed courage is of course the hidden part of Falstaff's character that Morgann most wants to unfold or infer. All the same, mere expediency seems an insufficient explanation for the frequency and evident interest with which Morgann returns to his doctrine that parts of Shakespeare's characters are available only to inference, and not directly accessible. Indeed the *Essay* can read as if its acquitting Falstaff of cowardice were merely an excuse for keeping the doctrine of partly hidden character to the fore.

Morgann uses his notion of character, as integral and definite and yet partly hidden, to ground one of the most famous "heavier parts" (144) of the *Essay*, the theoretical note that ends,

> A felt propriety and truth from causes unseen, I take it to be the highest point of Poetic composition. If the characters of *Shakespeare* are thus *whole*, and as it were original, while those of almost all other writers are mere imitation, it may be fit to consider them rather as Historic than Dramatic beings; and, when occasion requires, to account for their conduct from the *whole* of character, from general principles, from latent motives, and from policies not avowed. (168–68n)

Unseen, latent, not avowed—*of course*, we may wish to say from the vantage of our psychoanalytic and hermeneutic ideologies. After we set aside what seems to have gone stale for us (for example, the emergent or pre-Romantic valorization of originality), what remains looks rich and a bit strange. In particular Morgann's positing the truth of dramatic character as something "felt," together with similar remarks elsewhere in the *Essay*—"And yet this is not our *feeling* of *Falstaff*'s character" (149)—can be taken as constituting part of a phenomenology of dramatic character.

Morgann is little-known in the half-century after his publication, and underappreciated in much of the time following. By the mid-twentieth century, however, he receives routine, if usually ambivalent, acknowledgment. Some of the ideology determining his status shows in the observation that Morgann "is now regarded as the true ancestor of such criticism as Hazlitt's, and of the elaborate 'character analysis' which was a staple of Shakespeare criticism until the dethronement of Bradley in the 1930s" (Kermode, *Criticism* [1965] 330).[18] With the scare quotes and the caveats in "elaborate," "staple," and "dethronement," serious containment seems in progress here. Indeed Frank Kermode writes almost as if, while the battle is won, Bradleyan criticism of the sort L. C. Knights attacked a generation earlier in "Children" (1933) remains something of a pretender in exile, still the main enemy.

One main enemy, at least. Another—and of course there are relations between the two that figure in questions of character and ideology—may show in Kermode's mention of Hazlitt. While Kermode's apparent sense of Hazlitt as the most important commentator on Shakespearean character between Morgann and Bradley seems unexceptionable, Kermode may have other reasons for bracketing Hazlitt with Bradley, reasons that show in his "Introduction."

Here, after a discussion of "Coleridge, who has long and very properly been regarded as the chief source of modern Shakespeare criticism" (21), Kermode turns to "smaller men" (22), the other English Romantic critics including Hazlitt. While Kermode accords him genuine praise and no quite explicit dispraise, a political disaffection seems to show in the characterization of the "passionate, radical and disputatious nature" (23) Hazlitt brings to the plays.

As we from the vantage of 1989–90 watch Kermode on the threshold of 1968 watch Hazlitt in the wake of 1789 watch Shakespeare, political subtexts leap to mind, including rich and intricate subtexts about characterology worth considering at length. Here there is time for only a handful of observations prompted by my stroll in Shakespearean characterology from Morgann to the 1930s.

First, recent work including Annabel Patterson's *Shakespeare and the Popular Voice* helps us to read political subtexts in the processing of Shakespeare by Kermode's favored, "very properly . . . chief," Romantic, Coleridge. These subtexts are conservative, anti-Jacobin agendas, opposed to Hazlitt's far more explicit politics. The situation begs for more thorough critiques than we yet have of the political ideologies of Hazlitt's and Coleridge's respective characterologies. Character, however conceived, matters incalculably more to Hazlitt, and especially in earlier works nearer the French Revolution such as *Characters of Shakespeare's Plays* (1817) and *Lectures on the English Poets* (1818). The politics that lead Kermode to call Hazlitt radical (117) and Patterson to call him a democrat (5) figure in manifold ways in the value character has for Hazlitt, and that value itself figures in a tendency to belittle Hazlitt—no dethronement ever needed with him—by commentators writing from the politically conservative and more or less unacknowledged standpoints apparent in Coleridge and in much anglophone Shakespeare study from the first two thirds of our century.

Then, although Coleridge by contrast is in some respects so little concerned with character as to seem anti-characterological, what he does say of character is of interest. Indeed his remark about Iago's motive-hunting[19] opens a consequential aporia in the discourse of character and motive, and instigates a line of discussion in which we read through character's and author's conscious motives into an unconscious that itself dislimns. Whether virtually reiterating Morgann—"Shakespeare's characters are like those in life, to be *inferred* by the reader" (1:201)—or turning a nice paradox out of advanced current theory, as when he notes that characters of other writers are "so characteristic (*i.e.*, psychologic portraiture) as to be characterless" (1:201), Coleridge's characterology repays scrutiny.

Bradley may seem by now to have spent enough time in exile to be allowed some sort of return for the centenary of *Shakespearean Tragedy* (1904), no reaccession but perhaps something more like the last emperor's return to Communist China. One of our main pieces of unfinished business with Bradley seems to be an accounting for the ideology of character's genre theory, and specifically the very strong and usually implicit linkage of character with the genre of tragedy. Bradley hardly originates that link, which we can trace at least as far as Aristotle, but Bradley gives the link a powerful authorization that helps it survive scarcely touched by L. C. Knights and other iconoclasts, to constitute part of our own ideology of character that bears more looking into.

With an eye toward operative ideology, we may divide Shakespearean characterology since Knights into two periods, the transition occurring around about the otherwise charged year 1968. In the first period, with Bradley recently dethroned, and characterology in some official disrepute, hermeneutic and axiologic Shakespeare study operates under the sway of the New Criticism, whose linked premises tend to exclude character from consideration. During these years of course character study does appear, some residual and Bradleyesque, and some that is both vital and very much of its time. This latter characterology is typically—characteristically—written somewhat against the prevailing grain, as with Stewart (1949) and Sewell (1952).[20]

More recently, the decline of the prestige of the New Criticism and of other sorts of mid-century totalizing stances such as that of Northrop Frye might have been expected to signal a re-legitimization of characterology. As it happens, however, character remains offstage in most of the originary texts—Foucault, Derrida—that with their newer totalizings have most influenced criticism of the recent past, when character has been proscribed with unprecedented explicitness.[21] Furthermore, while the anti-characterological impetus has gathered most head outside Shakespeare study, some Shakespeareans as well have been inclined to exclude from their discourse not only Lady Macbeth's children but also the lady herself.[22]

On the other hand, character, though banished by some regnant critical stances, and more or less ignored by others such as feminism and the new historicism—with only psychoanalytic criticism giving anything like a blessing—survives in Shakespeare study not only of the past two years but also of the preceding two decades. Important characterology of this period is less embattled than some characterology of the preceding period, and at times its theoretical sophistication outranks any to be found in all earlier Shakespearean characterology. This period too has its share of routine reliance on the category of character, but in such landmarks as J. Leeds Barroll's *Artificial Persons* (1974) and the essays collected in *Shakespeare Survey* 34 (1981), new ideology stirs, if ideology it is: the recognition of the richly problematical constructedness of the very category of character.

Barroll's theoretical statements seem useful not only in their particulars but also in their general acknowledgment of the problematics of characterology. Despite—because of?—a certain slipperiness, Barroll's study remains seminal, initiating the present phase of Shakespearean characterology.[23]

Still more useful is *Shakespeare Survey* 34, with essays on character by Muir, Vickers, Weimann, Nuttall, Weil, Salingar, Melchiori, and Goldman, most delivered at the first International Shakespeare Conference, in Stratford-upon-Avon, 1980. Several of these writers have played key roles in Shakespearean characterology of the seventies and eighties, and the volume is too rich for more here than a pair of observations.

First, the fact that none of these writers pays much attention to concurrent anti-characterological forces seems to signal not characterology's provincialism but rather its vigor: defense seems needless and anyway too much else is on the agenda. At the same time, the general tendency to treat character as a given looks like an effect of ideology. Only Weimann is much concerned to scrutinize, problematize, or deconstruct the very concept of character, and his own treatment has some reductive, and ideological, neatness.[24]

Shakespearean characterology at the present time stands in the most richly unstable moment of its history, and ideology figures in it everywhere. The modern Western idea of character or individuality, like other modern Western ideas, is currently in flux within Shakespeare study as without, and further change seems likely in the shape and function of the idea and its associated ideology. Without risking further prediction, I wish to conclude with a glance at two areas that look ripe for development.

First, regarding our usages of character, "character," character-effect, characterization, and so forth: while it seems at least partly the case that character is itself ideological, for Shakespeare, for us, and for the discourse that intervenes, at the same time it seems also partly the case that character—at least character as individuality—is non-ideological, at least insofar as anything is; and it should be useful to have more of this combination of truth and ideology uncovered and untangled.[25]

And then it seems that there ought to be ways to grant more scope to the actual experience of character. Whatever anyone determines character to be, and however ideology figures in that determination, we all seem undeniably to have experiences of recognizing the characteristic as such. Early and late, left and right, the experience is documented through Shakespeare study, albeit usually in passing because the experience is taken for granted.

Nevertheless that experience—the recognition of character in, say, the characteristic turn of phrase—does seem important in more ways than can be enumerated here, particularly for Shakespearean drama. That experience also seems somewhat mysterious. What happens when I recognize the characteristic resembles what happens when I recognize a face, and here the Shakespearean character-visage link resonates. Analogies from other senses work too: just as thousands upon thousands of scents prompt instant recognition, so too, it seems, with a very large number of characters both fictional and nonfictional, a number far too large for any imaginable taxonomy of character to take into account at all usefully.

The sorts of accounts of the experience of recognition of character in the characteristic that I can almost envision sound—smell?—phenomenological. In any case, whatever sort of discourse might acknowledge the experience of character with the most generous fidelity, some ideology would alloy its truth.

## NOTES

1. Why then not title the essay accordingly? The reasons have to do not only with tidiness but also with an amalgam of convention and ideology, much as with the title of our premier quarterly of Shakespeare study, *Shakespeare Quarterly*.

2. *Shakespeare: Annotated World Bibliography for 1988*, *Shakespeare Quarterly* 40 (1990), "Descriptive Terms," lists twenty-two entries under *ideology*, and 156 under *characterization*. The latter number is larger than for all other entries except *opera* with 240.

3. My understanding of what ideology is and does grows out of the standard line that leads from Marx through Althusser, into literary studies through such texts as William's *Marxism and*

*Literature*, and into Shakespeare study through such texts as Dollimore's *Radical Tragedy*, and the essays in Howard and O'Connor. Cf. Bristol: "Ideology differs both from knowledge *and* from deliberate or malicious deception. Ideology is false consciousness or distorted communication that nevertheless has a functional equivalence to truth" (*Shakespeare's America* 9); Belsey: "[Ideology is] the very condition of our experience of the world, unconscious precisely in that it is unquestioned, taken for granted" (*Critical Practice* 5); and Greene: "[Ideology is] that system of beliefs and assumptions, unconscious, unexamined, invisible, by which we imagine and represent the world, that pervades every aspect of our thought and defines our imaginative horizons" (this volume).

The *SQ* gathering of twenty-two items from 1988 under the descriptor *ideology*, by the way, seems surprisingly small. In the current volume alone we have essentially the same total, so that this year's entry will presumably be considerably larger. The variation shows at least how volatile this area of Shakespeare study is at the moment. The term itself still seems new or foreign in some areas of Shakespeare study (as with the surrounding culture), although elsewhere in our bailiwick it has become as naturalized as in my desk dictionary (*American Heritage*, 1976), in which Watkins, "Indo-European," routinely includes an account of "Ideology" (1501–02).

4. That Berger finds the industry "flourishing" could support my claim about the current viability of the notion of character. Of course one might ascribe the flourishing rather to a current vigor in ethical judgement, but such a presumption seems riskier, in Shakespeare study as elsewhere. Berger (160) cites a "brief bibliography of judgmental criticism" of character, and a discussion of the issue, in William L. Godshalk (85–86, n. 19).

5. When Berger notes the importance of "flexibility in the deployment of such concepts as character" (145), one may glimpse behind the remark some of the history of ideology and character in Shakespeare study.

6. Here, as at other points, Young seems to have profited from States, *Reckonings*, a rich study bearing importantly on the theory of dramatic character. Young acknowledges the debt in his discussion of *Hamlet* (143–44).

7. Cohen does acknowledge general characterological problematics, at least indirectly, as when he writes of "the sheer difficulty of individual identity . . . the fusion of ideologies and impulses which constitute the self" (19–20).

8. My retrospective pretends neither to comprehensiveness nor orthodoxy. While I am aware of no comprehensive survey of Shakespearean characterology, see the useful bibliography in Skura, "Psychology" (587). The orthodox story is widely available piecemeal. See for instance Cavell 39ff.

9. For this subject as for most others, the OED richly rewards attention. For instance, new material in the current edition under *character* and related words foregrounds some of the late nineteenth- and twentieth-century networks of ideology surrounding the concept. Character as something good to have shows in such combinations as *character-formation* and *-building*, and in the adjective *characterful*, whereas a more transparently gendered and less favorable meaning of character, as something to be, shows in the entries for "16b. *colloq*. A person, man, fellow, (freq. slightly derogatory . . . )." The OED, furthermore, suggests an increase in the conceptual currency of *character* with a notable increase of citations of *characteristic* from the twentieth century.

The critical discussion prompted by Derrida's prioritizing the written language over the spoken is germane to questions of the theory and ideology of character; as a linguistic category, "character" is a feature exclusively of the written language. In recent Shakespeare study, Goldberg, esp. *Voice* 68–100, treats relations between character as personage and as grammatologeme.

10. The scriptive overtones of "character" might not suit it to all drama and drama study, but they do seem to suit it peculiarly to Shakespeare and Shakespeare study. Furthermore, the imposed vs. innate tension in *character* figures ideologically in the history I want to sketch, and seems to do so more subtly and tenaciously than the somewhat similar tension visible in *person* with its etymological meaning of "mask." The two terms, by the way, have tantalizing congruences. The OED lists as one denotation of "character," obsolete but current for Shakespeare, "10. The face or features as betokening moral qualities; personal appearance."

11. Kerrigan and Braden call "the conceptual center" (10) of *Civilization of the Renaissance in Italy* Burckhardt's famous contrast between the middle ages when "Man was conscious of himself only as member of a race, people, party, family, or corporation—only through some general category" (Burckhardt 143) and the Renaissance when "an *objective* treatment and consideration of the State and of all the things of this world became possible. The *subjective* side at the same time asserted itself with corresponding emphasis; man became a spiritual *individual*, and recognized himself as such" (143). Kerrigan and Braden touch on Shakespeare repeatedly in their handling of the topic of Renaissance individualism and relevant scholarship of the last century and a half. For the links they draw to theater and drama, see 55–69.

12. "Character-effect" works a bit less well as a rough synonym for Fineman's "poetic subjectivity" because character's continuing subtext of imposition from without gives character a persistent otherness. Other people have character or are characters, while I the subject have a persistent characterlessness. " 'Character,' one might say, is what other people have, 'consciousness' is ourselves" (Bayley, *Characters* 33). Ideology of course figures in these usages, and a consideration of ideology and character outside Shakespeare might lead almost anywhere in Western culture of the past four hundred years. Musil, *Qualities*, for instance, comes to mind, especially in contrast with Dickensian hyper-characterization.

13. I survey some characterology of this sort in *Mercutio* (166–77). In the same study and in *Drama* I touch *passim* on related ideological matters. Treatments of the general topic before Morgann include Richardson (1774); the composition of Whateley's *Remarks* (1785) also predates Morgann. See Vickers' "Emergence" for a full account of characterology in the last quarter of the eighteenth century.

14. Especially post-structuralist and deconstructionist Shakespeare study. See for instance Goldberg, "Characters," and Knapp.

15. Brief as this sortie into Johnson is, it has started still other hares that might be hunted through most Shakespeare study. One of these is gender, specifically the widespread and almost never explicit assumption that character is something else that men have and women lack. Better camouflaged but still discernible is the assumption mentioned above, n. 12, that character is marked other.

16. Morgann differs enough for later historians of Shakespeare study to have classed him with the Romantics more than with Johnson. Daniel Fineman, "Introductions," takes pains to distinguish Morgann's characterology "from the Romantic system of character-study which is usually attributed to him" (101).

17. Similar figurations appear *passim* in Morgann, as with the suggestion that Falstaff might have "considered his wit not as *principal* but *accessary* [sic] only" (152–53), and traces of them can be found in Shakespeare.

18. I find the words dutifully marked in the paperback *Four Centuries of Shakespearian Criticism*, ed. Kermode, that I purchased new in 1967 out of a graduate student's meager budget.

The anthology unaccountably fails to appear among those Pechter (165 n. 1) lists as available in 1970, although it was still in print then.

19. The famous or notorious phrase is "the motive-hunting of motiveless malignity" (*Criticism* 2:44).

20. It is tempting here to apply the model from Williams (*Marxism* 121–27) and say that the most useful characterology of the second third of the twentieth century is, within the domain of general Shakespeare study, marginal, or even emergent. Other characterological landmarks of the period include J. Dover Wilson's *The Fortunes of Falstaff* (1944); Palmer's *Political Characters* (1945) and *Comic Characters* (1946), Stirling's *Unity* (1956); and Matthews's *Character* (1962). Skura includes Mack's *King Lear in Our Time* (1965) in her bibliography. Kirschbaum's *Character* (1962) is more routine. Other commentary in books, articles, and editions of Shakespeare, as well as editions such as those of Overbury (1936) and Hall (1948), contribute to this lively minority discourse of the period. One might also grant honorary membership in this company to slightly earlier studies such as Schücking (1922); and Wales (1923).

21. See for example Culler: "Although for many readers character serves as the major totalizing force in fiction . . . a structuralist approach has tended to explain this as an ideological prejudice. . . . This notion of character, structuralists would say, is a myth" (230). Culler's own "would say" here itself looks ideological.

22. At the 1986 World Shakespeare Congress in Berlin, Joel Fineman from the audience challenged my very mention of Shakespearean characters, holding that "we can't talk about characters any more," or words to that effect. That gallant spirit's challenge partly prompts my present reply.

23. Cf. the claim that "It is neither necessary to subordinate the problem of Shakespearean characterization to an . . . interest in the ideology of the plays nor to reject historicity for a critical approach informed by the subtleties of modern personality depiction . . . " (Barroll 21).

24. According to Weimann, "the basic paradox in Shakespeare's conception of character can be viewed in relation to both past history and present meaning: as drawing upon that basic contradiction according to which the individual ultimately, in the course of modern history, does not achieve his particularity and individuality in isolation from, but only in connection with, the social process" ("Society and the Individual" 30). Weimann treats the subject less schematically and more usefully in "Mimesis."

Important Shakespearean characterology 1968–1988 also includes Goldberg, "Characters"; Holland; and the reference work of Berger and Bradford, as well as portions of other works including Felperin, *Representation*. Also useful are Pinciss, *Creations*; and Wolterstorff, "Characters."

25. Here syncretism seems appropriate. Psychological and psychiatric accounts of character could prove useful as well as sociological accounts including, for instance, those of Abercrombie, Hill and Turner. The relevant philosophical discourse seems to grow particularly useful in analytic treatments stretching from Strawson (1959) to more recent treatments including those in Perry (1975); Amélie Rorty (*Identitities* [ 1976]); and French, Uehling, and Wettstein (1988). Other sorts of discourse could prove useful as it were unwittingly—in works from within Shakespeare study, such as Mary Cowden Clarke's *Girlhood of Shakespeare's Heroines* (1891), and from without, such as the numerous books about character-building that appear from the late nineteenth century through the first half of the twentieth.

# 12

# Violence and Gender Ideology In *Coriolanus* and *Macbeth*

Marilyn L. Williamson

## Ideology and Literature

In terms of the debate that informs this volume, I should say that my position about ideology is necessarily complex and also that I consider the concept indispensable. An ideology is a set of representations that makes sense of material conditions and social formations (Donald and Hall ix). Ideologies are both conscious (the "isms" mentioned by Bristol in this volume) and unconscious: we are spoken by the languages of our cultures and we are socially constructed (Althusser 160–62). Ideologies govern our imaginary relations to our material and social world. Ideologies deny contradictions, seek to make the historical natural, and work to reproduce social formations. Therefore, we should not, in my view, abandon Marx's notion of "false consciousness" entirely: religion is not the only opiate of the masses; gender ideology has implicated women in their own oppression for centuries.

I resist tendencies to totalize a single ideology in Marx and other thinkers, such as many of the new historicists. First, the totalizing features of Marxist thought have proved simplistic: feminist thought has shown that class will not explain the oppression of women across cultures; nor can aspects of the fascist ideology attach to a given social group (Sprinker, *Imaginary Relations* 215–16; Laclau 81–142). Second, ideology usually presents itself as a false totality (Macherey 85). Third, gender, religious, and political ideologies are semi-autonomous, but also related in complex ways to one another and to class and race (Sprinker 271).

Moreover, aesthetic ideology operates differently for various theorists, and I find Macherey's formulations most congenial, possibly because they allow for the critique of ideology I think I find in literary texts. For Macherey, literature demystifies and challenges ideology by using it in a form that tries to appear non-ideological:

> A work is established against an ideology as much as it is from an ideology. Implicitly, the work contributes to an exposure of ideology, or at least to a definition of it. . . . It could be said that the work has an ideological content, but that it endows this content with a specific form. Even if this form is itself ideological there is an internal displacement of ideology by virtue of this *redoubling;* this is not ideology contemplating itself, but the mirror-effect which exposes its insufficiency, revealing differences and discordances, or a significant incongruity. (133)

As a consequence of these formulations, the object of the critic is very different from what it was for the New Critic, who was the accomplice of ideology by emphasizing the unity of the work and rationalizing its ruptures and contradictions. For Macherey, the critic "is to seek not the unity of the work, but the multiplicity and diversity of its possible meanings, its incompleteness, the omissions which it displays but cannot describe, and above all its contradictions" (Belsey, *Critical Practice* 109). Such readings produce knowledge of the limits of ideological representation.

Such a criticism assumes that both author and reader are inscribed in discourses, social formations, and material conditions of a historical moment: Shakespeare had ideological horizons he could not transcend, and so do I. Thus I attempt to define aspects of the historical moment from which Shakespeare wrote. And I acknowledge that I write of gender ideology from a feminist interest and of violence because I live in one of the violent places in an increasingly peaceful world. Yet I resist giving up a partially self-made subject and the author (Lee Patterson 70–72). I continue to stress the changes Shakespeare made in his sources and how his representations compare with those of his contemporaries.

We should not think that theory about ideology is settled: it is still developing (Donald and Hall xx). The theoretical and political issues are complex at a time when to be Communist is in many parts of the world to be conservative, if not reactionary. My position, therefore, is simply where I am now comfortable. What I hope to contribute to this debate is insight into the way gender ideology relates to political ideologies and the violence they employ, as these representations interact in the same aesthetic space. Specifically, I hope to show that the gender ideology, about which *Coriolanus* and *Macbeth* are silent, functions in very different ways from the political ideologies that also function differently in the two plays: one with a single ideology that governs the action and one with multiple perspectives, resolved only by an individual decision. I hope also to show how violence, which serves the political ideologies represented, but is heavily gendered, remains an unresolved surplus in both actions.

## The Plays

*Macbeth* and *Coriolanus* use political ideologies in very different ways, a topic interesting in itself. In *Macbeth* the ideology of kingship answers the forces of rebellion, male and female, through the king as virtuous authority and the representation of tyranny: pre-feudal Scots are made into Jacobeans through a series of silent historical shifts (Michael Hawkins 160–65). *Macbeth* concludes with a single ideological orientation, through which the cultural problem of violence and other contradictions peep, to be sure, but the end seems to be a victory for natural, virtuous, legitimate sovereignty. The threats to that sovereignty are implicit at the end. *Coriolanus*, on the other hand, never rests on a single political perspective: it shifts from the tribunes to the patricians to the military hero, never settling on a single orthodoxy (Sorge 232). The resolution in which Rome is saved through the assertion of familial values is still threatened after Coriolanus's destruction by the enemies of Rome.

### Political Ideology in *Coriolanus*

When Menenius is confronted with the angry and rebellious citizens at the beginning of the play, he presents them with the famous belly speech, a parable that employs the body metaphor for the state. One characteristic of the use of the body metaphor in *Coriolanus* is revealing: the head is without its usual authority. The Senate is the belly in Menenius's parable, suggesting the desire of the patricians to profit from the dearth that afflicts the city. To be sure, the court is referred to as the heart, as are limbs that are diseased to be lopped off, but the "kingly-crowned head" lacks a crucial authority that would control all the other parts (Andrew Gurr 66–67; Bristol, "Lenten Butchery" 213–15). Thus, each part of Rome, the patricians, the plebs, and the military man, is given a voice about the action, with which to criticize the others, but without any single group having final authority. The patricians support Coriolanus, but without the power to make him tame his choleric use of force for the good of the state. The encounters between him and the people reveal this fact, as Menenius cannot curb the warrior's hatred of the people, even for the time needed to obtain the consulship. The tribunes are criticized for manipulating the people, but they rightly fear Coriolanus's tyranny and lack of loyalty to Rome. The tribunes may represent the cowardly, Hydra-headed masses, but they see through the charismatic warrior as ruler, one who despises the people because they detest war, the only condition he savors. In the scene with his family before Rome's gates, Coriolanus acknowledges his tyranny to Virgilia, validating the tribunes' fear (5.3.43).[1] Brief scenes in Rome before Aufidius and Coriolanus invade Roman territory and challenge the city itself also validate the tribunes' vision of a peaceful, productive city (4.6). As soon as the invasion begins, however, the patricians excoriate the tribunes for having led to Coriolanus's banishment.

Coriolanus himself is in battle the automatic man, the harvester, the butcher, the thing of blood (Bristol, "Lenten Butchery" 216–17). He may be the "rarest man in the world" (4.5.169), but he is so among the Volscian followers of Aufidius, who find peace "is nothing, but to rust iron, increase tailors, and breed ballad-makers" (4.5.234–35). Coriolanus senses his own predicament when he is pressed by his mother to pursue the consulship: he would rather serve the state in his way than sue the people for power in theirs. One of Coriolanus's favorite words is *service*. The problem is that he does not respect the state he serves: his mother is the author of his wars.

The single ideology not subjected to critique in *Coriolanus* is that of the patriarchal family, to which Coriolanus and Volumnia submit in their famous confrontation at the gates of Rome. The family, imaged early as forming Coriolanus and his small son, and without a father, finally sets limits on violence within Rome.

## Political Ideology in *Macbeth*

In *Macbeth* Shakespeare uses the discourse of kingship to define the moral and natural legitimacy of rule through primogeniture, even though his sources presented a much different political situation (Michael Hawkins 171–76). In Holinshed, Macbeth had a good claim to the throne by Scottish custom, whereas Shakespeare's Macbeth is partly goaded to the murder by Duncan's designation of Malcolm as Prince of Cumberland and Duncan's successor. In Holinshed, Macbeth had ten years of good rule, while in the play he instantly becomes an ideological tyrant, arranging murders, destroying the family, and employing a spy in every thane's household. The play moves from the demonic unnatural to the natural, as even the invading army disguises itself to look as if it were "planted," a favorite word of Duncan and Malcolm. So the ideological effect of *Macbeth* is to assert a single perspective, one that legitimates and makes natural Malcolm's claim of the throne by force, because of primogeniture that makes succession seem natural rather than social, and because Macbeth seized the throne unlawfully and ruled as a tyrant, the only kind of ruler who could be deposed under the ideology of virtuous kingship.

Yet Shakespeare gives us one scene in which he allows the historical conditions of the play to show through its dominant ideology: the meeting of Malcolm and Macduff in England. It is a strange scene, one frequently cut from productions because it is long and boring to modern audiences. But it is valuable for the insights it gives us about Shakespeare's relation to the ideological material of his tragedy.[2] Because Macduff has deserted his family in Scotland, Malcolm suspects that Macduff may have been sent by Macbeth to trap the claimant to the throne. Malcolm therefore pretends not to have the virtues of a legitimate ruler, that he is lustful, avaricious, and has "none of the king-becoming graces," such as are defined in books on kingship like *The Basilicon Doron* James I wrote as advice to his son. When Macduff laments the fate of Scotland thus: "O nation miserable,/ . . . When shalt thou see thy wholesome days again/ Since that the truest issue of thy throne/ By his own interdiction stands accurs'd,/ And does blaspheme his breed?" (4.3.103–08), Malcolm retracts his self-description, swearing that his first lies were those about himself just uttered. Malcolm asks Macduff, "Why are you silent?" The thane answers, "Such welcome and unwelcome things at once/ 'Tis hard to reconcile.". Here Shakespeare allows the audience to glimpse the historical conditions not quite masked by the ideological statements of the scene.

That Macduff has left his family defenseless in Scotland makes his motives suspect, and he is desperate for a candidate with whom to challenge Macbeth. His responses to Malcolm's first assertions about his lust and avarice reveal the depths of Macduff's need for a legitimate heir to the throne to unseat the tyrant. Malcolm's claim to the throne, his virtues, and Macbeth's tyranny are the ideological constituents necessary to support the invasion of Scotland from England. Malcolm's manipulation of the ideology within the meeting and Macduff's dire circumstances, soon to be intensified by the news of the slaughter of his family, allow us to see the urgencies of power and revenge usually masked by the legitimizing and naturalizing process of ideology. In fact, Macduff's almost comic reactions to Malcolm's claims about his lust and avarice demonstrate the degree to which ideology may be manipulated to fit the needs of the historical moment. Malcolm's statement at the end of the play assures the audience on and off the stage that his behavior will not transgress the ideological bounds of Renaissance kingship; instead he draws the national community together, including the whole island, England and Scotland, in a gesture dear to the first royal audience of *Macbeth:*

> We shall not spend a great expense of time
> Before we reckon with your several loves,
> And make us even with you. My thanes and kinsmen,
> Henceforth be earls, the first that ever Scotland
> In such honour nam'd. What's more to do,
> Which would be planted newly with the time,
> As calling home our exil'd friends abroad
> That fled the snares of watchful tyranny;
> Producing forth the cruel ministers
> Of this dead butcher and his fiend-like queen,
> Who, as 'tis thought, by self and violent hands
> Took off her life; this, and what needful else
> That calls upon us, by the grace of Grace,
> We will perform in measure, time and place;
> So, thanks to all at once and to each one,
> Whom we invite to see us crown'd at Scone. (5.8.60–77)

The use of force has been legitimized by Malcolm's conformity to the lawful exercise of power in relation to the peers of the realm and by the tyranny and unnaturalness of the Macbeths. Rescue of Scotland has come from England, but from a saintly king without ambition, who has healed Scotland as he does his diseased subjects. All is sanctified by the grace of Grace.

*Macbeth* resembles *Coriolanus*, however, in that *Macbeth* also reveals patriarchal underpinnings that are not questioned in the text. As both Peter Stallybrass ("Witchcraft" 197–98) and Janet Adelman ("Born of Woman" 109–10) have shown, the play is haunted by the need for progeny, by destroyed families, by images of truncated lives and maimed rituals. Macbeth admits, "That which should accompany old age,/ As honour, love, obedience, troops of friends,/ I must not look to have" (5.3.24–26). Earlier a Scottish lord yearns for days when "we may again/ Give to our tables meat, sleep to our nights,/ Free from our feasts and banquets bloody knives,/ Do faithful homage and receive free honours" (3.6.33–35). If, in the play's ideology, the family and the state are models for one another, then the witches and Lady Macbeth are threats to both (Stallybrass 196–98). Macbeth's defeat, the disappearance of the witches, and the taming of Lady Macbeth reassure the audience that natural, patriarchal forces are equal to unnatural and demonic challenges.

Before we explore these matters, we need to deal with the issue of violence in the plays' historical context.

## The Tudors and Violence

In *The Crisis of the Aristocracy 1558–1641* Lawrence Stone remarks, "The greatest triumph of the Tudors was the ultimately successful assertion of a royal monopoly of violence both public and private, an achievement which profoundly altered not only the nature of politics, but also the quality of daily life" (97). The work of Stone and others provides ample evidence, moreover, that Shakespeare's world was still a much more violent place than we usually imagine (T. R. Gurr 300; Stone, "Interpersonal Violence" 25–27). Stone describes the process by which the Tudors brought a fractious and brutal society under control without a standing army. Although the Tudors tried systematically to reduce and control the size of the body of retainers that overmighty subjects might attach to themselves, the monarchs still depended on the forces of noblemen and gentry in time of emergency. Although "Henry VII passed a series of Acts asserting without any possibility of doubt that the prime loyalty of every subject was to the Crown, and only secondly to his 'good lord,'" a dual military system, partly quasi-feudal and partly national, persisted through the reign of Elizabeth (Stone, *Crisis* 99). The retinues of liveried retainers and household servants were gradually reduced, and the younger sons of gentry came to regard personal service to a great lord as socially humiliating. There was a corresponding decline in the use of castles as fortifications or the building of private arsenals.

For all the gradual implementation of royal policy, however, the daily behavior of aristocracy changed very slowly: "In the sixteenth and seventeenth centuries tempers were short and weapons to hand. The behavior of the propertied classes, like that of the poor, was characterized by the ferocity, childishness, and lack of self-control of the Homeric age" (Stone 108). And the actions resulting from such a cultural temperament were only gradually checked because Elizabeth still had to fear the most powerful peers of her realm. Open rebellions were repressed savagely, but aristocrats frequently got away with murder. Several factors gradually contributed to the growth of order: long periods of peace in which the nobility did little military service, growth in litigation as a means of solving disputes, and above all, the code of the duel which restricted violence to the principals of a dispute, rather than to armed bands of followers. Although James I disapproved of the code, the duel did not threaten the security of the state. The growth in the importance of the court loosened the ties of nobles to their tenants and retainers, and gradually loyalty and obedience to the Crown replaced local ties:

> The crucial victories of the Crown over the nobility were won between about 1570 and 1620. It was then that the great territorial empires were at last broken up, then that the massive bands of armed retainers were cut down to size, then that the nobility abandoned their age-old habits of casual violence, which now became the mark of dangerous eccentricity. The new sense of responsibility was affecting both old and new by the early years of the seventeenth century, and recorded acts of violence by the nobility declined sharply after 1600. (Stone, *Crisis* 133)

It seems plausible that a society moving through such a process might greet warmly representations of violence that could be tamed within recognizable social structures, but that the violence of privileged subjects might also be a source of anxiety as it continued to threaten within or without the social fabric. Such representations Shakespeare achieves in *Macbeth* and *Coriolanus* through the strategy of having the female—Volumnia and the synthetic figure of Lady Macbeth and the witches—be the source of violent action within the drama.

## Violence and Gender

Violence is heavily gendered in both plays. Only males are expected to be violent: both plays begin with heroes' bloody deeds sanctioned because they are directed at enemies of their states. Both heroes then turn their force against the state and are defeated by spectral figures: Aufidius and Macduff who are as bloody as their victims. In both plays Shakespeare violates and then reasserts the gender ideology, whereby women abhor violence and register its horror, through splitting the female figure into Volumnia and Virgilia and by psychic changes in Lady Macbeth. As destructive mothers, Volumnia and Lady Macbeth engender violence in son and husband, and one is associated with demonic powers, while the other expresses transgressive anger that drives her son's choler. Yet both are ultimately tamed by the patriarchy: one uses family loyalty to save Rome, while the other ends a mad woman in the care of a physician who records her feminine registering of the original murder (Callaghan). Both dramatic actions imply that the patriarchal society can control violence because both women fall into their traditional roles within the gender ideology. Yet there exists in both plays a surplus of violence, expressed in the spectral figures, Macduff and Aufidius, who slaughter or arrange the slaughter of the heroes in a vengeful rage. Both Macduff and Aufidius are highly ambiguous figures, who seem to be peaceful at play's end, but actually are close to the position from which the hero started his action. As a consequence, despite their very different political ideologies, both plays have similarly ambiguous implications for violence.

## Violence in *Coriolanus*

As the plays opens, the citizens understand that Marcius acts to please his mother and not Rome (1.1.40), and in several scenes of his entire invention, Shakespeare develops the relationship between mother and son. Although Janet Adelman ("Anger" 111–18) has given an excellent account of the mother-son relation, she has not touched on the issue of Volumnia's authorization of Marcius's violence. I argue that as we come to understand that Coriolanus is his mother's creation, we see why his violence may be turned against Rome: Volumnia and not Rome is the authority on which he acts, and that is why, at the crucial moment in the action as he marches against Rome, only she can turn him away. In a chilling scene, Volumnia is shown to be the source of brutal killing for her son and grandson. To the dismay of Virgilia, a gentle register to such actions, Volumnia, the destructive mother, exalts in killing, turning milk to blood:[3]

> Methinks I hear hither your husband's drum,
> See him pluck Aufidius down by th' hair,
> As children from a bear, the Volsces shunning him:
> Methinks I see him stamp thus, and call thus:
> "Come on, you cowards! you were got in fear,
> Though you were born in Rome:" his bloody brow
> With his mail'd hand then wiping, forth he goes,
> Like to a harvest-man that's task'd to mow
> Or all or lose his hire.
> *Virgilia.* His bloody brow! O Jupiter, no blood!
> *Volumnia.* Away, you fool! it more becomes a man
> Than gilt his trophy: the breasts of Hecuba,
> When she did suckle Hector, look'd not lovelier
> Than Hector's forehead when it spit forth blood
> At Grecian sword, contemning. (1.3.32–46)

A moment later Valeria describes Marcius's son as tearing apart a butterfly in a rage: "and over and over he comes, and up again; catched it again; or whether his fall enraged him, or how 'twas, he did so set his teeth and tear it; O, I warrant, how he mammocked it!" (1.3.68–71). The wanton destruction of the harmless butterfly reinforces the impression that the actions Volumnia authorizes are not restrained service to Rome, but the wanton expression of infantile rage, uncontrolled by purpose and therefore with no limits.

Like all creators of violent agents, Volumnia must withhold reward because she cannot lose control of Coriolanus. After his splendid military victory, she insists that he seek the consulship, which he does not desire and which will bring disaster upon him:

> *Volumnia:* I have liv'd
> To see inherited my very wishes
> And the buildings of my fancy: only
> There's one thing wanting, which I doubt not but
> Our Rome will cast upon thee.
> *Coriolanus:* Know, good mother,
> I had rather be their servant in my way
> Than sway with them in theirs (2.1.215–19)

Coriolanus understands what little concerns Volumnia, that because his use to the state is managing force on its behalf, careful limits must be set on his service to the polity, and that moving into the political arena means the potential release of force within or against the state. Volumnia, the transgressive woman, does not care for limits other than her own. When we next see her, she is trying to get Coriolanus to apply the rules of war to politics, to justify deceit of the electorate because they are like the enemy:

> If it be honour in your wars to seem
> The same you are not, which, for your best ends,
> You adopt your policy, how is it less or worse,
> That it shall hold companionship in peace
> With honour, as in war, since that to both
> It stands in like request? (3.2.46–51)

The scene reveals how ill-suited Coriolanus is for dealing with the political world of peace and negotiation, moving from the casque to the cushion, and how well he knows his role in Roman society. His mother cannot accept the same limits, and thereby she destroys her son. The scene establishes another significant pattern. Coriolanus is able to resist his mother as long as she begs him to alter his course of action. As soon as she reverts to the reactions she has taught him, he is hers: when she stops begging and exclaims, "I mock at death/ With as big heart as thou," (3.2.125) and "Do your will," (3.2.127), he immediately capitulates and agrees to go to the marketplace. Just as he cannot beg, so he cannot resist defiance that mirrors his own.

After Coriolanus's banishment, Volumnia turns her rage on the tribunes, raising her voice to them so that she embarrasses Menenius. When both Volumnia and Virgilia express their anger at Coriolanus's banishment, Sicinius asks Virgilia, "Are you mankind?" (4.2.16). Those who rail at tribunes must be men or they are, apparently, unnatural. The tribunes express the wish that Coriolanus had preserved his service for his country, but they take no responsibility for turning the citizens against him. Volumnia ends the scene so angry that she cannot eat: "In anger, Juno-like."

Shakespeare's Volumnia can fulfill her historical role as a woman who saved Rome, but she differs substantially from the heroic Roman matron of the histories of women.[4] She is angry, defiant, ambitious, and loud. In so representing Volumnia, Shakespeare sets up her and the son to whom she has taught anger and violence to be conquered by the patriarchal family. She cannot resist the heroic role in which she is thrust, even if she destroys her son. She is entirely authoritative and magisterial in appearing before Coriolanus at the end, and she brings with her the familiar train: Valeria, Virgilia, and the grandson. Volumnia's scene with Coriolanus involves a double capitulation: he gives up his warrior's anger and violence to his mother and the patriarchal family, and she gives up her transgressive anger and ambition to the patriarchal city, Rome, for which she sacrifices her creature. Volumnia uses the rituals of family relations—and their reversals—to play on Coriolanus's emotions: kneeling to him and the assertion that he is her "warrior," the naming of his wife and son, gestures not present in Plutarch's version of the scene. The pattern of Coriolanus's yielding only to defiance is here too:

He turns away:
Down, ladies; let us shame him with our knees.
To his surname Coriolanus 'longs more pride
Than pity to our prayers. Down: an end;
This is the last; so we will home to Rome,
And die among our neighbors. Nay, behold's:
This boy, that cannot tell what he would have,
But kneels and holds up hands for fellowship,

> Does reason our petition with more strength
> Than thou hast to deny't. Come, let us go:
> This fellow had a Volscian to his mother;
> His wife is in Corioles and this child
> Like him by chance. Yet give us our dispatch:
> I am hush'd until our city be afire,
> And then I'll speak a little. (5.3.168–82)

She has said all the fine words from Plutarch on behalf of Rome, but at the end she is her son's match, facing death with courage and defying her enemy. The difference is that she and his family are now Coriolanus's enemy: the cycle is complete, for violence authorized by any other than the state can be turned against the state. Volumnia is the only Roman who can defeat Coriolanus because he remains true to their relationship in acting for her; he imitates her in disregarding his own death; and he is the one in control of the action—he decides to accede after she withdraws pressure. Thus, as Coriolanus is destroyed, Volumnia is now Rome's hero; Menenius exclaims, "This Volumnia/ Is worth of consuls, senators, patricians,/ A city full; of tribunes, such as you/ A land and sea full" (5.4.55–58). In finally conforming to her patriarchal role, Volumnia makes the family seem very powerful because she has been so angry, so transgressive of the gender ideology. She is made even more awesome by the presence of Virgilia, whose role is to register horror at violence: "Angry displays of force may belong to the male, but crying, cowering, screaming, fainting, trembling, begging for mercy belong to the female. Abject terror, in short, is gendered feminine" (Clover 212). Virgilia hates blood and wishes to avoid conflict: she hopes Coriolanus will be spared by Aufidius, while Volumnia imagines her son standing on the Volscian's neck, an eerie foreboding of their reverse positions at the end of the play. Yet Virgilia is by no means craven: she stands up to Volumnia and Valeria in her wish to emulate Penelope and remain home while her husband is away, and she joins Volumnia in taking on the tribunes after Coriolanus's banishment. She is a voice of protest when Menenius and Volumnia gloat over fantasies of Coriolanus's wounds (2.1.132). When she weeps at Coriolanus's safe return, he reproves her, "Wouldst though have laugh'd had I come coffin'd home?" (2.1.193). Coriolanus's reversal makes the warrior's code partially grotesque, but because she is surrounded by those who share the code, including her small son, Virgilia seems quite alone in her feminine resistance to the code of violence. Her conformity to conventional gender ideology, however, serves to make Volumnia's transgressions and her submission to patriarchal values more striking.

Yet there is a surplus of violence that occurs outside the city that Volumnia has rescued: although in the last moments of the action Volscian lords are careful not to let the conspirators who have killed Coriolanus ravage his body, Aufidius, in a rage, stands on the body and must be ordered to stop treading on it. In Shakespeare we have no sense that the divisions within Rome will heal. Historically it was the Volscians that missed Coriolanus: without him they were soon defeated by the Romans and Aufidius was killed. In Shakespeare, violence remains at the gates of a divided city.

## Violence in *Macbeth*

If we move to *Macbeth*, we find that the play again opens with civil rebellion, which is represented as outside the society, and a hero who deals violently with the enemies of the state. First, Macbeth defeats the "merciless Macdonwald": "he unseam'd him from the nave to th' chops/ And fix'd his head on the battlement" (1.2.22–23). A participant in the conflict, the bleeding sergeant, is the narrator of the events, which are soon augmented by Ross's account of Macbeth's defeat of the traitorous Thane of Cawdor:

> Norway himself, with terrible numbers,
> Assisted by that most disloyal traitor
> The Thane of Cawdor, began a dismal conflict;
> Till that Bellona's bridegroom, lapp'd in proof,
> Confronted him with self-comparisons,
> Point against point rebellious, arm 'gainst arm,
> Curbing his lavish spirit: and, to conclude,
> The victory fell on us. (1.2.50–58)

The imagery of the description suggests a mirroring of Macbeth with the traitor, whom he defeats on behalf of king and country, but whom he is soon to imitate. Even an audience unfamiliar with the story might suspect from the language that the warrior was a spectral image, and the impression is reinforced by Duncan's giving Macbeth the Thane of Cawdor's title.

Here, as in *Coriolanus*, we are presented with a hero soon tempted to turn his much admired and rewarded use of force inside his own society. In *Macbeth* the process is more vivid, more rapid, and psychically more complex. It is obvious that Macbeth's violence against the king is released and inspired by the witches and Lady Macbeth, who early in the play seem to function as a single female figure. That is, the witches' prophecies encourage and rekindle previous ideas of assassination, which Lady Macbeth then reinforces to the sticking-place. The witches and Lady Macbeth are associated with the phallic, destructive mother, and, unlike Volumnia, they are also connected to perverse female sexuality (Biggins 256–66). The female figure, then, is complicated not only by being represented by the transgressive witches, but also by the fact that Lady Macbeth is both wife and mother in her self-representations and in her relations to Macbeth.

The witches are not only associated with rampant sexuality ("I'll do, I'll do, and I'll do") and sexual inversion in their beards, but also with the destructive mother: "Finger of birth-strangled babe/ Ditch-deliver'd by a drab" (4.1.30–31); "Pour in sow's blood, that hath eaten/ Her nine farrow" (4.1.64–65). In the same transformation made by Volumnia, Lady Macbeth vividly turns mother's milk into blood.

> I have given suck, and know
> How tender 'tis to love the babe that milks me:
> I would, while it was smiling in my face,
> Have pluck'd my nipple from his boneless gums,
> And dash'd the brains out, had I so sworn as you
> Have done to this. (1.7.54–59)

Although Lady Macbeth's lines may have created problems for critics wishing to make consistent a text that otherwise renders the Macbeths childless, and significantly so, the effect of the lines is clear: Shakespeare takes pains to imagine Lady Macbeth as a destructive mother. Moreover, Lady Macbeth wishes for the sexual inversion of the witches:

> Come, you spirits,
> That tend on mortal thoughts, unsex me here,
> And fill me from the crown to the toe top-full
> Of direst cruelty! make thick my blood;
> Stop up th' access and passage to remorse,
> That no compunctious visitings of nature
> Shake my fell purpose, nor keep peace between
> Th' effect and it! Come to my woman's breasts,
> And take my milk for gall, you murd'ring ministers,
> Wherever in your sightless substances
> You wait on nature's mischief! (1.5.41–51)

For Lady Macbeth, violence is so gendered that she must transform herself into a monster in order to persuade her effeminized husband to perform the murder of Duncan. No sooner does she know of the witches' prophecies than she declares, "yet I do fear thy nature:/ It is too full o'th' milk of human kindness/ To catch the nearest way: thou wouldst be great; / Art not without ambition, but without/ The illness should attend it . . . " (1.5.17–21). Macbeth is full of the milk she would turn to blood or gall. Volumnia had an entire childhood and youth to fill a hero full of rage; Lady Macbeth has a few hours in which to redirect Macbeth's already developed, but often wavering, violent impulses toward his king, kin, and guest. She therefore chooses a hyperbolic rhetoric and calls upon all the demonic resources that might come to her aid (Adelman, "Born of Woman" 97–99).

Men who react to the horror of violence, as Macbeth does, are feminized, and Macbeth maintains a female reaction to violence until his second encounter with the witches. Before he performs the murder, Macbeth is an eloquent register of his reluctance to do the deed, and Lady Macbeth is as eloquent a temptress. It is she who smears the grooms with blood; she who is certain that water clears them of the deed. As soon as the assassination is made public, their roles are reversed by gender: Macbeth has killed the grooms, and Lady Macbeth faints as he describes Duncan's corpse and their bodies in vivid detail.

In his own engendering of violence, Macbeth uses the technique that Lady Macbeth has taught him: he questions the manhood of the murderers of Banquo. He wonders if they will be too pitiful toward Banquo or his issue. When the first murderer replies, "We are men, my liege," Macbeth replies that they must be above the average run of men to do his bidding:

> Now, if you have a station in the file,
> Not i' th' worst rank of manhood, say 't;
> And I will put that business in your bosoms,
> Whose execution takes your enemy off,
> Grapples you to the heart and love of us,
> Who wear our health but sickly in his life,
> Which in his death were perfect. (3.1.102–08)

But his own feminized reaction to deeds which his agents carry out continues even through the banquet scene where the ghost of Banquo torments him, and Lady Macbeth continues her gendered reaction to Macbeth's experience of the ghost: "Are you a man?" she asks to bring Macbeth to his senses. Indeed, Macbeth imagines himself "the baby of a girl," when the ghost reappears, but as soon as it vanishes, he says, "I am a man again" (3.4.107). The Macbeths' psychic paths traverse one another after he visits the witches to scan the future. Then he resolves to raid Macduff's castle and that "from this moment/ The very firstlings of my heart shall be/ The firstlings of my hand" (4.1.145–47). From this point in the action Macbeth is anesthetized to the slaughter he orders, males have deserted their country ("It cannot/ Be call'd our mother" 4.3.165–66), and Macduff has deserted his defenseless family. The country, the family, and finally Lady Macbeth become the female register of Macbeth's violence. Macduff's family is slaughtered first, victims of the mixed loyalties in a time of civil rebellion, for "cruel are the times, when we are traitors/ And do not know ourselves" (4.2.18–19). Ross, who tries to warn Lady Macduff of her impending slaughter—and justify her husband—is later eloquent about Scotland's sufferings:

> Alas, poor country!
> Almost afraid to know itself. It cannot
> Be call'd our mother, but our grave; where nothing,
> But who knows nothing, is once seen to smile;
> Where sighs and groans and shrieks that rend the air
> Are made, not mark'd; where violent sorrow seems
> A modern ecstasy: the dead man's knell
> Is there scarce ask'd for who; and good men's lives
> Expire before the flowers in their caps,
> Dying or ere they sicken. (4.3.164–73)

As Macbeth hardens and becomes brutal in his tyranny, Lady Macbeth is gradually driven mad by the deed she engendered. She is transformed from a domineering, unnatural wife into a helpless madwoman in the charge of a male physician, who records her symptoms, which now may be perceived as natural because conforming to the play's gender ideology (Callaghan). To render her a suitable register to the murder Shakespeare transforms her psychic state: in her sleep Lady Macbeth can be eloquent about the horror of the assassination and the slaughter of Macduff's family. In her sleepwalking, Lady Macbeth retains just enough of her old attitudes ("Fie, my lord, fie! a soldier, and afeard?") to make the needed contrast with the searing impression the murder has made upon her, which she tries to expiate in the ritualistic washing of her hands. At the time she told Macbeth, "A little water clears us of this deed," but now she confesses, "Yet who would have thought the old man to have had so much blood in him" (5.1.44–45). The horrific effect increases as she reminds us of Lady Macduff, and again of the blood that cannot be washed away, and then of the smell of the blood in her conclusion, "All the perfumes of Arabia will not sweeten this little hand" (5.1.56–57). Her exclamation evokes an earlier one of Macbeth's: "this my hand will rather/ The multitudinous seas incarnadine,/ Making the green one red" (2.2.61–63). The linkage illustrates that the feminized male and the conforming female are the registers of the horror of violence. The audience is also reassured with a sense that Lady Macbeth's earlier unruliness was a temporary aberration as her true feminine nature is revealed in her sleep. The witches have disappeared, and Lady Macbeth is tamed to her true nature, controlled by a patriarchal figure, and finally self-destructive.

The end of *Macbeth* returns to the beginning of the action, but with greater subtlety than *Coriolanus*. Macduff is, as we have noted, the totally male instrument of inherited authority. "I have no words:/ My voice is in my sword," he tells Macbeth. Macduff, we remember, was the thane to find the murdered Duncan, and the one thane who resisted attending Macbeth's banquet. He has also been identified by his wife as wanting the natural touch after he has deserted his family, which is almost immediately slaughtered. In an ambiguous moment in England, Ross waits until he knows Macduff intends to invade Scotland before Ross tells him about the slaughter of his family. The male reaction to grief is appropriately, as Malcolm urges at this point when he needs Macduff, rage which may easily be converted to aggression against Macbeth: "Dispute it like a man" (4.3.220), but Macduff is clearly stunned at his loss. Sympathy for him complicates, but does not overwhelm, a sense that his challenge to Macbeth is in part personal vengeance. Macduff was untimely ripped from his mother, and, in the tradition of Caesarean births, may be destined for greatness or associated with the Antichrist (Blumenfeld-Kosinski 125–42). Macduff's linkage with the demonic—he is the only person specifically named by the witches—takes us back to the Macbeth with whom the play began, and Macduff remains the single unnatural presence in a play that insists on becoming more natural in all its aspects than when it began. At the end Siward shows qualities similar to those of Macduff in that Siward refuses to mourn his son as long as the son's wounds are on the front of his body. Macduff replaces Macbeth as violent agent of the state, while another head of another Cawdor is paraded before the audience. And we have Malcolm, who is willing to mourn Siward's son, and whose demeanor evokes that of his gentle victim-father. He is Macduff's creature: "Hail, king! for so thou art," but his having been named Prince of Cumberland was a spur to Macbeth's murder of his father. Although Malcolm's final speech emphasizes ritual in naming titles for those who helped him, in evoking the "grace of Grace," and in looking forward to his coronation, the repetition of elements raises a question about whether the time is truly free. The surplus of violence silently remains at the end of the play.

This analysis reveals the variety of ways in which different kinds of ideology may function within the same or similar aesthetic structures, and why, therefore, methods that seek a totalizing ideology or cultural system cannot account for all that happens with ideology in art or society. Such approaches resemble New Criticism in being accomplices of ideology in its own totalizing claims. The fact that "gender is implicated in the entire social domain" (Dollimore, "Cultural Materialism" 474) does not mean that gender or patriarchy disappears into the state or cultural elites.[5] But it does mean that gender ideology should not be totalized, as in psychoanalytic feminist scholarship, but should always be addressed in its complex relations to political, economic, and religious ideologies.[6]

The fact that Shakespeare saw gender as essentialist does not mean that the critic cannot consider changes in the way gender and patriarchy are constructed in each play Shakespeare wrote. For example, the patriarchal family is represented differently in our plays. In *Coriolanus* the family is almost entirely a social structure: the gods look down once on the unnatural scene of Volumnia kneeling to her son. But it is the only authority in a deeply divided polity, and so when Volumnia restrains her anger at the patriarchal city and stops her son, we have a sense of enormous power in the family, which can save the state. The sense of power comes largely from the strength of the individuals, Volumnia and Coriolanus, who make decisions to obey ideological roles when they have been unruly earlier. In *Macbeth* the state needs the family in male genealogies (Goldberg, "Speculations" 259–60), but both the state and the family are threatened by demonic females, who are then conquered or erased by patriarchal authority in league with nature. The healthy state is one in which the patriarchal family may flourish; the patriarchal family becomes a site of nostalgic longing for a civil society. All patriarchies, in short, are not alike, and all do not have the sole function of oppressing women, as I have tried to demonstrate earlier about Shakespeare's comedies and romances (Williamson). I hope to continue to complicate what Elizabeth Fox-Genovese (217) calls the "mindlessly simplistic category" of patriarchy, which for Shakespeare was the hinge between the personal and the political.

If psychoanalytic feminist criticism has the totalizing characteristics I have been answering here, it is still useful in alerting the critic to one effect of Shakespeare's having made—in variance from his sources—the instigators of violence destructive mothers who relish images of killing nursing children. Surely for audiences, even over the centuries, the effect of Shakespeare's choice to develop those characters in precisely that way is momentarily to horrify audiences about the violence in both plays. Because the fear that a destructive mother evokes is infantile, an audience may derive a strong sense from such figures that the violence released is limitless and overwhelming. Violation of the gender ideology has an important affective function in both plays. This effect is reinforced by the unresolved and repetitious endings of both plays, where although there is formal submission to patriarchal authority and definite attempts by the participants to set limits on violence, the elements that resulted in the action of the drama are again present, and the fundamental relation of the use of force to the civil polity is still urgent but unresolved.

## NOTES

1. All quotations from *Coriolanus* and *Macbeth* are taken from *The Complete Works*, eds. Craig and Bevington.

2. By this analysis I do not mean to imply that Shakespeare simplistically asserts the theory of kingship here or appeals slavishly to James I throughout, but rather that he is showing the gap between theory and the urgent moment, which ideology smoothes over. For example, Malcolm's claim to the throne is murky, even in the play's terms; yet his status as the late king's eldest son makes him a claimant by nature in a patriarchal society: the ideology almost conceals the ambiguity.

3. Adelman says, "The unspoken mediator between breast and wound is the infant's mouth: in this imagistic transformation, to feed is to be wounded; the mouth becomes the wound, the breast the sword" ("Anger" 131). Nursing, milk, and blood are traditionally identified by medieval thinkers, influenced by biblica!, Christian imagery, reinforced by metaphors of the Eucharist. See McLaughlin; and Bynum.

4. Volumnia, or Veturia, as Coriolanus's mother was sometimes called, is repeatedly cited as a heroine who saved Rome in the histories of women. Works which so represent her are Edward Gosynhyll, *The Praise of All Women* (1542); William Becher, *The Nobility of Women* (1559); Anthony Gibson, *A Woman's Worth* (1599); Lloyd Lodowick, *The Choyce of Jewels* (1607); Daniel Tuvil, *Asylum veneris* (1616); Constantia Munda, *The Worming of a Mad Dogge* (1617); Abraham Darcie, *The Honour of Ladies* (1622); and Nahum Tate, *A Present for the Ladies* (1692). Shakespeare's representation of Volumnia is unique in its complexity and in its motivation for her actions. Nothing in Plutarch, for example, prepares us for the scene in which Valeria describes Marius's and Virgilia's son and the butterfly; nothing is a source for the scene in which Volumnia urges Coriolanus to go again to stand for the consulship. Shakespeare's representation of Volumnia is remarkable in its unruliness, when compared to all the others mentioned.

5. Walter Cohen shows, for example, how patriarchy disappears as an oppressor of women in Jonathan Goldberg's work, while representations of women disappear into representations of

the state or into male self representations in the work of Stephen Greenblatt and Leonard Tennenhouse (37–38).

6. Examples would be the work of Adelman or Coppélia Kahn, in which there is little attempt to historicize the psychoanalytic material or to relate it to other elements of the drama. Of *Macbeth*, Madelon Gohlke (now Sprengnether) says, "The hero's equation of masculinity with violence as a denial defense against femininity leads to his destruction" (Gohlke 158).

## 13

# "A Woman's War": A Feminist Reading of *Richard II*

**Graham Holderness**

Two of the pioneers of feminist Shakespeare criticism, Linda Bamber and Coppélia Kahn, in their respective discussions of the history plays, offered interestingly divergent accounts of the relations between femininity, masculinity and history in *Richard II* (Bamber; Kahn, *Man's Estate*). For Bamber, there can be no dialectical relation here between femininity and history, since history is a grand narrative of male achievement, a "masculine-historical struggle for power" (135), a "military-political adventure" (142), which specifically denies any significant space to "feminine Otherness" (141). Those contrasting images of apparently powerful and aggressive women—such as Joan of Arc or Queen Margaret—which can be found in the earlier historical cycle *Henry VI-Richard III*, do not resolve this problem, since they may more appropriately be considered as male impersonators who unsex themselves in order to ape the violence and cruelty of men: though they participate in history, they do not participate in history *as women*.

Bamber therefore posits "a female principle apart from history" (140), a positive image of feminine Otherness which can issue, albeit from a position of acknowledged impotence, a challenge to the priorities of *his*tory. Richard's Queen Isabel is described for example as "queen of an alternative realm" (135) in which the female principle is "fully differentiated from the masculine Self" (135); and it is only as such that the imagery of woman can hope to assimilate any degree of power: "Only as the Other are women in Shakespeare consistently the equals of men. Only in opposition to the hero and the world of men, only as representatives of alternative experience do the women characters matter to Shakespeare's drama as much as the men" (141). Since the genre of the historical drama could not contain a full expansion of this female principle, which would subvert its very *raison d'être*, feminine Otherness has to wait for the genre of tragedy to provide it with an occupiable space. The relationship between "femininity" and "history" is thus constructed in Linda Bamber's argument as a binary opposition of mutually incompatible contraries.

In this early feminist polemic can be found the origins of that enduring sense of incompatibility between the Renaissance history play and the priorities of feminist analysis, which has deflected such critics from that dramatic genre, and which has its theoretical counterpart in current disagreements between feminism and other new theoretical perspectives such as new historicism, cultural materialism and deconstruction.[1] If indeed the kind of historiographical vision produced by such drama effectively expels the female as a significant dramatic presence, then the much more pronounced interest displayed by feminist criticism in tragedy, comedy and romance would be strategically intelligible.

Coppélia Kahn's treatment of the history plays in *Man's Estate* discovers an alternative to this resigned acknowledgment of female occlusion: she is not primarily concerned with the representation of women, but rather with dramatic explorations of masculine ideology: "The patriarchal world of Shakespeare's history plays is emphatically masculine. Its few women are relatively insignificant, and a man's identity is determined by his relationship to his father, son or brother" (47). Kahn's theoretical approach thus enables a direct address to the dramatized historical context as a patriarchal structure, the ideological site of a crisis of masculine identity. In this approach there is no irreconcilable split between masculine and feminine principles: Kahn is able to delineate effectively Richard II's attempts to assume a maternal sovereignty over his kingdom, or Falstaff's appropriation of female potentialities, his "curiously feminine sensual abundance" (72). The methodology employed is claimed as both "psychoanalytic" and "historical" (47). But in practice the former approach is far more constitutive than the latter: both family relationships and problems of identity tend to be seen as independent of history, gravitating towards the immanent structure of a psychological archetype.

It seems to me that the methodologies employed here by both Bamber and Kahn remain extremely important, despite the theoretical problems they raise,[2] and I have no intention in this context of offering the condescending tribute of a corrective critique. The arguments advanced above have an important place in the historical development of feminist Shakespeare criticism, and though they have certainly been relativized, they have been neither exhausted nor superseded by subsequent theoretical work. I want therefore not to oppose but to expand and develop the positions of Bamber and Kahn, by linking their arguments more formally with a historical approach. In this respect I am of course following those feminist critics who have consistently resisted any divorce between feminist theory and historical knowledge—especially Catherine Belsey, Kate McLuskie, Lisa Jardine and Juliet Dusinberre.[3]

This proposed application of a "materialist feminism" seems to me potentially capable of resolving some of the theoretical problems implicit in existing work, and of making a practical contribution to one of the questions central to the debate addressed by this book: Is any feminist reading purely an ideological strategy, or can such readings in certain circumstances claim the authority of objective knowledge? Must a feminist reading of *Richard II* necessarily be a reading "against the grain" of the text, theoretically defensible from the perspective of an overtly political criticism, but also wide open to the sort of attack against tendentious and ideologically "interested" criticism launched in the pages of *PMLA* by Richard Levin? ("Feminist Thematics"). In the midst of a debate in which too many critics are anxiously creeping under the authoritative shelter of some theoretical absolute, it seems to me particularly important to test these basic, original applications of feminist theory against some representative example of that hitherto resistant material, Shakespeare's history plays. I want in this paper to examine *Richard II* through a strategic conjuncture of feminism, historicism and the politics of gender. I propose to address, through the method of a detailed and specific textual practice, the play's representation of femaleness and its explorations of femininity; to analyze its interrogation of masculine identity; and to adumbrate the dramatized historical context within which these ideological interventions are activated.

In the course of that elaborate exchange of formal speeches which constitutes the opening scene of *Richard II*, where Henry Bolingbroke accuses Thomas Mowbray of treason, Mowbray offers a useful commentary on the relations between gender and history, between masculine and feminine identities:

> Let not my cold words here accuse my zeal.
> 'Tis not the trial of a woman's war,
> The bitter clamour of two eager tongues,
> Can arbitrate this cause betwixt us twain.
> The blood is hot that must be cooled for this.
> (1.1.47–51)[4]

It is hard to imagine a more precise or more decisive definition of an absolute and irreconcilable difference between the sexes. Fighting, an active and positive enterprise, is done with the "blood" and the body, and it can only be done by men. The only kind of fighting Mowbray can imagine women being involved in is a scolding squabble between "two eager tongues." The energy and vigour that characterize masculine militarism are absent from the latter activity: the woman's words are "cold," while the warrior's blood is "hot." There is even a latent accusation of constitutional cowardice on the part of women, who are far more "eager" to engage in the cold clamor of a verbal quarrel than they would be to undertake the physical challenge of a real battle. The patent substance of Mowbray's words is of course an accusation against Bolingbroke, tantamount to a charge of effeminacy: he (Mowbray) is too manly to join in this humiliating conflict of words, and cannot wait to get onto the field where the real "trial" can begin.

It should seem odd from our modern conceptions of law and justice that the value of words and of argument to a legal process should be so discredited. But that of course is the nature of a chivalric trial by combat. Both Mowbray's misogyny and his superstitious reliance on physical force as a means of securing justice are clearly, to us (and were, in my view, to the historical consciousness that found its way into Shakespeare's plays[5]), visible as anachronisms; dated, old-fashioned, antiquated beliefs, belonging to a particular historical society. Mowbray's words are dramatically located into that post-feudal society of the late fourteenth century in which, according to the dominant systems of belief, men were warriors and women a protected species.

This disclosure of masculine identity has its counterpart in the representation of female character. In one of the key scenes of *Richard II*, that which contains the play's best-known speech—John of Gaunt's famous patriotic celebration of "this earth, this realm, this England"—King Richard marks his departure from the stage by speaking, almost as an afterthought, to his Queen Isabella:

> Come on, our queen; tomorrow must we part.
> Be merry, for our time of stay is short. (2.1.222–23)

A reader of the printed play-text (as distinct from the spectator of a performance) could be forgiven for wondering, at least momentarily, where this Queen came from. In the course of the 150 or so lines during which she occupies the stage, she speaks only one line, and is neither spoken nor referred to. For a reader it is almost necessary to look back to the stage direction which announces the arrival of the king (at line 68) to see that the Queen enters with the King and a group of nobles. The reader of the play (whose attention is necessarily focused on those characters who manifest their presence in speech) encounters a virtually silent, self-effacing character, who is also ignored by everyone else in the room, virtually as an absence, a non-existence. In a stage production of course things are different. The text calls for the Queen to be physically, visibly present among the King's entourage, and her passive presence could actually be made quite significant: the female body is as eloquent a theatrical sign as the presence secured through verbalization. But when deciding what to do with the Queen, actors and directors are left entirely to their own devices, reliant on the resources of their own imaginations: for the verbal text itself has almost nothing to say about the strange quiet presence of Queen Isabella.

Scene 2.1 involves eleven characters, only one of whom—the Queen—is female. That disproportionate marginalization of the female population is typical of this play as a whole. Only five female characters appear in a cast of over thirty identified parts (not counting various supernumerary servants, attendants, soldiers, who are also overwhelmingly male): these are the Duchess of Gloucester, who appears only in 1.2 (her death is then reported in 2.2.97); the Duchess of York, who appears only in 5.2; and the Queen, who appears in three scenes—2.2., 3.4., 5.1.—in addition to her gestural presence in 2.1.

Now a number of common-sense arguments naturally present themselves to suggest that there is really nothing remarkable in this. There is never more than a handful of female parts in any of Shakespeare's plays—a fact obviously connected with the Elizabethan practice of using boys to play the roles of women. *Richard II* is a history play, and Elizabethan history plays were drawn from historical writings which did not particularly emphasize the presence or agency of women in history: history was largely thought of as an account of the actions of men. Lastly, this particular historical drama deals with the kinds of political and military crisis which necessarily excluded women from active participation: political struggles, trials by combat, military campaigns. Those active and enterprising heroines who appear in other Shakespeare plays seem to belong to a later age when a formidable "queen" showed herself capable (in a sense) of fighting her own battles, such as that against the Spanish Armada; and they appear naturally sympathetic to our own later age in which the principle of female equality is, though hardly universally attained, at least generally accepted. That exclusion of women from the decisive and determinant activities of a society is something we would naturally, from the perspective of modern ideas, decry; but it is a historical injustice for which we can hardly blame Shakespeare. In the historical story of the deposition of Richard II, he found no remarkable or influential women: so that absence was duly and dutifully reflected in the play.

A moment's consideration will reveal that all these apparently "common-sense" arguments are extremely suspect. It is a fact that only a small number of female roles is to be found in Elizabethan plays. But the women characters who occupy those roles usually have a disproportionate influence within the world of the play: Viola, Rosaline, Portia; Cordelia, Desdemona, Lady Macbeth. It is even often the case that they show strengths and abilities, kinds of determination and resourcefulness, not displayed at all by their menfolk. As we witness Portia dominating and winning Antonio's trial in *The Merchant of Venice*, or Cordelia leading an army in *King Lear*, or Lady Macbeth returning to the murdered Duncan's chamber, we are unlikely to derive from Shakespeare's plays any simple notion of women as "the weaker sex." This is certainly not the case in *Richard II*, where the Queen is a pathetic melancholy spectator of her husband's downfall.

The Elizabethan dramatist's relationship with his historical sources was not a passive and automatic subservience. Although the Tudor period saw the emergence of a modern conception of historical "fact," all the history plays of this period mingle fact with interpretation, historical authenticity with imaginative elaboration. When Shakespeare dramatized other periods of history in which women are described as having some kind of prominence, he gave them more assertive roles in his plays—Joan of Arc and Queen Margaret in the *Henry VI* plays are obvious examples. After *Richard II* Shakespeare started to interpolate fictional comic subplots into the "factual" material of the chronicle drama, thus providing more space for the participation of women: in the *Henry IV* plays, women like the Hostess and Doll Tearsheet have active and important (if distinctly "low-life") roles to play. It was quite open to him to make more of Queen Isabella than the historical sources themselves warranted. In fact he did, since the young woman who appeared in the play to express her unfocused melancholy, to complain of her husband's declining fortunes, and to lament his tragic overthrow, has no real historical authority at all: Isabella was a child of ten when these events occurred. Her passive role in the play is then, we might say, historically appropriate; her dramatic characterization is all Shakespeare's invention.

The third argument from "common-sense," that the particular historical character of this action excludes the active agency of women in a particularly decisive and intractable way, has rather more force than the other two. It is one thing to invent an interesting dramatic character for Isabella; but if women did not (outside romances like Spenser's *The Faerie Queene*), take part in chivalric combats, Shakespeare could hardly clap his Queen in armor and let her fight the King's battles for him. But that exclusion of women from the central and constitutive activities of a society can either be accepted as a natural condition, or foregrounded and interrogated as an arbitrary structure of patriarchal authority, a carefully-engineered inequality in the disposition of power.

It seems to me possible that the marginalization of women in a play like

*Richard II* is not simply the symptomatic expression of an unconscious misogyny, or a passive reflection of predetermined historical conditions. It is rather a historical reality of the past, grasped by the specific mode of historical consciousness active in the play, a reality which the play in turn foregrounds, interrogates and criticizes. Women may not be much in evidence in the play, but femininity is. Let us take a closer look at the scene with which we began (2.1), the scene of Isabella's strangely absent presence. As I noted above, Isabella appears there in a scene otherwise populated entirely by men. The problems and issues debated in the scene are specifically "masculine" preserves: politics, war, economics, law, property. Throughout the scene what the characters say about their specific situation carries with it wider dimensions of reference, so that other groups of people are continually being alluded to and moving into temporary focus. Again, these are all groups of men. Young men, sick men, dying men, living men, flattering courtiers, lawyers, Englishmen ("this happy breed"), Frenchmen, Irishmen, fathers, grandfathers, brothers, sons, uncles, kings, knights, commons, nobles, ancestors, "men of war." It would be hard to imagine a world more thoroughly cleared of any sign of the female gender.

Yet if we look a little closer, vestigial traces of femininity begin to surface: the repressed returns. John of Gaunt sings the praises of that "happy breed of men" (2.1.45) who under the strong government of warrior kings like Edward III had excelled in the conquest of other nations. Englishmen are famous for their strength, their military successes, their masculinity. But to describe a category of men, however unimpeachably manly, as a "breed," is to draw attention to the fact that somehow they must have been "bred," and that therefore members of the female sex must have played in the process something more than a marginal role. Gaunt also talks about "birth" (2.1.52), though he is there perhaps talking less about the biological process by which children are delivered than about the male-dominated dynastic system of lineage. More distinctively revealing are his references to England as a "nurse" and as a "teeming womb of royal kings" (2.1.51), metaphors which draw attention to the specifically female capacities of gestation and suckling (see Kahn, *Man's Estate* 67). As Gaunt's celebration of the achievements of the English aristocracy extends to include the crusades, he actually finds space to mention a woman's name:

> This nurse, this teeming womb of royal kings,
> Feared by their breed and famous by their birth,
> Renowned for their deeds as far from home
> For Christian service and true chivalry

> As is the sepulchre in stubborn Jewry
> Of the world's ransom, blessed Mary's son. . . .
> (2.1.51–6)

The allusion to the Virgin Mary is perhaps representative of Gaunt's view of women. Whatever cults of worship may attach to Mary, her primary significance is the fact that she gave birth to a remarkable man, Jesus. In Gaunt's feudal and aristocratic perspective, women appear as the passive vehicles by means of which the patriarchal seed is procreated, the patrilinear dynasty secured. Even the femininity of his metaphorical "England" is ultimately spurious, since that maternal symbol is so completely a construction of the kings and warriors who have served their country in loyalty, fidelity and truth. Nonetheless, however strenuous Gaunt's efforts to suppress the reality of the feminine, it continues to appear, if only in the interstices of his metaphorical language. You cannot really talk about nurses, and wombs, and birth, and breeding, without bringing into play a feminine dimension of meaning. Once that meaning occupies a space inside the imaginative universe of the play, it proves remarkably hard to expel.

I will now examine the part played in the drama by its three female characters. All three are present in the play not in their own right, or because they have any distinctive individual contribution to make to the play's action, but in terms of their relationships with men. They are all, primarily and even exclusively, wives and mothers. The Duchess of Gloucester is there to lament and preserve the memory of her murdered husband. The Duchess of York is there to plead, successfully, for the life of Aumerle her son. Queen Isabella has literally nothing to do in the play except to feel sadness and pity for her husband.

The Duchess of Gloucester seems to represent a potentiality for female assertiveness, which is nonetheless deflected and turned to self-destructive grief and melancholy. Her husband Woodstock has been murdered (or summarily executed: see Holderness, *History* 42–50; and Holderness, Potter and Turner 30) by the king. In her view Gloucester's murder was a dreadful crime, since it was not only an unlawful killing, not only an offence committed against a kinsman, but a violation of the royal family itself. Where Richard sees royalty as inhering in his own person, the Duchess conceives of it as a shared possession dispersed across the family of Edward III, and rooted in each of his seven sons. In killing Gloucester Richard has struck at the very root of the aristocratic kinship system itself.

But the Duchess's very strength and courage are self-denying, self-annihilating, since the noble family she idealizes, the dynasty of Edward III, consists entirely of men; the role of women in the composition of this dynasty is silently effaced, and they have no place or position in the family tree. The royal "blood" that privileges and sacralizes the aristocratic family is a peculiarly masculine substance: it can be spilt by murder, or redeemed by blood-revenge, but it possesses none of the capacities biologically associated with blood in the female body. Christian patience is scornfully dismissed as the natural subjection of the common, the "mean" man; for the aristocratic subject, *noblesse oblige*, and principal among those duties is the responsibility for avenging the death of a murdered kinsman.

The Duchess seeks to persuade Gaunt to take revenge against Richard; but Gaunt is committed to preserving the security of the crown, however much he may disapprove of the particular king who wears it. The Duchess's hopes of revenge focus therefore on the possibility of Bolingbroke's emerging victorious from the combat with Mowbray. If Bolingbroke were to kill Mowbray, then a kinsman of Gloucester's would have succeeded in killing his murderer, and in casting a guilty shadow over the instigator of the murder, Richard himself. Revenge would be satisfied, her dead husband's ghost appeased.

> O, sit my husband's wrongs on Hereford's spear,
> That it may enter butcher Mowbray's breast!
> Or if misfortune miss the first career
> Be Mowbray's sins so heavy in his bosom
> That they may break his foaming courser's back,
> And throw the rider headlong in the lists
> A caitiff recreant to my cousin Hereford!
> (1.2.47–53)

Such militant violence of language proves the Duchess capable of that hot-blooded martial vigor defined by Mowbray as the peculiar prerogative of the male sex. But however strong her feelings, and however forceful their expression, this is still "the trial of a woman's war": for the Duchess is prevented by the impotence of her gender from acting upon her impulses towards revenge and restitution. She can only ask men to act for her, or support their struggles from the sidelines like a superannuated cheerleader. Her femininity is negated twice over, first in her espousal of masculine feelings and values that repress the female, and second in the social prohibitions restraining her from taking any personal role in the activities she deems essential if her personal honor—which is defined entirely in terms of the honor of the men to whom she is related—is to be effectively defended. Her energies of principle and pride thus frustrated, they turn inwards with a damaging impact upon her vital self-esteem—"Grief boundeth where it falls" (1.2.58)—and produce the emptiness and inconsolable sorrow that destroy her:

> Desolate, desolate will I hence and die.
> The last leave of thee takes my weeping eye.
> (1.2.73–74)

Sadness and melancholy are the natural fate of women in this play. Our introduction to Queen Isabella is to a mood of unfocused sadness, a grief without cause, which yet proves to be a prophetic monitor of imminent calamity. Isabella naturally uses the imagery of pregnancy and birth, but displaces such possibilities from her own body, envisaging the birth of nothing but misfortune:

> Some unborn sorrow ripe in fortune's womb
> Is coming towards me. . . . (2.2.10–11)

Silent in her husband's presence, when left alone on Richard's departure to Ireland, the Queen is released to self-expression: but her only experience is that of self-abnegation, since she is possessed by a vague melancholy which seems both a disproportionate response to her lord's absence, and an ominous foreboding of his impending tragedy. When Green brings the news of Bolingbroke's return from banishment, that phantom pregnancy is delivered of its burden of sorrow:

> So, Green, thou art the midwife to my woe,
> And Bolingbroke my sorrow's dismal heir.
> Now hath my soul brought forth her prodigy
> And I, a gasping new-delivered mother,
> Have woe to woe, sorrow to sorrow joined.
> (2.2.62–66)

Isabella's "inward soul" (2.2.11 and 28), that subjectivity valorized by Linda Bamber (139) as a vessel of female Otherness, actually contains nothing of her own: only grief for the absence or future suffering of another. To describe this experience of unfocused sorrow awaiting a cause to which it may be attached, the Queen uses the imagery of pregnancy and birth. Isabella means that her prophetic sadness joins with her real sorrow to give her a double "woe"; but also that as a "mother" whose symbolic confinement delivers her of a tragic destiny, she suffers twice—from the pain of childbirth, and from the pain of discovering her "child" to be the "prodigy" of Bolingbroke's usurpation. Isabella's language specifically draws attention to the way in which women in this play are condemned to suffering by the patriarchalism of the aristocratic dynasty: their only function in this masculine world is that of bearing sons for their powerful husbands; so that even in the successful achievement of their biological function, their own lives are negated. The more illustrious and legendary the lives of their husbands and sons, the more completely are they themselves eclipsed from the significant structure of the family. Isabella's lot is particularly hard since she will not bear Richard's children (the historical Isabella was a child of ten when these events occurred): her "dismal heir" (2.2.63) is the succession of Bolingbroke. Deprived by fate of what is seen as the only kind of power women can possess—the capacity to reproduce powerful men—Isabella's life seems unspeakably and inconsolably sad. In place of the child she will not bear, the Gardener plants in elegiac remembrance of her sorrow a "bank of rue":

> Rue even for ruth here shortly shall be seen
> In the remembrance of a weeping queen.
> (3.4.106–7)

In the Queen's last scene (5.1) where she takes leave of the deposed King, Isabella laments Richard's fall, and in doing so she acknowledges the blossom of her own life to be "withered":

> But soft, but see, or rather do not see,
> My fair rose wither. (5.1.7–8)

Again, her function is literally marginal: to stand by the roadside and observe the "woeful pageant" of the King's disgrace. Here however Isabella makes her one display of strength, manifesting that potentiality for resistance already seen in the Duchess of Gloucester:

> The lion dying thrusteth forth his paw
> And wounds the earth, if nothing else, with rage
> To be o'erpowered. And wilt thou pupil-like
> Take the correction, mildly kiss the rod . . . ?
> (5.1.29–32)

But again, whatever reserves of strength and defiance the woman has, she cannot act for herself: she can only ask men to act for her. Richard's response to this encouragement is to declare that he is, in effect, already dead, and the Queen already ("Good sometime queen," 5.1.37) a widow.

The only other female character in the play, the Duchess of York, offers what is in effect a contrasting success-story, precisely because she accepts and embraces the subjected and marginal role of women. Her significance is that she is mother to Aumerle, the close companion and supporter of Richard who joins the Abbot of Westminster's conspiracy against the life of Henry. She is a mother: now past the age of child-bearing, the prospect of losing her son would rob her of her very existence, reduce her to the shadowy unreality of the childless Isabella:

> Is not my teeming date drunk up with time?
> And wilt thou pluck my fair son from mine age?
> And rob me of a happy mother's name?
> (5.2.91–93)

In her appeal to her husband to save their son, the Duchess brings out the contradictions of this ideology of patriarchal maternity. Her suffering in childbirth to deliver Aumerle predisposes her to a pity her husband cannot feel:

> Hadst thou groaned for him
> As I have done, thou wouldst be more pitiful.
> (5.2.103–4)

Although she does not question the patriarchal principle that a woman's only proper profession is that of bearing sons, the Duchess does at least suggest that femininity may have its own peculiar experiences and values, in some ways quite separate from the world of masculine ideology. But this potential affirmation of femininity is soon eclipsed, since in order to save Aumerle the Duchess has to plead with men, and to argue on their terms. She tries to persuade York that Aumerle resembles only him, not her or any of her relatives:

> He is as like thee as a man may be;
> Not like to me, nor any of my kin. . . .
> (5.2.109–10)

To save her son the Duchess is not only prepared to humiliate herself—"For ever will I walk upon my knees" (5.3.92)—but even to sacrifice from her boy the personal traces of her maternal inheritance: only as the exclusive property of his father will Aumerle appear to be worth saving. Though she resists her husband, who is determined to incriminate his son, the Duchess can do so only by appealing to a greater, symbolic father, who represents the paternalistic principle of divinity ("God the father") in mortal form, the King: "A god on earth art thou!" (5.3.135).

The play's representation of its female characters shows quite clearly that in this male-dominated society women are consistently marginalized and subjected to a passive social role: they are the instruments and vehicles of masculine power, possessing no effective or positive social identity of their own. This severe limitation on the active presence of women, which is so unusual in Shakespeare's plays, seems to me an aspect of the play's historical vision. This is the unenviable lot of women in a feudal, patriarchal and chivalric society: they may be romanticized as mothers or idealized as lovers, but in themselves they are nothing—they derive their significance only from their relationships with husbands, brothers, sons. It is not a representation of the natural lot of women, or a depiction of women as they existed in Shakespeare's England, where the most powerful member of society was after all, a woman. The condition of female self-abnegation, discovered within that dramatized fifteenth century social formation, provokes in the sixteenth century play a consistent and comprehensive response of pity and compassion (like the Gardener's planting, in elegiac remembrance of Isabella's sorrow, of a bank of the herb rue, symbol of sadness and regret); an anachronistic solicitude which is then read back into the theatrical simulation of a fifteenth century world. And when in 2.2 Bushy attempts to comfort and console the Queen's nameless grief, he unwittingly discloses the strange and insubstantial existence allowed to women by this feudal and patriarchal society. In an elaborate conceit, Bushy argues that grief and sorrow multiply themselves into numerous "shadows," so that when observed from an angle, like perspective paintings, they appear greater than their real substance. The Queen's sadness at her lord's departure is thus exaggerated into a disproportionate anxiety. But how then is the sufferer supposed to distinguish shadow from substance, reality from illusion? If Isabella looks correctly at the real conditions of her life, she will see "naught but shadows/Of what is not" (2.2.23–24). Thus we see the woman's life de-realized by the very pity that is offered as her consolation.

The play reveals clearly that in this kind of patriarchal society, dominated by powerful men and their concerns, women have a purely marginal function. It cannot convincingly be argued that the play simply presents that condition as natural and unremarkable, since the women in the play are the objects of a powerful sense of pity. Of course it is easier to offer pity than to secure justice: and it could be argued that Shakespeare's own ideology is as patriarchal as John of Gaunt's, since the play cannot imagine women as anything other than the instruments of men and the bearers and protectors of male children: the saddest thing that can be said of a woman is that she has no children. Some feminist critics might argue that this kind of pity is a more dangerous enemy to the cause of female emancipation than open injustice, since though it appears to have the interests of women at heart, yet it still cannot conceive of women as anything other than the passive instruments of masculine oppression or compassion.

My own conviction is that the play can be read as demonstrative of a deep-seated structural injustice in the way this society positions women. If we read the play historically, we can see that it goes further than the utterance of mere compassion for the unfulfilled lives of its female characters. It reveals quite clearly that as long as women are positioned in society in the way they are here, there can be no realization or fulfillment of female existence. Whether a woman has children or is denied them, whether her husband is successful or a failure, the woman's own life remains empty and sterile. In 5.3 Bolingbroke, now Henry IV, reveals for the first time that he has a son: the young Prince Henry who will not appear in this play, but whose personal and political development will be the principal subject of the remaining plays in this historical sequence. There is nowhere in this play or any of the others any indication that Bolingbroke must have had a wife, Prince Henry a mother. He is his father's son.

Is the kind of reading I have offered here purely a strategic ideological appropriation? Does it interpret *Richard II* against the grain of the play's own ideological tendencies, using it simply as a mirror capable of reflecting back the critic's own preoccupations and concerns? In the most obvious sense, a reading undertaken from a feminist perspective cannot but be ideological, in the sense of partisan, tendentious, politically committed—otherwise the "ism" of feminism would have no significance. But if our feminist reading takes the form not of an essentialist universalization, but of a materialist practice, then the critic's activity of reconstruction comes up against something resistant to a radical indeterminacy of the text, or the uninhibited play of textual signifiers: it confronts, in a word, the historical. In the continual dialogue between present and past that we call history, the past can only ever be alive in the present; but it is still the past that we encounter, to be known through its historical difference.

The past in question is one that we know from those modern historiographical attempts at reconstructing the social practices and institutions which inscribed within the Renaissance drama its potentialities for releasing gender-political discourse. From the historiography of Christopher Hill, Lawrence

Stone and others, we derive an understanding of the period as characterized by large-scale and far-reaching changes in the institutions of marriage and the family, changes active throughout the Tudor period, and accelerated and consolidated by the rise of Puritanism and the Revolution. Christopher Hill speaks of a "sexual revolution" which eventually replaced property marriage by "a monogamous partnership in the affairs of the family" (306ff.); Lawrence Stone has argued for the view that in this period an older dynastic and familial concept of marriage as a property and kinship relationship was beginning to give way to "companionate marriage" and to the "nuclear family."

Though few would seriously argue that the period saw widespread female emancipation (and Stone believes that Puritan marriages actually enhanced rather than diminished patriarchal power) it is evident that there was, as Catherine Belsey puts it, "a contest for the meaning of the family in the sixteenth and seventeenth centuries which unfixed the existing system of differences ("Disrupting"). Such "unfixing" of traditional stereotypes and social roles is naturally of interest to feminism. Juliet Dusinberre emphasizes the Puritan revaluation of marriage—"replacing the legal union of the arranged marriage with a union born of the spirit" (104)—as a significant factor in the development of female independence, a principal emphasis of the new conception of "companionate marriage" being the importance of free choice for the partners, as against the old system of parental arrangement: the voluntary emotional contract of a couple becoming more important than the legal and financial contract engaged in by the parents. This in turn produced a new version of patriarchy, which emphasized reciprocal obligation and mutual respect, and which had to recognize—as Charles I discovered to his cost—the possibility of a false fatherhood from which it was legitimate to withhold consent. We are familiar enough with the frequent expressions in Elizabethan culture of that orthodox vision of social hierarchy and state power, in which the subordination of subject to prince, child to parent, wife to husband and citizen to magistrate, was a fundamental principle of civil order. Yet the logical end of Puritanism was a radical questioning of state authority, which in turn created the further possibility of questioning patriarchy: in 1641 the Leveller Mrs. Chidley argued that just as a magistrate had no right to control a man's conscience, so in turn that man had no right to control his own wife's.

We have also become accustomed to accepting that Shakespeare's plays, despite their evident complexity and apparent intellectual independence, may still be shown ultimately to speak for the dominant ideologies of state power and patriarchal authority. Criticism has become perhaps in this respect too exclusively concerned to identify the political and cultural powers Renaissance theater can be conjectured to have spoken *for:* at the price of neglecting the fundamental truth that all art—particularly the art of the Renaissance theater—is a dialogue between producers and audience, and that these plays spoke *to* that audience as well as *for* certain powerful vested interests in society. A fundamentally anti-democratic bias characterized the historicist criticism of the Tillyard school and has by no means been expunged from newer kinds of historical criticism. We have to be very wary of the assumption that quoting the letter of state propaganda or the dominant aesthetic language is an adequate way of describing the cultural life of a people. Arguments from demography and reception are of course notoriously more difficult to construct than arguments from centralized authority and cultural power. The agents of patriarchal authority in church and state recorded their views on the nature of marriage and the necessary subordination of women: while most of Shakespeare's audience went to their graves in silence.

It remains nonetheless possible to attempt some speculations about probable contemporary reactions to these plays. Almost without exception Renaissance plays express a positive appreciation of free choice, companionate relationship and romantic individualism in marriage, as opposed to parental authority, domestic inequality and impersonal contract. The audiences were metropolitan, more likely to be attuned to the more modern currents of contemporary thought: it was certainly illegal in London to batter a wife or even to call a woman a whore. We know that the Elizabethan audiences consisted of more than one social class, so that the variations in attitude towards marriage, noted by historians, between one social group and another, would probably be reflected. Lastly the audiences contained women as well as men: and the two genders could be differentiated and addressed by the actors as separate constituencies within the unified audience (as in the epilogue to *As You Like It*) capable of differences of opinion and response.

If sixteenth-century patriarchy was an unstable ideological system, a site of contestation and struggle, then it was capable of producing a drama in which the historical contradictions entailed in the construction of gender could be foregrounded and interrogated. Furthermore if, as I have argued elsewhere, sixteenth-century intellectuals had access to a historical consciousness, and to forms of historiographical discourse, in which the past was becoming visible as past, intelligible as difference rather than continuity, the possibility would arise of projecting the reactionary oppressiveness of Elizabethan patriarchy into a remote historical period where its routine marginalization of women could be clearly apprehended as a functioning system of injustice, a global apparatus of systematic, structural inequality. Feminist interpretation of Renaissance drama can therefore claim, as my reading of *Richard II* attempts to show, that its procedures are valid methods of finding something "in" these texts, as well as political strategies for relocating the texts into a necessary contemporary debate. Our immediate concern should be to construct a history of femininity, as well as to accomplish a feminization of history.

## NOTES

1. "It is, for example, a little disappointing that feminist criticism has continued to follow traditional assumptions about the established hierarchy *within* the canon, privileging the tragedies above all, then the middle comedies and the problem plays. . . . I regret that feminist criticism has so far neglected the earliest plays (apart from the fairly inevitable promotion of *The Taming of the Shrew* and the history plays" (Anne Thompson 85). The feminist predication of a hidden patriarchal agenda in much post-structuralist criticism can be encountered at its sharpest in Neely, "Constructing the Subject."

2. Kate McLuskie incorporates Bamber and Kahn into a general polemic against the essentialism of much feminist criticism ("Patriarchal Bard").

3. See Belsey, "Disrupting"; McLuskie, "Patriarchal Bard" and *Renaissance Dramatists*; Jardine; and Dusinberre. A forthcoming volume from Harvester Press offers a compilation of such work (Valerie Wayne).

4. All quotations from *Richard II* are taken from the Penguin edition, ed. Stanley Wells.

5. See Holderness, *Shakespeare's History* 27–32; Holderness, Potter and Turner 16–19.

# 14

# *Julius Caesar,* Allan Bloom, and The Value of Pedagogical Pluralism

**Darryl J. Gless**

Writing in the late 1970s, Richard Levin maintained that "interpretation . . . should begin with our actual dramatic experience, in its unique and concrete particularity" (*New Readings* 204). The uncomplicated touchstone labeled "our actual dramatic experience" is readily discoverable because "the most reasonable hypothesis about a play of this period . . . is that . . . it is in its primary aspect what it appears to be, and what it has been taken to be by the overwhelming majority of viewers and readers down to the present—namely, a literal representation of particular characters engaged in particular actions. It would follow, therefore, that the contour of these actions constitutes the basic form or structure of the play, and the response they evoke" (199; cf. 202). Similar advice—to seek the reliable touchstones of "our" dramatic experience or "the" response transparently signalled in the self-evident "contour" of "literal" actions as received by the "overwhelming majority of viewers and readers"—underlies Levin's earlier work on dramatic plots as well as his most recent series of attacks on feminist, Marxist, and cultural materialist interpretations of Shakespeare (*Multiple Plot* 16; "Bardicide" 494).

Without conceding that interpretation is the only thing one might do with literary texts, I nevertheless find it impossible to disagree with the notion that interpreters ought to follow carefully the concrete, particular structures of texts in an effort to discover ways such structures seek to condition the responses of audiences or readers. But we will be discovering probable *responses*, not as Levin so consistently has it, "*the* response of the audience." Effective teachers who seek not only to help students learn, but to help them think clearly and creatively about what they learn, know the limits of so simple a notion of audience response. Effective teaching requires that we maintain a disciplined receptivity to views other than those that maintain established residences in our lecture notes. If we remain alive to interpretive possibilities students' perceptions can bring home to us, we are also likely to receive repeated reminders that the group to whose responses Levin appeals, "the overwhelming majority of viewers and readers," is an illusion erected from partial evidence: the critical writings chiefly of privileged men. Throughout critical history, the majority of Shakespeare's readers and viewers, excluded from social, economic, and professional locations from which to speak, have remained silent.

That literary meaning is always in part a consequence of projection, of the kind of questions we ask of texts and the information, attitudes, and interpretive strategies we bring to them, requires no demonstration for many members of our discipline today. That readers play an extensive role in creating the meanings they "find" does, however, require repeated demonstration for students. As Gombrich has shown in his account of the process, the "illusion" that takes possession of us when we "find" a pattern in art or a meaning in language is an insistent force. Under its spell, we have trouble admitting that the pattern in question may not be empirically there (*Art and Illusion* part 3). We can hardly bear to admit, even years later, that a literary interpretation to which we have committed ourselves resulted from effects of illusion that no longer possess us. The departed illusion, like the newly certain one that has supplanted it, is a product of (1) the necessarily selective attention readers give to the profusion of linguistic detail literary works present, and (2) readers' projections—constructed of materials their own interests, preoccupations, information, and the underlying effects of ideology supply—onto the "places of indeterminacy" that always remain in our apprehension of literary works (Iser). Not all interpretations will enjoy equal respect, however, and they should be subjected in the classroom to the processes of validation many interpreters more or less consciously employ. According to Paul Armstrong's lucid recent formulation (12–16), these processes include tests of "inclusiveness" (the interpretation's capacity to account for an extensive array of the text's details), "intersubjectivity" (the interpretation's power to persuade people that it is reasonable), and "effectiveness" (the interpretation's ability to solve interpretive difficulties without creating new ones).

Though we seldom acknowledge the contribution illusion makes to interpretation, its power becomes evident whenever people who have spent time with a work begin to discuss it with each other. Our understandable resistance to other people's perceptions tends to transform discussions at scholarly conferences into comic exercises in intransigence. But when teaching, and when preparing classes in the safe privacy of our studies, it is important that scholars labor to recognize something of the specialized information as well as the psychic, social, and political energies that determine what we create of the meanings we believe we find in the texts we teach.

The importance not only of undertaking this enterprise but of learning to describe it to students and to non-academic audiences has recently been suggested by the extraordinary popular success of Allan Bloom's characterization of American higher education (*Closing*). The preconceptions that govern Bloom's indictment of the academy also determined his reading of Shakespeare's *Julius Caesar*, published more than twenty years earlier. Bloom's *Caesar* illustrates the power illusion exerts in all our acts of perception and literary interpretation. Because it incorporates a recurring tendency of mainstream *Caesar* criticism, it exhibits patterns of thought in which many of us may unconsciously participate. Bloom's *Caesar* also exhibits the ease with which unexamined assumptions can enable interpreters to render Shakespeare an agent of their own ideological commitments. The role of unexamined assumptions seems to me the fundamental issue raised by Richard Levin's sustained critique of feminist and cultural materialist studies of Shakespeare.

Bloom names his source of assumptions, without describing them, when he announces that his reading of *Julius Caesar* was proposed by Leo Strauss (*Politics* 75n). The essence of Strauss's *Caesar* had been briefly stated by Bloom's fellow Straussian, Harry Jaffa, whose creative and febrile readings discover in Abraham Lincoln the "master villain of American history" (184). This Lincoln's yearning to realize the *Übermensch* in himself requires that he transcend the laws by which democracies ineluctably inhibit or destroy true greatness (Jaffa ch. 9, esp. 215–19; cf. *Closing* 330–31). Whatever else the Straussian genealogy of Bloom's *Caesar* might lead us to foresee, it certainly predicts (1) an adulation of "great men" of the sort aristocracy is assumed to engender, (2) a corresponding contempt for democracy and ordinary people, and (3) an advocacy of "machismo," the attribute Bloom praises in *Closing* as the "ambitious, warlike, protective, possessive character" that constitutes "the souls of men," now being destroyed by the "nasty" coercions of feminism (*Closing* 329–30, 129, and *passim*).[1] As forceful reviewers have pointed out, convictions like these underlie Bloom's profoundly anti-democratic notion of the purposes of higher education. In his view, "the university exists within democracy to call chosen 'natures' away from the corrupt judgments of 'the many' and teach them the superior value of the contemplative life" (Nussbaum 21).

Despite relentless invocations of the classics, Bloom's convictions receive neither documentation nor specific argument. They are supported only by rhetorical strategies that envelope literary and philosophic texts in numinous haze and then urge veneration of the haze: "Men may live more truly and fully in reading Plato and Shakespeare than at any other time, because then they are participating in essential being and are forgetting their accidental lives. . . . The books in their objective beauty are still there, and we must help protect and cultivate the delicate tendrils reaching out toward them through the unfriendly soil of student's souls" (*Closing* 380). How does Bloom enable us to share in essential being when he reads one of the great books? His reading of *Julius Caesar*, I hoped, would yield a specific instance of that promised epiphany. And it does, in a sense. Seldom have I read an academic essay, by someone who tries "to read [great books] as their authors wished them to be read" (*Closing* 344), that makes the dependence of perception on preconception so conspicuous. Seldom is that dependence so feebly tested against the play's details, especially by a perceiver who claims to take the systematically skeptical Socrates as his model for the intellectual life.

The adulation of great men and their "Roman" brand of "machismo" dominates Bloom's perceptions of major figures in *Julius Caesar*. For him, "[t]he Romans were the greatest political people who ever existed. . . . [They] were unabashedly ambitious of glory. . . . They were an extraordinary number of able men, none recognizing a master, each honed to a superb edge of emulation." Like any interpreter possessed by the effects of illusion as Gombrich describes it, Bloom is certain that the playwright's enthusiasms matched his own: "In *Julius Caesar,* Shakespeare has chosen to depict the greatest of these great men" (78). The greatest of the great, the *Übermensch* himself, is the Caesar Bloom constructs from the presuppositions that determine his version of the play: "Shakespeare . . . demonstrates the inadequacies of ordinary men to overcome the force of a man like Caesar. . . . Caesar seems to have been the most complete political man who ever lived. . . . A true philosophy would have to be supple enough to grasp the mind of Caesar," who "seems to defy the principle of contradiction" (104–05).

Having chosen to depict such great men, the playwright Bloom imagines as the author of his Straussian *Caesar* displays decidedly aristocratic values: his Rome "is not one city, but two—the city of the rich and the city of the poor. . . . The city of the rich contains all that is noble and interesting; these are the men who make up the Senate and lead the wars. They are the soul of Rome. Shakespeare is no democrat." Bloom's Shakespeare "is convinced that certain important virtues can be possessed by only a few and that those few require special training and long tradition. It is this concentration on virtue, and particularly certain political virtues, that leads him to emphasize the special rights of the patricians," and in other ways to conclude that "the man who has greater qualities should be preferred to those who have lesser ones" (79–80). Although it harbors a class of exceptional leaders, Rome's political health is endangered in *Julius Caesar*. The fault for this lies with its "lazy, brutal populace," which Shakespeare portrays as "a real urban proletariat.

They are accustomed to dominating, and they are insolent; they have the habit of being flattered." These "imperious arbiters of the civil war to whom the whole rhetoric of the conspiracy is directed" (81) make their appearance in the first scene of *Julius Caesar*.

Many readers or viewers of *Julius Caesar* will be startled, I think, by Bloom's description of the commoners (so they are called in the opening stage direction) whom Flavius and Marullus confront in this scene.[2] Perceptions less absolutely predetermined by preconceptions could construe the scene differently. Speaking the play's opening words, Flavius initiates what will be one of its linguistic norms, the persistence of the imperative mood:

> Hence! Home, you idle creatures, get you home!
> Is this a holiday? What, know you not,
> Being mechanical, you ought not walk
> Upon a labouring day without the sign
> Of your profession? Speak, what trade art thou?
> (1.1.1–5)

The response seems cooperative, perhaps registering surprise at the vehemence of the tribune's demand: "Why, sir, a carpenter" (1.1.6). When Marullus responds with scolding interrogatives ("Where is thy leather apron . . . ") and imperiously demands "You, sir, what trade are you?" (1.1.9), is it any wonder the cobbler responds with evasive quibbles?

Although an actor could certainly make him insolent, the cobbler could as easily be shown to make a defensive retreat into evasion and humor, and as the scene develops, the commoners' simple decency receives emphasis. It seems worthy of note that these people are "mechanical," and the emphasis is on their trades. Bloom's construction of the scene depends, it appears, on views about the Roman proletariat which he has brought to the play from extrinsic sources. His authorities appear not to include Plutarch, whose occasional reports about the people (like his accounts of their leaders) provide grounds for varying evaluations (e.g. *Shakespeare's Plutarch* 97, 126). Whatever Bloom's sources, they must have been energetically rewritten by his reading of them. It is certainly true that late-Republican Rome comprised a large population brutalized by unemployment, the corn dole, and the assiduous wooing and bribery of politicians (Scullard 18–20, 32–33, 116, 179–80), but it is difficult to find evidence that the "imperious arbiters of the civil wars" were any other than the oligarchs Bloom idolizes. Conscientious scrutiny of the evidence reveals instead that the Roman plebs never mounted a popular movement, that they wanted stability rather than power, and that they "influenced political life only when used by the politicians for their own ends." The "Roman nobility," which supplied those politicians, "was consumed within itself by a fierce and incessant competition for position" (Earl 15–16).

This view of incessant Roman competitiveness corresponds to Augustine's analysis, which established an attitude toward Rome that persisted in Shakespeare's time. On that judgment, the greatest virtue of Rome's best men, their eager desire for glory to be earned through virtuous service to their country, was also a great vice—one that can easily slide into the appetite for shear domination (*City of God* 5.12–19). Typically, this incessant competition induced members of the oligarchy, when their personal ambitions were thwarted in the Senate, to make the popular assembly their means of ascent. The leaders of the "popular" Party, including Pompey and Caesar, "asserted the rights of the people, [but] they were all . . . seeking personal power rather than establishment of the rights of the sovereign people." And with one exception, these leaders were "all members of the hereditary nobility" (Taylor 21).[3] The mob violence of Republican politics, was, in short, organized from above, by the group Bloom admires for comprising "all that is noble and interesting."

The evaluation offered by responsible historians conforms closely to an interpretation Shakespeare's text appears to invite. The plebs in *Julius Caesar* are not inherently vicious, but they can be manipulated; Antony's manipulation is what transforms them into a murderous mob. A primary means of that transformation is his appeal (at 3.2.173–86) to a sensitivity Marullus's oration had revealed to be characteristic of the mechanicals in 1.1. Marullus's speech, the first in a series of self-consciously oratorical occasions which pervade the play (see Greene, "Power"; Velz, *inter alia*), deploys its schemes of repetition and its graphic depiction of the entire populace unanimously joined in celebrating Pompey's previous triumphs (1.1.32–51) to enforce a simple moral indictment:

> Run to your houses, fall upon your knees,
> Pray to the gods to intermit the plague
> That needs must light on this ingratitude.
> (1.1.52–54)

"Tongue-tied in their guiltiness" (1.1.62), the plebs break off their celebration for Caesar. Sensitive to a simple notion of fair play, the tradesmen who constitute "the people" in Shakespeare's *Julius Caesar* are embarrassed to appear ungrateful for the achievements they had earlier celebrated on Pompey's behalf.

An interpreter intent on constructing an inclusive reading might readily notice that Marullus's oratory determines the meaning the commoners now believe their behavior has signified. Having transformed the people's celebration for Caesar into a sign of ingratitude to Pompey, the tribunes set off to modify the meaning of other signs. By removing "Caesar's trophies" from "the images," the tribunes hope to deprive those images of the special significance Caesar's admirers had dressed them in. So deprived, the images will announce that Rome's admiration for Caesar remains within previously established limits, an implication that will, the tribunes hope, "make him fly an ordinary pitch" (1.1.73). The crucial point is that 1.1 enables us to watch political meanings in the making, first through forceful interpretive rhetoric, then through the manipulation of "ceremonies" (1.1.65).

Meanings remain visibly in the process of manufacture when Caesar himself enters, eager to "leave no ceremony out" (1.2.11), then to redefine another reader of signs (ceremoniously and coercively scrutinized, 1.2.20–22) from sayer of sooth to "dreamer" (1.2.24), then to participate in a ceremonial drama that stages his own magnanimous reluctance to accept a crown and (to his dismay) demonstrates the crowd's admiration for that very reluctance (1.2.235–59). Meanwhile Cassius has misconstrued Brutus's recent aloofness as a symptom of diminishing love (1.2.32–36); Brutus misconstrues the offstage shouts as evidence that "the people / Choose Caesar for their king" (1.2.78–79); and Caesar shrewdly reads Cassius as an instance of men who are "never at heart's ease / Whiles they behold a greater than themselves" (1.2.208–09).

Interpreters who focus on these recurrent acts of construal and misconstrual are responding to a concern our own time shares with Shakespeare's—a concern with ways in which language creates what we perceive as "reality." Waswo's recent book effectively argues that a constitutive conception of language was developing among Italian and Northern Renaissance humanists. Powerful interpretations of *Julius Caesar* have likewise focused on the skepticism toward language and rhetoric which the play shares with or draws from influential contemporaries, Montaigne and Bacon among them (Barton, "Roman"; Gayle Greene, "Power," *inter alia*). Greene provides an especially masterful study of "Shakespeare's depiction of Rome as a society of skilled speakers whose rhetorical expertise masks moral and political truth." This depiction implies "a criticism of rhetoric and of language . . . a skepticism of the word" ("Power" 69, 71). Such skepticism becomes manifest, for instance, in Brutus's soliloquy in 2.1, where "[h]is thought moves . . . between general observations about human behavior and metaphors that illustrate them, and nowhere does he look outside this self-referential linguistic construct to the supposed subject, Caesar himself" (81).

Although theoretical preoccupations of our own time will have prepared critics to notice such things, the resulting interpretations establish their validity by meeting the tests of inclusiveness, efficacy, and (to judge from recent criticism) persuasiveness. An interpretation which recognizes, for example, that "Caesar is virtually constituted of the guesses made about him" (Danson, *Tragic* 57) can persuasively account for an impressive selection of the play's features. The incompatible acts of construing which constitute Caesar constitute other characters as well. Those acts also constitute the categories within which the characters understand themselves, and the lofty ideals on which the same characters ground their actions. Although critics often take the play's honorific key words as names for stable objects of linguistic reference, the play invites us to watch those objects being invented. Speakers employ these terms so vaguely that interpreters (within the play and outside it) perceive them as screens containing inchoate but suggestive materials; the interpreters themselves complete these materials by projecting favored assumptions onto them.[4] Terms so invented include "Rome," "Roman," "noble," "honor," "honorable," "love," "freedom," "tyranny," "woman," and "man." The occasion for this essay leads me to focus on some instances concerning the last two of these terms.

The incapacity of the critical tradition accurately to represent what Renaissance plays have "been taken to be by the overwhelming majority of viewers and readers down to the present" becomes clear when we focus a little attention on women in *Julius Caesar*. Recent political and social preoccupation with gender roles is what might first move us to think more carefully about Portia and Calpurnia than most critics have suggested we should. Ripley's stage history of *Julius Caesar* affords them a single footnote, for example, which reports that "[t]here is surprisingly little to be said of Portia and Calphurnia [sic]. Although they have been played by actresses of the calibre of Peg Woffington, Sybil Thorndike, and Edith Evans, no one has won much critical acclaim in these roles" (314n). In its combination of conscientious neglect and unexplained praise, Bloom's single comment on Portia represents the wider critical tradition with some fidelity: "Brutus reveals that Portia is dead. This is indeed a terrible loss, and we have seen what a wonderful couple they were" (*Politics* 101).

In Bloom's analysis as in most of the major criticism, we have not in fact "seen what a wonderful couple" Brutus and Portia are; we have simply been told. Eager to interpret Brutus's domestic relations as indices of his nobility of character, MacCallum asserts that Portia's brief appearances leave an "impression . . . indelible and overpowering . . . of the perfect union in which she and Brutus lived. There is no obtrusion of their love: it does not exhale in direct professions" (272). Palmer avers that "[t]he gentle Brutus is never more likeable than when he answers Portia in the orchard at daybreak" (*Political Characters* [1948] 10–11). Employing a phrase often echoed by subsequent critics, Stewart comments not only that *Julius Caesar* "is a direct and manly play . . . filled with straight talk" but that it presents Brutus as a character "whose personal relationships are . . . beautiful and whose politics are . . . insufficient" (Stewart 50, 55). Humphreys remarks that "in the orchard scene . . . the devoted intimacy between [Brutus] and Portia . . . touches the heart" (13).

Quotations like these have lately been provoking satiric laughter from students who read the scene with attention. Why? For one thing, changes in our society's attitudes and in the population of the classroom have rendered less common the presuppositions and values that in part created what the critics I have quoted saw in Portia's scene with Brutus. When women's subservience could be considered "natural," it was easy to see Portia's extraordinary, self-mutilating act of persuasion only as an occasion for Brutus's winning display of admiration for his wife. Students now are more likely to look at Portia's actions themselves, as we shall in a moment. Moreover, the meeting of Brutus and Portia occurs in a context that has begun to question the stability of the unchanging essence Brutus believes his character to be and of the ideals he employs to guide his actions. Although terms like "honor" and "noble" have received no specific definition at all, earlier speeches have by now invited readers or spectators to guess, if only semi-consciously, at what those grand labels might intend. In 1.2.99–131, Cassius's long "story" about honor obliquely defines it as a function of dominance displayed in an athletic competition that carries an unavoidable political subtext. So conceived, honor disappears when others gain preeminence:

> Age, thou art sham'd!
> Rome, thou hast lost the breed of noble bloods!
> When went there by an age, since the great Flood,
> But it was famed with more than with one man?
> (1.2.150–53)

To be of "noble blood" is to ensure that no one gains preeminence so complete that the athletic, military, and political competition for honor ceases—when "there is in [Rome] but one only man" (1.2.157). Against Caesar's potential monopoly, Cassius would enlist a figure who has as "fair a name" as "Caesar" (1.2.142–44), whose ancestor "would have brooked / Th'eternal devil to keep his state in Rome / As easily as a king" (1.2.159–61), and whose strictly balanced, logically ordered language expresses confidence in the steady and reasonable principles summed up in his own name:

> That you do love me, I am nothing jealous.
> What you would work me to, I have some aim.
> How I have thought of this, and of these times,
> I shall recount hereafter.
> . . . . . . . . . . . . . . . . .
> Till then, my noble friend, chew upon this:
> Brutus had rather be a villager
> Than to repute himself a son of Rome
> Under these hard conditions as this time
> Is like to lay upon us.
>
> (1.2.162–75)

For Brutus as for Caesar, to refer to one's self in the third person is to guarantee utterance. In a world disordered by the waning of senatorial power and by civil war between former triumvirs and their issue ("Pompey's blood," 1.1.51), a stable, identifiable self supplies the only reliable foundation for meaning. Persuasive argument under these circumstances depends, more completely than it otherwise might, on the speaker's capacity to represent himself, or herself, as a person of intelligence and integrity (cf. Cicero, *De Officiis* 9.33). Hence, Cassius's temptation of Brutus begins by establishing a persuasive *ethos* ("Were I a common laughter . . . " 1.2.72–78); Brutus's successful oration at Caesar's funeral depends heavily on *ethos*, ("Believe me for mine honour, and have respect to mine honour, that you may believe," 3.2.14–16; Greene, "Power" 82–85); and Antony's appeal to the people relies upon *ethos* as fully as it does on *pathos*—he is merely a "plain blunt man," who loved his friend (3.2.85, 105–07, 210–12). And in every case, the touchstone of self is as reliable as Caesar's: as "constant as the northern star . . . That unassailable holds on his rank, / Unshaked of motion . . . *Et tu, Brute?* Then fall, Caesar!" (3.1.60–76).

In every case, that is, the steady point of self is itself a vulnerable fabrication of language—of the brisk third-person gestures of Caesar and Brutus, the more elaborate self-presentations that ground acts of oratorical persuasion, or the still more persistent patterns of thought and behavior that we take to add up to an essence called "character." By the time we reach Brutus's much-admired meeting with Portia in the orchard, the detached and rational character he presented in 1.2 (the man who can look upon death or honor with equal indifference, 1.2.86–87) has begun to display surprising elasticity. His soliloquy at 2.1.10–34 replaces the imageless, rational-sounding isocolons of earlier speeches with self-deceiving metaphors ("think him as a serpent's egg"), designed to "fashion" the "quarrel" to suit the speaker's predilections (Greene, "Power" 79–81; Barton, "Roman" 45; cf. Shuger 210). Brutus's first acts as leader of the conspiracy are to overrule all three proposals made by others, and extensively to elaborate a misleading metaphor to justify the most important of those decisions: "For Antony is but a limb of Caesar . . . " (2.114–40, 150–52, 166–84). Brutus concludes this fateful interview by supplementing Cassius's final adjuration to the conspirators ("show yourselves true Romans," 2.1.224) with a telling coda:

> Good gentlemen, look fresh and merrily;
> Let not our looks put on our purposes,
> But bear it as our Roman actors do,
> With untired spirits and formal constancy.
> (2.1.225–28)

"Telling" because Brutus now implies so forthrightly that to be "true Romans" the conspirators must imitate "Roman actors" who "put on" dramatic roles that hide emotional disturbance beneath an expression of decorous steadfastness. To be a "true Roman" in this sense is to act outwardly ("formally") the unperturbed rational man Brutus characteristically presents himself to be.

Although Plutarch's Brutus does play this role, reasoning his way with impressive consistency to military and political decisions from recognizably coherent principles (*Shakespeare's Plutarch* 105, 147–48, 151, 152–53, 155), Shakespeare's Brutus indulges more in persuasion than in ratiocination, as we have seen. Portia's complaint now supplies evidence of more visible inconsistencies in Brutus's performance of the role of rational man:

> You've ungently, Brutus,
> Stole from my bed; and yesternight at supper,
> You suddenly arose, and walked about,
> Musing, and sighing, with your arms across;
> And when I asked you what the matter was,
> You stared upon me with ungentle looks.
> I urged you further; then you scratched your head,
> And too impatiently stamped with your foot.
> Yet I insisted; yet you answered not,

> But with an angry wafture of your hand,
> Gave sign for me to leave you. So I did. . . .
> (2.1.238–48)

"What a wonderful couple"? Perhaps; wonderful couples can have bad moments. Yet the scene suggests less simplistic interpretations which the critical tradition—in its habit either of admiring or condemning, of silencing or being silent about women—has seldom been prepared to consider.

Among those possibilities is the one Portia herself states. Brutus's "formal" features have been so much transformed by his inner disturbance that

> could it work so much upon your shape
> As it hath much prevailed on your condition,
> I should not know you Brutus. (2.1.254–56)

The self-validating character of "Brutus" depends so far on his capacity to preserve "formal constancy" that he becomes unrecognizable when inward passion reshapes him outwardly. At supper yesternight, he adopted the role of tyrannical husband, and for the time, that is what Brutus in fact was. That role expresses a recurrent impulse. Despite his opposition to monarchy, Brutus's readiness to exert unchallenged authority over the conspirators has already suggested that an appetite to dominate exists in Brutus. The same appetite will emerge again, nakedly in Brutus's quarrel with Cassius ("Must I budge? / Must I observe you? . . . from this day forth, / I'll use you as my mirth . . . " (4.2.96–101), and fatally when Cassius's "[g]ood reasons must of force give place to better" (253). The most persuasive of those better reasons turns out to be a rhetorically powerful image of a "tide in the affairs of men" (268–74). The regularity of tides renders them inadequate analogies for the chaotic activity of late Republican politics, the disorderly action of the latter half of *Julius Caesar*, and the irregular movements of military campaigns. The metaphor expresses Brutus's will to maintain control; it fails to describe the world in which he must function.

As this scene suggests, the play provides striking opportunities for spectators to identify "the spirit of Caesar" (2.1.168)—when that elusive quality walks onto the stage and identifies itself as "[t]hy evil spirit, Brutus" (4.2.332)—as Brutus's own unconscious but powerful "Roman" appetite to gain honor by dominating those around him. Artemidorus calls this appetite "emulation" (2.3.13). The first words Brutus speaks to Cassius register an overtly scornful and (less obviously) competitive technique of self-definition: "Will you go see the order of the course?" Cassius asks. Brutus replies in gratuitously comparative terms: "I am not gamesome. I do lack some part / Of that quick spirit that is in Antony" (1.2.28–29). This impulse to represent himself through negative comparisons with others persists. Like other men in the play, Brutus labors to stabilize his identity by distancing it from stereotypes about women:[5]

> But if these . . . bear fire enough,
> To kindle cowards, and to steel with valour
> The melting spirits of women, then, countrymen,
> What need we any spur but our own cause
> To prick us to redress? (2.1.119–24)

In his final speech, Brutus's primary concern is to establish his sense of honor by topping his competitors:

> My heart doth joy that yet in all my life
> I found no man but he was true to me.
> I shall have glory by this losing day
> More than Octavius and Mark Antony
> By this vile conquest shall attain unto.
> So fare you well at once, for Brutus' tongue
> Hath almost ended his life's history.
> (5.5.34–40)

The ambivalent evaluation history granted Brutus before Shakespeare wrote of him (Schanzer) helps to render a simple response to this speech nearly impossible. The irony which for many interpreters will qualify Brutus's words helps to focus attention on the point that, for him, it is decisively "Brutus' tongue" that ends his "life's history." What counts at death is the dignity he can draw from a story he now finds himself able to construct and to credit.

Many viewers can detect the presence of inaccuracy and oversimplification in this speech and yet grant that the mental tricks Brutus here plays are recognizable and forgivable defenses of a character whose world has collapsed. In its complexity, this reaction matches the richly textured patterns of response the play enables interpreters to enact. Antony's closing panegyric provides for a correspondingly varied final response:

> His life was gentle, and the elements
> So mixed in him that Nature might stand up
> And say to all the world, "This was a man!"
> (5.5.74–76)

Already engaged in undeclared struggle for dominance with Octavius (5.1.2–4, 7–12, 16–20; 5.4.26–29; 5.5.61–62), Antony has political motives for an exaggerated display of noble generosity, beyond that which the norms of deathbed testimony require. Brutus has often been moved by passions he has sought consciously to deny, and his mixture of elements has been less than perfect. Precisely because he was "a man" whose behavior must be interpreted by other men and women, he necessarily becomes a focus for varying gradations both of sympathetic and critical response.

An inclusive interpretation will find grounds for varying and mixed reactions in the orchard scene, to which we may now return. Because Brutus persists in replying in curt dismissive terms (2.1.258, 261), Portia's speeches become more emphatically oratorical. These speeches consequently participate in the play's habit of endowing its characters' grand idealistic labels with meanings that vary as a succession of forceful orators variously construct those meanings. What Portia's oration does here is to recreate the reality of their marriage as she believes it rightly to exist. Her rhetoric produces a performative speech act, which realizes her meaning when Brutus is won (or won again) to share her view that marriage can only exist when two souls live as one. Portia's rhetorical authority derives in part from allusions to the Platonic and Neoplatonic notion that two souls in love are in reality loving their "other half"—that alter ego provided by beneficent providential arrangement.

> I charm you, by my once-commended beauty,
> By all our vows of love, and that great vow
> Which did incorporate and make us one,
> That you unfold to me, your self, your half,
> Why you are heavy. . . . (2.1.272–75)

Shakespeare's Portia also echoes a Pauline notion that the historical Portia could never have known. Many members of Shakespeare's earliest audiences could automatically have included that idea in their perception of her words ("he that loveth his own wife, loveth himself" [Booty 297]):

> Am I yourself
> But as it were in sort or limitation,
> To keep with you at meals, comfort your bed,
> And talk to you sometimes? Dwell I but in the suburbs
> Of your good pleasure? If it be no more,
> Portia is Brutus' harlot, not his wife.
>
> (2.1.283–88)

Brutus's response is striking because it expresses a degree of passionate devotion:

> You are my true and honourable wife,
> As dear to me as are the ruddy drops
> That visit my sad heart.
>
> (2.1.288–90)

Deeply impassioned, of course, this is not. Lovers and husbands in Shakespeare's plays often do better, and it is worthy of note that Brutus's favorite touchstones of merit initiate his remark: "true and honourable." Moments ago, Brutus implied that those panegyric terms have substance, though as is always the case in *Julius Caesar*, their substance remains for interpreters to construct. An oath is unnecessary for the conspirators, Brutus has said,

> when every drop of blood
> That every Roman bears, and nobly bears,
> Is guilty of a several bastardy
> If he do break the smallest particle
> Of any promise that hath pass'd from him.
>
> (2.1.136–40)

As obliquely described here, to be true to one's blood as "Roman," "nobly" Roman, requires absolute fidelity to one's promises. Portia meets the requirement, making clear that she means fully to live up to that "great vow" that made them one.

To win her point, however, the role she has so far presented in this scene—Portia as rigorously logical rhetorician ("excellently well seen in philosophy," Plutarch 118)—must conclude with an extraordinary passage of dramatic self-fashioning. It constitutes one of the most impressive uses of argumentative appeal to *ethos* in a play rich in comparable appeals:

> I grant I am a woman; but withal
> A woman that Lord Brutus took to wife.
> I grant I am a woman; but withal
> A woman well-reputed, Cato's daughter,
> Think you I am no stronger than my sex,
> Being so fathered and so husbanded?
> Tell me your counsels, I will not disclose 'em.
> I have made strong proof of my constancy,
> Giving myself a voluntary wound

> Here, in the thigh. Can I bear this with patience,
> And not my husband's secrets?
>
> (2.1.295–303)

This speech draws from Brutus the much-admired concession: "O ye gods, / Render me worthy of this noble wife!" The sequel is not staged, but Brutus provides a promise of what it will contain:

> Portia, go in awhile,
> And by and by thy bosom shall partake
> The secrets of my heart.
> All my engagements I will construe to thee,
> All the charactery of my sad brows.
>
> (2.1.306–10)

Brutus will "construe" his "heart" for Portia. His promise employs the term Cicero earlier used to stress the problematic consequences of interpretation: "But men may construe things after their fashion, / Clean from the purpose of the things themselves" (1.3.34–36).

Although he promises complete self-revelation, Brutus's construction will be blind to some parts of its subject, and it will misrepresent others. He should be forgiven that, but we may in turn be forgiven for guessing that his uncharacteristically impassioned expression of admiration for Portia dramatizes love of other as love of self. Portia has achieved her husband's admiration for fashioning herself into a version of the "noble" man he seeks to be. In authentically Roman manner (Miles 259–60), Brutus derives his character as inveterate anti-monarchist from his ancestor; Portia credits her capacity to transcend the limitations of her sex to her father, and at the same time flatters Brutus with the view that that strength derives partly from her husband. Her *coup de théâtre*, however, is to display the "voluntary wound." This represents her capacity to exert absolute control, by force of reason and will, over sensations people are expected naturally to feel, including especially the "natural" female incapacity to keep secrets.[6] Although many signs in the play derive meaning chiefly from the rhetoric that presents them, the meaning Portia's rhetoric here assigns to her wound is the meaning her actions earlier gave it.

Existing outside the male sphere, in which military and political action can supply evidence of constancy, the one action Portia can take is self-destructive. In taking it, she has transformed herself into an image of Brutus's ideal self. That he can love the Portia who now stands before him suggests how inextricably love and self-love intermingle—in a more narcissistic sense than the marriage service intended. But Portia is also like Brutus in her incapacity to subdue emotional reflexes to which human beings are normally subject. After she has been made aware of the conspiracy, her disempowered place ensures that her frustration and fear will turn inward and that further action will become self-destructive.[7]

On her next appearance, Portia reverts to self-explanatory generalities that conflict with the character many interpreters will have thought they came to know in 2.1.235–309 (Cf. Woodbridge 326–27):

> I have a man's mind, but a woman's might,
> How hard it is for women to keep counsel!
> (2.4.8–9)

> Ay me, how weak a thing
> The heart of woman is!
> (2.4.39–40)

Many could of course accept the scene as standard sixteenth-century misogyny, faithfully recorded or authentically felt by Shakespeare. Others, however, will notice that Artemidorus has expended more than half of the preceding scene (2.3.1–9) listing for us the names of all the conspirators, whom he seeks to betray to Caesar. The male conspiracy has been conscientiously and completely broadcast, without the aid, it seems, of Roman women. Like Hotspur (*1 Henry IV* 2.3.28–31; cf. 1.3.292–93, 2.3.108–111), these men have themselves betrayed their purposes. The stereotypical proneness to verbal leakage our Renaissance predecessors assigned to women (Paster) could have done little to increase the celerity with which the conspirators had themselves spread the news. That Popilius Lena soon terrifies Cassius by revealing that he also knows of the conspiracy ("I wish your enterprise today may thrive" [3.1.13]) renders this point all the more apparent.

Such scenes have not prevented critics from making the stereotype part of their perceptions of 2.4. As MacCallum puts it, "[w]e presently find her all but ruining the conspiracy by her uncontrollable agitation. . . . She may well confess: 'I have a man's heart, but a woman's might' " (273). This places a heavy burden of responsibility on Portia, as Gertrude and Isabella have been similarly burdened by major critics (Rose). There is little point, however, in dwelling on the negative stereotypes that controlled the vision of a good interpreter of the Roman plays who was working at the beginning of our century. There is a great deal more point in reflecting on the processes of reading which have helped make Allan Bloom a popular cultural commentator, and helped him make Shakespeare father to his own patterns of blindness and bias. And there is much that should give us pause in witnessing any established critic mount repeated attacks on feminist Shakespeare scholars, always reading their work with the aim more of discovering weakness than of grasping the point.

It is true that our shared place in the hermeneutic circle induces all of us to contribute much of what we find in the texts we read. Yet different readings can be subject to tests of relative validity that nonetheless respect the diversity of their origins in diverse readers. When we take this diversity—and our teaching—seriously, we must also take interpretive pluralism seriously. I refer not to the "intuitive pluralism" or "dogmatic monism" students often bring with them to the classroom, nor to the charged pluralism that disguises ideological positions even from those who occupy them.[8] I refer instead to the "considered pluralism" that has learned generously and persistently to try out unfamiliar or alien ways of thinking and finally also to honor "the plurality of human centers that any classroom holds" (Booth 473, 479).

Reading students, colleagues, and Shakespeare pluralistically will not bring on a revolution, but it will be authentically educative. Such reading enables students to take up their legitimate role in the community endeavor which is the simultaneous finding and making of meaning in literature. Misreadings like Bloom's, unable to account for the bulk of Shakespeare's text, can take effect in the classroom, of course, but they will do so less through reason than through an authoritarian teacher's charismatic power.[9] Levin's studied hostility to new ways of reading Shakespeare tends in the same authoritarian direction. By assuming that "we" already know "the" meaning of Shakespeare's plays, Levin establishes himself and his readings of a narrow selection of past interpretations as sole arbiters of what Shakespeare can be allowed to mean. Pluralistic reading, by contrast, will not only better reflect the ways in which literary texts actually do mean; it will also promote education that is authentically transformative—a goal which authoritarian teaching, either from the Left or the Right, can seldom reach.

## NOTES

1. This, and other expressions of vicarious pleasure in and defenses of aggressively dominant men, has probably enhanced Bloom's popularity with people who hold positions of political power—people who, whether male or female themselves, enjoy the game that got them where they are.

2. All citations to *Julius Caesar* refer to the Oxford Shakespeare edition, ed. Arthur Humphreys.

3. Despite exceptions, the tribunate had long since become subservient to oligarchic senatorial control. See Scullard 8; Taylor.

4. For the analogous effect in visual arts, see Gombrich 199–200, 216–22, and elsewhere. "The indistinct parts of the canvas become a screen" for the beholder's projective faculty, "provided that certain distinctive features stand out with sufficient force . . . " (222).

5. Cf., for example, 1.2.128, 271; 1.3.84. Cf. Miola 94–97.

6. For the Renaissance stereotype, see Woodbridge 79, 86, 125, 259, 308. See also Paster's convincing description of the conspirators' efforts to associate Caesar with a stereotypical view of women, which focuses on their incapacity to control bleeding; Portia's deliberately inflicted thigh wound reverses that stereotype (290–94, and *passim*). For an apropos and frequently expressed Renaissance comment on the Stoic ambition to achieve rational control by banishing emotion—an achievement which "leaves . . . no man at all, but rather . . . a marble simulacrum of a man"—see Erasmus 39–40.

7. On separate occasions, two perceptive students, John Woodmansee and Lisa Granered, first brought this point home to me, and suggested that Portia's suicide, effected when she "swallowed fire" (4.2.207), will have especially powerful implications for interpreters aware that the need for control of one's circumstances plays a large role in the psycho-dynamics of eating disorders. My reading of the scene (and the play) owes a large and more general debt to Kevin Farley, Mary Floyd-Wilson and Victoria Reed Gless.

8. On this point, see Bristol; Greene; and Kahn (this volume).

9. On some consequences of Allan Bloom's own charisma—"the splendid pedagogic charms of this great popularizer (of this great teacher)"—acutely analyzed by a former student, see Sedgwick 148–52.

# 15

# Transfer of Title in *Love's Labor's Lost*: Language, Individualism, Gender

**Katharine Eisaman Maus**

Influential feminist critics of Shakespeare have rarely dealt with Shakespeare's early, linguistically extravagant work.[1] Most have confined themselves to discussing Kate's capitulation scene in *The Taming of the Shrew*, or to tracing in the first years of Shakespeare's career basic plot or image patterns that recur in what is often considered the "mature" *oeuvre*. Understandably, feminists have preferred to concentrate upon the later comedies, the histories, the tragedies, and some of the romances. Proponents of a new critical discourse can most efficiently demonstrate the power of their approach by influencing the ways the most impeccably canonical Shakespearean texts are discussed in professional publications and conferences, and taught in the undergraduate and graduate classroom. Moreover, the perennially fascinating characterological complexity of Shakespeare's later work has proven congenial to feminist critics, allowing them an ample field upon which to display the insights that become available when gender becomes a primary analytical category.

Nonetheless, these critical predilections have some unfortunate consequences. Suspicion of a depoliticized formalism, whether New Critical or deconstructive, has sometimes encouraged feminists to imply dubious distinctions between the language of the plays and poems and their politics. In "The Rape in Shakespeare's *Lucrece*" Coppélia Kahn, for instance, complains that its "rhetorical display-pieces invite critical attention for their own sake, offering readers a happy escape from the poem's insistent concern with the relationship between sex and power" (45). In Kahn's formulation the feminist critic must resist such temptations, must look beneath the linguistically ornate surface to

I would like to thank Fred Maus, Clare Kinney, and the members of the University of Virginia Renaissance Area Discussion Group for their comments on a draft of this essay.

discern the social and characterological realities which make the work interesting and important.

In this repudiation of "mere rhetoric" Kahn follows, intentionally or not, a host of earlier critics who find themselves apologizing for the early Shakespeare's unseemly linguistic superfluity. In Harley Granville-Barker's account, *Love's Labor's Lost* seems the symptom of a Shakespearean artistic pubescence: "To many young poets of the time their language was a new-found wonder; its very handling gave them pleasure. The amazing things it could be made to do!" (9). For James Calderwood, *Love's Labor's Lost* shows the young Shakespeare "passing from a sensuous enchantment with language, a wantoning with words, to a serious consideration of his medium, his art, and their relation to the social order" ("Wantoning" 318). Calderwood sees *Love's Labor's Lost* as a rite of passage after which Shakespeare, having sown his verbal wild oats, shakes off such adolescent temptations to indulgence, settles down to become the artistic equivalent of a responsible husband, and begins to write the history plays and romantic comedies we value today. Feminist criticism might well question the assumptions about manly adulthood upon which such a critical practice relies, but by and large it has not bothered to do so.

Meanwhile critics who do not concern themselves with gender, but who do confront directly the remarkable linguistic elaborateness of *Love's Labor's Lost*, have developed an interesting critical perspective upon the play. William Carroll and Keir Elam discuss *Love's Labor's Lost* in terms of sixteenth-century Neoplatonic linguistic philosophy, popularized in Elizabethan England as part of a new self-consciousness about the expressiveness and literary potential of the vernacular. An essentialist theory of language derived from Plato's *Cratylus* proved particularly influential: a theory, that is, that "there is an inherent rightness in names, that names are not arbitrary signs but are in some sense themselves the essence of what is named" (Carroll 12).[2] Carroll and Elam maintain that *Love's Labor's Lost* is both deeply invested in, and deeply critical of, a Cratylanism they associate with Navarre's Academy. In the course of the play, both critics argue, the inadequacy of this linguistic theory becomes increasingly obvious. Its plausibility is hopelessly undermined by elaborate puns, daring tropes, novel epithets, multilingual malapropisms, ambiguities intended and unintended by the characters: all the verbal exorbitance for which *Love's Labor's Lost* has long been condemned.

By demonstrating that important sixteenth-century philosophical debates about words and meaning inform the play's linguistic self-consciousness, Carroll and Elam are able to make impressive sense of features of *Love's Labor's Lost* previously considered trivial. In their account, the play is not just a display of linguistic possibilities; it is *about* linguistic possibility. My own focus upon issues of naming and reference in the pages that follow bespeak my indebtedness to their arguments. Nonetheless, their thesis has its limitations. Both critics abstract the linguistic issues in *Love's Labor's Lost* from the sexual politics of its comic plot, ignoring the misogynist assumptions upon which Navarre's failed Academy is founded, the affinities insisted upon in the play between verbal invention and erotic energy, and the tense sexual dynamics of the unexpectedly anti-comic conclusion. In consequence their readings seem deracinated from and unenlightened about psychological or generic concerns.

Is it possible for feminist criticism to avoid, on the one hand, treating Shakespearean verbal complexity as a distraction from politics or psychology, and on the other, treating politics or psychology as a distraction from verbal complexity? Perhaps we ought to wonder not merely why Shakespeare writes a play overtly concerned with linguistic problems and with problems of figuration, but why these problems become important in this unusual comedy, in which a group of men and a group of women fail to reconcile their differences. To answer this question, we need to understand how apparently abstract intuitions about linguistic meaning acquire psychological and political urgency in the court of Navarre. For in fact, I shall argue, some of the important linguistic issues in *Love's Labor's Lost* are inseparable from its generic, comic concern with sexual politics and with the construction of a gendered identity in a social context.[3]

As *Love's Labor's Lost* begins, the King of Navarre is completing his plans for an "Academy" devoted to celibate study and to the mortification of the senses, and requiring his courtiers to sign a document listing the conditions by which they propose to live for the next three years. He explains his rationale in an intricate opening speech, the complexities of which deserve close attention:

> Let fame, that all hunt after in their lives,
> Live register'd upon our brazen tombs,
> And then grace us in the disgrace of death;
> When, spite of cormorant devouring Time,
> Th'endeavor of this present breath may buy
> That honor which shall bate his scythe's keen edge
> And make us heirs of all eternity.

> Therefore, brave conquerors—for so you are,
> That war against your own affections
> And the huge army of the world's desires—
> Our late edict shall strongly stand in force:
> Navarre shall be the wonder of the world;
> Our court shall be a little academe,
> Still and contemplative in living art. (1.1.1.–14)[4]

What is the appeal of this project? As a way for a king to spend his time, it would have been inconceivable a few generations earlier. In the course of the sixteenth century, however, the humanist emphasis on the education of secular leaders makes intellectual pursuits, previously considered fitting only for churchmen, newly respectable for an aristocrat.[5] Thus while we learn in the second act that Navarre's late father involved himself in military adventures, the son, like the young Hamlet in a later play, turns to scholarship. As a result, the conflicts he anticipates are largely spiritual or internal. The new enemies are one's own affections, the huge army of the world's desires.

Interestingly, however, Navarre assumes that the metaphors of the battlefield remain appropriate, and the anticipated gratification similar. In the *Courtier* Castiglione writes: "Where the courtier is at skirmish, or assault, or battle upon the land, or in such other places of enterprise, he ought to work the matter wisely in separating himself from the multitude, and undertake noble and bold feats which he hath to do, with as little company as he can, and in the sight of noble men that be of most estimation in the camp . . . for indeed it is meet to set forth to the shew things well done (95).[6] Castiglione's courtier neither concerns himself with military discipline, nor sees himself as carrying out part of an overall strategy involving an entire army. Rather he uses the circumstances of conflict to detach himself from the group and cut an unmistakable figure in the eyes of others. In *Love's Labor's Lost*, Navarre wants the same rewards from scholarly asceticism. Traditional forms of contemplation, dissolving the individual in the apprehension of the absolute, are not for him. Rather he imagines himself undergoing the contemplative life as if it were a heroic ordeal, emerging victorious and universally admired. Self-mortification becomes a means to self-exaltation, a way to acquire the traditional aristocratic *desiderata*, honor and fame.[7] The potential absurdities of such a combination will be suggested later in the play in the figures of Armado, the bombastic soldier, and Holofernes, the militant pedant, who burlesque from opposite directions, so to speak, Navarre's idealized conflation of martial valor with learning and eloquence.

Navarre's opening speech, as well as the scene that follows it, connects his particular kind of identity-formation with a particular rhetorical anxiety. *Love's Labor's Lost* begins with edicts proclaimed, contracts endorsed, and promises extracted—a flurry of what J. L. Austin calls "performative utterances." This kind of language is not referential; it performs actions rather than describe or point to an extralinguistic reality. As such, performative utterances seem to close the gap between signifier and signified, *verba* and *res*, word and world. Closing that gap is something Navarre seems to find highly desirable. In his opening speech he suggests that the fame he expects for his ascetic heroism will take the form of a stable description, a name permanently "registered" on a tomb. "Navarre shall be the wonder of the world!" In the meantime he demands another sort of stabilization of and through the name, asking his courtiers to ratify their promises with their signatures.

Navarre's desire for the permanence of his own name and those of his friends is quite comprehensible, because proper nouns seem to attach uniquely and immutably to their referents as other identifying features might not. They are, as Hobbes puts it, "singular to only one thing."[8] If, moreover, William Carroll is right that Navarre would like to believe that names "are not arbitrary signs but are in some sense the essence of what is named," if *verba* and *res* are really inseparable, then ensuring the permanence of the name becomes a magical way of ensuring the permanence of the self. Thus the King sees an inscription upon the tomb as a way of overcoming death. If his logic seems specious here, it is no more so than that of many Renaissance writers of love poetry, Shakespeare included, who assert that their words grant the beloved a kind of immortality.[9]

Navarre's opening speech suggests, however, that the permanence he desires is not merely an automatic consequence of the usual relationship between names and things. Rather, it is a hard-won achievement. He describes a kind of transaction: hardships in the present "buy" an honor that mitigates the effects of mortality. In this passage he seems less the Cratylan essentialist than the prudent investor who has learned how to make a profit from "cormorant devouring Time," contractually assenting to deprivation in the short term in order to realize a long term gain. This long term gain is represented as an inheritance: the King expects that he and his friends will become "heirs of all eternity."

What are the implications of these metaphors? Why should the problem of stabilizing the name, of making an indissoluble connection between signifier and signified, be formulated in terms of exchange or inheritance? Perhaps an association between naming and inherited property seems "natural" for the

King because the aristocratic male name—Navarre, Berowne, Dumaine, Longaville—is normally an inherited name; moreover, it is the name of *what* is inherited, the piece of property that guarantees its owner income and status.

The close connection in the aristocratic mind between a name and a title to property is adumbrated later in the play, when Longaville catches sight of a lady, immediately falls in love with her, and "desires her name" of Boyet. Boyet playfully refuses to tell him, so Longaville rephrases his request:

Pray you, sir, whose daughter?
*Boyet:* Her mother's, I have heard.
*Longaville:* God's blessing on your beard!
*Boyet:* Good sir, be not offended.
She is an heir of Falconbridge.
*Longaville:* Nay, my choler is ended.
She is a most sweet lady. (2.1.201–07)

And Longaville exits forthwith, satisfied despite never, apparently, receiving an answer to his question. For it is Maria's place in the network of aristocratic entitlements that matters to Longaville, that constitutes her "name."

The inextricability of person and property has important consequences for the way the King is able to formulate his desire for immortal fame. When he declares, in his opening speech, that "Navarre shall be the wonder of the world!" it is unclear whether he is referring to himself—the founder of the Academy—or rather to the site upon which it will be located. (Likewise, when Boyet tells Longaville that Maria is "an heir of Falconbridge," there is no way of knowing whether Falconbridge is *what* or *from whom* she will inherit.) A related ambiguity confuses the claim Navarre makes in his opening speech, when he imagines himself and his associates as the "heirs of all eternity." Is he thinking of eternity as testator or as bequest?

Perhaps Navarre sees no reason to distinguish the two possibilities because for him they have amounted to the same thing: he has inherited the territory of Navarre from a father named Navarre. But becoming the "heir of eternity" is more problematic, since inheritance requires the death of the previous possessor, and eternity is precisely what does not die. The dream of a fixed name, called forth by an anxiety about "the disgrace of death," turns out paradoxically, as the King has formulated it, to need what it wants to resist or avoid.

In other words, the King demands a name that will refer permanently and uniquely to *him*, but he is frustrated by the fact that the aristocratic male name is a doubly transferred name—transferred in space, so to speak, from possession to possessor, and then again in time, down the generations from one possessor to the next. The names the courtiers "subscribe" to Navarre's document in the first scene are metonymies in both a synchronic and a diachronic sense.[10] And an aristocrat's name seems, as proper names go, an unusually unstable matter, since if his father or older brother dies, then his name changes to reflect the alteration in status and property rights.

Moreover, the Cratylan position is stronger than is required to maintain the aristocratic privilege of Navarre and his courtiers. The landowning class as a group needs not fixity of reference but predictability of reference: regular and orderly methods of managing the necessary transfer of title from father to child, from debtor to lender, from buyer to seller. The propriety of the aristocratic proper name actually rests not upon an essential, immutable connection to the individual whom it denotes, but upon the legitimacy of the means by which that name has been acquired and by which it will be passed along. Thus when Boyet praises Navarre as "the sole inheritor / Of all perfections that a man may owe" (2.1.5–6), he uses "owe" here in its common Renaissance sense, a variant of "own." But the language simultaneously invokes the sense still current today, suggesting not possession but its apparent opposite, debt—the obligation to relinquish ownership. These two senses are not as inconsistent as they might seem. The fact of death, which makes possible the acquisition of property from one's ancestors, also necessitates its eventual surrender.

For Navarre, however, this is not good enough. To be "matchless," in his terms, is to take possession of his proper name once and for all. But this desire is covertly, illogically linked to an incompatible order of inherited transfer, in which the possessor of a name is merely the temporary bearer of a title acquired from the father and passed along to the son. Resisting the inevitability of his own mortality, Navarre resists at the same time the effect his mortality has upon the meaning of his name. Without acknowledging it, he asks to be installed forever in a place that he is only allowed to occupy for the time being. The imagery of inheritance that comes naturally to him thus seems ill-suited to the aggressively meritocratic and competitive quality of the sentiments he uses that imagery to express. Navarre makes, as it were, an excessive demand upon the very system to which he owes his preeminence.

The linguistic confusion here is structurally identical with an ambiguous feature of Renaissance aristocratic psychology first discussed by Jacob Burckhardt and analyzed more recently by Stephen Greenblatt. Well-off, educated men in early modern Europe manifest a powerful desire to distinguish themselves from each other, to demonstrate their freedom and uniqueness. But because the aristocratic impulse to individuality is the cultural construction of a particular class, the aristocrat's convictions about his own independence and originality are themselves inevitably derivative, part of a group *ethos*. What seems like a meritocratic claim has subterranean links to a system of inherited entitlement it seems to oppose or subvert. In *Love's Labor's Lost*, the meritorious aristocrat desires an identity based upon his own individual exploits, but in fact derives his prestige not from his own heroic exertions, but from the transferred glory of accomplished ancestors.

Given this incoherence, it is not surprising that the intelligent Berowne finds Navarre's scheme objectionable. He suggests a different way of conceiving of the relation between name and referent:

> These earthly godfathers of heaven's lights,
> That give a name to every fixed star,
> Have no more profit of their shining nights
> Than those that walk and wot not what they are. (1.1.88–91)

The "name" for Berowne's purposes is the first or Christian name, bestowed by a godfather who has no proprietary interest in the child, rather than the last or family name, derived from a father whose stake in his own offspring is far more consequential. Berowne suggests that the names of the fixed stars have nothing to do with how they originated, whether they shine, or who profits from them. Language is merely arbitrary, unconnected to facts about inheritance and social privilege.

Berowne's separation of naming from paternity has a number of advantages. Not only does his account avoid the contradictions of Navarre's essentialism, but it promotes more radical possibilities for individuation, since if signifiers are no longer strictly aligned with signifieds, then the topic of an utterance no longer determines usage. The idiosyncratic pressures of the speaker's personality and choices—his individual *style*—determines how he speaks and what he says. Not surprisingly, most critics of *Love's Labor's Lost* have seen Berowne as the most "realistic" or "fully realized" character in the play, a harbinger of the highly particularized protagonists of the romantic comedies Shakespeare writes a few years later.[11]

Nor is it surprising that despite his expressed doubts, Berowne does agree to participate in Navarre's project, for despite their difference the two men share important common ground. For both of them, the linguistic problem of what and how names mean is inextricably linked to a psychological problem of self-construction. They both want to be "individuals," though they envision different paths to that goal. As such they are both caught up in what might be called the quintessential humanist problem, that is the relation of original to copy, archetype to type, model to imitation, source to derivation, ancestor to heir.[12] Much of the so-called action in *Love's Labor's Lost*, a virtually plotless play, concerns the manifold ways in which one thing can stand in for another, replacing and displacing it: Dull's representation, or reprehension, as he calls it, of the King's authority; Armado's search for precedents in love; the oddly prolonged discussion about whether Cain can substitute for Adam in an old joke about the moon; the bizarre argument about how many actors are going to "pursent" (present, personate) the Nine Worthies. On a dramatic level the problem might be seen as intrinsic to the theatrical medium, in which a character is always an impersonation or counterfeit. On the linguistic level the problem is one of the substitutability of one word for another, and finds expression in the play's obsession with figures of synonymy: coelo, the sky, the welkin, the heaven; wench, damsel, virgin, maid; carry-tale, please-man, zany, mumble-news, trencher-knight. The most elaborate and gratuitous example of the anxiety generated by such substitutions is the curiously exaggerated hostility the courtiers displayed at the masque of the Nine Worthies near the end of the play. Their ridicule suggests a discomfort at the way the names and attributes of quintessentially exemplary individuals—Hector, Hercules, Alexander, Judas Maccabeus—are subject to appropriation by incompetent place-holders, degraded even at the moment of memorialization.

*Costard:* I Pompey am,—
*Berowne:* You lie, you are not he. (5.2.541)

While the masque purportedly celebrates the immortal fame of virtuous heroes, it actually conducts a final assault upon the aristocratic fantasy of an absolute heroic identity, unalterable by death or by the passage of time.

The issues about language and meaning that Navarre and his courtiers debate in the first scene of *Love's Labor's Lost*, and which continue to arise in many of the scenes thereafter, are thus profoundly implicated in their own sense of themselves as men of a particular class and generation. In Navarre's case the unacknowledged incoherence of this self-conception is connected with a refusal to acknowledge women, whose role in the production of a new generation involves them indispensably in the process of title transfer. Navarre establishes "Academe" as an entirely male community, protected from female incursion by a penalty reminiscent of Tereus's abuse of Philomela: any woman who approaches the court will have her tongue cut out. With some help from Longaville, who devises this threat, Navarre wishfully defines language as a wholly male possession, and imagines women as speechless and passive. Their attitude is consistent with that expressed in English Renaissance linguistic and historical writing, which often associates linguistic slippage and transfer with a female sexuality both indispensable for social and familial order and potentially uncontrollable by that order.[13] William Camden, for instance, looking back at the English spoken before the Norman invasion, admires the Anglo-Saxon preference for expressing complex or abstract ideas in compound words derived from native elements, rather than importing words, as sixteenth-century speakers do, from French, Latin, or Greek:

> Our ancestors seemed . . . as jealous of their native language, as those Britons which passed hence into Armorica in France, and marrying strange women there, did cut out their tongues, lest their children should corrupt their language with their mothers' tongues. (32)

By means of a violence identical to that contemplated by Navarre and his courtiers in the first scene of *Love's Labor's Lost*, the British fathers maintain the fixity and purity of their language by passing it directly to the next generation, without the intrusion of the women who under ordinary circumstances would introduce their children to language. The accurate transfer of the mother tongue from generation to generation requires the silencing of actual mothers. Like Navarre in *Love's Labor's Lost*, Camden associates originary language, true naming, with the male. By contrast, the openness of modern English to alien influence constitutes a kind of corruption of its bloodline, which perhaps contributes to its hybrid vigor but which also defines regulation and makes purity impossible. Navarre's desire to clarify the relation between names and things thus not surprisingly requires the exclusion of female sexuality, associated as it is with a corruption of the truth. Since Berowne is not so heavily invested in this particular notion of truth—since for him signifiers are arbitrarily applied anyhow—Navarre's interdictions make no sense to him, and he attempts to make a case for a more accommodating attitude toward women.

If Navarre's fantasy of a fixed name represents a kind of excessive attempt to guarantee *aristocratic* privilege, the fantasy of the silent woman represents a similarly excessive assertion of *male* privilege. The connections between these two kinds of privilege quickly become clear. The Princess of France arrives to enquire about title to Aquitane, a title disputed because of a deal made between her father and Navarre's father. As she enters for the first time at the beginning of the second act, her courtier, Boyet, is describing her mission to her:

> Consider who the King your father sends,
> To whom he sends, and what's his embassy:
> Yourself, held precious in the world's esteem,
> To parley with the sole inheritor
> Of all perfections that a man may owe,
> Matchless Navarre; the plea of no less weight
> Than Aquitaine, a dowry for a queen. (2.1.2–8)

In Boyet's account the Princess seems to exemplify woman's place in a strict patriarchal system, an item of exchange among men. While Navarre's position, as we have already seen, is that of an heir ("the sole inheritor / Of all perfections") the Princess is by contrast a valued object, something "held precious in the world's esteem." Her task requires her to act as an intermediary between father and potential husband, representing her father's interest in a negotiation for a territory described as a "dowry." Nonetheless, her arrival forces "matchless Navarre"—matchless not only in the sense of being unique, but in the sense of being still unmarried—to confront everything he has tried to repress: the involvement of women in the process of title transfer, the dependence of the present generation upon the actions of its predecessors, and the possibility that the title itself may be ambiguous, subject to conflicting claims.

Moreover, since the paternal source of her authority is remote, offstage, the Princess seems to operate in the world of the play as a power in her own right. Her first action is to command one of her male followers to act as deputy or "fair solicitor" between herself and the young King. The drama of title transfer, in other words, casts the Princess as both object and subject in a system of exchange. Another way of describing this doubleness is that the women in *Love's Labor's Lost* turn out to talk, as well as to listen to themselves being talked about.[14] Their lovers imagine them attending silently to sonneteering monologues, the topics and recipients of an erotic discourse they themselves are not permitted to speak. But the Princess and her ladies are, in fact, vocal and witty critics of the poems and gifts sent to them by the men. The female tongues the men imagine excising in the first scene turn out to be cutting, not cut: by 5.2 Boyet is remarking gleefully that "The tongues of mocking wenches are as keen/ As is the razor's edge invisible" (5.2.256–57). As the play proceeds the women appropriate many of the postures associated with the subject-position conventionally occupied by an aggressive male lover. In 4.1 Rosaline, skillfully launching arrows at a target, indulges simultaneously in a bawdy dialogue with Boyet in which she identifies herself as the shooter / suitor who "hits" (copulates with) the "mark" (female genital) with a "prick." In the hunting scenes, the Amazonian princess penetrates her deer / dear with a similar phallic efficiency; as Holofernes puts it, "The preyful Princess pierc'd and prick'd a pretty pleasing pricket" (4.2.55–56). Helpless at last, Berowne presents himself to Rosaline as a target:

> Here stand I, lady; dart thy skill at me;
> Bruise me with scorn, confound me with a flout;
> Thrust thy sharp wit quite through my ignorance;
> Cut me to pieces with thy keen conceit. (5.2.396–99)

The mutilated Philomela of the first scene is here replaced by the male victim Orpheus, dismembered by unruly female Bacchantes.

How are we to understand the kinds of power and prestige the women in the play find it possible to acquire and deploy?[15] In theory, the role of the female in the passing down of titles is merely instrumental. In *Love's Labor's Lost* the women do not have surnames at all, and in Shakespeare's England, a woman's property like her surname ordinarily disappears into her husband's when she marries. Aristocratic men are endowed with the goods, power, and equipment they need to become Renaissance self-fashioners and heirs of all eternity, while the female role seems in contrast to be defined as purely ancillary. Thus when Boyet tells the enamored Longaville that Maria is her mother's daughter, Longaville finds it a mere impertinence. He imagines the mother as a necessary but ideally unnoticed conduit between the father who possesses wealth and the child who will inherit it. For ideally, under the rule of primogeniture, the patriarch passes the bulk of his property to his eldest son, who succeeds to his position of power over the resources of the family.

In practice, however, things do not always work this way. To function smoothly, primogeniture requires a son who survives to manhood. When there is no surviving son, inheritance customs diverge; in some systems, title to the property goes to the next surviving relative, even if that relative is female, and in others, title passes over the females to the next surviving male, if one can be found. In England, where *Love's Labor's Lost* is written, the first practice was normal; in France, where the play is set, the second prevailed; but in both cases an absence of male heirs could allow women to occupy places in the inheritance system supposedly reserved for men. So even while Longaville belittles the role of the mother he is gratified to learn that the lady he desires is "the heir of Falconbridge." Just as the conventions of sonneteering courtship employed by Navarre and his associates deny women a position from which to speak—a position the women nonetheless find it possible to appropriate for themselves—so in some circumstances the conventions of inheritance grant aristocratic women the very power they seem at first glance designed to preclude. But this does not really feminize power, since the woman's possession of it is accidental, perhaps temporary, and most importantly remains defined in male terms. For despite their apparent independence, the Princess and her ladies never have available to them a specifically *feminine* subjectivity, a special claim upon the cultural or material resources available to the men. Camped for the duration of the play in a field just outside the borders of the male domain, they find it possible to insinuate themselves precariously into a subject-position normally defined as male, taking advantage of the absence, naiveté, or inattentiveness of those who are its normal occupants. This is why Rosaline's and the Princess's seizure of initiative is figured by phallic attributes (pricking the pricket) and why the men may react by accusing them of a usurpation which, in fact, they have in a way committed.

The possibility of a woman inhabiting such roles, however, does function to cut social facts loose from biological ones and to blur or complicate the significance of gender difference. Moreover, it suggests that the sharp demarcation between men and women Navarre insists upon early in the play involves a significant mystification of the facts of male lives. For it is possible to think of men, too, as conduits through which the family title passes from generation to generation. Unlike their mothers and sisters, male heirs are allowed some control over their property in their lifetimes, but as we have already seen this may not satisfy those to whom the fact of mortality itself seems unacceptable. Perhaps the men exaggerate the passivity and discursive inconsequence of the women in order to displace onto them an anxiety generated by their own inconsistent sense of identity: how are they to reconcile an inherited status, which must eventually be relinquished to the next generation, with an energetic egoism that refuses to give up what it has acquired, defying "cormorant devouring Time" with a demand for eternity?

And there are further complications. Since a woman can function as a subject rather than a mere object or a conduit, with a mind and a speech of her own, she possesses the power to interrupt or derail the orderly process of transferring names from father to son, from original to likeness. This disruptive potential is the subject of many of the notoriously bawdy double-entendres in *Love's Labor's Lost*. One class of such jokes implies fantasies of simply bypassing female subjectivity altogether: by rape, in which the woman's desires are overruled, or by homosexuality or onanism, in which they become irrelevant. Another class of jokes recognizes the indispensability of female subjectivity for the functioning of kinship networks and property transfers, but stresses the unreliability built into such a system. The constant witticisms about light women, horns, and cuckoos constitute reminders that although fathers may possess titles, their relationship to the children who will inherit those titles is always open to question.[16]

Many critics have noticed that the aristocratic women in *Love's Labor's Lost* seem more "serious" than their male counterparts about the ways language can be used—a seriousness evident in the attitudes they express toward language rather than in any plain-style austerity of usage.[17] The Princess, for instance, repeatedly deplores the "painted flourish" of flattery and professes horror at oath-breaking; Rosaline regrets Berowne's uncontrolled wit. It is hardly surprising that the women are more likely than the men to construe the referentiality and reliability of words as a specifically *moral* issue. They cannot help knowing that the truth of names in patriarchy is the consequence not of some intrinsic connection between names and things but of female sexual fidelity.

While "truth" for the men, in other words, is an issue of right definitions—a matter of correctly aligning words and things-in-the-world—for the women "truth" is a behavioral matter, the keeping of a marital vow that demands submission to a patriarchal order. For the women, truth is an exercise not of the intellect but of the will: and not, moreover, of an ambitiously self-assertive will but of a will that disciplines itself, that brings desires into accord with social requirements. For the Princess and her ladies are not revolutionaries. They do not want to undermine or escape from patriarchy, but to find themselves a secure and relatively advantageous position within it. Thus Berowne's skepticism, with its refusal to acknowledge a connection between words and practice, is despite its apparent tolerance at least as threatening to their interests as Navarre's rigid misogynist exclusivism. For the happiness of their lives will depend upon their husbands' scrupulous fulfillment of their contractual obligations in marriage.

The aristocratic women's relatively earnest association of truth with virtuous self-restraint has, however, a flip side—a playful awareness of the way they can, by their own initiative, alter the relationship between sign and referent. When they learn that their lovers, disguised as Muscovites, are coming to woo them, the ladies mask, and exchange among themselves the love-tokens the men have just sent them. They know that the lords will not think of questioning the symbols of male entitlement—that they will be, in the Princess's phrase, "deceived by these removes" (5.2.135). As Berowne laments when he learns of the ruse, "we/ Following the sign, wooed but the sign of she" (5.2.469). The ladies in *Love's Labor's Lost* perform the equivalent of a bed-trick on the level of the signifier. The way the Princess describes the deception suggests that the aristocratic concern with property can be as pressing for the women as for the men:

> There's no such sport as sport by sport o'erthrown,
> To make theirs ours and ours none but our own. (5.2.153–54)

Appropriating male sport and subsuming it under the rubric of a sport "owned" by the women, she reverses the direction in which property and power ordinarily flow in patriarchal marriage. Although it is never as ambitious, the Princess's desire for self-ownership—"ours none but our own"—resembles Navarre's competitive individualism in some respects. But while Navarre's strategies of self-assertion involve thinking of the relationship of name and thing as a clear and permanent matter, the Princess's self-assertion involves subverting that clarity and permanence, rupturing the connections between desire and its objects, signifier and signified. These reversals are, however, limited ones, unlike Berowne's more wholesale subversions: a game in which rules and durations are carefully specified.

The significant conceptual differences between the sexes become starkly evident at the end of the play, when Jacquenetta's pregnancy is announced, the death of the King of France is reported, and the aristocratic women refuse to marry the men. The men have sworn to abjure the company of women, but they find themselves in love nonetheless. Berowne satisfies them that their perjury can be overcome by a process of redefinition, that the performative utterances with which the play began do not really matter. In Berowne's account the eyes of women become sources of truth:

> From women's eyes this doctrine I derive:
> They are the grounds, the books, the academes,
> From whence doth spring the true Promethean fire.
>
> . . .
>
> For where is there any author in the world
> Teaches such beauty as a woman's eye?
>
> . . .
>
> Then when ourselves we see in ladies' eyes,
> Do we not likewise see our learning there? (4.3.298–312)

Berowne reformulates the place of sexual desire in the pursuit of knowledge, repudiating Navarre's original conception of passion as an enemy to the scholar's "still and contemplative" mind. The truth-seeker comes upon himself not directly, but as a displaced image, reflected in the object of his passion. Berowne rejects Navarre's notion that by some strenuous effort of self-creation the scholar can achieve a perfect autonomy. Nonetheless, like Navarre, Berowne assumes that truth is a *place*, a locus of authority from which originary meaning issues. Although he installs women in that place of privilege, his assumptions are very different from those of the women themselves, whose conception of truth is social and contractual.

Unfortunately for the men, the women insist upon the seriousness of male vacillation far more vigorously than might be expected. The Shakespearean heroine—Julia in *Two Gentlemen of Verona*, Helena in *A Midsummer Night's Dream*, Hero in *Much Ado*, Mariana in *Measure for Measure*, Imogen in *Cymbeline*—typically asks not that her lover has kept faith throughout the play, but that he promise improvement in the future. Comic endings require a certain female charity, or laxness of standards, that the Princess and her entourage refuse to endorse. In *Love's Labor's Lost*, the women's refusal to credit the men's apparently sincere declarations of ardor makes the predictable unions impossible. Instead, in the last lines of the play, the women impose tasks upon the lovers. The Princess insists that Navarre perform a version of his original project, sequestering himself in a hermitage for a year, learning to keep his word. Rosaline sends Berowne away to try jesting with the sick at hospital beds:

> A jest's prosperity lies in the ear
> Of him that hears it, never in the tongue
> Of him that makes it. (5.2.851–53)

These tasks involve a re-education in the nature of truth as the women conceive it: as the faithful submission to the command of another, and as a speech-act completed not when it is uttered but when it is heard and assented to.

The ending of *Love's Labor's Lost* is derailed, then, because the women find it impossible to believe the men. But issues of belief, trust, and faith are implicated in relations of power. The death of fathers—Navarre's before the play begins, the Princess's as it ends—makes the transfer of title possible, indeed necessary, imposing the pleasures and obligations of reproduction upon the next generation. Making these transfers, however, requires the cooperation of women, and *Love's Labor's Lost* calls the inevitability of this cooperation into question. The only union in the play, Armado's and Jacquenetta's, provides a father's name to a child whose paternity is in fact very much in doubt. The aristocratic women disrupt the process of transfer by a different strategy, insisting upon the postponement of their nuptials. "Our wooing doth not end like an old play" complains Berowne, "Jack hath not Jill. These ladies courtesy/ Might well have made our sport a comedy" (5.2.864–66).

Patricia Parker has recently argued that the delay of closure in courtship and in literature is identified with women's interest and women's power, and the pressure towards an ending represents reimposition of a stable patriarchal order in which men can exert their control unchallenged (8–35). Courtship, reversing the normal currents of social authority, grants women a kind of power, a power Berowne casts in philosophical terms when he grants an originary status to women, instead of defining them as secondary, derivative, or ancillary. "O! I am yours, and all that I possess," he declares to Rosaline (5.2.383). This ownership of men by women is a temporary matter, however, and will be reversed in the event of their marriage. For normally, women finally submit to men, finally extend the "courtesy" that allows courtship to come to an end. But *Love's Labor's Lost* ends without closure, with the women's insistence upon further delay. They sustain the fiction of their power in order, they hope, to be able to dispense with it at last.

A refusal to provide the expected satisfactions of a comic denouement, then, is part and parcel with the play's inquiry into problems of signification. The socially prescribed ways the characters conceive of themselves, and the ways they try and fail to interact with each other across the psychic rifts of gender difference, are deeply implicated in anxieties about the naturalness of meaningful language, and with a closely related concern for the elusiveness and displacement of origin. The linguistic pleasures and perplexities of *Love's Labor's Lost* are inseparable from its sexual politics, as the play calls the relations between the sexes and the appropriateness of names into question by the same means and for similar reasons.

## NOTES

1. For instance, Carol Neely gets underway with *Much Ado About Nothing;* Peter Erickson with *As You Like It;* Marianne Novy with *The Taming of the Shrew.* Linda Bamber discusses *Twelfth Night* and *The Merchant of Venice* in the context of the histories and tragedies. The earlier plays addressed by the essays in *The Woman's Part* are *Richard III* and *The Taming of the Shrew.* Coppélia Kahn's *Man's Estate* contains a chapter on *Venus and Adonis,* but as in her essay on *The Rape of Lucrece,* she downplays Shakespeare's rhetorical self-consciousness in order to pursue other lines of inquiry.

2. Keir Elam, 114–58, makes a somewhat more elaborate philosophical argument with similar consequences for a reading of the play.

3. A fuller reading than I have room to present here would take account of class as well as gender. *Love's Labor's Lost* explicitly frames the interactions among aristocrats, professionals, and peasantry in terms of the possession of a literacy imagined in humanist terms as both the ability to read and write and as access to the classical past.

4. All references are to the Arden edition of *Love's Labor's Lost*, ed. Richard David.

5. Numerous historians of education have commented upon the significance of this change in the conception of the aristocrat, and its impact upon educational institutions and curricula. See, e.g., J. H. Hexter; Mark H. Curtis, *Oxford;* Lawrence Stone, "Educational Revolution".

6. I have modernized the spelling in this and other passages from Renaissance texts.

7. In fact, by the latter part of the sixteenth century changes in military technology have already rendered obsolete the individualistic military strategy Castiglione describes. With the widespread employment of weapons capable of killing at long range (muskets, cannons, etc.), sophisticated group maneuvers become more effective than uncoordinated one-to-one confrontations in the battlefield. For a succinct account of these changes see, e.g., Felix Gilbert. One reason Navarre may be searching for an alternative form of self-display is that older means of acquiring honor in hand-to-hand combat are no longer available, except in the artificial circumstances of the jousting ring.

8. Cf. Elam 120–21: "The great paradigm for language at large in *Love's Labor's Lost* is the proper name . . . the appeal, as it were, of appellation is evident first in the obsessive adamic ceremony of nomination as such and in the very range of names for naming drawn upon . . . and then in the carefully cultivated anxiety that the pedants in particular express over nominal propriety." Although she does not deal with *Love's Labor's Lost*, or with much other Shakespeare for that matter, Anne Ferry (69–80) usefully illuminates the privilege given to the proper name in sixteenth-century linguistic theory.

9. It is also a kind of error that Shakespeare elsewhere associates with royalty. What a king says or demands often happens, and the correlation between his words and the real world can present itself to him as an issue about the nature of language rather than about the nature of politics. Thus Sigurd Burckhardt writes about Lear: "The full, gapless identity of sentence and of power, of word and act, is the essence of Lear's conception of himself and his place" (276). But of course this is a mystification. The end of the first scene of *Love's Labor's Lost* demonstrates efficiently that the truth of the King's words requires the subject's participation: Costard, arrested in the company of Jacquenetta and asked if he had noticed the decree forbidding him the company of women, admits "much the hearing of it, but little the marking of it."

10. The sixteenth-century antiquarian William Camden remarks upon the impulse to suppress the metonymic transfer of the name from places to persons: "I cannot see why men should think that their ancestors gave names to places, when the places bare those very names, before any men did their surnames. Yea the very terminations of the names are such as are only proper and appliable to places, and not to persons in their significations. . . . Who would suppose hill, wood, field, ford, ditch, pole, pond, tower, or ton, and such like terminations to be convenient for men to bear in their names, unless they could also dream hills, woods, fieldes, [sic] fords, ponds, pounds, etc. to have been metamorphosed into men by some supernatural transformation" (104).

11. See, among many others, Bobbyann Roesen 415–18; Alexander Leggatt 79; Kenneth Muir, *Comic* 35.

12. For a discussion of the linguistic issues of origin, copy, and translation in humanist texts from Erasmus to Montaigne, see Terence Cave.

13. For a discussion of the way fears of female uncontrollability are figured in Renaissance rhetorical treatises, see Patricia Parker 103–13.

14. It is perhaps easy to exaggerate what seems to be a validation of female subjectivity in

this play; the Princess and her insouciant ladies are, after all, boy-actors speaking lines written for them by a male playwright. Nonetheless love-comedy virtually requires a different and more active fictional role for women than does the sonnet sequence: one needs to put female characters on the stage, and once they are there they must be given something to say.

15. Claude Lévi-Strauss (60–61) comments on women's ambiguous position both as signifiers in a kinship system that works as "a kind of language," and as producers of signs in their own right: "words do not speak, while women do."

16. A recognition of the mutual dependence of the sexes is, Berowne suggests, one of the differences between falling in love and indulging the rape fantasies that beguile the men in the early scenes; he recommends that the courtiers abandon their original oaths "for men's sake, the authors of these women/ Or women's sake, by whom we men are men" (4.3.356–57).

17. The usual way of interpreting this difference is in terms of the greater "maturity" of the women: see, e.g., Thomas Greene.

# 16

# On the Continuity of the *Henriad*: A Critique of Some Literary and Theatrical Approaches

Harry Berger, Jr.

## 1

By italicizing the name of Shakespeare's second tetralogy in my title, I mean to signal my commitment to the idea that it *is* a tetralogy—that it possesses tetralogical continuity, but a continuity that I distinguish from diachronic conceptions of linear sequence on the one hand and, on the other, from synchronic conceptions of organic wholeness or thematic unity. My notion of continuity is briefly touched on in the closing pages of this essay, but it is writ large in the study-in-progress in the *Henriad* from which the essay is excerpted. That study gets its energy and organization from the crossing of two interpretive procedures each of which picks out an analytically distinct aspect of the *Henriad*'s language. The first explores language as the medium of interlocutory drama that unfolds between and within individual speakers; the second explores language as the medium of collective language-games or discourses that circulate through the *Henriad* community. Together, the two procedures supply the textual evidence that supports the argument for tetralogical continuity. I have defined, discussed, and illustrated these procedures in previous studies, the first in *Imaginary Audition* and the second in "What Did the King Know and When Did He Know It?" The present essay is devoted mainly to a critique of the approaches to the *Henriad* in response to which the two procedures were developed. Section 2 reviews several literary approaches and section 3 examines an approach generated by the practical obstacles to the representation of continuity posed by the attempt to stage the tetralogy.

Before starting my critical survey, I think it will be helpful to distinguish, in a cursory way, my sense of the *Henriad*'s singleness from that of critics who insist on its "artistic integrity," "thematic unity," and "organic" wholeness.[1] These critics, who advance divergent accounts of the patterns holding the *Henriad* together even as they agree on its structural or sequential coherence, tend to be academic interpreters, armchair readers, rather than theater-centered interpreters. There are three reasons why I don't find their claims and accounts persuasive. The first is that no one arguing for the unity of the *Henriad* has confronted the objections of theater-centered critics who insist that the unifying features picked out by academic critics defy the conditions of performance. The occasional literary critic mentions this problem only to dismiss it,[2] but the objections are serious, and to meet them requires a critique of the basic assumptions that underwrite theater-centered attacks on armchair interpretations.[3]

The second reason is that all the accounts of the unity of the *Henriad* I have read treat either *Henry V* or its protagonist or both as flawed in some way, and it is often hard to determine whether what they find problematical is a praiseworthy effect of the text or a blameworthy defect in the author or an indecisive combination of the two. I think this uncertainty is symptomatic of theoretical as well as interpretive shortcomings in the various conceptions of tetralogical unity. The third reason is related to the general theoretical weakness inherent in appeals to thematic or aesthetic "unity," "artistic integrity," and "organic wholeness": such phrases hover uneasily between evaluative and descriptive status—"integrity," for example, denotes a virtue as well as the state (for better or for worse) of being whole, or intact—and such appeals glance toward criteria of aesthetic value and autonomy that have, in my opinion, been convincingly discredited. My concern is not with unity or integrity *per se,* and if I invoke the singleness of the text I do so in terms not of structure and synchrony but of dynamic transformation and diachrony. Thus, to illustrate these alternatives, on the one hand E. M. W. Tillyard locates the unity of the *Henriad* in a series of static contrasts (of style, character, and action) and a "network of cross-references" that boil down in his account to an uninterpreted list of anticipations and echoes; Tillyard premises that "Shakespeare knew what he was doing from the start and deliberately planned" the *Henriad* as a "single organism."[4] On the other hand, D. A. Traversi approaches the *Henriad* as a "closely integrated series" the continuity of whose argument "does not . . . imply that the four plays were originally conceived as a single unit, but simply that the latter terms of the series recognized the existence of the earlier" (2). I propose to put into play a stronger version of Traversi's thesis: the later terms are radically modified by their relation to the earlier terms, which are in turn modified by that modification.

For me, what makes the *Henriad* a single text is that it unfolds a process of continuous revision in which earlier textual moments persist like ghosts that haunt and complicate later moments, and thus take on new meaning. Its most highly charged vectors of meaning circulate through the sequence of four plays in such a manner that if you disconnect any one play from the others and read it independently you short those vectors out. This is especially true of the language and motivation of the three kings, in whose figures and relationships the system of the *Henriad*—the political and psychological dynamics of the system—becomes most perceptible. To continue the electrical metaphor, the three kings are hooked up in series, so that if any one of them goes out the others do too. Richard's power charges up Henry, whose resistance to it charges up Harry. Harry's resistance increases Henry's and Richard's power, just as Henry's increases Richard's. To disconnect any play from its tetralogical source is to impoverish the power of its drama and the resonance of its language. *Henry* V suffers most from disconnection, as the critical record testifies, and much of what follows will be directed not so much toward a new view of Harry as toward a new way of conceiving the interpretive problems his language poses when the *Henriad* is read as a single text.

## 2

The reading that supports this argument is organized by the practices of imaginary audition and discursive analysis. These provide the interpretive armature of the present study. Their orientation toward the text is conditioned by my concern to put into play the model of stage-centered reading described in *Imaginary Audition*, a model that attends to the structure and circumstances of theatrical performance (and of its intrafictional representation) without sacrificing attention to the demands and opportunities peculiar to reading. No approach develops out of thin air, and mine is situated at the center of a complex network of ongoing negotiations with other critical approaches and their practitioners. It owes much more to their imaginative, responsive, and generative encounters with Shakespeare than the references scattered throughout my text and footnotes can adequately indicate. The debt deepens when I consider how much I have learned in the struggle to wean their insights from their interpretive frameworks to my own.

One way to characterize the combination of borrowing and critique that constitutes the process of appropriation is to proclaim it nasty. I, of course, prefer a milder sentence: if my gratitude for the gifts donated by precursors manages to keep from toppling over into the abyss of anxiety and impotence, it is because their various positions are strongly and clearly enough staked out to enable me to differ with them, and so to go on. And if at times I seem more intent on harrying them than thanking them, that can only increase their generosity and my gratitude. I shall now perform this double service by describing some of the things they have taught me to avoid in the course of working out my own approach. To facilitate such a positioning or space-clearing move, I reduce the targets of my little critique to the following seven categories of reductionism.

(1) *Theatrical* reductionism restricts the interpretive possibilities inherent in the reader/text relation according to criteria more appropriate to the playgoer/performance relation. Theater-centered critics are concerned primarily with the actability or performability of plays and interpretations, thus they do not give high priority to the *Henriad* as a continuous text. The reductive effect produced by diminishing the links among the plays or ignoring their interactivity is especially noticeable—as one might expect—in theater-centred treatments of the last two plays in the sequence.

(2) *Metatheatrical* and *metadramatic* reductionism insists that whatever else the plays are about their most important and interesting themes are reflexive. That is, they are ultimately about theatricality, or mimesis, or role-playing, or language. The *metapoetic* version of this reduction shifts the focus of reflexivity to the author: the plays are about the artist's struggle with his material.[5] Since this concern tends to be coupled with attention to the artist's development it edges into another category,

(3) *developmental* reductionism, whose basic premise, "later is greater," adversely affects plays dated earlier in the chronological canon. So, for example, it is argued that *Julius Caesar* and *Hamlet* deal more adequately with "tragic" themes imperfectly treated in *Henry* V.[6] Another form of developmentalism finds its way into

(4) *psychoanalytic* reductionism, or, to be more precise, Freudian reductionism. The Freudian interpreter uses epigenetic (developmental) schemes of explanation, with their focus on the repression, displacement, etc., of oedipal and preoedipal relations as if they and the fictional subjects they are applied to were natural rather than constructed. The plays are sometimes evaluated according to the adequacy with which those schemes are represented: one of the reasons given for the superiority of *Hamlet* to *Henry* V is the mother's presence in the former play and her absence in the latter. Critics have occasionally connected this to the developing maturity of the playwright. In "What Did the King Know?" I suggested that the Lacanian critique of epigenesis applies to Freudian interpretations of Shakespeare, and that certain features of Lacanian analysis safeguard it from Freudian reductionism.

(5) *Ethical* reductionism channels interpretive energy into the project of judging whether and explaining why characters—Henry V, for example—are good or bad. This is a kind of voyeurism, and it is reductive because it ignores the central concern of the plays with the internal dramas of conscience, self-judgment, self-evasion, self-esteem. Ethical critics worry more about what they think of characters than what characters are shown to think of themselves. Yet the desire and danger of self-judgment are inscribed in both the interlocutory and discursive registers of the characters' language.[7] It has been too easy for critics to find reasons for praising or blaming, liking or disliking, Harry, and although my own practice betrays the same tendency I try to minimize it, first, by distinguishing between what I think of Harry and what my reading of his language suggests to me about his self-representations and self-perceptions, and second, by bracketing out the former and isolating the latter as the only relevant object of interpretive concern. The aim of the practice of imaginary audition and the theory of discourses is to avoid ethical reductionism by facilitating these moves. More specifically, the aim is achieved by two procedures: the first is to pick out and unpack from a speaker's language the particular terms of his or her inner conflict, which in Harry's case is the desire and struggle for moral legitimacy; the second is to explore the effects of the conflict not only on the interlocutory politics of dialogue but also on the scenarios or projects embedded in language and objectified by its performative action into patterns of emplotment.

(6) *Historical* reductionism occurs whenever an overall diachronic scheme is imposed on the tetralogy in a manner that encourages disregard of complex interlocutory and discursive effects that don't fit the scheme. In what is probably the most generally favored scheme the movement of the *Henriad* from *Richard II* through *Henry* V is characterized as "a passage from the Middle Ages to the Renaissance and the modern world," from "feudalism and hierarchy to the national state and the individual," and from the failure of weak King Richard II to the triumph of strong King Henry V.[8] This is the familiar story of disenchantment in which religious attitudes toward history and politics give way to secular and humanistic attitudes. Whether this is treated as a fall from a sacramental to a Machiavellian conception of kingship, or as the emergence of a triumphant Renaissance humanism, or as some combination of both, the story positions the three kings in a politico-historical context that narrows the framework of explanation; it obscures the extent to which their interlocutory politics and psychological warfare produce sequences of plot that compose into a larger story. I say *a* rather than *the* larger story because disenchantment may not be the only story, and, in the form outlined above, it may have lost some of its cachet. There are two reasons for this, one

connected with a new emphasis emerging in many recent studies of *Richard II* and the other with the reading I propose to give of Harry's career through the tetralogy.

The studies of *Richard II* don't question the disenchantment thesis so much as complicate it and rearrange the relation of the sequence of plays to the sequence of "historical" changes. In effect, they move the sequence of changes forward in time so that, from the opening lines of the first play, we encounter a community already disenchanted with the feudal and medieval ritualism to which everyone pays lip service. The work of many recent critics has made it possible to see how much the first play and its titular character question or demystify the traditional ideology. The pressure of this revision, which influenced my account of *Richard II* in *Imaginary Audition*, can be felt in reinterpretations of the other three plays, especially in the controversies that center on the moral assessment of Harry and the aesthetic assessment of *Henry V*.

My response to these controversies—and this is the other reason why I think the disenchantment story needs to be changed—is to treat with utmost seriousness the importance Harry's question "May I with right and conscience make this claim?" has *for him*. I maintain that the cause behind the claim to the French throne is morally dubious, if not reprehensible; that since this cause, which can be traced back to Harry's first appearance in *1 Henry IV*, leads him to make war more in his own than in the national interest, his subjects are asked to risk their lives for reasons that might not stand up at the bar of his conscience; that his language betrays the cost of his need to persuade himself, and not merely the world, that the cause is just; and that his frequent appeals to God therefore spring less from the desire to give himself political legitimacy and his war religious sanction than from concern for his ethical probity and spiritual welfare.

This view of Harry calls for a radical readjustment, if not a reversal, of the disenchantment scheme. For if a historico-political approach to the sequence traces the passage out of the declining ritualism and religious ideology of medieval kingship, the psycho-political approach I am proposing traces increasingly strident appeals, cresting in *Henry V*, to God, religion, and the scenario of salvation and damnation we associate with the Morality Play tradition. Both Henry IV and his son rehabilitate religious motifs to guarantee more efficient guilt management. Henry's longing for Jerusalem, Harry's enactment of the Prodigal Son parable, Falstaff's Puritan parodies (aimed at Harry), and the persistent if varying use made by the royal protagonists of the imagery of Christ's betrayal and sacrifice, all point to the abiding desire for the punishment, justification, absolution, and forgiveness that only God can give. The climax of this movement occurs in the fourth act of *Henry* V. The fear of damnation and desire of salvation embedded in the language of the Chorus and of the first scene register by their very hyperbolic quality how much Harry has at stake in the battle ahead of him. As he moves through the *Henriad* from Shrewsbury to Westminster to Agincourt the need for personal justification becomes more critical and hence more dependent on religious as well as secular validation. This increase in the necessity of God is proportional to that of Harry's famous victories at home and abroad. The "mirror of all Christian kings" has won loud applause for the splendor of his Renaissance humanism and loud catcalls for his lurking Machiavellianism and his skill in shifting responsibility, but the irritability of his filial and Protestant conscience has only recently begun to excite the attention it merits. Thus in my reading of the *Henriad* the story of disenchantment is crossed by the no less familiar story of the Protestant reenchantment that intensifies both the intimacy and the vividness of the spiritual warfare which transpires in the subject's dialogue with himself and God. This warfare is represented in the conflict of discourses that animate the language of the three kings and Falstaff—represented, that is, in the dialectical and self-regenerating struggle of the sinner's discourse with those of the victim/revenger, donor, hero, and saint. And I submit that this configuration of discourses, grounded in the sinner's desire for self-recognition and judgment, is historically specific—is, in a word, Protestant—and accounts for the religious reenchantment whose power vivifies the *Henriad*. Given this reading, it should be clear what I find wrong with the final category of reductionism,

(7) *political* reductionism. To begin with an example, the thesis of Sigurd Burckhardt's striking and original essay on the *Henriad* is that Shakespeare deployed "two mutually inconsistent . . . models of succession," primogeniture and combat, in a relation of complementarity, and Burckhardt's sophisticated development of the thesis amounts to an analysis of the disenchantment process that corrodes the legitimacy of the traditional belief system. But his analysis remains at the level of political structure. Thus, for example, when he observes of the encounter over the crown between Henry IV and Harry in 2 *Henry IV* (4.5) that "even under primogeniture succession seemed to be by combat," this is offered as a strictly political comment on the bloody transmission of the crown from the time of Richard II to that of Henry VII (183,172). The political thesis is put forth as *a sufficient explanation* of the encounter. Burckhardt thereby misses both the specific dramatic impact of the episode and its representation of the more pervasive theme that dominates the tetralogy:

combat between father and son marked by the volatile interplay of ethical discourses—those enumerated above—that wound all their efforts at reconciliation or atonement.

Another form of political reductionism appears in the more recent wave of commentaries that go by the name of cultural materialism and new historicism. The project of politicizing and de-aestheticizing interpretation too often leads advocates of "political Shakespeare" or "alternative Shakespeares" to adopt new rules of evidence that restrict the scope of intratextual reading while expanding that of inter- and extratextual reading. Their narrow focus on the Thing they call "power" prompts them to construe legitimation in purely political terms as the effect of successful manipulation of the resources of idealization. Their reliance on selective citation and paraphrastic foreshortening deprives them of the interpretive resources required for an adequately sophisticated view of a theme that interests many of them, the theme of self-legitimation. For example, Jonathan Dollimore and Alan Sinfield locate Henry V's problems not in the struggle to protect his conscience from the ethical contradictions inscribed in his language but in his struggle with the vulnerability of power they attribute to the transitional character of "the Elizabethan state" reflected in the history plays:

> What really torments Henry is the inability to ensure obedience. . . . Not surprisingly, he has bad dreams. The implication [of his soliloquy on ceremony] is that subjects are to be envied . . . because as subjects they cannot suffer the king's fear of being disobeyed and opposed. Henry indicates a paradox of power only to misrecognize its force by mystifying both kingship and subjection. ("History and Ideology" 218)

This, the authors assert, is the "sub-text" of the speech in which Harry reaches "the height of his own program of self-legitimation" (218). But they confuse a subtext with a displacement: what really torments Harry is not a failure in political legitimacy but—as I noted earlier—fear of a failure in moral legitimacy, a fear whose source is registered by the traces of discursive warfare that wound his language.

When political reductionists fix on the representation of power, ideology, and strategies of legitimation, they occlude all such traces, and, along with them, the politics of interlocutory, psychological, and spiritual conflict. To argue, as one political Shakespearean does, that the *Henriad* is about the legitimization of misrule, that its hero is a figure of carnival, that its major conflict is between two conceptions of political order ("hagiographic" and carnivalian) and that what it demonstrates is that "legitimate order can only come into being through disruption" (Tennenhouse 82–84)—to argue this way is to reduce the moral struggles of the *Henriad*'s royal protagonists, their psychological warfare with themselves and each other, to Shakespeare's critique of ideology and analysis of the contradictions that drive the motor of institutional change. I don't mean to imply that such a critique and analysis (whether "Shakespeare's" or the critic's) cannot or should not be elicited, only that in this new politicism it is the product of too soft or fast or blurry a reading of the text.

Since, as I observed above, the chief obstacle to my major thesis, the singleness of the *Henriad*, is posed by theater-centered interpretation, I shall devote the remainder of this discussion to an example in which the problem of tetralogical continuity is viewed from the standpoint of actual theater practice. This perspective is not vulnerable to the charge of reductionism because it puts a different set of aims into play. Its proponents are not engaged in a polemic against reading—unlike those I discussed in *Imaginary Audition*—and the problem they have in staging the tetralogy offers the strongest obstacle to my thesis.

## 3

Anthony Quayle notes in the foreword to *Shakespeare's Histories at Stratford, 1951* that his production of the complete cycle was only the second on record since Shakespeare's time. Nevertheless, Quayle, who was the Director of the Shakespeare Memorial Theater, argued forcefully for the advantages of cycle presentation:

> We well knew that each play was strong enough to stand theatrically on its own feet, and that economic necessity for many years had forced them to do so; but the more we studied the more we felt that this practice of presenting the plays singly had only resulted in their distortion, and that their full power and meaning only became apparent when treated as a whole. It was not only that many of the characters lived and developed through several of the plays; it was not only that literary and dramatic echoes reverberated backwards and forwards through the text of all four; it was because what appeared to be puzzling psychological inconsistencies when the plays were treated singly disappeared when they were considered as a whole, and became clear as purposeful and masterly writing. (Wilson and Worsley vii)

The coauthors of this volume, J. Dover Wilson and T. S. Worsley, agree with Quayle on the specific differences produced by the cycle conception: personal dramas are more firmly contained within the larger political story and, analogously, the "star vehicle" aspects of such roles as Richard, Hotspur, and Falstaff preempt less attention from the cycle's political scenario, morality design, and epic theme. Thus Richard's "personal tragedy" gives ground to his function as "the last of the kings who is claiming the Divine Right" (27); Bolingbroke becomes more important from the beginning of the tetralogy, and is a more complex figure in the *Henry IV* plays; the unfolding of the Prodigal Son drama clarifies Falstaff's role and just deserts as the Prince's "Tempter" (21); finally, the portrait of Harry becomes more understandable as the "long sweep" allows the apparent inconsistency between Prince Hal and Henry V to be resolved in the heroic king's favor.

Because the authors are sensitive to the demands of the theater and the practical obstacles to serial presentation, their assessments of Shakespeare's intention are cautious. Wilson thinks "it would be going too far . . . to suppose that he planned the four plays from the beginning as one historical masterpiece in serial parts," and assumes instead that Shakespeare added "links . . . to give them a measure of unity and coherence" (4). Although Worsley supports and fully articulates the above rationale, the production failed to convince him that the plays were designed for performance in cycle. In his opinion "the most probable way in which the plays came to be written in the condition of Elizabethan playwriting" was "that they *happened* one after the other": because *Richard II* was successful Shakespeare wrote another history play in which he "developed a better chronicle method," then responded "to the public's demand for 'More!', particularly more of Falstaff," with a much weaker sequel, and finally met "a different demand from the audience" with *Henry V*.

I think both the occasion of this volume and the volume itself testify to the justness of Worsley's verdict. For if Quayle's is only the second cycle performance recorded since Shakespeare's time, and if "the economic and organizational difficulties in the way of presenting the cycle as a whole are so formidable" (vii), and if Shakespeare was as smart a practical theater man as everyone says, it stands to reason that he would not have written *for the theater* a sequence whose overall meaning depended on conditions of performance it was not likely to receive *in the theater*. From this, however, it is not at all necessary to conclude that such a sequence didn't get written, only that it didn't get written *for*—or at least not exclusively *for*—the theater. To put it barbarically, whatever it got written for, whatever it was intended for, *it got written as writing*. And as writing it can be read as well as staged. Buried in Quayle's foreword is a single phrase that points to the alternative which is thrown away by the theatrical orientation of the volume as a whole: "literary and dramatic echoes reverberated backwards and forwards through the text of all four" plays. I am not sure what the aural metaphor means in the temporal context of theatrical performance: could we anticipate or identify a forward reverberation or pre-echo before it is registered as an echo reverberating backwards? But the figure makes good sense if we imagine "the text" stabilized in a material inscription that makes all parts of it theoretically accessible in any or all moments of reading. It is conceivable that the *Henriad* lends itself to a kind of interpretation radically different from that which guides both the staging of the plays and their reception by a theater audience. But it is also conceivable that such a reading makes enough dramatic and theatrical sense to lend itself at least in part to performance. I now want to explore this possibility, but before doing so it will be helpful to review very briefly some distinctions I explored in *Imaginary Audition*.

When reading the *Henriad* I do not think of it as a dramatic poem. Nor do I conceive of it as the blueprint for a film or video performance. Nor do I approach it as a system of signs whose referent is to be visualized in some extratheatrical context of actual experience. What I visualize or imagine while reading are the conditions, conventions, and positional relations (among actors, directors, audience, and characters) of theater, and specifically of Elizabethan theater as Shakespeare uses it. This includes, for example, the conventions that govern staging, scene division, role performance (representing oneself as another), the choreography of violent action, the variations of prose and verse, and the forms of interlocutory relationship (soliloquy, dialogue, eavesdropping, etc.). These offer themselves to the armchair interpreter as *theater effects* that help him interpret the speech and language of fictional speakers.

Text-centered reading is in this respect as parasitical on theater-centered reading as it is on theater itself. For it must always attend to the ways any theatrical interpretation reflects the interests, values, powers, dangers, and privileges embedded in the very structure of theatrical relationships as they were institutionalized in Shakespeare's time and are represented by his texts. His individual plays are clearly written *for* theater, and aspects of the theatricality with which this purpose invests them are often thematized as constituents of their meaning. At the same time, his texts are just as clearly underdetermined by their theatrical purpose, and thus although the text-centered reading I propose is modified by stage-centered concerns and is parasitical on theater, it is not bound to theater in the same way because it reverses the means/end relationship: theater becomes a means to the transtheatrical reading of the play as a book; such a reading submits to the seductive generativity, the exploding semiosis, of an *écriture* that transcends the digestive capacity of the performed play without, however, abandoning its theatrical circumstances. Those circumstances are *represented* as effects in the text.

The tension between these two perspectives may help us appreciate the problem posed by the *Henriad*. My argument is that the themes that bind the four plays together, and do so increasingly as the sequence proceeds, are largely buried in the language of the *Henriad* community and call for the sort of literary excavation on which theater-centered critics frown because it violates the constraints and opportunities peculiar to performance; and that for this very reason the odds are against any production's achieving success in dramatizing the psycho-political "system" of motives and interests that drives the sequence through a coherent pattern of change. It is unlikely that the *Henriad* as a whole will come to occupy a place in the Shakespeare repertory similar to Wagner's *Ring*. Practical theater people have much more reason than theater-centered critics to give the individual plays primacy as self-contained producible units and to interpret each play as much as possible on its own terms. The trouble is that as the sequence proceeds this strategy tends to be self-defeating. The rich interplay of shadow and light becomes more intense, the motivational drama more powerful, in the last two plays precisely because of their position in the sequence. Yet in strictly theatrical terms, 2 *Henry IV* and *Henry V* have less independence, lose more in being isolated, than the first two plays. Because this is clearer in the case of 2 *Henry IV*, it has not had a distinguished theatrical career and has not been appreciated by those whose criterion is the self-contained play. Because it is less clear in the case of *Henry V*, that play has attracted more theatrical and literary attention, but until fairly recently both its advocates and its detractors have judged on the dubious basis of interpretations that presuppose its independent status.[9] Both plays—*Henry V* more subtly but no less certainly—are haunted by the figure of "the times deceas'd." Since those times are depicted in the first two plays, a more comprehensive burden is placed alike on the theatrical and literary interpreter, and since the tetralogy is not readily available as a theatrical unit, the first two plays will at least have to be read.

But the problems go beyond this relatively mechanical level. For the third and fourth plays not only presuppose the material of the first two, they represent and continually revise that material, entraining a dialectic between each play and its predecessors. This demands more of us than reading to refresh our memory; it demands a process of reinterpretation that sends us back and forth between the earlier and later plays in order to determine (1) how the characters' motives and interests affect their memory, and (2) whether the themes and emphases of the earlier plays are substantially altered by their development in the later plays. Thus, for example, when *Richard II* is viewed in the light of the whole tetralogy, the relation between Gaunt and Bolingbroke is retroactively situated in the thematic center in such a way as to belie its peripheral appearance. This happens because strains that were damped down by the ritual surface of the play and the focus on Richard are exposed, repeated, and exacerbated in later plays. It is as if the passage of the first father-son relationship through the echoing corridor of the *Henriad* amplifies its resonance. Or—to shift from aural to visual imagery—as if the original context of that relationship represents it in an anamorphic blur which we bring into focus by viewing it through the peephole of the frame the rest of the *Henriad* places around it. These adjustments change the mood of the present time as well as of the time deceased. For (to shift figures once more) the textual rhizome does not grow upward like a tree or forward in a vertical or horizontal line but twines and twists omnidirectionally back on itself.[10]

It is very difficult to stage the psycho-political thematics embedded in the rhetorical texture of the language that carries the Gaunt-Bolingbroke conflict, especially since the silent king's silence about it remains unbroken. Yet I think that the failure to ground the tetralogy in this conflict may contribute to the exponential increase of misunderstanding that attends the traditional theatrical view of *Henry* V. Consider, for example, the brief and genuinely perceptive outline of the tetralogy which Sally Beaumann gives in assessing the importance of Quayle's production:

> No company had ever embarked on an exploration of all four plays, attempting to trace their continuing themes, their poetic structure, and their development of characters. The workings of Richard II's curse had never been followed through; the contrasting of three kings, one anointed, one a usurper, one attempting to merit kingship, had never been examined. Their central story, the expiation of guilt and Hal's transformation from renegade boy to the mirror of all Christian kings, had never been given by one company on one stage. The intricate sub-plots of the plays, the way in which actions throw ahead of them long shadows, the continuing revenges of sons for fathers—these could never be fully appreciated when they were played singly, or out of sequence. (206–07)

Beaumann blames the critics' "traditional preconceptions" and star-gazing tendencies for their failure to appreciate the cycle which, she notes, was a box office success and which had much influence on subsequent interest in as well as production of Shakespeare's histories (207–09). But if we give her final sentence the weight I think it deserves, and make it the basis for a practice of close reading, we may ultimately find ourselves recombining the terms of her account to produce a significantly different emphasis. First, although Beaumann astutely censures critics who found Michael Redgrave "insufficiently moving and sympathetic" as Richard—"few questioned the degree to which Richard *should* be sympathetic" (207)—she maintains the flat contrast between the anointed king and the usurper. What her statement implies, however, points in another direction: If Richard moves us insufficiently it is because he works so hard at moving himself and his subjects with his play, The Tragic Deposition and Death of King Richard, while attempting at the same time to merit deposition—even, indeed, selecting and seducing his usurper. This in turn throws an odd light on the increasing corrosiveness of the "inward wars" that Bolingbroke's sense of culpability afflicts him with, and which he manages to bequeath to his son in the uneasy language of the atonement scene. As a result, finally, Harry's language in *Henry* V betrays the cost of "transformation" from a "renegade" to a king who never ceases trying to merit kingship and expiate guilt. If this last point is hard to conceive, and harder to implement, in theatrical terms, it is partly because it presupposes minute adjustments of interpretive response inching slowly through the four plays considered as a single text.

Were this the only obstacle, it is still conceivable that such interpretive microadjustments could eventuate in a cycle which, however different in meaning, would still be stageable. But in my opinion there are two further obstacles. The first, which I discussed briefly in *Imaginary Audition*, is that Shakespeare builds into his text a critical thesis about theater in particular and theatricality in general; that in writing *for* theater he also writes *against* theater, and represents this ambivalence in his dramatic fictions. However much difference there is between the conspicuous theatricality of *Richard II* and that of *Henry* V, it works in both plays to raise moral questions about the projects of Richard and Harry—about the motives informing self-presentation, self-justification, self-doubt, and self-evasion. While Shakespeare's texts proclaim their ability to do justice to theater, they question the ability of theater to do justice to them, and this questioning thematically informs the representation of royal actors who, in staging themselves, simultaneously delight in their political performances and fail to be fully persuaded by them. A theatricality which is reflexively ironic is entirely within the limits of theatrical production, though, as the plays often suggest, it may demand a temperance and modesty that goes against the grain of the performer's sensibility.

The second obstacle may be more difficult to surmount because its basis is structural. If we assume that earlier plays in the sequence are in effect rewritten by later plays, and if this alters our sense of the later plays, then sequence has to be violated; even seeing or reading the plays in a manner that respects their sequence will not suffice. The synchronic but dynamic structure of the *Henriad* as a whole is greater than the sum of its diachronic parts. If we approach the structure as a textual rhizome whose twisted pathways ramify synchronically through all the parts, we can abstract it from the dramatic time of its serial events and from the theatrical time of serial performance. Burrowing under narrative and performative sequences to those omnidirectional pathways is something we can do only in the time line of reading. For performance, sequence is the only alternative, but for reading it is not.[11] This does not mean that sequence is to be thrown out the window, only that its role in the reading process needs to be more carefully situated. One of the privileges specific to reading is the violation of apparent sequence (beginning to end, front to back, top to bottom, left to right) by synchronistic operations that presuppose the presence of the complete text in a visible inscription; operations based on the intrinsic possibility that all parts of the inscription are simultaneously accessible to the reader's gaze. The packaging of the material and perceptible inscription in sequential form is an arbitrary practice, a cultural representation and organization of meaning that controls the flow of the first reading of a text more fully than that of subsequent readings. When the text becomes the *déjà lu* (in a sense different from that intended by Barthes), it offers itself for decomposition and recomposition. That is, it gives way to the synchronization that makes the whole text copresent and establishes the basis on which to reconstruct its diachronic form as the site of the production and play of meanings. Interpretation shuttles back and forth between these synchronistic and diachronistic moments. The point I want to emphasize is that although the reconstructed sequence may seem identical with the given sequence—with the narrative before-and-after secured by conventions of inscription—it differs in being recomposed from the synchronistic analysis of all textual registers (lexical, syntactical, rhetorical, prosodic, semantic, thematic, etc.). Relative to the given sequence, the reconstructed sequence is *virtual*. The given sequence has to be decomposed before it is reimagined so that interpretation may fold the synchronic structure into it. We recall that Anthony Quayle and his company found in their study of the plays "that literary and dramatic echoes reverberated backwards and forwards through the text of all four." But how could the reverberation be touched off unless one could "listen" backward from the last play to the first while "listening" forward from the first to the last? For if, as I do, one imagines the polyphonic structure of the text to be rhizomatic rather than linear, then the directionality of reading can't be confined to the linear sequences of dramatic narrative and theatrical performance. In order to set up the field of reverberation within which imaginary audition can proceed, one has to practice a kind of omnidirectional reading that does not ignore dramatic and theatrical linearity but, on the contrary, consistently interrogates their relation to the rhizome.

## NOTES

1. See, for example, Coursen 4; Ornstein 221; and Tillyard 236. More specific examples of unitarian interpretation are noted and discussed in the following pages.

2. Thus Ornstein argues that since "the tetralogies, so far as is known, were never performed as such on the Elizabethan stage, Shakespeare had no practical artistic reason or professional obligation to concern himself with their unities. Few members of his audiences would have recognized and objected to inconsistencies of characterization from play to play, just as few would have been able to appreciate the continuities, parallelisms, and symmetries which a critic can discern. Nevertheless, there are in the tetralogies . . . reaches of art that lie beyond the grasp of theatergoers . . ." (*Kingdom* 221).

3. I have tried to do this in part 1 of *Imaginary Audition*.

4. *History Plays* 235–37. See also Norman Rabkin 35–36. For a brief survey of the critical debate over the structural unity of the two *Henry IV* plays see Bevington 37–41.

5. Examples: Burckhardt; Calderwood, *Shakespearean Metadrama*, *Shakespeare's Henriad*; Blanpied.

6. Examples: Traversi; Blanpied; Calderwood, *Shakespearean Metadrama*, *Shakespeare's Henriad*; Baxter; Hibbard; Wheeler, *Development*, *Journey*.

7. My critique of a response to this form of reductionism is laid out in detail in "What Did the King Know?"

8. Examples: Tillyard ch. 4; Barber ch. 8; La Guardia 68–88; Kernan, "The Henriad" 245–75; Calderwood, *Shakespearean Metadrama*; Porter, *The Drama of Speech Acts*; Coursen.

9. Cf. Beaumann 206–07.

10. See part 2 of *Imaginary Audition*.

11. It may be useful to distinguish *objective sequence* from *subjective sequence:* the former denotes the time line of the performed plays and the different time line of the fiction it represents; the latter denotes the time line of the playgoer and that of the reader.

# 17

# "The King Hath Many Marching in His Coats," or, What Did You Do in the War, Daddy?

**David Scott Kastan**

Out of many, one: a logical impossibility; a piece of poetry, or symbolism; an enacted or incarnate metaphor; a poetic creation.

—Norman O. Brown, *Love's Body*

If *1 Henry IV* can be said to be "about" anything, it is about the production of power, an issue as acute in the early years of the reign of Henry IV as in the final years of the aging Elizabeth when the play was written. Henry has, of course, the problem of how to consolidate and maintain his authority, having deposed Richard who ruled by lineal succession. Elizabeth inherited her crown, but, in the complex religio-political world of post-Reformation England, her ability to succeed her Catholic half-sister was in some considerable doubt until the day before her accession, and, like Henry, she would rule over a divided country and similarly face a rebellion of Northern nobility led by the Percy family.[1]

Understandably "shaken" and "wan with care" (1.1.1),[2] Henry recognizes the fragility of his delegitimized political position. In deposing Richard, exposing the insubstantiality of the assertions of sacred majesty, Henry's own claims of rightful authority ring hollow. His access to the powerful ideology of order is necessarily limited, as his presence on the throne reveals its tendentiousness. "Thus ever did rebellion find rebuke" (5.5.1), Henry chides Worces-

I would like to thank David Bevington, Barbara Bono, Art Efron, and Coppélia Kahn for generously arranging occasions on which parts of this paper were delivered and discussed. In addition to the valuable responses I received on those occasions, the comments and criticism of Jean Howard, James Shapiro, Peter Saccio, and Peter Stallybrass have continually pointed me toward the essay I should be writing.

ter, asserting the inevitability of the victory of legitimacy, but certainly Henry's own rebellion found no such "rebuke," as he successfully opposed Richard's legitimate kingship.

Henry rules over a nation whose boundaries are insecure and whose integrity is under attack from within. He is at war with the Scots in the North, the Welsh in the West, and the very nobles that helped him to power now oppose his rule. Henry's discussion of his intended crusade is then both an understandable fantasy of national unity and a strategy for its production. The national identity torn by civil war would be reformed in common purpose. The unitary state, "All of one nature, of one substance bred" (1.1.11), would be produced in opposition to an alien and barbaric "other," almost precisely the way an idea of an orderly and coherent English nation was fashioned in Elizabethan England largely by reference to the alterity and inferiority of the Irish.[3] Henry promises

> To chase these pagans in those holy fields
> Over whose acres walk'd those blessed feet
> Which fourteen hundred years ago were nail'd
> For our advantage on the bitter cross. (1.1.24–27)

Henry would construct through the agency of the holy war the national unity he desperately seeks. The nation that

> Did lately meet in the intestine shock
> And furious close of civil butchery,
> Shall now, in mutual well-beseeming ranks,
> March all one way. . . . (1.1.12–15)

Henry knows, of course, that in fact his nation does not "march all one way," but is sharply divided by class loyalties, ethnic conflicts, and regional concerns, differences purposefully organized in hierarchies of inequality. The reality of his kingdom—of any kingdom—is that it is multiple and heterogeneous, a loose aggregation of individuals, families, counties, etc., all with local and sectarian interests and commitments. The desire to undertake the crusade articulates a familiar fantasy of political incorporation, a utopian solution to the problems of difference; but Henry must acknowledge it as a fantasy denied by present circumstance:

> But this our purpose now is twelve month old,
> And bootless 'tis to tell you we will go. (1.1.28–29)

A similar insistence upon an imaginary unity marked the production of power in Elizabethan England. The familiar political metaphors of the well-ordered body or the patriarchal family articulate the would-be absolutist state's desire for an integral wholeness, and the multiple historical and mythological typologies of Elizabeth did the same. Elizabeth, the Tudor Rose, representing the unification of aristocratic factions, was also Deborah, uniting secular and divine authority, and Diana, expressing in her chastity the inviolability of the Queen's body and the body politic.[4] A nation that since mid-century had experienced five forms of official religion, endured four changes of monarch, the reign of each marked by a significant rebellion, and that now faced further instability as Elizabeth ruled without an heir and over a country whose traditional social and economic structures were changing with the pressures and possibilities of a nascent capitalism, no doubt demanded the various tropes of the integrity of the virgin Queen and the sovereign nation for which she stood. In the prologue of Dekker's *Old Fortunatus* (1599), an old man speaks of Eliza: "Some call her Pandora, some Gloriana, some Cynthia, some Belphoebe, some Astraea, all by several names to express several loves. Yet all those names make but one celestial body, as all those loves meet to create but one soul." And, if almost hysterically, Nicholas Breton, in his "Character of Queen Elizabeth," similarly finds a radical unity in the representations of the Queen:

> was shee not as she wrote herself *semper eadem* alwaies one? zealous in one religion, believinge in one god, constant in one truth, absolute vnder god in her self, one Queene, and but one Queene; for in her dayes was no such Queene; one Phoenix for her spiritt, one Angell for her person, and one Goddesse for her wisedome; one alwayes in her word, one alwayes of her word, and one alwaies, in one word ELIZABETHA *βασιλεθέα*, a princelie goddesse, Elizabeth a deliverer of godes people from their spirituall thraldome and a provider for their rest: one chosen by one god to be then the one and onlie Queene of this one kingdome, of one Isle. . . . (Breton 2, n.p)

Not least of the inadequacies of this is that the "one isle" contained in fact *two* kingdoms: England and Scotland, as well as the conquered principality of Wales; but such fantasies of imperial unity, however attractive, always occlude the reality that their unity is constructed only through acts of exclusion and homogenization. In Elizabethan England this was achieved by ideological configuration and political repression that either violently eliminated marginal subgroups—such as gypsies, witches, vagabonds, the Irish—from the articulation of the English nation or discursively arranged them into stable and stabilizing hierarchies. In *1 Henry IV*, with the rebels routed, Henry orders his forces to follow up their advantage and extinguish the remaining pockets of resistance:

> Rebellion in this land shall lose his sway,
> Meeting the check of such another day,
> And since this business so far is done,
> Let us not leave till all our own be won. (5.5.41–45)

The homonymic pun (inexact but recognizable in late sixteenth-century London English) between "won" and "one" exactly enacts the political process of unification, verbally reconciling what can only be coerced. "Winning" is "one-ing," we might say, but the processes of incorporation involve always a more violent repression of difference than can be admitted. In complex society, only what is "won" is "one."

The play registers its unreconciled social disjunctions generically. The comic plot voices what the unitary state would repress, indeed exactly what the unitary *plot* would repress. Criticism has delighted in demonstrating the play's aesthetic unity by showing how the comic plot "serves" the historical plot, functions as a *sub*plot clarifying the "main" plot. But the play seems to me less coherent—not therefore less interesting or good, but less willing to organize its disparate voices into hierarchies—than such demonstrations of its putative unity would allow. The formal coherence that critics have demanded from the play can be achieved only by subordinating subplot to main plot, commoners to aristocrats, comedy to history—by imposing, that is, the same hierarchies of privilege and power that exist in the state upon the play. But the play does not so readily subordinate its comedy. Though Thomas Fuller in 1662 objected that Falstaff was merely "the property of pleasure" for Hal "to abuse" (408), the fat knight resists all efforts completely to subjugate him to the prince's desires or designs. "The humorous conceits of Sir John Falstaff" in fact share the title page of the 1598 Quarto with "the battell at Shrewsburie . . . " as the most notable aspects of *The History of Henrie the Fovrth*. And indeed throughout the seventeenth century, the play was as likely to be called *Falstaff* as *Henry IV*. On New Year's Night in 1625, for example, the play entitled *The First Part of Sir John Falstaff* was presented before the Prince at Whitehall.

If this striking inversion of the traditional relationship of history and comedy perhaps overestimates the domination of Falstaff, it does reveal the inadequacy of the familiar critical demonstrations of the play's unity. Certainly the comic plot gives voice to what is silent in the historical plot. I don't mean by this merely that the comic plot includes social elements absent from the "main" plot or even that the comic plot speaks the reality of class differentiation and domination that the aristocratic historical plot ignores or idealizes, though no doubt Hal's arrogant joking at the expense of Francis, for example, does do this. I mean something more radical: that the very existence of a comic plot serves to counter the totalizing fantasies of power, to expose and disrupt the hierarchies upon which they depend. History is displayed as something other—something more extensive, however less stable—than merely the history of what Renaissance historians characteristically called "matters of state." The play, however, insists that history is not identical with state politics, indeed that the history of state politics inevitably and purposefully erases other histories—histories of women or of the poor, for example—histories whose very existence contests the story that the hegemonic state would tell of itself.

To find in the play the ready subordination of comedy to history that has become the norm of formalist accounts of *1 Henry IV* is to accept Hal's version of events for Shakespeare's, or rather, it is to *behave* as Hal, to presume that the Tavern world exists only for the production of aristocratic pleasure and value. Yet most accounts of the unity of the play's two plots do exactly this. They analyze the comic plot's thematic relation to the "main" plot, finding that it parallels or parodies the historical action. In either case, the analysis reproduces the priority and privilege of aristocratic history. The comedy is seen to exist primarily to clarify the meaning of the serious plot, thus unwittingly performing a formalist version of Stephen Greenblatt's elegant demonstration of the containment of subversion in the play and in Renaissance England.

For Greenblatt, as he argues in his influential article, "Invisible Bullets," the play, like the culture of Renaissance England, contains, in both senses of the world, the potential subversions of its counter-cultures. The play's comic energies are never able effectively to challenge the claims and claimants of power: "The subversiveness which is genuine and radical . . . is at the same time contained by the power it would appear to threaten. Indeed the subversiveness is the very product of that power and furthers its ends" (Greenblatt, *Negotiations* 30).[5] Thus, the actions and values of the Tavern world are denied any disruptive effect; they serve to legitimate and consolidate political power rather than to contest it. Hal is seen as a master actor, merely playing at prodigality to achieve a purchase on rule. "The unyoked humour of [his] idleness" (1.2.191), which seems a potential subversion of Hal's political destiny and desire, is revealed instead to be a "product" of that desire, designed to further "its ends," a carefully calculated intemperance designed to make his "reformation" the more extraordinary. Hal's insistent role-playing, which finds its essential form in the Tavern, Greenblatt concludes, is then not opposed to power but rather "one of power's essential modes" (46); and the comic plot is, therefore, not an alternative to the monological voice of aristocratic history but finally its justification.

This discussion of what could be called Hal's power play leads to Greenblatt's argument that the play enacts precisely the forms of power that dominated Elizabethan England. Certainly Elizabeth's rule was marked by an insistent theatricality, as perhaps it had to be in the absence of effective agencies of coercive control. Sir Robert Naunton said that he knew

> no prince living that was so tender of honor and so exactly stood for the preservation of sovereignty, that was so great a courter of her people, yea, of the commons, that stooped and descended lower in presenting her person to the public view as she passed in her progresses and perambulations. . . . (44)

From the moment her accession to the throne was assured, Elizabeth was almost compulsively concerned with "presenting her person to the public view," that is, with representing herself, aware that her rule could be—and perhaps could *only* be—constituted and confirmed theatrically.

While certainly we need to recognize the relationship between Shakespeare's dramatic practices and Elizabethan political conditions if ever we are to historicize our understanding of his plays, nonetheless, it seems important, and fortunately possible, to distinguish between the theatricalized world of Elizabethan politics and the politicized world of the Elizabethan theater. "Royal power" may be, as Greenblatt claims, "manifested to its subjects as in a theater" (65) but the simile must not be quickly collapsed into an identity as it has often been by those who see the theater merely producing and legitimizing the ideology of royal power. *Nullum simile est idem*, as was said proverbially. Royal power is not manifested to its subjects *in* the theater, only *as* in the theater. The simile would make the various modes of a culture's production homologies, occluding their uneven development that becomes a source of social contradiction, a space for the resistance to power that Greenblatt's argument precludes. The labile and unlegitimated representations of the popular theater prevent the drama, regardless of any overt political intentions of its playwrights or patrons, from simply reproducing the dominant ideology, and clearly theatrical representation was never, as the insistent governmental efforts to supervise and control its production attest, merely a vehicle for the reproduction of royal authority.

As much recent scholarship on the institution of the Elizabethan theater has demonstrated, Shakespeare's theater was oddly liminal—geographically, socially, and politically.[6] Located in the Liberties, it was both part and not part of the City, which no doubt was appropriate for the home of a commercial acting company that was both dependent and not dependent upon its aristocratic patron; and actors, deemed rogues, vagabonds, and beggars by the 1572 Poor Act, became formally members of aristocratic households, in the case of the King's men even entitled to call themselves gentlemen. These contradictions of the theater were the inescapable conditions of its playing and suggest that the spectacle of rule was not merely reproduced in its representations but redistributed and dislocated.

The modes of representation in the popular theater of Elizabethan England, as Robert Weimann has shown, refuse to privilege what is represented. Its staging practices, which shifted the action between an upstage *locus* and a downstage *plataea*, continually displace the dominant aristocratic ideology, submitting its postures and assumptions to the interrogation of clowns and commoners (*Popular Tradition* 208–55). Both on stage and in the playhouse itself, the popular theater mixed linguistic and social consciousness. "The toe of the peasant," as Hamlet says, or, at least of the artisan, "comes so near the heel of the courtier, he galls his kibe" (*Hamlet* 5.1.136–38). Artisan and courtier confronted one another in the theater as they confronted one another on the stage. The public theaters thus produced the situation that Bakhtin saw as characteristic of the Renaissance itself, in which the aristocratic and the common, the sacred and the vulgar, the elite and the popular "frankly and intensely peered into each other's faces" (*Rabelais* 465).[7] Diverse accents and dialects, styles and values sounded, clashed, and sometimes blended, the polyphony challenging the homogenizing and unifying pressure of the theater of state: a drama that in presenting the spectacle of power reveals the fantasy of univocality that must be exposed and modified by the heterogeneity it anxiously denies.

But in the public theater that heterogeneity found full expression, its diverse social and formal modalities expressed in the generic hybrids that came to dominate the stage. John Florio, in his *Second Frutes*, includes a dialogue about the state of the English theater which holds that the plays are "neither right comedies, nor right tragedies," but "representations of histories, without any decorum" (Sig. D4$^{r}$). Florio, of course, is echoing Sidney, who had grumbled that the native drama contained "neither right tragedies, nor right comedies, mingling kings and clowns, not because the matter so carrieth it, but thrust in the clown by head and shoulders to play a part in majestical matters with neither decency nor discretion, so as neither the admiration and commiseration, nor the right sportfulness, is by their mongrel tragi-comedy achieved" (114). Words like "mongrel," "mingle-mangle," "gallimaufrey" appear again and again to describe, or at least to protest, these increasingly common miscegenated forms. In 1597, probably the year *1 Henry IV* was first performed, Joseph Hall, in his *Virgidemiarum*, complained about what he termed the "goodly *hoch-poch*" that results "when vile *Russetings*/ Are match't with monarchs, & with mighty kings" (*The Poems* 15). But in the popular theater, and certainly in *1 Henry IV*, kings and clowns did mingle; disparate languages and conventions regularly—or better, irregularly—shared the stage, competing for attention and control.

But this brings us back to Falstaff. No doubt it must be said of him, in Sidney's words, that he plays "his part in majestical matters with neither decency nor discretion." Indeed Hal does say it, as he upbraids Falstaff on the battlefield for having a bottle of sack instead of his pistol: "What, is it a time to jest and dally now?" (5.3.55). But Falstaff refuses to privilege "majestical matters" any more than the play does. Hal privileges them. They provide the telos of his Prodigal Son play, but not of Shakespeare's mingle-mangle. Falstaff's lack of decency and discretion is the sign of the play's resistance to the totalizations of power, massive evidence of the heterogeneity that will not be made one. His exuberance and excess will not be incorporated into the stabilizing hierarchies of the body politic.

Revealingly, when he imagines his life in the impending reign of Henry V, he thinks in terms of his social role:

> let us be Diana's foresters, gentlemen of the shade, minions of the moon; and let men say we be men of good government, being governed as the sea is, by our noble and chaste mistress the moon. . . . " (1.2.25–29)

This is the exact fantasy of social order in the England of Elizabeth, the virgin Queen. She of course was Diana in one of the familiar political mythologies that surrounded her, and her loyal subjects would be "men of good government, being governed . . . by our noble and chaste mistress." But for Falstaff this is not a submission to authority but an authorization of transgression; he serves not the monarch whose motto, as Nicholas Breton insisted, was "*semper eadem* alwaies one," but only the changeable moon, "under whose countenance we steal" (1.2.29).

Falstaff, then, is one of "the moon's men" (1.2.31), endlessly ebbing and flowing instead of filling a fixed place in a stable social hierarchy. He resists incorporation either into the hierarchical logic of the unitary state or that of the unified play. Nonetheless, Hal attempts to fix him. However much the Prince enjoys his banter with Falstaff, it is clear that Hal is using the fat knight to construct his own political identity. Hal is only a temporary inhabitant of the underworld of Eastcheap, and that only to make his inevitable assumption of responsibility the more remarkable and desired:

> I . . . will awhile uphold
> The unyok'd humour of your idleness.
> Yet herein will I imitate the sun,
> Who doth permit the base contagious clouds
> To smother up his beauty from the world,
> That, when he please again to be himself,
> Being wanted he be more wonder'd at. . . . (1.2.190–96)

This is, of course, exactly the political strategy of King Henry, though the King mistakes his son's behavior for real rather than a carefully managed prodigality. In act 3, scene 2, when he rebukes Hal for his "inordinate and low desires," the King worries that Hal has put his authority at risk. Henry is not worried about the state of Hal's soul but about Hal as the soul of the state. Clearly the issues are political not moral; what is at stake is the production of power.

> Had I so lavish of my presence been,
> So common-hackney'd in the eyes of men,
> So stale and cheap to vulgar company,
> Opinion, that did help me to the crown,
> Had still kept loyal to possession. . . . (3.2.39–43)

Henry would turn his aristocratic aloofness into a political asset: "By being seldom seen, I could not stir/ But like a comet I was wonder'd at . . . " (3.2.46–47). Henry anticipates Edward Forset's assertion in 1606 that "seeing that both God and the Soule, working so vnlimitably, be yet vndiscerned, in their essence, as hidden and concealed from the eyes of men; it may seeme to stand more with maieste, and to work more regarding, more admiring, and more adoring if (howsoeuer their power doth shew it selfe) yet their presence be more sparing & lesse familiarly vouchsafed" (Sig. E1$^{r}$). No doubt Forset here reflects King James's particular imperial style, his distaste for, as opposed to Elizabeth's apparent delight in, the theatricalizations of power by which it is constituted. But James, no less than Elizabeth, knew that it was precisely in the ability of the monarch to "work more regarding, more admiring, and more adoring" that sovereign authority resides. The spectacular presence of rule is the very condition of its power.

Certainly it is Henry's understanding that power is not merely confirmed but actually constituted theatrically that leads him to fear that Hal has alienated opinion with his "rude society" (3.2.14). Hal seems to Henry too much like Richard, who

> Grew a companion to the common streets,
> Enfeoff'd himself to popularity
>
> . . . . . . . . . . . . . . . . . . . . . . . .
>
> So, when he had occasion to be seen,
> He was but as the cuckoo is in June,
> Heard, not regarded; seen, but with such eyes
> As, sick and blunted with community,
> Afford no extraordinary gaze,
> Such as is bent on sun-like majesty
> When it shines seldom in admiring eyes. . . . (3.2.68–69, 74–80)

In his carousing, Hal has become similarly familiar, a "common sight" (3.2.88), affording no "extraordinary gaze" to the people and so apparently derogating his authority as Richard had his own: "thou hast lost thy princely privilege/ With vile participation" (3.2.86–87).

Though obviously his father misrecognizes Hal's behavior, what is interesting is that for Henry, "participation" is "vile," "community" sickens, "popularity" enslaves. The familiar watchwords of modern democracy sound dangerously to the King who in deposing Richard has brought power into range of popular contestation or control. Nonetheless, in spite of the distinction Henry draws between a "common sight" and an "extraordinary gaze," his conception of majesty as what Hobbes resonantly termed "visible Power" (129),[8] silently demands and authorizes an audience of commoners as a condition of its authority. If a spectacular sovereignty would construct power in its "privileged visibility" (Greenblatt, *Negotiations* 64), it risks, as Christopher Pye has written, reducing "the sovereign to the object of the spectator's unseen and masterfully panoptic gaze" (43). However reluctantly, a spectacular sovereignty must acknowledge the people's constitutive role even as it seeks to constrain, if not deny, it. "Opinion did help [him] to the crown," Henry knows, but it is a hypostatized "Opinion" that he acknowledges, erasing the agency of the people who must hold it.

Similarly, in his emphasis upon the "extraordinary gaze," Henry seeks to escape the destabilizing political implications of the subjection of the sovereign to the "admiring eyes" of this subjects. The unacknowledgeable power of the viewing subject is registered in Henry's disgust that Richard was "daily swallow'd by men's eyes" (3.2.70), and his own escape from the threat of this power is achieved through verbal magic: "My presence, like a robe pontifical, / [was] Ne'er seen but wondered at. . . ." (3.2.56–57). Most immediately, of course, this means that each time he was seen he was an object of wonder, but the lines must also mean that he was "ne'er seen" at all, only wondered at. This is the strategy by which spectacular sovereignty denies that its viewing subjects are the source of its power. The king is never seen, never subjected to the gaze of his subjects; he is only wondered at, subjecting them to his spectacular presence. The spectacle of the monarch must dazzle those it would captivate. Sidney calls Elizabeth "the only sun that dazzeleth their eyes" (52), and, with a similar understanding, in *Henry V*, Hal, now King, promises to unleash his power in France:

> I will rise there with so fully a glory
> That I will dazzle all the eyes of France,
> Yea, strike the Dauphin blind to look on us. (1.2.278–80)

But the English monarch must first "dazzle all the eyes of" England, eyes that are at once constitutive of and captivated by his spectacular sovereignty, and strike them "blind" that they not recognize their productive power; and it is this fundamental contradiction—unacknowledged and unresolved—underwriting the notion of spectacular authority that leads Henry IV to identify the legitimate Richard with the apparent political liabilities of Hal, and his own course with the rebel Hotspur.

> As thou art to this hour was Richard then
> When I from France set foot at Ravenspurgh,
> And even as I was then is Percy now. (3.2.94–96)

No doubt, in part this represents a residual class loyalty. Hotspur's aristocratic ambition would hold an inevitable appeal for the man who, in returning from exile to reclaim his ducal inheritance and achieving the crown, similarly asserted aristocratic privilege against the absolutist assertions of the King. But Henry has always been attracted to Hotspur, earlier admitting his envy of Northumberland and his hope that "some night-tripping fairy had exchang'd / In cradle-clothes our children where they lay, / And call'd mine Percy, his Plantagenet!" (1.1.86–88). But however much Hotspur is the child of Henry's desire, clearly Hal is the child of his loins. Henry's hope is only a displacement of his knowledge of the illegitimacy of his rule. His identification with Hotspur is his unintended acknowledgment that his conception of sovereignty opens a space for resistance, empowering precisely those whom it would subject.

Henry's unnecessary advice to Hal is based on the idea that the destabilizing potential glimpsed in the conception of spectacular sovereignty can be kept under control by carefully managing its representations, by controlling what is made available to "admiring eyes" to ensure that it dazzles. But the play recognizes a similar instability lurking in the representations themselves, and nowhere more obviously than in act 5, in scenes 3 and 4. There the play explicitly becomes a representation *of* representation, as the rebels at Shrewsbury encounter various nobles "semblably furnish'd like the King himself" (5.3.21). Holinshed reports that Douglas "slew Sir Walter Blunt and three other appareled in the King's suit and clothing, saying, I marvell to see so many kings thus suddenlie arise one in the necke of an other." But Holinshed's narrative of the battle immediately goes on to emphasize the King's own actions: "The king in deed was raised, & did that daie manie a noble feat of armes, for as it is written, he slue that daie with his owne hands six and thirtie persons of his enimies" (Sig. Eee2$^r$).

Shakespeare's dramatic account of Shrewsbury, however, erases the King's powerful and decisive intervention in the battle. Royal power appears in the play exclusively in represented form, and where the King is present on the battlefield, he must be saved in his confrontation with Douglas by the intervention of the Prince. In a sense the multiple representations of the King at Shrewsbury (literally his lieu-tenants, his place-holders) can be seen not to weaken the idea of sovereign power but to literalize its operations; the state depends upon the authority of the sovereign being successfully communicated in acts of representation in various modalities. Power is both the effect of representation and its authorization. Nonetheless, the scene reveals the inevitable contradiction of representation. It is always an agent both of production and loss. If it communicates sovereign authority, it is necessary only in the absence of that authority; in standing as surrogate it cannot help calling attention to what is not there. Representation thus at once constructs and subverts authority, at once enables it and exposes its limitation.

This doubleness is what Derrida calls, in another context, the "risk of *mimesis*" (241), the risk that any form of figuration will reveal the gap between the representing agent and what is represented, will admit their relation to be arbitrary and fragile, will expose the emptiness that it would fill. Representations mark the absence of a presence that is never fully available in and of itself, and they are, therefore, always more mobile, both less legitimate and legitimating, than theories of cultural dominance allow. Douglas, when he sees yet another representation of the King in the field at Shrewsburg, says with weary irritation: "They grow like Hydra's heads" (5.4.24), ironically using the familiar figure of rebellion to describe the replications of sovereignty he encounters, but thus articulating exactly the destabilizing potential, the possibility of a chaotic reproduction, that resides in the very notion of representation. At best, then, power might be understood as the effect of its representations; at worst, power might be seen actively to be undone by them.

Seeking the King, Douglas encounters a surplus of royal representations that he believes can brutally be dispatched to reveal their authorizing presence.

> Now, by my sword, I will kill all his coats;
> I'll murder all his wardrobe, piece by piece,
> Until I meet the King. (5.3.26–28)

Yet, although he works his way through the King's wardrobe with murderous efficiency, he is unable to recognize royalty when he finally confronts it. In *The Merchant of Venice,* Portia confidently asserts that "A substitute shines brightly as a King / Until a king be by" (5.1.94–95), but when Douglas does at last "meet the King," Henry shines no more brightly than any of the substitutes Douglas has killed.

> *Douglas:* What art thou
> That counterfeit'st the person of a king?
> *Henry:* The King himself, who, Douglas, grieves at heart
> So many of his shadows thou hast met,
> And not the very King. . . .
> *Douglas:* I fear thou art another counterfeit. . . . (5.4.26–30, 34)

The language of difference here—"shadows" and "counterfeit"—clearly implies an authentic regal presence against which these imperfect representations can be measured; however, on the battlefield at Shrewsbury the King cannot be distinguished from his representations. Henry's majesty can be effectively mimed. Though Douglas admits to Henry that "thou bearest thee like a king" (5.4.35), royal bearing proves no guarantee of royalty. But the implications of the episode are not merely that Henry unheroically, if prudently, adopts a strategy in the interests of his safety, that appearances are manipulated to disguise the king. They are far more disturbing: that kingship itself is a disguise, a role, an action that a man might play. Even Henry can bear himself only "*like* the king"; he has no authentic royal identity prior to and untouched by representation. In dispossessing Richard from his throne, Henry, no less than Blunt, has only a "borrow'd title" (5.3.23), but he must manipulate the verbal and visual symbols of authority as if they were rightfully his own.

Yet the play perhaps registers even a deeper skepticism about the nature of authority: that Henry's inability to partake of an authentic majesty is not merely a result of his usurpation of Richard's crown but is indeed a condition of rule. To counterfeit "the person of the king" is always to counterfeit a counterfeit, for "person," as Hobbes observes, derives from the Latin *persona*, which "signifies the disguise or outward appearance of a man, counterfeited on the stage; and sometimes more particularly that part of it, which disguiseth the face, as a mask or vizard" (125). The "person of the king" is, then, always already a representation, unstable and ungrounded, and not the immanent presence of what Henry calls the "very King."

The language of Renaissance absolutism, responding to the same crisis of authority, attempted to resolve the regress of representation by locating authority finally in God. Thus Henry VIII in the Act of Succession of 1534 insisted upon the "grants of jurisdiction given by God immediately to Emperors, kings and princes in succession to their heirs." If the monarch knew that to rule was to be "like the King," he (or she, in the case of Mary and Elizabeth) knew also that to be "like the king" was to be, in the system of hierarchical homologies that organized experience, like God; the monarch rules in God's name and in His manner. James, in his treatise on rule, *Basilikon Doron*, claimed that

> God gives not Kings the stile of *Gods* in vaine,
> For on his Throne his Scepter doe they swey. (3)

However, the appeal to divine authority is itself unsatisfying without a convincing account of how this sanction is transmitted and transferred. The King "by birth . . . commeth to his crowne" (69), as James familiarly put it, but the principles of patrilineal inheritance providing for the succession of the eldest son occlude the question of origin. Even in an unbroken line of rule somewhere there must be an originating act which, except perhaps in the case of Saul in *1 Samuel* in the Old Testament, is something other than an immediate ordination by God. Sovereignty would construct itself upon a vertical axis of authorization, a synchronic principle of divine authority. But however much the state wishes to conceive of itself as timeless, permanently existing, the discontinuities of history must be acknowledged. The crown exists also upon a horizontal, diachronic axis of coercive power. Bodin held that "Reason, and the verie light of nature, leadeth vs to beleeue very force and violence to haue giuen course and beginning vnto Commonweals" (Sig. E6$^r$). Even James had to admit the coercive origin of monarchical rule. In part to escape the dangerous implications of what has been recently called translation theory, the idea that monarchy begins with a transfer of power from the people,

James acknowledged that the authority of the Scottish crown derived directly from the conquest of the Irish King, Fergus, though James attempted to defuse the potentially destabilizing implications of grounding authority in power by insisting that the "people willingly fell to him" and that, in any case, the country was "scantly inhabited" (61–62).

But if authority must concede these coercive origins, the distinction between, for example, Richard II's legitimate rule and Henry IV's usurpation soon begins to blur. What is the difference in legitimacy between the rule of a usurper and the rule of a usurper's heir? English monarchs habitually based their authority "on the goodness of the cause of William the Conqueror, and upon their lineal, and directest descent from him," as Hobbes notes, but, as he wryly continues, "whilst they needlessly think to justify themselves, they justify all the successful rebellions that ambition shall at any time raise against them, and their successors" (506). Deriving legitimacy from conquest risks, however, not merely authorizing rebellion but delegitimizing rule itself. William Segar in 1590 skeptically wrote that "Kings, Princes, and other soveraign commanders did (in the beginning) aspire unto greatness by puissance and force: of which Cain was the first" (Sig. S6$^{r}$). And once authority acknowledges its customary origins in "puissance and force," recognizing the mark of Cain upon the throne, the distinction between legitimate and usurped rule no longer can be made absolute. If authority is grounded only in power and sanctioned only by custom then all titles are merely "borrowed" rather than in any significant sense rightfully belonging to those who hold them.

Lacan notoriously asserted that the man who believes himself king is no more mad than the *king* who believes himself king;[9] that is, it is madness to believe that kingship resides magically in the person of the king rather than in the political relations that bind, even create, king and subject. But this is precisely Hal's enabling knowledge, the authorization of his impressive improvisations. He never confuses the charismatic claims of kingship with the political relations they would accomplish. In 2 *Henry IV*, King Henry anxiously admits the "indirect, crooked ways" by which he achieved the crown, but for Hal the matter is almost comically simple, untouched by political irony or moral complexity:

> You won it, wore it, kept it, gave it me;
> Then plain and right must my possession be. . . .
> (4.5.221–22)

Hal knows that the crown is always illegitimate, that is, always an effect of social relations and not their cause, and therefore must (and can) endlessly be legitimated by the improvisations of each wearer. Legitimacy is something forged, no less by kings in Westminster than by Falstaff in the Boar's Head. The king's state, scepter, and crown have no more intrinsic link to sovereignty than Falstaff's chair, dagger, and cushion. All are props in the representation of rule. If "the raised place of the stage" continuously refers to "the raised place of power," as Raymond Williams has said (15), the reference works to materialize and thus demystify the gestures of authority, exposing their theatricality in its own. Puttenham speaks of "the great Emperour who had it usually in his mouth to say, *Qui nescit dissimulare nescit regnare*" (Sig. X4$^{r}$).[10] But rather than an admission of the necessary tactics of rule, this is an acknowledgment of its inescapable nature. Certainly Hal knows how to dissemble, is able and willing to "falsify men's hopes" (1.2.211). If Falstaff insists on the distinction between "a true piece of gold" and "a counterfeit" (2.4.491), Hal blurs the difference. He is always aware that kingship is only a role, however much a major one; and he is well-prepared to play it, to "monarchize" (*Richard II*, 3.2.165), in Richard II's shocking word, with the same authority that Hal has played heir-apparent. He is indeed what Henry terms him scornfully, "the shadow of succession" (3.2.99), not in the sense that Henry intends "shadow"—that, unlike Hotspur, Hal is a weak and unworthy successor—but in a more characteristic Renaissance colloquial sense of "actor." And Hal will successfully *act* his succession.

Indeed he literally does act it, in the "play extempore" in act 2, scene 4. He deposes Falstaff from the "joint-stool" that is the throne, instantly capable of the language and gestures of sovereignty, and more, instantly aware that rule depends on the exclusion of what resists the incorporation of the unitary state. "Banish plump Jack, and banish all the world," Falstaff warns, and the future is chillingly etched in Hal's "I do, I will" (2.4.473–75).

But it really isn't that simple. Hal will, of course, banish Falstaff in 2 *Henry IV*, but the popular energy of comic misrule is not so easily excluded or contained. At the end of 2 *Henry IV*, the victory over misrule is announced as a linguistic purification, a triumph of the monoglot aristocratic hegemony: "all are banish'd till their conversations / Appear more wise and modest to the world" (5.5.101–02). But although, as Bakhtin says, the monological voice of authority always "pretends to be the *last word*" (*Poetics* 318), in 2 *Henry IV* the "wise and modest" aristocratic voice does not have the final say; literally that belongs to the epilogue—and to the clown, I would argue, who has played Falstaff.[11] And *his* speech, like the dance that concludes it, exuberantly undermines both the unifying fantasies of charismatic kingship and the coherence and closure of the represented history that such kingship appropriates for its authorization, insisting precisely on the social, ideological, linguistic, and aesthetic multiplicity that both the unitary state and the unified play would deny.

## NOTES

1. Lily B. Campbell has called attention to the ways in which Shakespeare's presentation of the events of the reign of Henry IV necessarily recalled for "an English audience of the last years of the sixteenth century" recent English history and contemporary concerns (229–44). While her sense of the political meanings of Shakespeare's play seems to me unduly prescriptive, her reconstruction of the contemporary resonances of the events of the reign of Henry IV provides a useful corrective to almost exclusive focus of historical critics on the parallel provided by Elizabeth's notorious "I am Richard II, know ye not that?"

2. All quotations are from the Arden editions of the plays: *1 Henry IV* (ed. A. R. Humphreys.), *2 Henry IV* (ed. A. R. Humphreys), *Richard II* (ed. Petter Ure), *Henry V* (ed. J. H. Walter), *The Merchant of Venice* (ed. John Russell Brown), and *Hamlet* (ed. Harold Jenkins).

3. Recently a number of studies of English colonialism have insisted that "the cultural products which celebrated the supremacy of Englishness were based upon differences and discrimination and ensure that the positional superiority of the English was produced through the 'otherness' and inferiority of alien people of which the Irish were one" (Cairns and Richards 7).

4. For extensive discussion of these mythological identifications, see Elkin Calhoun Wilson's *England's Eliza* (*passim*), as well as Frances A. Yates's *Astraea* (88–111).

5. Compare C. L. Barber's argument that "misrule works . . . to consolidate rule" (205), and Leonard Tennenhouse's assertion that in the history plays "the figures of carnival will play a particularly instrumental role in the idealizing process that proves so crucial in legitimizing political power" (83).

6. See, for example, Mullaney, esp. 26–39; and Montrose, "Purpose" 53–76, each of whom provocatively discusses the contradictory institutional, social, and geographical locations of Elizabethan playing.

7. Cf. Annabel Patterson's suggestive account of the "complex social phenomenon" that was the popular theater, comparing it to the cafe-concerts in the Paris of Napoleon III: both were "scandalous in their apparent jumble of classes, itself a result of new social mobilities; and, more subtly, this very social mélange was itself a form of theater, a two-way impersonation" (18).

8. Christopher Pye has brilliantly applied Hobbes to the problem of political and theatrical representation in the Renaissance, finding in Hobbes's account of the constitution of sovereignty a means to explore "the vulnerability and the terrifying power of the monarch's visible presence" (43–81). See also Kastan 459–75, from which a few sentences in this present essay have been borrowed.

9. " *. . . si un homme qui se croit un roi est fou, un roi qui se croit un roi ne l'est pas moins*" (Lacan 170). See also the discussion by Slavoj Žižek, who invokes Lacan in considering the "fetishistic misrecognition" by both king and subject that the "the king is already in himself, outside the relationship to his subjects" (25).

10. Sir Anthony Weldon claimed disparagingly in his "Court and Character of King James" that this, along with the more familiar *Beati pacifici*, was actually the King's motto (Scott 1, 421).

11. See David Wiles's excellent account of Falstaff and clowning, esp. 116–35. Wiles argues that Falstaff's role "is structurally the clown's part" and that the part was written specifically for Kemp (116). The epiloque, or jig, Wiles sees as part of a convention of clowning which when understood would force us "to discard the old critical notion of the unity of the text, and seek instead the unity of the theatrical experience" (56). Recently John Cox has also suggestively recognized Falstaff as the dramatic heir of the stage clown, particularly Tarlton (121–24).

# 18

# A Tale of Two Branaghs: *Henry V*, Ideology, and the Mekong Agincourt

Chris Fitter

*We no longer are defensible* (3.3.50)

Kenneth Branagh's 1989 film version of *Henry* V, darkly powerful in its primitive interiors of hewn oak in penumbra and its primordial Agincourt of morassed slugging, has been widely eulogized both for restoring the *drama* of Shakespearean drama, and for the intelligent candor of its tough realism. Reviewers have often defined the latter through contrast with Olivier's 1944 version, with its clowning (rather than conspiratorial) clerics in the opening scene, its excision of scenes that morally undercut Henry (Scroop and the conspirators, the Harfleur speech, Williams's challenge to the king over his responsibility for the war, the reference to Richard II and Henry's dubious title), and the pretty chivalry of its battle scene, all racing knights on caparisoned steeds, their pennants aflutter in brilliant sunshine. Branagh's *Henry*, we are told, restores the cuts and thus the honesty, gives us a credible, pained, demotic Henry, and an Agincourt that will not hide from us that war is hell.

This perspective, I will argue, is insupportable. It is credible—initially—only due to the film's contrast with two commanding legacies: the overtly (and dazzlingly successful) propagandist character of Olivier's film, which was structured to boost patriotic morale in the months prior to the D-Day offensive; and the deadening influence of the Victorian and Tillyardian tradition of Shakespeare as committed upholder of monarchical ideology ("The Tudor view of history"), which bequeaths here a Henry naively glorified as the "mirror of all Christian kings." (Among editions of *Henry* popularly used by students, John Russell Brown in the Signet writes of "a simple plot. . . . with an undoubted hero," [xxiv], while the Arden, edited by J. H. Walter, sings of "Henry's perfection, physical, intellectual and spiritual," likening him to Aeneas. Matchless in its serene devotion to the English monarchy, this Arden can even claim, "It is noteworthy that the French display degenerate breeding, disunity, dishonour and impiety in waging a 'bellum impium' against Henry the rightful inheritor" [xxi; xxiv and xxix; xxx]. Clearly, moral duty lay in immediate abdication to a usurper's son, who didn't even speak the language.) Although many critics have disliked Henry, finding his character "limited," his "efficiency" instrumentalistic and deficient in human affection or depth, critics have nonetheless been overwhelmingly reluctant to concede that Shakespeare was deliberately writing an anti-imperialist drama critical of the monarchical system. It has become increasingly difficult to sustain in any version, however, the traditional, "loyalist" reading of Shakespeare's political perspective, given the growing number of recent publications that recognize Henry's double standards and evasiveness, and the radical ambiguation of his stature within the drama.[1] Just such a riddling, demystifying reading has also in fact been staged recently, at the Royal Shakespeare Company; and it starred as Henry our new screen idol, Oscar nominee Kenneth Branagh (nominated in the categories of Best Actor and Best Director). There are thus two Branagh versions of *Henry* V, and we shall see that they are politically polar. Knowledge of the first—directed by Adrian Noble at Stratford in 1984—casts transforming light on the supposed toughness and honesty of the second, directed by Branagh himself. This paper seeks to scrutinize the two productions, assessing each in the light of a close reading (my own) of the text the seventeenth century has left us; and to suggest that, at the level both of content and form, the "new" film has in fact tenderly remodelled the critically exploded hagiography of the conservatives, restoring a fellowly, idealized Harry. Its narratological politics are carefully assimilated to those of the mainstream popular culture of the contemporary USA in such a way as to secure Branagh resounding personal success, a commercial Agincourt. Branagh, I suggest, like some literary Oliver North, has deliberately shredded vital documentation, provided by the text and the RSC production, and his Henry therefore emerges as a familiar figure: the handsome military hero and godly patriot at the heart of an establishment coverup.

Superficially, Branagh's movie much resembles the Stratford production. Branagh again is Henry, and Brian Blessed once more wonderful with his Exeter as ursine thane. Christopher Ravenscroft is again the refined, disdainful yet gradually impressed Montjoy, and Richard Easton the majestic, exasperated statesman, the Constable of France. The staging of Bardolph's execution at 3.6.109[2] directly before the eyes of the king, performed by Exeter in full armor, is borrowed from Noble's production (at Stratford, Bardolph is garroted from behind, in the film he is hanged from a woodland tree), as are deft moments of psychological highlighting: Henry collapsing, battle-worn but victorious, to be caught and supported by the massive Exeter, as a father cradles a son; Henry dragging Montjoy to the floor in an ecstasy of sudden savagery at his final appearance (4.7.70); Henry wavering, weakened, between exhausted tears and laughter after Agincourt at Fluellen's patriotic prattle over Welshness; the lengthy rendition of "Non Nobis, Domine" as the soldiers exeunt from the battlefield (sung by the actors at the RSC). Also borrowed is the visual impact of the towering door in a blacked-out wall through whose strange light and primal immensity Henry enters, ominously, his council chamber. At Stratford, figures had exited rearstage through a normal door until, as Agincourt's sudden commencement, an unsuspected portal the height of an aerodome hangar abruptly opened, looming overhead, to swallow the warriors in its swirling light as if into some monstrous apocalyptic plain.

Beyond the cast and such "special effects," however, likeness ends.

### *Piece out our imperfections with your thoughts* (Prologue, 23)

Interjacent between classes, Shakespeare problematized the ideology of each, and excelled in playing off against one another various groups in his heterogeneous audience. Adept at smuggling past the censor effects innocent on the page but explosive on the stage, he preserved a subversive subtext within dramas outwardly supportive of traditional authority and harmonic in finale. The "hidden critique" of *Henry* V can be located, I suggest, in (among others) six crucial textual moments and devices, and it is by focusing these moments of political shibboleth that I wish to expose the operations of Branagh the shredder at work on the coverup. First crux is the treatment of the demystifying and satiric populist vignettes juxtaposed to the guiding narrative of regal idealism and nationalist solidarity; others consist of the nocturnal debate of Henry with Bates and Williams, the function of the Chorus, the presentation of Agincourt, the "insulation" or otherwise of the final wooing scene; and finally the representational mode itself, and the political gains of collapsing artistic illusionism. In his treatment of each of these matters, I suggest, Adrian Noble's *Henry* is rendingly true to the sardonic exposures in Shakespeare's text.

Shakespeare's structural rotation of attention between the decision-making aristocratic class-fraction and the common people whose lives are convulsed by them (or the "low-life" characters, as middle-class critics are in the habit of insultingly styling them) makes clear the human cost of imperial ambition; and likewise the insistent references to the outcast heartbreak and death of Falstaff ("the King has killed his heart"), capping and critiquing even the victory of Agincourt (4.7.40–54), obtrudes upon a thwarted Globe audience the cost of Henry's tactical moral *volte face*, to make in fact his fault glitter o'er his reformation. Noble squarely foregrounds the sufferings and terrors of the ordinary soldiers. Act 4, with the Chorus's lines on the "poring dark" and "foul womb of night," begins in absolute blackness and silence. Gradually the Chorus, whom we see to be wearing a First World War greatcoat, picks his way along a trench-like row of slumped, sleeping soldiers that spans the breadth of the set. His flashlight illuminates the taut, white faces of one soldier after another, who flinch, or stare hopelessly into the darkness and distance. Again, at the seige of Harfleur, the song into which Pistol's band breaks ("Would I were in an alehouse in London" [3.2.12–20])[3] is made a moving and spirited chorus, so that Fluellen's intervention to drive them into combat becomes a brutal act of class coercion. Howard Blake's musical setting of the song is a lilting, elegiac lament, whose naive, sorrowing cadences are thereafter used in a wordless soprano voiceover to haunt and highlight the carnage: the objectified consciousness of the play is thus a grieving proletarian consciousness. By contrast at the same siege the king's egotistic, rhetorical self-intoxication is underscored. Harfleur at 3.1 is a smooth, vast wall of gleaming grey steel that extends the breadth of the set, its apex soaring above view. Ascending this height are three parallel scaling ladders, onto the middle of which Henry throws himself after "Once more unto the breach, dear friends, once more, / Or close the wall up with our English dead." As soldiers swarm eagerly up the two flanking ladders, Henry abruptly freezes, three rungs up, and to the astonishment of the troops now above him, who exchange puzzled glances on their heights, Henry breaks into the lengthy and now redundant grandiloquence of a further thirty-two lines. At his ardent climax, crying "God for Henry, England and St. George!" he throws up his arms in surrender to euphoria and topples stiffly backwards from the ladder into the arms of Exeter and his "brothers." His troops thus recommence the assault alone, Henry being below in fraternal delirium.

Politically companion masterstrokes of Noble are the decisions to make the commoners' sufferings visible, in bringing onstage the killings of Bardolph and the Boy. Bardolph kneels, hands tied, with the armored Exeter looming at his back, before the silent Henry some feet away—with a long, transfixing wordless gaze. When, at Henry's nod, he is abruptly garroted, he offers no struggle. Gently, submissively, his head and shoulders sag forward onto his chest as he bows in death to become a kneeling corpse. The Boy, having at the conclusion of 4.4 interpreted Pistol's French knight, and delivered a second merry soliloquy to the audience, hoists the knight's double-handed sword over his shoulders. Hooking a hand casually over each end, he makes to exit. He is encircled suddenly by a knot of French soldiers, and frozen thus in a crucifixion position, he is butchered. The lights dim over his corpse, as a distant boy's voice sings "Would I were in an alehouse. . . . "

Henry's debate with Williams at 4.1 forms another site of decisive ideological construction, in the text's first inscription and in the reinscription of any subsequent production. In falling out with Pistol and then goading Williams into violent outrage, Henry's actions flatly contradict the Chorus's panegyric assurance that pining troops "Beholding him, pluck comfort from his looks" (4 Chorus 42). Although the King's attempts to exculpate himself from responsibility for his troops' death (4.1.150–192) are, I submit, palpably contradictory and facile (although we lack space here to pursue this), clearer still is that Henry lapses thereafter into immediate contradiction of his own experience. His self-pitying soliloquy envies the peasant who "can sleep so soundly" and "never sees horrid night, the child of hell" only minutes after quitting lowly followers insomniac in nocturnal terror. Adrian Noble perhaps glances at the irony here, and in Henry's reference to the peasant's "profitable labour" in the fields (4.1.283), by staging Williams, Bates and Court as clothed in indigent rags, and as equipped, with terrible poignancy, with nothing save simple agricultural implements to combat the French cavalry.

To the best of my knowledge no critic has commented on the strategic surplus of Alexander Court here. Guaranteed presence on stage through allocation of a single, opening line that could easily have gone to Williams or Bates ("Is not that the morning which breaks yonder?"), yet wordless thereafter throughout, Court constitutes, in an indeterminacy of role installed at the heart of a major debacle, a formidably unconstrained commentative resource. He may of course just sit; he may also sneer during the exchange, laugh derisively, turn his back on Henry, weep, or bite his thumb at the King. Such *structural* articulations of silence—where the dramatic conjuncture converts silence into nonagreement, or compels directly involved protagonists into undisclosed framing action—link Court with the resolutely undeclarative Katharine in act five (from line 275, her final sentence being a furious rebuke: "il n'est pas la coutume de France"); and with the pregnant onstage silences of such as Jessica in *The Merchant of Venice*, when in act 5 her father's death is merrily anticipated in racist terms. The deployment of such flexible, textually invisible resources to embarrass a textually dominant ideology is, I would suggest, a prime device of Shakespearean stagecraft for outwitting the Elizabethan censor. Although Noble does not articulate the densely potential silence of Court in terms of direct commentative gestures, his Alexander Court is yet visually eloquent throughout. Skeletal, ghastly in pallor, clad only in a thin grey vest and armed with a scythe, trembling incessantly and with dilated eyes, Court is silent because he is imbecile with terror.

The questionable function of the Chorus has consumed much ink, and still keeps word processors clacking. The Arden edition, as ever dazzlingly inept, noddingly accepts the Chorus's self-validation, and finds Shakespeare "apologetic," cognizant that "on the common stage he laid himself open to the scorn and censure of the learned and judicious (xv). Other critics, less disposed to think Shakespeare a penitent theatrical ham embarrassedly playing sycophant to pedants, have looked beyond a surface meaning so pointedly contradictive of Shakespearean valuation of drama in *Hamlet* and elsewhere. In my view, the Chorus is indeed sycophantic, but toward Henry, not embryonic Arden editors of the late sixteenth century, and his propagandist, "official" narrative of immaculate Henry provides Shakespeare with a respectable alibi which his staged action can then proceed to question, contradict and subvert. The Chorus is thus not the Bard enunciating *ex cathedra*, but is one of the *dramatis personae*; and, mindful of the many links of this play with *Hamlet*, I suggest that he is something of an anticipation of Polonius. Characterized as a courtly and high-minded flatterer (note the relentlessly insincere sycophancy toward the audience as "gentles" (Prologue 8, 34; 2 Chorus 35) which conspires with the King's duplicitous class rhetoric: "he . . . that sheds his blood with me . . . shall gentle his condition"), he is yet fatally out of touch with common people: his assurance, "We'll not offend one stomach with our play" (2 Chorus 40) would disappoint or amuse a lusty audience, familiar with the bear-baiting pit across the grass, who have come to revel in a war play. In these aspects he resembles the pompous, misdiagnosing Polonius, who misconstrues Hamlet and stands alien to the sensibility of the common players. Polonial again is the repeated disruption of the drama: "these tedious old fools" is precisely what the audience must have felt as he strode in yet again to shatter the racing momentum of the action. (One could imagine him listening stiffly at side-stage, peremptorily opining " 'half-achieved Harfleur' is good.")

The disruptions are political. They constitute, I submit, deliberate frustrations and coolings of the audience by Shakespeare. The Chorus's foregroundings of the play's fictive devices disallow the audience self-transcendence and jingoistic fellowship with the King's "brotherhood," and thereby they compel a "Brechtian" alienation and critical relation to the action upon the disgruntled consciousness of an ineluctably "exilic" audience.

Noble's production compromises here. His Chorus, Ian McDiarmid, is not given characterization, and he possesses quite magnetic subtleties and range of voice. Moreover, the disruptiveness of his speeches is reduced through his retention throughout on stage, as viewing from the sidelines, and through the maintenance of a swirl of preparatory activity around his speeches. Against this, however, he often kindles proletarian sympathies, when for instance his flashlight lingers tenderly, differentiatingly, on the slumped soldiers in the nocturnal "trenches." Whilst Henry's imperialism is not subjected to critical estrangement by the breaking of the spell, it yet is problematized by the mourning of its manifest costs, laid bare by an *exploratory* Chorus.

Equally prominent a frustration effect (and a point apparently unremarked in criticism hitherto) is that this play of Agincourt in fact refuses to stage a single scene of combat. At the close of the sixteenth century when the English monarchy had long lost its medieval military importance in Europe, Agincourt burned in the national memory as having ascended the brightest heaven of English martial pride and continental achievement. At least three other plays on Henry V were acted in London in the 1590s. Many among the Elizabethan genteel classes being trained in fencing, moreover, stage combats would be the more keenly relished for sleight of swordsmanship. Under such conditions, an Agincourt with no fighting was a phenomenon perilously close to a Rambo movie with no shootout for today's teenage audiences, or a *Rocky* sequel that skips the boxing. Shakespeare's combination of rapid-fire scene changes, French panic, confusion on both sides, and lushly narrated off-stage violence (Exeter on York's death, Montjoy on French steeds "fetlock deep in gore") serve to substitute for combat and to contain audience disappointment, while the narrative shuttles on to the safety of comic gratifications with Fluellen's crooning Welshness and Henry's trick on Williams. The Shakespearean disallowance of a single duel or killing (though the chroniclers recount a personal duel with Alencon, to which the text draws our attention at 4.7.158) aims, I suggest, again to abort inebriated chauvinism, just as pronounced narrative details—the feral threats of mass rape and infanticide that Shakespeare invented for Henry at the Harfleur siege, the slitting of the French prisoners' throats in cold blood (mentioned twice, so as not to be missed [4.6.37; 4.7.10]), and the massacre of the boys—again steep our minds in the horrifying cost of Harry's imperialist "honour."

Integral to this logic is a humanization of the enemy—and during Agincourt itself—to the point where perversely we actually fear for his life. The Noble production projects just this logic, resisting the temptation to stage thrilling unscripted duels and easy heroics, and instead heightening the comedy and latent brutality of the scene between Pistol and the French knight. The latter, his headpiece ripped off, transpires to be middle-aged, balding and avuncular, hysterical with fear, and helplessly entombed inside a hundredweight of primrose-colored armour. At the scene's conclusion the Boy has to help lever him from his knees; and he exits, with melancholy clanking, on a comically excruciated "Merci!"

Sensitive, too, to Shakespeare's planting of Fluellen, in 4.7, as a minefield of accidental arraignments of his sovereign, Noble sustains *across* the scene the inconsolable breakdown with which it opens ("Kill the poys and the luggage! 'tis expressly against the law of arms"). Fluellen's "Alexander the Pig" and his analogy with Henry as one that "killed his best friend" are the ramblings of a mind driven by horrors into an agnostic *metanoia*, questioning, in grieving stupor, the coherence of its foundations. "There is a river in Macedon, and there is moreover a river at Monmouth," stumbles Fluellen, as one incapable of his own distress. "It is called—Why?" The staggering pun on Wye trails downwards unanswerably along the mourning Welsh vowel into deadly silence. Henry, at his entry, shares in the collapse, sobs on Fluellen's shoulder at his address (from line 94). Fluellen, seeking finally to raise both their spirits, catastrophically reassures him: "I *need* not be ashamed of your majesty, praised be God, so long as your majesty *is* an honest man. . . . " Agincourt has become infamy.

Adrian Noble's final *coup de théâtre* of ideological destabilization comes with his staging of act five. Shakespeare's wooing scene functions, of course, as a climax of triumphalist euphoria, the skilled and victorious duel with Katharine in part working on the audience as unconscious compensation for the austere interdiction of fighting action preceding it. (This aspect, naturally, is habitually lost on "the learned and judicious": the indomitable Arden editor declares that "The Christian prince to complete his virtues must be married. Bouvaisteau, following Aegidius Romanus, is most emphatic on this point.") Yet Shakespeare's scene offers also a characteristic, and virtuoso, split-level ending, the jubilation and romance of one plane repeatedly punctured and jabbed through by the upthrusts of a subtext always just beneath, like some shark's black fin breaking the surface of sunlit waters. Henry's "love" of a Katharine he had refused earlier (3 Chorus 29–32), his "plain" and "downright" wooing as in reality a farce of juridical rape, constitute one such dark ambiguity, particularly as she is subsequently left aside for a rondo of collusive patriarchal smut between Henry and Burgundy. Retrospective to the action of the entire play, however, is that Henry's rhetoric now belittles the common man and celebrates monarchical autonomy in pointed contradiction of his earlier speeches, thus preserving to the end the play's political disquiet. Henry, always alert to the value of being a People's Prince (a lesson observed, no doubt, from the downfall of Richard II) has sought, following his disastrous encounter with Williams and Bates, to overcome class disaffection by a rhetoric of demotic solidarity and class transcendence (see especially the Crispian speech), thereby ironically repositioning his subjects in instrumental conformity and obedience. The scene in the French king's palace presents a glittering, sequestered, privileged finale, immediate upon the destitute Pistol's limping off bereaved, penniless, and assaulted by Henry's trusted officer. Safely out of his footsoldiers' earshot, Henry makes a snobbish joke about simple farmers (122–26), and asserts himself, like all "great kings," the source, not follower, of behavioral norms (284–89). "The liberty that follows our places stops the mouth of all find-faults" confesses a chilling truth, and this merriment over his power of life and death may uneasily remind us of the hanging of Bardolph and the royal intimidation and bribery of Michael Williams. Noble gives the split-level structure ingenious visual projection through bisecting the set. Just before the palace scene opens, the bodies of the wounded and murdered boys and troops are seen rearstage, laid out in a row as in a battlefield hospital. Amongst them, in low lighting, moves a female nurse in Victorian attire, pausing to set a candle beside each motionless body. She moves slowly, and her candle flickers quietly in the dusk, as a soprano voiceover sings once more at its most still and most lilting the wordless melody of "Would I were in an alehouse." As the nobility enter sumptuously attired for the gladding "courtship," a thin gauze veil or "scrim" falls midstage. Throughout the remaining action, as Henry, frontstage, jests and charms and celebrates his privilege, perceptible at rearstage through the scrim are the flickerings in twilight of testimonial candles.

***Never came reformation in a flood,***
***With such a heady currance, scouring faults*** **(1.1.33–34)**

Turning to Branagh's own production of *Henry* V five years later, "we must needs admit the means / How things are perfected," in Canterbury's cynical words (1.1.68–69). Branagh's film version expels almost every progressivist political gain from its RSC predecessor, triumphantly flattening down its multiple levels into a basic tale of sterling venture. Amputating the democratic limbs of the work, it excises the populist subtext out of effective existence. *Glasnost* it is not. Its opening omits the *facts* of the current parliamentary bill, and thus conceals the consequent structural antagonism established from the outset of the interests of the common people against those of state and church leaders, who conspire to strip the ill, aged and weak of "A hundred almshouses right well supplied." A long list of shredded textual "secrets" further includes: excision of the praise (by Fluellen) of Pistol for courageous fighting, immediately prior to denying him Bardolph's life; the later assault on Pistol by Fluellen; Pistol's capture of a French solider for ransom, and the subsequent dispossession of this ransom as the King orders all prisoners killed; the lines on "Alexander the Pig"; the song of Pistol and friends, "Would I were in an alehouse"; Henry's second argument to Williams, that many of the troops deserved their imminent deaths, as murderers, thieves, and pillagers; and the jolly colloquy between Henry and Burgundy over "virgin crimson" and the future nakedness of Katharine. The Boy's two soliloquies (at 3.2 and 4.4) are also cut, news of his subsequent death thereby affecting us little. Henry's scheming deployment of Fluellen to quarrel with Williams is eradicated, along with Henry's buying off of Williams's criticisms with a gloveful of crowns: instead the film shows Henry wordlessly return the glove with a sardonic, hearty slap on Williams's shoulder, as he exits, in glory, to hear tally of the dead. Expurgated too is the final touch of Henry's ruthless coercion: he compels France to agree to his designation as French "son and heir," an article the French king had avoided to the very last (353–65)—and a point used by Shakespeare to contradict certain chroniclers, who had written that Katharine's beauty made Henry soften his demands.

Another device tilting the movie away from involvement with Henry's victims and toward admiration of the King is Branagh's skillful recontextualizing of the fiendish Harfleur threats. Henry here delivers the speech in solitude from horseback, his men having fled the breach in panic. It thereby functions as a brilliant trick to win a city apparently lost: through dazzling and solitary oratorical fiction he has won what his soldiers could not. A further royalist coup by Brandagh is the class transference of an emotional crux he has remembered from the Noble production. The RSC vignette of the sudden French encirclement and hacking to death of the Boy is displaced in the movie onto the loyal Duke of York. The martyrological exaltation of the incident is thus transferred from the sphere of proletarian suffering and onto the heroized fidelity of the nobility.

It is the three flashbacks, however, that most would please an Arden editor (though they lack the authority of Bouvaisteau and Aegidius Romanus). The first, at 2.1, "explains" Falstaff to the audience, as we see the fat knight revelling at the fireside with quips from *Henry IV*. He greets an entering Hal roaringly, and at once asks him not to banish plump Jack. The scene, however, elevates rather than subverts the Branagh Henry. Falstaff is hard and cold-eyed, witty but menacing. Henry's "I know thee not, old man" is given only in voiceover, thought but not stated by a Hal dewy-eyed, grieving. Henry has thus an aching interiority opened up in him for us, begins a journey of sensitive, lonely inwardness. Far from being the royal machiavel, or relishing his status as "maker of manners," he is here the silent sufferer, victim not origin of necessity.

For most viewers, the on-screen execution of Bardolph will appear a principal innovation of the film, and a locus of "mature realism" concerning Henry.

But the innovation, we have seen, was borrowed from Noble, and Branagh's own innovation—a second flashback at this point—works again to strengthen our identification with the King. Where the text gives us a stonily silent monarch (3.6.110), Branagh reopens a bravely agonized Henrician interiority, with a closeup on his tear-filled eyes as memory delves fondly back to carousals. In this vignette, like the last, Henry is set off from the drinkers, alone and watchful as if compassionately prescient—no inciting cheerleader of a close-knit band. The flashback's effect is to prioritize Henry's consciousness over that of Bardolph, simultaneously marginalizing Bardolph while ennobling the King as a hero of pious discipline. Loyalty to staunch Henry is further rallied as, minutes later, conspicuous in a knot of soldiers, we see a non-alienated Pistol clearly enjoying Henry's rejoinder to Montjoy's contumely.

The final flashback comes during Burgundy's speech on battered France, as Henry's mind, patriotically impervious to it, recalls his own exhausted soldiers on the field of battle, then Falstaff, Mistress Quickly, Bardolph. Again the effect is to heroize, even sentimentalize, the King, his Romantic heart high-sorrowful, a mourning Mnemosyne, unrelapsing even here from an inner solidarity with loyal troops and beloved friends. The contrast with the RSC staging, with the scrim's ironic suggestion of amnesia and sequestration, could not be sharper in political polarization. Combined with its outright excision here of the bludgeoning of Pistol, the film preserves immaculate a blue-eyed People's Prince.

Branagh's gifted narratological intelligence similarly reconnotates and recuperates the nocturnal quarrel and soliloquy. This Williams, Bates and Court are well-clothed soldiers, with thick, dark jerkins. Untextually, this Williams jumps up to attack the King and must be hauled back by his companions, so that Henry becomes the wronged disputant. His lines on his army as harboring base criminals are cut—for they contradict earlier speeches, by himself and the Chorus, hymning the valor of his "cull'd and choice-drawn cavaliers." As Henry, now walking the dark alone, dispraises "ceremony"—whose "rents" and "comings in" are in ample evidence in act 5—Branagh transfigures the self-pity of privilege into objective oppression by having Henry pace here past a wagonload of pikes and helmets. His nonsense on the fortunate peasant, who never sees horrid night, is abruptly justified, as somnolent commoners heave suddenly into camera view. Where Shakespeare subverts, Branagh inventively validates.

The Chorus is easily made Branagh's ally. Entering below the feet of Bardolph lynched, he looks up and tut-tuts, before a truncated speech on cheerleading Henry and "a little touch of Harry in the night." Any alienation effect is easily removed by a systematic and massive reduction of his lines to a minimal narrative supply: at the opening of act 3, for instance, he is a mere voiceover as we follow a parchment map tracing English movement from Southampton to Calais and Harfleur. Rather than disrupt, intrude and problematize, this Chorus conversely adds momentum and coherence to the action. Branagh retains him perhaps as a technical problem for resourceful resolution, and he mainly succeeds; but this badly backfires, given the inherent naturalism of the cinematic medium, where Derek Jacobi deprecates "four or five most vile and ragged foils" as scores of armed soldiers catapult in front and behind him, roaring to war, whilst he picks his way gingerly between huge wooden stakes jutting across an emerald meadow.

Only the battle scene appears to come close to an RSC-like questioning of all the King has set afoot. It is filmed for regret and sorrow, not battle-joy. We have slow motion, facial closeups of men in fatigue, laboriously swinging and reswinging broadswords as they slither in rain and mud. Their faces express doggedness, immense effortfulness, as they heave and pant, their actions rhythmically punctuated by the fall of horses and riders, of anonymous footsoldiers, into the spattering slush, in protracted, hopeless inevitability. Over the gruelling dying is elegiac, mourning music. Henry is seen open-mouthed in panting fatigue, transparently exhausted, but there are no individuated combats followed. All is mêlée, pain, reluctant duty; there is not even naturalistic sound. Instead is an eerie, distant simplification and magnification of key noises—the fall of Exeter's axe on a French shield comes as through a mist as a slow, torpid rhythm, reverberating and diffusing afar through the great emptiness.

Much in the tonality seems taken from a brutal British rugby match, yet "the undefeated will" recalls Maldon. The tone of action could almost be mediated from Branagh's physique: this is a victory not of deft coordination or slender speed or intellectual strategy, but a triumph from dogged chunkiness, the bulldog's indomitable determination. Simplified and relentless, this doughty self-rootedness corresponds perfectly to Henry's cadencing:

> We would not seek a battle as we are;
> Nor, as we are, we say we will not shun it. (3.6.169–70)

But the structure also owes much, I suggest, to Vietnam movies of the 1980s, particularly its moral ambiguity: war is hell, but it heroizes. Far from antiheroic, the technique offers a different *style* of heroism: that of an ethical, courageous resolution. This is but heroism in a paradoxical garb. And it is illicit. We have, for example, only *honorific* blood in this film: virtually always a facial ornament, a red badge of courage, a thin, valorific smatter on cheekbone or jaw. Here is no gore of opened entrails or severed limbs, despite axes, double-handed swords and the specific enunciation of the text: "When all those legs and arms and heads, chopped off in a battle . . . " (4.1.137). In Henry's triumphal march at the close, all the corpses he passes are unbloodied, with calmly closed eyes and sleeping faces. Not one rictus of death yawns on Branagh's Agincourt. The stakes we have seen driven in by mallets, which at the historical Agincourt spitted ranks of cavalry, are hygienically untenanted. (Contrast of the overall effect with Polansky's *Macbeth* will make my point very clearly.) Branagh, thus, has gorged us on the climatic battle which Shakespeare had doubly refused in denying his audience both staged combat and illusionist enablement. Yet this "hellish" war will "not offend one stomach" and imperil Henry's stature.

As the climax to this climax comes a long, and I think brilliantly innovative, four-minute scene (for which so much dialogue was cut—the excellent jokes in the French tent at 3.7, for instance), which we might refer to as the long path of grief. In it, Henry bears on his shoulder an anonymous dead boy far across the strewn field of battle, amongst the slain and the scavenging and the weary, to lay him on a wagon. Needless to say, the passage is an anthem of heroization, as, in this gesture of unity with the fallen, his simple followers gather to his path, move with him, while rich music swells over, and the corpses passed are each bloodless and clean. This is the apotheosis of the caring King, of whom the stoniest anti-monarchist might relent to murmur, "An honorable murderer, if you will . . . " Structurally extraordinary, it is the precise opposite of a military march-past or a formal procession: it is a march-*with*, and we have thus the final *frisson* of an authenticated solidarity in the weary, unassuming, democratic trudge of a King spontaneously at one with his people.

"He that sheds his blood with me . . . shall gentle his condition." The long path of grief puts this into reverse. Constrained by text and sense from actualizing this instrumental bluff, Branagh must have Henry become a "plain," "good-hearted," "downright" man, as he characterizes himself to Katharine while rhetorically outfoxing her. This "downward" class transcendence lasts all the way to the Palace.

***If it be a sin to covet honour,***
***I am the most offending soul alive*** (4.3.28–29)

Turning, finally, to observe the operations of ideology at the level of representational form, we must concede that any modern production of *Henry* is

predestined from the outset to betray the first inscription of Shakespeare's play. The Elizabethan conditions of performance are irrecoverable, and probably beyond all modern analogy (although for bawdy anti-authoritarian relish, devoted attention to *ipsissima verba*, and jubilant audience participation, *The Rocky Horror Picture Show* staged at a North American student theater offers gusty points of comparison with feasts of misrule, and thus one dimension of affairs at Shakespeare's Globe). Yet it has been well observed that "Elizabethan stage conditions are potentially productive of plurality of meaning: whereas films operate to close the plural work into a single dimension of significance." The Elizabethan theater unfolds its spectacle across an apron stage, the audience surrounding it on three sides or more, and the consequent irreducibility of the action to a single visual perspective helps breed multiplicity of interpretive perceptions, impressions and meanings. Contrariwise, "the introduction after 1660 of the proscenium theatre with perspective backdrops radically changed the relationship between the audience and the stage. . . . Film is the final realization of the project of perspective staging. The framed rectangle contains a world which is set out as the single object of the spectator's gaze, displayed in order to be known from a single point of view.[4] Modern stage and film productions thus invite a "tyranny" of directorial control of meaning, and encourage a relation of docile, passive empathy from an audience distanced from the plane of action in far-reaching tiers.

To disrupt monological meaning and "parasitic" audience empathy in the modern playhouse, by the kind of Brechtian frustration effects that Shakespeare has built into *Henry* V through the Chorus, blundering pompously onstage to shatter the illusionism and repel us into skeptical detachment, is thus all the more urgent yet all the more dangerous an experiment in defamiliarization, if we are to try to be "true" to this ambiguating and interrogative drama. The 1984 production took place in a divided RSC uncertain of its direction and politics. A prestigious, "intellectual" theater granted experimental latitude within the security of national subsidy and a guaranteed audience of tourists and students, nonetheless its "Royal" Charter, absence of proletarian audience, high prices and menace by Thatcherite cuts in arts spending towed it regularly toward the safe waters of naturalist drama. While Noble's production effected, as we have seen, a socialist restitution of political tensions, and resisted sensationalist possibilities at Agincourt and elsewhere, it opted against narrative disruptiveness and estrangements. The alienation effects of the Chorus were diminished by the continuation of action around his speeches, and the ungranted battle briefly adumbrated by turbulent lighting and a sudden violence of color lashed from the streaming of titanic banners. Illusionist excitements could not be entirely surrendered, nor linear drive arrested. Against this, however, the framing of the huge Stratford stage by tall, "Victorian" red-brick walls, with doors into which characters in armor regularly vanished, as well as the use of the scrim in act 5, served as a mild, recurrent undercutting of the naturalism, and to activate the imagination toward associations with modern imperialist wars which the trench scene and the Florence Nightingale nurse confirmed.

Primitivist medieval *frissons* notwithstanding, Branagh's movie is a tamed tale, narratologically familiar, and sufficiently domesticated to thrive in the Oscar market in George Bush's USA. It slides away at every point from a Shakespearean interrogation of the action and liberation of the imagination, into the political and financial security of transparent and singular meaning. Deftly disambiguated by its director's hand, instantaneous intelligibility and firmly manipulated empathy are secured by supervening music-over at almost every scene, to aid a pulsing speech or moisten a baffled eye. (The closing music, to which the credits roll, is once more an endorsement of the noble King: the film's summation, its musical self-characterization, it is written in Henry's own major key, being the pious and majestic anthem "Non nobis, domine." No horror, indignation, skepticism or wit linger here to embarrass the final and regal record.)

That the Chorus's rupturing of the film's illusionism is reduced to a curiosity-value minimum ensures the continuous involvement of the audience at the emotive level; indeed its enveloping, even saturating, visual immediacies—its varied wardrobes, fall woodlands, brazier-lit interiors—help discourage "thinking above the action." (Testimony to its atmospheric seductions, the film won the Oscar for Best Costume.) The Elizabethan skeptical emphasis on the play as simulation is rejected, and along with it, critical plurality of meaning.

Furthermore, the very familiarity of the film's screen conventions works to naturalize ideology rather than interrogate and defamiliarize the action. By contrast with such films of Shakespeare as Peter Hall's *A Midsummer Night's Dream* and Grigori Kozintsev's *King Lear*, where normal habits of cinematic perception are subverted by mannered and disjunctive cinematography, this one assimilates itself at many points to the mainstream lineage of Vietnam movies. The rendering of Branagh's Agincourt owes much, for example, to Kubrick's *Full Metal Jacket:* the slow-motion silence as trainee marines stagger, topple and founder on through heavy rain together in swampish mud, or the reverberant stylized sound of the rifle shot within slow motion as the sniper's victim writhes on the ground. For the long, rich climax of cut-sound and elegiac music-over, the battle has much in common with the same devices in *Platoon* where Sergeant Elias (Willem Dafoe) is pursued and killed by Viet

Cong in tragic slow motion. Henry's "long path of grief" as he bears the dead boy in wide passage before the moving camera recalls the triumphant end of *An Officer and a Gentleman* where Richard Gere carries forth Debra Winger in a similarly climatic and protracted ennobling rite. (The rearing of the Lone Ranger's white stallion before the walls of Harfleur we would prefer to forget.) Branagh's *Henry*, though thrilling entertainment, gives us a work whose center comprises, as in the tradition of United States versions of the Vietnam War, a young male rite-of-passage movie rather than a critique of institutional power and class injustice. Branagh's motto might almost have been Pistol's: "Let senses rule, the word is 'Pitch and Pay" (2.3.50). And pitch and pay the masses have; Branagh, already famed in the United Kingdom, has successfully crafted a star-vehicle for himself, to conquer overseas the nation of Hollywood.

Shakespeare's play, however, satiric, ambiguating and interrogative, is clearly an exposé of imperialist rhetoric and a critique of the institution of monarchy. Compelled to provide panegyric and chauvinist surfaces to the play (the Chorus's encomia of Henry, the occasional moments of French-baiting) in order to please the royal censor and to secure the play commercial success, Shakespeare systematically proceeded, as we have seen, structurally to undercut such jingoism and hymning of royal authority through the *action* of the play. Monarchical interests, Shakespeare repeatedly shows, are inimical to those of the common people, whose support must thus be ideologically reinforced through oratorical inductions of false consciousness. As such, the play lays certain foundations of *Hamlet*. Hamlet is another People's Prince, but one, as it were, who has read *Henry V*: who knows that thrones are assumed in "Polonial" courts, in the state-rooms of Canterbury and Ely and of royal machiavels, and that to ascend them is to pass inevitably into enmity and betrayal of Pistol and Mistress Quickly, of the Boy and the Players; that to assume monarchy is thus helplessly to inherit contamination: the contamination of a determinate location within a pre-existing and corruptive structure of class exploitation and rhetorical duplicity. His torn cry "We are arrant knaves all, trust none of us" is a reinfusion of indignation into Pistol's steady cynicism: "Trust none . . . Caveto be thy counsellor" (2.3.51,54).

Kenneth Branagh has done us, as lovers of Shakespeare, a quite wonderful cultural service, in giving us a Shakespeare that is genuinely popular, intelligent and enthralling, unforgettable if also unfaithful. His screen persona is entirely winning, and his debut as film director certainly precocious. But he has done the ordinary people of the English-speaking world—which is coming to mean, at this time of global Anglophone hegemony, the majority of the citizens of the world—an irresponsible political disservice, in whitewashing traditional autocracy and the logic of imperialism. What Shakespeare has demystified, Branagh, persuasively, affably, immorally, has resanctified.

## NOTES

1. Critics who have disliked the character of Henry, while not reading the play as designedly subversive of authority or imperialism, include William Hazlitt (chapter on *Henry V* in *Characters of Shakespeare's Plays*); A. C. Bradley ("The Rejection of Falstaff"); and Mark Van Doren (170–79). Gerald Gould and Harold C. Goddard (215–68) appear the sole champions of the view that Shakespeare intentionally writes a mordant satire on imperialism and monarchical government: an interpretation with which I align myself. Other major accounts of the play that acknowledge its subversive dimensions and extend our perception of its terrible ironies, while recoiling nonetheless from the conclusion of a deeply anti-authoritarian Bard into the safety of a neutrally ambiguating Shakespeare, include Norman Rabkin (33–62), who sees Shakespeare producing ambiguity for its own sake, and critics who, like John Palmer (*Political Characters* [1948] 180–249), Gordon Ross Smith and Karl P. Wentersdorf see Shakespeare simply holding the mirror up to nature as it was in those dark times. Honor Matthews (31–36, 51–66) posits the ambiguity of a reluctant machiavel, unable fully to repress his native good nature; Roy Battenhouse ("*Henry V*") construes the play's satire as sympathetic and "Chaucerian"; while Jonathan Dollimore and Alan Sinfield ("History and Ideology") doubt the possibility of resolving whether the disunitary tendencies in the play override the harmonic. Stephen Greenblatt ("Invisible Bullets") argues the drama's registration of regal hypocrisy, ruthlessness and bad faith within the context of celebration and panegyric; while Hazelton Spencer billows ambiguity of his own in lauding a superlatively virtuous monarch whom he casually notes in his concluding paragraph to embody "a semi-fascist ideal" (193–99).

2. All references to *Henry V* are to the Arden edition, ed. J. H. Walter.

3. Blake's rendition incorporates Pistol's prose line preceding the song ("Would I were in an alehouse in London!") into the song itself as its first line (and ends it at line 17). I have accordingly referred to the song in this version.

4. Holderness ("Radical Potentiality") cites (183) and quotes Catherine Belsey (184).

19

# Commentary: "In the Destructive Element Immersed"

**Lawrence Danson**

I've been asked to comment on the preceding eight very rich and diverse essays about "Ideology and Critical Practice," and to be brief about it. Briefly, then, some reflections, beginning with one about my own position as commentator on a group of essays responding directly or indirectly to the papers given at an MLA session called in response to a letter signed by twenty-four feminist critics to protest a critique of feminist criticism. The swarm of commentary in that sentence doesn't end the affair: most of the essays in this section begin with a statement of critical position or ideological commitment, and some make the working out of that position or commitment the substance of the paper. What might under a different dispensation have been an ancillary task—the commentary about the criticism—becomes in this volume the substance and burden of criticism itself; and in that respect my task, impossible as it is, begins to look like the typical, maybe inescapable, task of the academic critic, *circa* 1991, endlessly critiquing critiques of critiques.

Plunged so deeply in the critical *abyme* I can hardly claim an outsider's status. Still, with a naiveté only partly pretended, I ask how we've come to this pass, and whether in fact it's as entropic as my rhetoric makes it seem. And I begin, not with the eight essayists themselves but with Richard Levin, whose critique of feminist practice provided the immediate occasion for this volume about the place of ideology in the criticism of Shakespeare. Levin has a lot to answer for. Before 1979, the second section of the present volume might have been called "Readings," perhaps even "New Readings"; but then Levin published *New Readings vs. Old Plays*, and the world changed. It was about then that ideological self-consciousness became a paramount *desideratum* for Shakespeareans, and "insufficiently theorized" became the nastiest thing you could say about a critic's work. *Post hoc* is not necessarily *propter hoc;* among the complex historical forces that created the current academic dispensation, Levin's book was a lucky—but still a palpable—hit; it hastened the collapse of a structure (daub of New Criticism and wattle of old historicism) that was waiting to topple. Levin's more recent essays chiding the profession that followed his lead (in a direction he hadn't intended) can be seen as expiation or damage-control. But it won't work: his recent essays, like his volume of 1979, only involve us more deeply in the imbroglio of self-consciousnesses, in which the necessity to think about the process of thinking about Shakespeare keeps us from ever reaching the elusive object of our former "readings," the Shakespearean text itself.

In other ways too Levin is a precursor of the critical scene he deplores, and which the essays in this section fairly represent. Compare Levin's agonistic title, *New Readings vs. Old Plays*, with that of a fine collection of essays edited in 1954 by John Garrett, *Talking of Shakespeare*; they were such good essays that they summoned a companion volume, *More Talking of Shakespeare* (1959). Garrett's comfortable titles imply that criticism is friendly chat among like-minded folk (we were talking of Althusser just the other day), the most natural thing in the world. There is no such implication in Levin's title, or indeed his book. But it's not only contentiousness that marks Levin's book as precursor of the current scene. *New Readings vs. Old Plays* was frankly addressed to professional practitioners; its subject was not Shakespeare (or Renaissance drama) but the protocols of the academy. What used to be called methodology, and what is now, with differences of course, called ideology, was the central critical issue. The eight essays in this section of *Shakespeare Left and Right* belong to Levin's world, whether they or he like it or not.

There's this big difference between them, though: Levin wants us to get back to a place—the single authentic site of Renaissance drama—which some of the critics in this volume think never existed, except as the nostalgic or otherwise interested construction of critics who preceded them. In *New Readings vs. Old Plays*, Levin used the plurality of contradictory critical readings as evidence that criticism had carried us away from the single site of textual meaning. Some of Levin's opponents take the evidence the opposite way, to show that Shakespearean meanings exist precisely as contestation and contradiction, within the texts and within the critical community, and that the plurality of meanings *is* a significant meaning.

From that difference emerges a surprise for readers who, when they hear the word *ideology* combined with the word *criticism*, are afraid that we're about to be coerced in the name of a cause other than that of pure disinterested truth. A belief in historical contingency, which finds that "disinterested truth" is itself a historically variable and very impure notion, may turn out to be less coercive than its ostensibly non-ideological alternative, precisely because it's obliged to make its investments visible and therefore contestable. In this volume, Darryl Gless's essay, which explicitly addresses the larger struggle within and around the academy over Allan Bloom's claim that left-wing intellectuals are "closing the American mind," expresses, and then in its treatment of *Julius Caesar* enacts, the most important gain that I see in the tendency toward explicitly ideological criticism. On the one hand it shows the political tendentiousness of a criticism (in this case Bloom's) that lays claims to universality and objectivity; and with its own position clarified by contrast, it goes on to show alternative possibilities generated by the Shakespearean text.

Like Edward Pechter's witty essay "Against 'Ideology' " in section one, Gless argues for "the value of pedagogical pluralism." It's a comfortable doctrine in theory; in the actual heat of battle among committed positions, when it comes for instance (and it does) to tenure and curricular and publishing decisions, it is a most difficult and—as old-style liberals like myself better admit—a dangerous doctrine to maintain. Pluralism (as several essays in this volume imply) is the privilege of the already-empowered; it discovers its own limitations when it's confronted by once-empowered or not-yet-empowered forces both on the Right and Left which do not share its own culturally specific, historically contingent values. How to maintain it? As was said to a Marlow later than Christopher, "in the destructive element immerse," which in this case means keep the critiques coming. I think I understand the anger of the feminist critics who protested *PMLA*'s decision to publish Richard Levin's article; but his article, their response, the MLA session that followed, this volume, and so on and on suggest that the current age of ideology can also be one of liberal expansiveness. Such expansiveness is good for feminism as it is for other causes with which it may sometimes find itself at temporary odds but without which it could not have developed so far.

Several essays in this section draw simultaneously on apparently competing methodologies. And since those methodologies presumably reflect competing ideological investments, they sustain the prospects for pluralism (if, admittedly, a pluralism of the relatively Left). Graham Holderness makes a brave gesture in undertaking what he calls "a feminist reading," attempting to solve as it were by *fiat* the still-vexed theoretical issue of the male critic's status in (towards?) feminism. His essay on *Richard II* recapitulates an argument he's made elsewhere, that Shakespeare's history plays reveal a (modern) historical consciousness of the past's difference, and that Shakespeare represents on the screen of the feudal past the tensions of his own world's emergent capitalism. What strikes me is how that argument (which one might be tempted to pigeonhole as Marxist) has been complicated by what Holderness has learned from feminist discourse. A question otherwise not to be asked—why are women relatively unrepresented in *Richard II?*—becomes a question virtually mandated by his effort to join Marxist and feminist protocols of reading; and the question receives an interesting answer.

Katharine Eisaman Maus also asks the reader to engage in acts of inclusiveness, bringing linguistic concerns which have previously been useful in criticism of *Love's Labor's Lost* more closely in touch with gender-issues that have not previously seemed germane to the play. Like other contributors to this section, Maus carefully locates the ideological determinants of our critical methods—in this case, why feminist critics have found some parts of the canon more productive for their purposes than others. Her critical self-consciousness allows her to open more of the canon to feminists by forging in effect a (provisional) alliance between feminism and formalism.

Joseph A. Porter, in his prolegomenon to a study of Shakespearean "character," begins to recuperate a category that more rigidly policed ideological boundaries might exclude altogether. "Character" smacks of self, which smacks of humanism, which suggests that drama holds a mirror up to an unchanging world—all that hegemonic stuff that some people might want to consign to the rubbish heap of history. (A few years ago I wrote an article asking "how Shakespeare and Marlowe create dramatic characters as imitations of persons, and what idea of person the dramatic imitation implies" ("Character" 217)—which provoked an up-to-date editor to remark that it sounded like a question Harley Granville-Barker might have asked: so I confess an interest in the recuperation of the category of "character.") "Character-study" has played a complex role in the construction of Shakespeare studies generally, and precisely for that reason it's a valuable and available site for the ideologically astute critic's intervention.

One final instance of contentious pluralism from this section: Harry Berger's essay carries on a careful negotiation of the ancient critical controversy between page and stage, finding no easy rapprochement but a complex way of reading the theatrical text that remains mindful of both locales.

But I don't want to press too hard on the tendency to *glasnost* in these essays. I don't think that many of them will co-opt the critic (again, of the Left or the Right) whose primary commitment is not to seeing history but to making it over in her or his image. Certainly within the pluralistic tendency I'm noticing there's still plenty of room for political contention; or better, it's a tendency born precisely in contention and that couldn't continue without it. But some of the signs of political *Sturm und drang* may seem to an uncommitted reader to go beyond the demands of the occasion. Marilyn L. Williamson, for instance, contributes an essay that shows how the violence in *Coriolanus* has a gendered dimension; but she begins her essay by drawing firm theoretical lines between the critic who is "the accomplice of ideology" and the critic (like herself) dedicated to resistance. Does her essay need the declaration of political intent? I'd be tempted to dismiss the issue she raises as merely "academic," but Darryl Gless's essay reminds me that Jesse Helms and Company have done more than any Ph.D. of the Left to show that academic politics aren't merely academic.

One essay in the group is anomalous because its explicit agenda is the closing down of borders and the drawing in of perspectives. Chris Fitter's essay about productions of *Henry* V is committed to "proletarian" and "progressivist" positions; it treats different positions with contempt (the Arden edition is "dazzlingly inept") and implies that all difference is in fact intolerable opposition. Personally, I object less to Fitter's lack of proportion in comparing Kenneth Branagh's directorial choices to Oliver North's criminal offenses, than to his certainty about what's objectively "in" the text. That question—to what extent do our own historical positions, our ideologies or, as Gless calls them (following Gombrich) our "illusions," make the readings we think we find in the text?—is one of the things most profitably vexed by several other essays in this section. Fitter's way of resolving it is rough but ready: whatever gets his political imprimatur is genuine, whatever doesn't is a critical or theatrical misrepresentation. The evidence of diverse theatrical embodiments of *Henry* V might incline one to the view that the text is complex enough to support different readings. Fitter opts instead for univocality: "Shakespeare's plays . . . is clearly an exposé of imperialist rhetoric and a critique of the institution of monarchy."

Fitter's theory is that Shakespeare wrote the Chorus as a sop for the censors who would be so happy chewing on its praise of royalty that they wouldn't notice the audience behaving with the "bawdy anti-authoritarian relish" of modern college students at a showing of *The Rocky Horror Picture Show*. His politicized version of the theory of comic relief assumes (ahistorically) a "proletarian" us against an authoritarian them, ignoring what neo-Marxist criticism of the Althusserian sort and new historicist criticism of the Greenblattian sort have shown about the pervasiveness of power relations and the depths at which ideology operates.

There are dangers in making every critical disagreement also a political disagreement, and it's more than just a lapse in decency to demonize our opponents as class (or gender or racial) enemies. The damage is not only to sociability but to intellectual clarity. Critics who share a "progressive" politics may differ about the extent to which Shakespeare escapes inscription within some dominant assumptions of his time; conversely, many "middle-class" critics (as Fitter might stigmatize them) have in fact agreed with him about the ironic intentions of the Chorus in *Henry* V. Our critical choices are, no doubt, at some level politically conditioned, but they are not narrowly or completely determined; and there is no necessary relation between our own political views and our view of Shakespeare's politics. Norman Rabkin, in a well-known essay, drew on the idea of "complementarity" to write about a *Henry* V that couldn't be exhausted by a reading either pro or con, recognizing explicitly that the play responds to whichever point of view one brings to it. Rabkin's essay is ideological in the best sense, not because it's overtly "political" instead of "literary" (it's not) or because it's submerged in the unconscious constructions of its age (it's not that either), but because it works from an explicit awareness of how its own views are located within the field of competing views; and by respecting those views it gathers the strength of its provisionality.

Like Fitter's essay on *Henry* V, David Scott Kastan's on *1 Henry IV* attempts to modify, possibly even to overthrow, a traditional reading. It skillfully deploys a fashionable rhetoric—"hegemony," "representation," "monological"—in support of its premise, that critical relegation of Falstaff's anti-authoritarian energy to a subordinate position duplicates the hierarchizing strategy practiced by Hal—a strategy which is deconstructed by the play's fuller representation of royal authority. Intentionally or not, Kastan's fine essay also has a local interest as an ironic *homage* to Richard Levin's *New Readings vs. Old Plays*. Its first sentence ("If *1 Henry IV* can be said to be 'about' anything, it is about the production of power. . . ." parodically recalls Levin's strictures against "thematic readings." (The "anything" in Kastan's sentence makes an even niftier logical puzzle than the "about": *Can* the play be said to be about "anything"? If so, it might as well be about the production of power as about, say, three hours in the theater.) By overturning the main plot-subplot hierarchy, Kastan ingeniously produces what Levin called an "ironic reading." It's also an "historical reading" (Levin's third category of critical malfeasance), but one which deploys historical evidence to shatter the totalizing illusion of official historiographies.

Much as I admire Kastan's essay, it's his epigraph (from Norman O. Brown's *Love's Body*, a text which brings back warm memories, like films of Woodstock) that I'd like to focus on: "Out of many, one: a logical impossibility; a piece of poetry, or symbolism; an enacted or incarnate metaphor; a poetic creation." Kastan invokes Brown's text because of its relevance to his theme, the hegemonic state and/or play versus the state and/or play of exuberant multiplicity. But it has a wider bearing on the issues enacted in this volume. Is the democratic ideal, *e pluribus unum*, now worth less than the dime it's inscribed on? Is the dream of incorporation actually a nightmare of late-capitalist coercion? Those who are proud to call themselves ideological critics and those who see ideological criticism (when written with a leftward slant) as the writing on the wall may agree that "Out of many, one [is] a logical impossibility." Experience, if not authority, teaches me too that the best of pluralist intentions sometimes founder on the reality of unassimilable difference. And now that literary criticism carries the weight of the world on its shoulders, so that studies of Shakespeare's Tudor history plays seem determined to encompass the whole history of racial, sexual, and class oppression, our differences may appear greater than ever. I've tried to assure myself in this brief commentary that those differences can be invigorating, that they're signs of individual and institutional health. Still, with my attention drawn to Norman O. Brown, I conclude with a utopian leaf taken from his book: "To heal is to make whole, as in wholesome; to make one again; to unify or reunify: this is Eros in action. Eros is the instinct that makes for union, or unification, and Thanatos, the death instinct, is the instinct that makes for separation, or division" (80).

"treat the play as an enemy to be fought" ("Bardicide" 501), epistemological problems arising from charges of "hubristic objectivism" ("Bardicide" 499; this volume).[1] Levin's point about some feminists' crediting Shakespeare with a feminism in advance of his time is one Carol Cook makes in this volume; I have made it myself (*Women* 221–22).

Against Levin, I have no personal ax to grind—he ignores rather than attacks my main feminist work (not "thematic"?) and glances at my early work as one of feminist criticism's "first tentative efforts," apparently not too obnoxious ("Feminist Thematics" 125). But I signed the letter to *PMLA*, and attended (with most of the signers) an informal lunch at which its main ideas were sketched out. I signed because I perceived consequences of such an essay in that world beyond the page in which women must live.[2]

The lunch—at a conference of that hotbed of radicalism, the Shakespeare Association—was a larger gathering than analogous convocations in *Swetnam the Woman-hater* and other imagined congresses of outraged womankind; and what with the clattering of knives and forks and the din of discourse I couldn't catch the temper of the whole room. But people sitting near me were worried not about Levin's disagreement with our critical practices or theories—such healthy testing is the essence of academic life—but about a possible political agenda, part of a backlash against the women's movement they had encountered in many places. Some people think backlash talk is paranoid, just as others think talk of a feminist takeover is paranoid; to try to get beyond a cry of "help, the paranoids are after us," I will document the backlash I've experienced over the last two years. My context is Canadian, mostly western; my experience may not be representative. Readers in other places can test their experiences against mine.

I teach at Canada's second largest English-speaking university, in an English Department of seventy-one professors. We have a cosmopolitan staff, but we *are* isolated: Canada's most northerly university, we sit amid thousands of miles of rural conservatism, some of which rubs off on us. Affirmative action, entrenched in university policy, has almost never (to my knowledge) been practiced, either on gender or racial grounds; Women's Studies is in its infancy; there was a lot of resistance to setting up a day care center for staff children—after all, as a chemistry professor wrote to our staff newspaper only last year, the university shouldn't employ married women, who should be home raising children, a woman's true function. Readers may not recognize their own universities in this portrait of mine—yet mine has the advantage, as an example, that attitudes discreetly hidden in more southerly universities are voiced aloud here, with refreshing candor. Think of my university as a time machine, by which to go back a generation.

What has been happening here in the last two years? The fledgling Women's Studies program has been charged with being not a real academic discipline but an eruption of ideology in that otherwise doctrinally untainted preserve of objective thought, the university. A speaker was brought in to advocate Men's Studies—not to explore male imprisonment in gender stereotypes, but to disempower Women's Studies by showing that men do not really have more political power than women, that men have been victimized more than women (forced to go to war) and by women (false accusations of rape). (Cook's evidence that Levin regards men as victimized by women—specifically feminists—jibes with such complaints.) A visiting Women's Studies speaker was faced with the charge that her discipline favors admitting women writers into literary canons not for "merit" or "excellence" but solely on grounds of "ideology." (The same charge is made when women authors are added to English courses, or gender issues discussed in male works; again, "ideology" is the buzzword.) That Women's Studies is perceived as such a dire threat recalls Gayle Greene's remark on "how little a woman needs to accomplish . . . to provoke fear and rage, how terrified men are, how hysterical they are, about women making inroads into the professions" (this volume): Women's Studies here consists of one professor with an office in a trailer.[3]

Affirmative-action hiring has been assailed too. Since, as I've said, almost none of it goes on here, this has been a ghostly campaign. I must declare a personal interest in this one: I chaired our English Department when, in 1989, it had five junior tenurable positions vacant and hired five women. It was not an affirmative action hiring; they were simply the best candidates, as the department agreed with almost unprecedented unanimity—all five had books accepted for publication, and they were outstanding in many other ways. Inside the department, most people were very happy with the hirings; outside, rumblings began. No one approached me to ask if it had been an affirmative-action hiring, or if excellent male candidates had been passed over; I would happily have spoken with them. Instead, various professors began a campaign of hate letters to the Vice-President. Presently they took to the staff newspaper, where they attacked me in print over several months, calling my professional integrity into question on no grounds at all, for the crime of having hired women. The fact that during my previous years as chair the department had hired five men and one woman never excited the notice of these self-professed defenders against gender discrimination; nor did they take to print when my male successor as chair hired only men the following year. Our five new professors, during their first year here, found their credentials impugned in print by professors of economics, engineering, dentistry; a student asked one of them, in class, if it were true she was not qualified but was hired only because she was a woman. One of the five has now resigned her position.

Throughout this sordid business, three words kept sounding: "merit," "excellence," and "ideology." We want to hire only on the basis of merit and excellence, not of ideology: when men are hired it's merit and excellence; when women are hired it's ideology. The terms were identical to those of the attack on Women's Studies: the traditional way of hiring professors or canonizing writers was solely on the basis of merit; the feminist way of hiring professors or admitting writers to the canon is solely on the basis of ideology. Merit good, ideology bad. Me Tarzan, you Jane.

Against these professors' contention that fairness and merit are their only concerns, that they would protest any appointment in which politics and ideology helped exclude any candidate, one can adduce the fact that for nineteen years the university has complied with the federal government's "Canadians only" hiring policy, and I don't recall a single protest against this exclusion of meritorious candidates on *purely* political grounds. That no uproar occurs when only men are hired, or only Canadians, indicates that our noisy faction is not opposed to ideology or in favor of excellence; it is opposed to hiring women and in favor of hiring men. The ideology talk is a smokescreen. This I will return to. But back to my narrative.

It now began to be felt that the warm spirit of collegiality on campus was starting to chill; to mend things a colloquium on "excellence" was sponsored. Articulate, logical, witty, subtle, the speakers approached the topic like good academics, exploring the history of the concept "excellence," its polyvalent lexical resonances, philosophical implications, social ramifications. The one thing missing was any recognition of the way the word has been used by the attackers: as a code word, a masonic password by which the Merit Only league recognized each other at public gatherings.[4]

At just this time, when our English Department was being attacked for hiring women and Women's Studies for existing, an explosive event shook another Canadian campus. On December 6, 1989, one Marc Lepine entered an engineering class at the University of Montreal, armed with a semi-automatic rifle; separating out female students, he shouted, "You're all a bunch of feminists" and began shooting. Over the next twenty minutes he hunted down women, leaving fourteen dead. He left, on his suicide, a long letter raging against feminism and listing some ninety prominent women he hoped to kill. Over the next few days on radio phone-in programs, female callers linked Lepine's act with sexism and violence toward women in society, while most males dismissed Lepine as a lunatic and belittled charges of sexism;

many displayed hostility to feminism, a force they saw as disrupting family life, taking jobs away from men, threatening the fabric of society.

A big crowd of women and men held a vigil on the snowy steps of our administration building, for the women killed; I remember being especially shaken and moved by this vigil, since my own daughter was in Montreal at another university. One speaker, a young woman engineering student, spoke briefly and simply of sexism in our own Faculty of Engineering. A few days later at engineering Skit Night, long an occasion for puerile sexist skits, the woman who had spoken at the vigil appeared and the crowd chanted "shoot the bitch." Within a few days, she received a number of death threats, and finally dropped out of the university and moved away from the city, fearing for her safety. At about the same time, the engineering student newsletter made sexist remarks about the city's female mayor, and posters in the law school featured a woman with naked breasts slashed and bloody. The university at last responded by setting up a Commission on Equality and Respect.

Our local defenders of Merit were not silent through these times. One wrote to a city newspaper complaining that having a vigil for fourteen murdered students was an overreaction (*Edmonton Journal*, 10 December 1989). Understandably eager to put some distance between Lepine's views and their own, colleagues who had recently attacked women's programs and the hiring of women spoke out publicly to assure everyone that Lepine was a madman, whose insane act could not be linked with their rational views; one wrote to a national newspaper laying Lepine's behavior at the door of his mother. To many of us, Lepine's paranoia eerily resembled local views—women students are taking places in engineering and chemistry, males being excluded; Women's Studies is draining resources from "real" disciplines; women professors are being hired, costing men jobs; feminists are causing most of our problems. And we were told there was nothing to worry about because Lepine was only a paranoid psychopath with a gun. Our campus anti-feminists were indeed different. They didn't have guns.

In its hearings, the Commission on Equality and Respect heard a fair amount from the Knights of Merit. One, who claimed he'd attended every hearing, said in a radio interview that people telling the commission of campus sexism had uttered many falsehoods; he also appeared before the commission himself to decry "false accusations of sexism": those concerned about sexism on campus were "immoral" in "supporting a lynch-mob atmosphere in order to protect [their] own self-interest." He conceded that chanting "shoot the bitch" at a student "arguably might have reflected callousness toward women," but that this was the one and only possible sexist incident in recent campus history, and "even that case is less than clear" (*Folio*, 22 March 1990).

A graphic recent instance of male hysteria on our campus, the conviction that the university has been invaded or infiltrated by a fifth column of feminists, appeared in a letter from a colleague to the student paper (*Gateway*) on November 22, 1990. He demands, "Has not feminism been clearly identified as a political program having no place as part of the University's curriculum?" and in cold war spy-thriller language aludes luridly to "a larger political movement in which the intellectual operatives have been told to take over their own assigned segment of society, the University." On November 15, 1990, another professor wrote to the same paper proudly announcing the impossibility of "feminist ideology [being] forced on all women," assuring us that in his all-male department, fifty-seven percent of faculty wives had chosen to be full-time housewives; implicit was the specter of feminists as home-wreckers intent on giving ideas to contented housewives. The first letter envisions feminists as enemy agents, the second as wife-seducers; the first accuses feminists of carrying off-campus political concerns into the university's sacred halls; the second reveals that anti-feminist professors are carrying into the debate considerable baggage from *their* off-campus lives.

Such has been the antifeminist[5] backlash on my campus in the last two years. In this atmosphere I found myself, as I read Levin's attack on feminist criticism. Other backlashes mentioned at that lunch seem to differ from mine in degree, not kind, and are continuous with backlashes outside our ivory but not bulletproof tower, from the failure of the Equal Rights Amendment to restrictions on access to abortion. To attack feminist criticism in such a climate is not politically innocent. I know Levin slightly, and believe him when he says he "accept[s] feminist political ideology" and implies he meant no harm to it by his purely literary arguments (this volume); but to mean no harm is not necessarily to do no harm.

Levin's remarks have added one more string to the bow of those who don't want to hire women professors, fund women's studies, or approve for the curriculum courses dealing with women; they now have the authority of a prominent scholar and the *PMLA* to help them argue that no, it isn't that we're against women, it's that we're for merit, for excellence, and they after all are bad critics, not real literary critics at all but narrow ideologues, the sort of person who doesn't *belong* in a university but should be out picketing somewhere. Who recalls that Levin professed to attack feminist *thematic* critics? (There was a lot of slippage in his essay, from thematists to feminists in general.)[6] People just made a mental note that a well-known professor proved feminist criticism academically unrespectable.[7]

Levin's allusion to his earlier attacks on (male) thematic or historicist critics (this volume) is unhelpful: they aren't in the same vulnerable position. Feminism touches things that threaten people: it impinges on people's marriages, ideas about The Family, sexual hangups. *No* intellectual polemic can conjure up around thematic criticism the primal fears pulsating around the idea of the female. People don't blame thematic critics when their marriages break up, but they do blame feminism; people don't shoot thematically-inclined students when they can't get into a university themselves. Attacking a group as intensely vulnerable as feminists is *not* the same as attacking thematic critics. Whether Levin had a political agenda doesn't matter; consciously or unconsciously, he has played into the hands of those who do, giving them another way to pretend that their male supremacist views are actually expressions of high academic standards.[8]

To some extent, *Shakespeare Left and Right* sidesteps this problem. It *is* a fine collection. The essays of the second part exemplify good criticism: careful reading, interpretations tested against the text—no evidence here of programmatic forcings of the text into preconceived frameworks dictated by abstract ideology. The feminist essays show how far good feminist criticism is from the mere pratings about patriarchy to which "Feminist Thematics" reduces it. It's true that in the volume's first part Shakespeare isn't mentioned for pages at a time, while theory is debated, but so what? Shakespeare is hardly starved for attention, and theory is important. As I have argued elsewhere, though, theoretical debate can sometimes *mask* problems, as in the Swetnam controversy and other *querelles des femmes:* "Attacks and defenses were eruditely written; their classical form and their Christian-humanist opinions and *exempla* gave the impression of true intellectual theory; . . . the existence of so many treatises created the illusion that the topic was being discussed in a responsible way. The question of women, it must have seemed, was being taken care of" (*Women* 133); yet real-life women were steadily losing power and opportunity. And that's rather the sense I have in this volume, with its erudite scholarship and arguments often shrewd, at times brilliant: "ideology" is being thoroughly aired, but. . . .

I'm reminded of that stimulating but unsatisfying colloquim: serious scholars in treating "excellence" as an intellectual construct unwittingly deflected attention from the fact that it was serving as a password. The very intellectualizing of debate obscured what was going on: an institutional power struggle. The ideology talk was a smokescreen. There's a danger that by doing what academics do—responding intellectually to a complex problem—we are walking into a trap. Levin made a political move (attacking feminism) which he defined as an intellectual move; feminist critics responded politically (condemning his attack); he countered with the argument that he is intellectual while they are political. Responding, several writers in this volume keep the political question sharply in view; others accept the definition of the problem as largely intellectual. Intellectualizing is important: it provides theory crucial to both criticism and social action; but separated from a sense of local political reality it can be dangerous, and I have some sympathy with Michael Sprinker's suggestion that we stop responding to such attacks altogether.

Levin uses "ideology" in a different sense from that of most contributors to this volume, and the two senses belong not to different individuals but to separate discourses. It's not as if Wordsworth were arguing with Coleridge on the meaning of "heart"; it's as if Wordsworth were arguing with a cardiac surgeon on the meaning of "heart." Or, since, unlike "excellence," "ideology" often functions not only as a password but as a term of abuse in a smear campaign, it is as if a distinguished political science scholar were trying to discuss the meaning of "communism" with one who habitually calls enemies "commies." Most contributors are honestly trying to come to terms with "ideology" as an intellectual construct. They are not entirely innocent of using it as a password—it places them in a cluster of approaches (feminist, Marxist, new historicist, cultural materialist)—but they make honest attempts to define it, understand it, trace its intellectual pedigree; they don't use it as a term of abuse for denigrating groups of scholars. Levin's use seems to me much closer to just that: ideology for him is a term of abuse, as it is on my campus for those attacking women's studies, feminist interpretations in the classroom, the hiring of female professors.

I would expect holders of such reactionary views to align themselves with Right-to-Lifers, fundamentalist religion, Back-to-Basics in education, toughness on welfare bums, maintaining America's military might, respect for the police, warfare on drugs, allegiance to the flag, and putting Father back at the head of the family. Levin, however, says he's a liberal, which means saying what one likes under the banner of free speech—though liberals recognize that freedom of speech does not extend to yelling "fire" in a crowded theater, and I would say that in the present climate, attacking feminist criticism *is* such a yell.[9] Levin shouldn't be surprised to be thought neo-conservative, since he speaks the language of the Right—in his fanatical animus against Marxism and nearly-indecent gloating over the collapse of socialist regimes, his envisioning criticism as free enterprise (it "requires a free choice among competing approaches" just as "our democracy is based on pluralism, on the existence of different parties and interests that . . . compete in the public arena" [this volume])—*Laissez-faire* pluralism? If he doesn't want to be thought conservative, why conjure the McCarthy era and place himself on the anti-Communist side ("I am not now and never have been a New Critic" [this volume]), positioning himself among those who think feminist spy-masters tell "operatives . . . to take over their own assigned segment of society, the University"?

Whence comes this posture of the tolerant, benign, conciliatory gentleman, championing pluralism, live and let live: can this be the Levin of "Feminist Thematics," "Bardicide," and *New Readings vs. Old Plays*, charging into thematics, feminism, or historicism on a thundering steed, slashing away with a scimitar at idiocies to the left of him, inanities to the right of him? *That* was the Levin we knew and loved, the man who if he had your tribe alone in Arabia would make an end of thy posterity; a pox on this new pose of lovingkindness. It is of course an illusion anyway, since Levin's "pluralism" means that approaches compete until one wins, presumably silencing the others once and for all. Two models of competition flicker in and out of his imagery: first, one approach will triumph when it reaches the Truth and compels others to recognize it—the others will then wither away in embarrassment at their own inadequacy; and second, one approach always triumphs by main force, in a profession visualized as a King of the Mountain game, the king of "prestige" fending off attacks by the young from below, until one overwhelms him and reigns in his place—Freud's patricidal son meets Social Darwinism: the profession red in tooth and claw.

Given such imagery, there's something false about Levin's alliance with common readers against professional critics, as teased out by Gerald Graff (this volume). The common-reader passages have the drab tone of conventional piety: what really charges Levin's imagination is the cut and thrust of professional competition: here, his prose burns with a hard gem-like flame. He adopts the language of mass-attended sports: approaches compete in a public "arena" (this volume). Levin doesn't want peaceful co-existence with the common reader or anyone else; like any sportsman, he wants to win, and his criticism has always taken the stance of one braced for combat. (No wonder Cook counsels feminists to enter political criticism "armored" [this volume].) Seeking "victory" in the "arena," Levin is clearly piqued to find, as he thinks, the Feminist Flyers leading the league standings: proclaiming "the feminists' victory in the prestigious arena," he finds even Greene's complaints "evidence of their victory" in the gladiatorial carnage of a Shakespearean Super Bowl: "Young colleagues try to climb on their bodies because they are on top, . . . just as they themselves climbed on the bodies of the New Critics when they were on top, who in turn climbed on the bodies of the historical critics" (this volume). Those feminists got the desire, they got the momentum, they wanna win that ball game. We're used to men talking like this; but it's a long way from the simple pleasures of reading.

All this King of the Mountain, body-climbing talk—which Greene, not Levin, initiates, though she regrets it while he downright relishes it—may represent the way things are in our profession. But is this how things should be, and are we powerless to change them? Fearing that success for women will mean the same old dog-eat-dog competitive world, feminists have offered a cooperative model of human endeavor, against our culture's adulation of cut-throat competition. (Male critics Levin attacked didn't unite to answer—they didn't have years' experience banding together to start day-cares, lobby for changes in divorce laws, support sexual assault victims; to feminists, group action has become habitual. We can but pity thematic critics, suffering alone from Levin's assaults, unable to express their feelings in a thematist support group.) Levin's literary utopia where approaches battle it out and scholars claw their way to the top—the academy as corporate jungle—isn't one that warms *my* heart.[10]

Levin's attack on a tiny corner of the universe, feminist Shakespeare criticism, seems a ripple in a great tide: the old male-centered society stirring itself to reassert traditional values, reestablish old lifestyles, against alarming social change. Levin complacently reassures us, the "vast hinterland . . . full of people who resist feminism, . . . producing most of that 'rage' and 'backlash'," does not count "in the long run" (this volume). I think he's wrong: I think enraged hinterlanders outnumber feminist sympathizers a thousand to one. Many English professors oppose feminism, and as a group male English professors are if anything more liberated in their views of women than professors in most disciplines. That's just in the university—try sampling the views on feminism of construction workers, football players, truckers. That scholars who might have agreed with Levin declined to contribute to this volume ("Introduction" note 6) means an unfortunate imbalance that casts Levin as embattled underdog, a lonely voice; I think that, in fact, he has a vast majority behind him.

In the "long run," hinterlanders "count" by sheer numbers: traditionalists *do* regain control. When I was a child in the 1950s, when "she works outside the home" was uttered *sotto voce* as if this were a social disease, I came across my grandfather's medical school annual and noted a substantial number of women in the graduating class. What happened in the meantime was what always happens to women's movements—you relax after gaining the vote or being a wartime riveter and the next thing you know, you're back in the kitchen and women are invisible for another twenty years. The current backlash looks like the old push toward the kitchen sink. (Think of my university as a time machine by which to go *forward* a generation.)

Levin used to attack thematists or historicists for being wrongheaded; now he attacks feminists and Marxists for being ideological. (And wrongheaded.) What makes an approach ideological? What do feminism and Marxism share, that the others lack? First, both are consistently interested in the lot of a disadvantaged group (women, the working class)—not in itself a hateful trait, except to conservatives; second, both have always had one foot in the extra-literary world. Levin's claim that he "accepts feminist political ideology" in life but not in literature seems an attempt to cut the tie between life and literature.[11] Yet *can* one accept feminism without recognizing that tie? That literature impinges on women's lives has been a vital recognition of feminism from the start. It is no accident that women of letters have led feminism since Wollstonecraft, since Christine de Pisan: noticing how literature shapes our social roles and constructs our very identities is a first step to understanding how culture molds us. If social construction of identity is a feminist legacy to critical theory, the insight has been active far beyond canonical literature and the academy: hundreds of grass-roots feminists have protested stereotyping of girls in textbooks, have boycotted companies' products when their advertising shows men planning skyscrapers and women scrubbing floors.

As to whether feminist criticism is "in," of course it is. Walter Cohen was not far wrong when in 1987 he called it "the most widely practiced approach to Shakespeare in the United States" (22), and since 1987, journals haven't dropped it. It's a fashion, like character criticism or image patterns, and like earlier fashions it will pass. Getting essays accepted did get easier once the fashion was established, and the cynical might say this was after it was taken up by male critics (a suspicion this volume's gender balance does little to dispel), but let's not be cynical: only occasionally do I think, of male feminists, that men always find a way to take over—usually I value their help. When this fashion passes it will be mourned more intensely than most such deaths. An image hunter can easily retool into a thematist; but feminism has meant more than that to us.

As to whether "women enjoy literature" (Levin, this volume), one could answer, not all literature: I don't enjoy, say, act 5 of *The Taming of the Shrew*. Not to recognize that women have ambivalent feelings toward a cultural form that so often stereotypes, brutalizes, or excludes them is simply insensitive. Or one could situate the question in the ideology debate: pleasure is culturally constructed like any human activity; whether I take pleasure in sonnets or in bowling is hardly unconditioned by my social class, any more than whether I choose needlework or boxing is unrelated to my gender. But this said, I'll say yes, I *do* enjoy literature, and after the exhaustion of taking three degrees in English and the often repetitive business of teaching it for twenty years, I still read for pleasure, and literature still matters more to me than almost anything. That is why I decline the invitation to view it as a battleground or sports arena, where opponents bloody each other in the prestige stakes, or the invitation to seal it off from life. I value the moments when a student, angry at the sentiment "he for God only, she for God in him," blurts out "That offends me, that makes me feel women are some kind of appendage; I don't feel the same about church; the minister probably agrees with Milton." Feminist criticism has faults like any other sort; it has its inept or careless readers, its schematic oversimplifiers, its opportunists, its polemicists and its plodders. But one of its virtues is precisely that which those who smear it as "ideology" seem to count a vice: it constantly assumes that literature matters to people's lives.

In December 1989, just after the Montreal shootings, my daughter was coming home for the holidays; awaiting her plane from Montreal, I stood in the airport wondering what life held for her, what her chances of a satisfying career would be, what life would be like for women when she was my age. As she got off the plane I began to cry, thinking of those fourteen families whose student daughters would never come home from Montreal for this holiday. And I gave her books for Christmas, because she loves reading.

## NOTES

1. I share Levin's uneasiness with thematic criticism and readily acknowledge that *New Readings* helped me articulate and examine the uneasiness that was previously only intuitive. I have found some of the questions he raised in that book very useful in teaching as well as in my own reading.

2. Though Levin subsequently also attacked Marxist and Freudian criticism, I'll comment mainly on feminism, the focus of the essay that started all this.

3. The rather paranoid attribution of vast power and influence to feminists—power we certainly don't often feel ourselves—is a common feature of these attacks on women's programs; the nameless souls who write to Levin seem to share this anxiety: "many of my correspondents felt *PMLA* is now controlled by the feminist and other new approaches" (Forum 79).

4. Levin understands code words: see "Bardicide" note 19.

5. Should it be "anti-feminist" (opposed to feminism) or "antifeminist" (opposed to women)? It's both, I fear.

6. Levin announces at the outset in "Feminist Thematics" his wish to "to examine the nature of this criticism"—that is, "feminist criticism of Shakespeare . . . [and] of many other aspects of the canon," but space limits him to "one major trend" (125). He gives no reason for his choice, though his calling the trend "major" suggests that he chose it as being representative, which indicates again his real wish to attack *all* feminist criticism, given world enough and time. Or he may have chosen this "trend" because he saw it as the worst of feminist writing—he *has* virulently attacked thematic criticism in the past; if so, he deliberately made a choice he thought

would show feminist criticism in the worst possible light. I have little sympathy with his claim "I am not dealing with this entire approach but only with one strand" (Forum 78)—he has clearly offered a synecdoche in which one strand represents the whole. He doesn't even identify the "trend" as "thematic" until 850 words into the essay; before that, it remains a Mystery Approach, called "an interpretive approach," "this one approach," "this approach" (125). By the time he announces, like a triumphant sleuth, "these [quotations] should be enough to make the point, which is, quite simply, that this body of criticism is thematic," it requires a deliberate effort of memory to recall that "this body of criticism" refers not to feminist Shakespeare criticism in general but to a set of writings Levin himself has selected on the basis of their being thematic. And by page 131, he has slipped back into talking of feminist Shakespeare criticism as a whole—"this group of critics" and "this body of criticism" clearly refer to the whole thing, since both include the "early studies" Levin initially exempted from his critique of feminist thematic criticism.

7. And they needn't limit it to Shakespeare criticism—Levin himself says that "much of the discussion will also apply to similar kinds of feminist criticism in other fields" ("Feminist Thematics" 125).

8. To his opponents' charge that he failed "to understand the serious concerns about inequality and injustice that have engendered feminist analyses of literature," Levin replies, "what they were saying is that I did not accept feminist political ideology. I replied that I did accept it, but that this did not affect my judgment of those feminist readings"; he claims that feminists "made acceptance of their politics a prerequisite for judging feminist analyses of literature" (this volume). The equivocation between "understand" and "accept" is crucial; one who truly understood feminism's "serious concerns," whether he accepted them or not, would not display such political naivete in the timing of a publication.

9. Some of our campus merit defenders espouse free speech causes; under this banner, they have defended the right of publishers to purvey pornography, and of an Alberta high school teacher to teach that the Holocaust never occurred—it was a fabrication by an international Jewish conspiracy controlling the media. One *could* call these stances liberal, but that is not the only construction that might be put upon them. The recent volume of essays *The Sexual Liberals and the Attack on Feminism*, ed. Leidholdt and Raymond, documents the way liberals, approaching feminists "as friends offering support" (173), have defended female-subjugating institutions in the name of free speech. The information on funding of American Civil Liberties Union activities by pornographers (xii–xiii, 198–99) is especially revealing. One writer describes liberalism as "people with power defend[ing] their oppression of women as freedom" (4); another writes that "the history of liberalism, of libertarianism, and libertinism has been a history of gentlemen advocating liberty and license for gentlemen" (176).

10. I have used "attack" often, but it seems unavoidable; this word, with its connotations of aggression, combat, and/or sexual assault is one Levin applies to his own work (e.g., this volume). The historical Joseph Swetnam was a fencing master, and the language of argumentative discourse abounds in weaponry, a fact about which Levin's despised Freudians can draw obvious conclusions. The macho academy too, has its "big guns," its "hired gun" Department chairs, its task forces. Until feminists objected, our Commission on Equality and Respect was to be the Commission to Combat Sexism.

11. His contention "a just cause cannot justify interpretive faults" (this volume) sounds reasonable—except that what constitutes a "fault" will always be debatable—but he attacks not interpretive faults *per se*, but those faults presumed to have arisen from the blinkering effect of

enslavement to ideology. Marxism and feminism are "consciously produced from a political creed"; he discusses them separately because they are "significantly different from the others in the threat they pose" (7). If Levin were mainly interested in "faults" he could easily organize his attacks around kinds of fault rather than around groups of critics labelled ideological because of their involvement in the world beyond the page.

# Bibliography

Abercrombie, Nicholas, Stephen Hill, and Bryan S. Turner. *Sovereign Individuals of Capitalism*. London: Allen and Unwin, 1986.

Abrams, M. H. "A Reply." *High Romantic Argument: Essays for M. H. Abrams*. Ed. Lawrence Lipking. Ithaca: Cornell UP, 1981. 164–75.

Abrams, Richard. "*The Tempest* and the Concept of the Machiavellian Playwright." *English Literary Renaissance* 8 (1978): 43–66.

Adelman, Janet. "'Anger's My Meat': Feeding, Dependency, and Aggression in *Coriolanus*." *Representing Shakespeare: New Psychoanalytic Essays*. Ed. Murray M. Schwartz and Coppélia Kahn. Baltimore: Johns Hopkins UP, 1980. 129–49.

———. "Born of Woman: Fantasies of Maternal Power in *Macbeth*." *Cannibals, Witches, and Divorce: Estranging the Renaissance*. Ed. Marjorie Garber. Baltimore: Johns Hopkins UP, 1987.

Adelman, Janet, et al. Forum. *PMLA* 104 (1989): 77–78.

Adorno, Theodor. "Perennial Fashion—Jazz." *Prisms*. Trans. Samuel and Shierry Weber. London: Spearman, 1967.

Agnew, Jean-Christopher. *Worlds Apart: The Market and the Theater in Anglo-American Thought, 1550–1750*. Cambridge: Cambridge UP, 1986.

Alter, Robert. *The Pleasures of Reading in an Ideological Age*. New York: Simon, 1989.

Althusser, Louis. "Ideology and Ideological State Apparatuses (Notes Towards an Investigation)." *Lenin and Philosophy and Other Essays*. Trans. Ben Brewster. New York: Monthly Review P, 1972.

*American Heritage Dictionary*. Ed. William Morris. Boston: Houghton Mifflin, 1976.

# Bibliography

Armstrong, Paul B. *Conflicting Readings: Variety and Validity in Interpretation*. Chapel Hill: U of North Carolina P, 1990.

Aronowitz, Stanley, and Henry A. Giroux. *Education under Siege: The Conservative, Liberal and Radical Debate over Schooling*. South Hadley, MA: Bergin and Garvey, 1985.

Augustine, St. *City of God*. Ed. David Knowles. Harmondsworth: Penguin, 1972.

Austin, J. L. *How to Do Things with Words*. 2nd ed. Cambridge: Harvard UP, 1975.

Bakhtin, Mikhail. *Problems of Doestoevski's Poetics*. Trans. Caryl Emerson. Minneapolis: U of Minnesota P, 1984.

———. *Rabelais and his World*. Trans. Hélène Iswolsky. Bloomington: Indiana UP, 1984.

Balch, Stephen H. and Herbert London. "The Tenured Left." *Commentary* 82 (1986): 41–50.

Bamber, Linda. *Comic Women, Tragic Men: A Study of Gender and Genre in Shakespeare*: Stanford: Stanford UP, 1982.

Barber, C. L. *Shakespeare's Festive Comedy: A Study of Dramatic Form and Its Relation to Social Custom*. Princeton: Princeton UP, 1957.

Barker, Francis. *The Tremulous Private Body: Essays on Subjection*. London: Methuen, 1984.

Barker, Francis, and Peter Hulme. "Nymphs and Reapers Heavily Vanish: The Discursive Contexts of *The Tempest*." Drakakis 191–205.

Barroll, J. Leeds. *Artificial Persons: The Formation of Character in the Tragedies of Shakespeare*. Columbia: U South Carolina P, 1974.

Barth, Hans. *Truth and Ideology*. Trans. Frederic Lilge. Berkeley: U of California P, 1976.

Barthes, Roland. "The Death of the Author." 1968. *Image-Music-Text*. Trans. and ed. Stephen Heath. London: Fontana, 1977. 142–48.

———. *The Pleasure of the Text*. Trans. Richard Miller. New York: Hill and Wang, 1975.

Barton, Anne. "Introduction." *The Tempest*. Harmondsworth: Penguin, 1968. 7–50.

———. "*Julius Caesar* and *Coriolanus*: Shakespeare's Roman World of Words." *Shakespeare's Craft: Eight Lectures*. Ed. Philip H. Highfill, Jr. Carbondale: Southern Illinois UP, 1982. 24–47.

Battenhouse, Roy. "*Henry* V as Heroic Comedy." *Essays on Shakespeare and Elizabethan Drama in Honor of Hardin Craig*. Ed. Richard Hosley. Columbia: U of Missouri P, 1962. 163–82.

———. *Shakespearean Tragedy: Its Art and Its Christian Premises*. Bloomington: Indiana UP, 1969.

Baxter, John. *Shakespeare's Poetic Styles: Verse into Drama*. London: Routledge, 1980.

Bayley, John. *The Characters of Love: A Study in the Literature of Personality*. New York: Basic, 1960.

———. *Shakespeare and Tragedy*. London: Routledge, 1981.

Beaumann, Sally. *The Royal Shakespeare Company*. Oxford: Oxford UP, 1982.

Bell, Daniel. *The End of Ideology*. New York: Free, 1961.

———. *Cultural Contradictions of Capitalism*. New York: Basic, 1976.

———. *The End of Ideology: On the Exhaustion of Political Ideas in the Fifties: With a New Afterword*. Cambridge: Harvard UP, 1988.

Belsey, Catherine. *Critical Practice*. New York: Methuen, 1980.

———. "Literature, History, Politics." *Literature and History* 9 (1983): 17–27.

———. *The Subject of Tragedy: Identity and Difference in Renaissance Drama*. London: Methuen, 1985.

———. "Disrupting Sexual Difference: Meaning and Gender in the Comedies." Drakakis 166–90.

Bennett, William. "Lost Generation: Why America's Children Are Strangers in Their Own Land." *Policy Review* 33 (1985): 43–45.

———. "To Reclaim a Legacy." *American Educator* (1985): 21.

Berger, Harry, Jr. "Miraculous Harp: A Reading of Shakespeare's *Tempest*." *Shakespeare Studies* 5 (1969): 253–83.

———. "What Did the King Know and When Did He Know It?: Shakespearean Discourses and Psychoanalysis." *South Atlantic Quarterly* 88 (1989): 811–62.

———. *Imaginary Audition: Shakespeare on Page and Stage*. Berkeley: U of California P, 1989.

Berger, Thomas L., and William C. Bradford, Jr. *An Index of Characters in*

*English Printed Drama to the Restoration*. Englewood, CO: Microcard, 1975.

Bevington, David. Introduction. Oxford Shakespeare edition of *1 Henry IV*. New York: Oxford UP, 1987.

Bhaskar, Roy. A *Realist Theory of Science*. 2nd ed. Atlantic Highlands, NJ: Humanities P, 1978.

———. *Scientific Realism and Human Emancipation*. London: Verso, 1986.

———. *Reclaiming Reality: A Critical Introduction to Contemporary Philosophy*. London: Verso, 1989.

Biggins, Dennis. "Sexuality, Witchcraft, and Violence in *Macbeth*." *Shakespeare Studies* 8 (1978): 255–77.

Birnbaum, Milton. Forum *PMLA* 104 (1989): 357–58.

Blanpied, John W. *Time and the Artist in Shakespeare's Histories*. Newark: U of Delaware P, 1983.

Bloom, Allan. *The Closing of the American Mind: How Higher Education Has Failed Democracy and Impoverished the Souls of Today's Students*. New York: Simon, 1987.

Bloom, Allan, and Harry V. Jaffa. "The Morality of the Pagan Hero: *Julius Caesar*." *Shakespeare's Politics*. New York: Basic, 1964.

Blumenfeld-Kosinski, Renate. *Not of Woman Born: Representations of Caesarean Birth in Medieval and Renaissance Culture*. Ithaca: Cornell UP, 1990.

Bodin, Jean. *The Six Bookes of a Commonweale*. Trans. Richard Knolles. London: 1606.

Booth, Wayne C. "Pluralism in the Classroom." *Critical Inquiry* 12 (1986): 468–79.

Booty, John E., ed. *The Book of Common Prayer 1559*. Folger Shakespeare Library. Charlottesville: UP of Virginia, 1976.

Bourdieu, Pierre. *Reproduction: In Education, Society, and Culture*. Trans. Richard Nice. London: Sage, 1977.

Bradley, A. C. *Shakespearean Tragedy: Lectures on* Hamlet, Othello, King Lear, *and* Macbeth. New York: World, 1904.

———. "The Rejection of Falstaff." *Oxford Lectures on Poetry*. 2nd ed. London: Macmillan, 1909. 256–58.

Brecht, Bertolt. *The Messingkauf Dialogues*. Trans. John Willett. London: Eyre Methuen, 1965.

Breight, Curt. "'Treason Doth Never Propser': *The Tempest* and the Discourse of Treason." *Shakespeare Quarterly* 41 (1990): 1–28.

Brennan, Teresa, ed. *Between Psychoanalysis and Feminism*. London: Routledge, 1989.

Breton, Nicholas. *The Works in Verse and Prose of Nicholas Breton*. Ed. Alexander B. Grosart. London: Edinburgh UP, 1879.

Bristol, Michael D. "Lenten Butchery: Legitimation Crisis in *Coriolanus*." Howard and O'Connor 207–24.

———. *Shakespeare's America, America's Shakespeare*. London: Routledge, 1990.

Brown, John Russell, ed. *Focus on* Macbeth. London: Routledge, 1982.

———. "Introduction." *Henry* V. Signet Classic edition. New York: NAL-Penguin, 1988.

Brown, Norman O. *Love's Body*. New York: Vintage, 1966.

Brown, Paul. "'This Thing of Darkness I Acknowledge Mine': *The Tempest* and the Discourse of Colonialism." Dollimore and Sinfield 48–71.

Burckhardt, Jacob. *Civilization of the Renaissance in Italy*. Trans. S. G. C. Middlemore. New York: Harper, 1958.

Burckhardt, Sigurd. *Shakespearean Meanings*. Princeton: Princeton UP, 1968.

Burger, Peter. *Theory of the Avant-Garde*. Trans. Michael Shaw. Minneapolis: U of Minnesota P, 1984.

Burke, Kenneth. A *Rhetoric of Motives*. New York: Prentice, 1950.

Bynum, Caroline E. *Jesus as Mother: Studies in the Spirituality of the High Middle Ages*. Berkeley: U of California P, 1982.

Cairns, David and Shaun Richards. *Writing Ireland: Colonialism, Nationalism and Culture*. Manchester: Manchester UP, 1988.

Calderwood, James. "*Love's Labor's Lost*: A Wantoning With Words." *Studies in English Literature* 5 (1965): 317–32.

———. *Shakespearean Metadrama*. Minneapolis: U of Minnesota P, 1971.

———. *Metadrama in Shakespeare's Henriad:* Richard II *to* Henry V. Berkeley: U of California P, 1979.

Callaghan, Dympna. "Women and Children First: Violence and the Masquerades of Power." Renaissance Society of America. Toronto, Apr. 6, 1990.

Camden, William. *Remains Concerning Britain*. Ed. R. D. Duncan. Toronto: U of Toronto P, 1984.

Campbell, Lily B. *Shakespeare's Histories: Mirrors of Elizabethan Policy*. 1947. London: Methuen, 1964.

Carroll, William. *The Great Feast of Language in* Love's Labor's Lost. Princeton: Princeton UP, 1976.

Castiglione, Baldassare. *The Book of the Courtier*. Trans. Sir Thomas Hoby. London: J. M. Dent, 1974.

Cave, Terence. *The Cornucopian Text*. Oxford: Clarendon, 1979.

Cavell, Stanley. *Disowning Knowledge: In Six Plays of Shakespeare*. Cambridge: Cambridge UP, 1987.

Chase, Cynthia. "The Witty Butcher's Wife: Freud, Lacan, and the Conversion of Resistance to Theory." *MLN* 102 (1987): 989–1013.

Chodorow, Nancy. *The Reproduction of Mothering: Psychoanalysis and the Sociology of Gender*. Berkeley: U of California P, 1978.

———. *Feminism and Psychoanalytic Theory*. New Haven: Yale UP, 1989.

Chomsky, Noam. *Necessary Illusions: Thought Control in Democratic Societies*. Boston: South End P, 1989.

Cicero. *De Officiis*. Trans. Walter Miller. Cambridge: Harvard UP, 1975.

Cixous, Hélène and Catherine Clement. *The Newly Born Woman*. Trans. Betsy Wing. Minneapolis: U of Minnesota P, 1986.

Clarke, Mary Cowden. *The Girlhood of Shakespeare's Heroines*. 5 vols. London: Hutchinson, 1891.

Clover, Carol. "Her Body, Himself: Gender in the Slasher Film." *Representations* 20 (1987): 187–228.

Cohen, Derek. *Shakespearean Motives*. New York: St. Martin's, 1988.

Cohen, Walter. "Political Criticism of Shakespeare." Howard and O'Connor 18–46.

Coleridge, Samuel Taylor. *Shakespearean Criticism*. Ed. Thomas Middleton Raysor. 2nd ed. 2 vols. London: Dent, 1960.

Cook, Carol. "Unbodied Figures of Desire." *Performing Feminisms: Feminist Critical Theory and Theatre*. Ed. Sue-Ellen Case. Baltimore: The Johns Hopkins UP, 1990. 177–95.

Coursen, Herbert. *The Leasing Out of England: Shakespeare's Second Henriad*. Washington: U Presses of America, 1982.

Coward, Rosalind and John Ellis. *Language and Materialism: Developments in Semiology and the Theory of the Subject*. London: Routledge, 1977.

Cox, John D. *Shakespeare and the Dramaturgy of Power*. Princeton: Princeton UP, 1989.

Craig, Hardin. *Freedom and Renaissance*. Chapel Hill: U of North Carolina P, 1949.

Crews, Frederick. *Skeptical Engagements*. New York: Oxford UP, 1986.

Culler, Jonathan. *Structuralist Poetics: Structuralism, Linguistics and the Study of Literature*. Ithaca: Cornell UP, 1975.

Curtis, Mark H. *Oxford and Cambridge in Transition 1558–1642*. Oxford: Clarendon, 1959.

———. "The Alienated Intellectuals of Early Stuart England." *Past and Present* 23 (1962): 25–43.

Cutts, John. *Rich and Strange: A Study of Shakespeare's Last Plays*. Pullman: Washington State UP, 1968.

Danson, Lawrence. *Tragic Alphabet: Shakespeare's Drama of Language*. New Haven: Yale UP, 1974.

———. "Continuity and Character in Shakespeare and Marlowe." *Studies in English Literature* 26 (1986): 217–34.

Dash, Irene. *Wooing, Wedding, and Power: Women in Shakespeare's Plays*. New York: Columbia UP, 1981.

Dekker, Thomas. *Dramatic Works of Thomas Dekker*. Ed. Fredson Bowers. Vol. 1. Cambridge: Cambridge UP, 1953.

Delany, Paul. "*King Lear* and the Decline of Feudalism." *PMLA* 92 (1977): 429–40.

de Man, Paul. *The Resistance to Theory*. Minneapolis: U of Minnesota P, 1986.

Derrida, Jacques. *Margins of Philosophy*. Trans. Alan Bass. Chicago: U of Chicago P, 1982.

Dollimore, Jonathan. *Radical Tragedy: Religion, Ideology and Power in the Drama of Shakespeare and His Contemporaries*. Chicago: U of Chicago P, 1984.

———. "Introduction: Shakespeare, Cultural Materialism and the New Historicism." Dollimore and Sinfield, eds. 2–17.

———. "Shakespeare, Cultural Materialism, Feminism and Marxist Humanism." *New Literary History* 21 (1990): 471–94.

Dollimore, Jonathan, and Alan Sinfield. "History and Ideology: The Instance of *Henry* V." Drakakis 206–27.

———. "Culture and Textuality: Debating Cultural Materialism." *Textual Practice* 4 (1990): 91–100.

———, eds. *Political Shakespeare: New Essays in Cultural Materialism*. Ithaca: Cornell UP, 1985.

Donald, James, and Stuart Hall. *Politics and Ideology*. Milton Keynes and Philadelphia: Open UP, 1986.

Donoghue, Denis. "A Criticism of One's Own." *New Republic* 10 Mar. 1986: 34.

Drakakis, John, ed. *Alternative Shakespeares*. London: Methuen, 1985.

Durkheim, Emile. *The Elementary Forms of the Religious Life*. Trans. J. W. Swain. London: George Allen and Unwin, 1915.

Dusinberre, Juliet. *Shakespeare and the Nature of Women*. London: Macmillan, 1975.

Eagleton, Terry. *Criticism and Ideology: A Study in Marxist Literary Theory*. London: Verso, 1978.

———. *Literary Theory: An Introduction*. Minneapolis: U of Minnesota P, 1983.

———. "Ideology and Scholarship." *Historical Studies and Literary Criticism*. Ed. Jerome J. McGann. Madison: U of Wisconsin P, 1985. 114–25.

———. *The Ideology of the Aesthetic*. Oxford: Blackwell, 1990.

Earl, Donald. *The Moral and Political Tradition of Rome*. Ithaca: Cornell UP, 1967.

Elam, Keir. *Shakespeare's Universe of Discourse: Language-Games in the Comedies*. Cambridge: Cambridge UP, 1984.

Ellis, John. *Against Deconstruction*. Princeton: Princeton UP, 1989.

———. "Radical Literary Theory." *London Review of Books* 8 Feb. 1990: 7–8.

Erasmus. *The Praise of Folly*. Trans. Hoyt Hopewell Hudson. Princeton: Princeton UP, 1941.

Erickson, Peter. *Patriarchal Structures in Shakespeare's Drama*. Berkeley: U of California P, 1985.

Evans, Malcolm. *Signifying Nothing: Truth's True Contents in Shakespeare's Text*. Athens: U of Georgia P, 1986.

Felperin, Howard. *Shakespearean Representation: Mimesis and Modernity in Elizabethan Tragedy*. Princeton: Princeton UP, 1977.

———. *The Uses of the Canon: Elizabethan Literature and Contemporary Theory*. Oxford: Clarendon, 1990.

Ferguson, Margaret. "Afterword." Howard and O'Connor 273–83.

Ferguson, Margaret, Maureen Quilligan, and Nancy J. Vickers, eds. *Rewriting the Renaissance: The Discourses of Sexual Differences in Early Modern Europe*. Chicago: U of Chicago P, 1986.

Ferry, Anne. *The Art of Naming*. Chicago: U of Chicago P, 1988.

Fineman, Daniel A. "Introductions." Morgann, *Shakespeare Criticism* 1–140.

Fineman, Joel. *Shakespeare's Perjured Eye: The Invention of Poetic Subjectivity in the Sonnets*. Berkeley: U California P, 1986.

Fish, Stanley. "Commentary: The Young and the Restless." Veeser 303–16.

———. *Doing What Comes Naturally: Change, Rhetoric, and the Practice of Theory in Literary and Legal Studies*. Durham: Duke UP, 1989.

———. Forum Reply. *PMLA* 104 (1989): 219–21.

———. "Rhetoric." Lentricchia and McLaughlin 203–22.

Florio, John. *Second Frutes*. London: 1591.

Forset, Edward. *A Comparative Discourse of the Bodies Natural and Politique*. London: 1606.

Foucault, Michel. "What Is an Author?" 1969. Rev. version. *Textual Strategies: Perspectives in Post-structuralist Criticism*. Trans. and ed. Josue Harari. Ithaca: Cornell UP, 1979. 141–60.

Fox-Genovese, Elizabeth. "Literary Criticism and the Poetics of the New Historicism." Veeser 213–24.

Fraser, Russell. *Young Shakespeare*. New York: Columbia UP, 1988.

French, Marilyn. *Shakespeare's Division of Experience*. New York: Ballantine, 1981.

French, Peter A., Theodore E. Uehling, Jr., and Howard K. Wettstein, eds., *Ethical Theory: Character and Virtue (Midwest Studies in Philosophy XIII*). Notre Dame: U Notre Dame P, 1988.

Frye, Northrop. A *Natural Perspective: The Development of Shakespearean Comedy and Romance*. New York: Harcourt, 1965.

Fuller, Thomas. *Worthies of England*. Ed. John Freeman. London: Unwin, 1952.

Fuss, Diana. *Essentially Speaking: Feminism, Nature, and Difference*. London: Routledge, 1989.

Gadamer, Hans-Georg. *Truth and Method*. New York: Seabury, 1975.

Gallie, W. B. "Essentially Contested Concepts." *Proceedings of the Aristotelian Society* 56 (1955–56): 96–112.

Gallop, Jane. *The Daughter's Seduction: Feminism and Psychoanalysis*. Ithaca: Cornell UP, 1982.

Garber, Marjorie. *Shakespeare's Ghost Writers: Literature as Uncanny Causality*. London: Methuen, 1987.

Gardner, Helen. *In Defence of the Imagination*. Cambridge: Harvard UP, 1982.

Garrett, John, ed. *More Talking about Shakespeare*. London: Longman, Green, 1959.

———. *Talking of Shakespeare*. 1954. Freeport, NY: Books of Libraries, 1971.

Gayley, Charles Mills. *Shakespeare and the Founders of Liberty in America*. New York: Macmillan, 1917.

Guess, Raymond. *The Idea of a Critical Theory: Habermas and the Frankfurt School*. Cambridge: Cambridge UP, 1981.

Gilbert, Felix. "Machiavelli: The Renaissance of the Art of War." *Makers of Modern Strategy: Military Thought from Machiavelli to Hitler*. Ed. Edward Meade Earle. Princeton: Princeton UP, 1943. 3–15.

Goddard, Harold C. *The Meaning of Shakespeare*. Chicago: U of Chicago P, 1951. 215–68.

Godshalk, William L. *Patterning in Shakespearean Drama*. The Hague: Mouton, 1973.

Gohlke, Madelon. "I Woo'd Thee with My Sword': Shakespeare's Tragic Paradigms." *The Woman's Part: Feminist Criticism of Shakespeare*. Ed.

Carolyn Lenz, Gayle Greene, and Carol Neely. Urbana: U of Illinois P, 1980. 150–70.

Goldberg, Jonathan. "The Politics of Renaissance Literature: A Review Essay." *English Literary History* 49 (1982): 514–42.

———. "Shakespearean Inscriptions: The Voicing of Power." Parker and Hartman 116–37.

———. "Shakespearean Characters: The Generation of Silvia." *Voice Terminal Echo: Postmodernism and English Renaissance Texts*. New York: Methuen, 1986.

———. "Speculations: *Macbeth* and Source." Howard and O'Connor 242–64.

Goldman, Michael. "Characterizing Coriolanus." *Shakespeare Survey* 34 (1981): 73–84.

Gombrich, E. H. *Art and Illusion: A Study in the Psychology of Pictorial Representation*. 2nd ed. Princeton: Princeton UP, 1961.

Gould, Gerald. "A New Reading of *Henry V*." *English Review* 29 (1919): 42–55.

Graff, Gerald. *Literature Against Itself: Literary Ideas in Modern Society*. Chicago: U of Chicago P, 1979.

———. "The Pseudo-Politics of Interpretation." *The Politics of Interpretation*. Ed. W. J. T. Mitchell. Chicago: U of Chicago P, 1983. 145–58.

———. *Professing Literature: An Institutional History*. Chicago: U of Chicago P, 1987.

Gramsci, Antonio. *Selections from the Prison Notebooks*. Ed. Quintin Hoare and Geoffrey Nowell Smith. London: Lawrence and Wisehart; New York: International, 1971.

Granville-Barker, Harley. *Prefaces to Shakespeare: First Series*. London: Sidgwick, 1927.

Greenblatt, Stephen. *Renaissance Self-Fashioning*. Chicago: U of Chicago P, 1980.

———. "Invisible Bullets: Renaissance Authority and Its Subversion, *Henry IV, Henry V*." Dollimore and Sinfield, eds. 18–47.

———. *Shakespearean Negotiations: The Circulation of Social Energy in Renaissance England*. Berkeley: U of California P, 1988.

———, ed. *Representing the English Renaissance*. Berkeley: U of California P, 1988.

Greene, Gayle. " 'The Power of Speech/ To Stir Men's Blood': The Language of Tragedy in Shakespeare's *Julius Caesar.*" *Renaissance Drama* 11 (1980): 67–93.

———. "Feminist and Marxist Criticism: An Argument for Alliances." *Women's Studies* 9 (1981): 29–45. (Special issue on "Feminist Criticism of Shakespeare," ed. Gayle Greene and Carolyn Swift.)

Greene, Thomas. "*Love's Labor's Lost*: The Grace of Society." *Shakespeare Quarterly* 22 (1971): 315–28.

Gurr, Andrew. "*Coriolanus* and the Body Politic." *Shakespeare Survey* 28 (1975): 63–69.

Gurr, T. R. "Historical Trends in Violent Crime: A Critical Review of the Evidence." *Crime and Justice: An Annual Review of Research* 3 (1981): 295–353.

Habermas, Jürgen. *Communication and the Evolution of Society*. Trans. Thomas McCarthy. Boston: Beacon, 1979.

———. "Neo-Conservative Culture Criticism in the United States and West Germany: An Intellectual Movement in Two Political Cultures." *Habermas and Modernity*. Ed. Richard J. Bernstein. Cambridge: MIT P, 1985.

Hall, Joseph. *Heaven Upon Earth, and Characters of Vertues and Vices*. 1606. Ed. Rudolf Kirk. New Brunswick: Rutgers UP, 1948.

———. *The Poems of Joseph Hall*. Ed. Arnold Davenport. Liverpool: Liverpool UP, 1969.

Hardison, O. B. *Toward Freedom and Dignity: The Humanities and the Idea of Humanity*. Baltimore: Johns Hopkins UP, 1984.

Hawkes, Terence. *That Shakespeherian Rag*. London: Methuen, 1986.

Hawkins, Harriet. *The Devils Party: Critical Counter-Interpretations of Shakespearean Drama*. Oxford: Clarendon, 1985.

Hawkins, Michael. "History, Politics and *Macbeth*." Brown, ed. *Focus* 155–88.

Hazlitt, William. *Characters of Shakespeare's Plays*. London: 1817.

———. *Lectures on the English Poets*. London: 1818.

Hesse, Mary. *Revolutions and Reconstructions in the Philosophy of Science*. Bloomington: Indiana UP, 1980.

Hexter, J. H. "The Education of the Aristocracy in the Renaissance." *Journal of Modern History* 22 (1950): 1–20.

Hibbard, G. R. *The Making of Shakespeare's Dramatic Poetry*. Toronto: U of Toronto P, 1981.

Hill, Christopher. *The World Turned Upside Down*. Harmondsworth: Penguin, 1975.

Hobbes, Thomas. *Leviathan*. Ed. Michael Oakeshott. New York: Collier, 1962.

Holderness, Graham. "Radical Potentiality and Institutional Closure: Shakespeare in Film and Television." Dollimore and Sinfield, eds. 182–201.

———. *Shakespeare's History*. Dublin: Gill and Macmillan; New York: St. Martin's, 1985.

———, ed. *The Shakespeare Myth*. Manchester: Manchester UP, 1988.

Holderness, Graham, Nick Potter and John Turner. *Shakespeare: The Play of History*. London: Macmillan, 1988.

Holinshed, Raphael. *The First and Second Volume of Chronicles*. London: 1586.

Holland, Peter. "The Resources of Characterization in *Othello*." *Shakespeare Survey* 41 (1989): 119–32.

Horkheimer, Max. "Traditional and Critical Theory." *Selected Essays*. Trans. M. J. O'Connell. New York: Continuum, 1972.

Horwitz, Howard. " 'I Can't Remember': Skepticism, Synthetic Histories, Critical Action." *South Atlantic Quarterly* 87 (1988): 787–820.

Howard, Jean. "The New Historicism in Renaissance Studies." *English Literary Renaissance* 16 (1986): 13–43.

———. "Recent Studies in Elizabethan and Jacobean Drama." *Studies in English Literature* 27 (1987): 321–79.

———. "Renaissance Antitheatricality and the Politics of Gender and Rank in *Much Ado About Nothing*." Howard and O'Connor 163–87.

Howard, Jean, and Marion F. O'Connor, eds. *Shakespeare Reproduced: The Text in History and Ideology*. New York: Methuen, 1987.

Humphreys, Arthur, ed. *Julius Caesar*, by William Shakespeare. Oxford: Clarendon, 1984.

Hunt, Marvin. "Commotion in the Winds!" *Spectator* 8 Dec. 1988.

Irigaray, Luce. *This Sex Which Is Not One*. Trans. Catherine Porter. Ithaca: Cornell UP, 1985.

Iser, Wolfgang. *The Act of Reading: A Theory of Aesthetic Response*. Baltimore: Johns Hopkins UP, 1978.

Jacobi, Derek. "Interview: Derek Jacobi on Shakespearean Acting." *Shakespeare Quarterly* 36 (1985): 134–40.

Jaffa, Harry V. *Crisis of the House Divided*. New York: Doubleday, 1959.

James I. *Political Works of James I*. Ed. C. E. McIlwain. Cambridge: Harvard UP, 1918.

Jameson, Fredric. *The Political Unconscious: Narrative as a Socially Symbolic Act*. Ithaca: Cornell UP, 1981.

———. "Science versus Ideology." *Humanities in Society* 6 (1983): 283–302.

Jardine, Lisa. *Still Harping on Daughters: Women and Drama in the Age of Shakespeare*. Hemel Hempstead: Harvester Wheatsheaf, 1983.

Jay, Martin. *Marxism and Totality: The Adventures of a Concept from Lukács to Habermas*. Berkeley: U California P, 1984.

Johnson, Samuel. "Preface to Shakespeare" (1765). *Johnson on Shakespeare*. Vol. 7 of *The Yale Edition of the Works of Samuel Johnson*. Ed. Arthur Sherbo. New Haven: Yale UP, 1968. 59–113.

Kahn, Coppélia. "The Rape in Shakespeare's *Lucrece*." *Shakespeare Studies* 9 (1976): 45–72.

———. *Man's Estate: Masculine Identity in Shakespeare*. Berkeley: U of California P, 1981.

Kahn, Victoria. "Habermas, Machiavelli, and the Humanist Critique of Ideology." *PMLA* 105 (1990): 464–76.

Kastan, David Scott. "Proud Majesty Made a Subject: Shakespeare and the Spectacle of Rule." *Shakespeare Quarterly* 37 (1986): 459–75.

Kavanagh, James H. "Shakespeare in Ideology." Drakakis 144–65.

———. "Ideology." Lentricchia and McLaughlin 306–20.

Kermode, Frank. *The Art of Telling: Essays on Fiction*. Cambridge: Harvard UP, 1983.

Kermode, Frank, ed. *Four Centuries of Shakespearean Criticism*. New York: Avon, 1965.

Kernan, Alvin B. "The Henriad: Shakespeare's Major History Plays." *Modern Shakespearean Criticism: Essays in Style, Dramaturgy, and the Major Plays*. Ed. Kernan. New York: Harcourt, 1970. 245–75.

———. *The Death of Literature*. New Haven: Yale UP, 1990.

Kerrigan, William, and Gordon Braden. *The Idea of the Renaissance*. Baltimore: Johns Hopkins UP, 1989.

Kirschbaum, Leo. *Character and Characterization in Shakespeare*. Detroit: Wayne State UP, 1962.

Kittredge, George Lyman. *Shakespere* [sic]: *An Address Delivered on April 23, 1916 in Saunders Theatre at the Request of the President and Fellows of Harvard College*. Cambridge: Harvard UP, 1916.

Knapp, Robert S. *Shakespeare—The Theater and the Book*. Princeton: Princeton UP, 1989.

Knights, L. C. "How Many Children Had Lady Macbeth?" 1933. *Explorations*. London: Chatto, 1946. 1–39.

Kolodny, Annette. "Dancing Through the Minefield: Some Observations on the Theory, Practice, and Politics of a Feminist Literary Criticism." *The New Feminist Criticism*. Ed. Elaine Showalter. New York: Pantheon, 1985. 144–67.

Lacan, Jacques. *Écrits*. Paris: Editions du Seuil, 1966.

Laclau, Ernesto. *Politics and Ideology in Marxist Theory: Capitalism-Facism-Populism*. London: NLB, 1977.

La Guardia, Eric. "Ceremony and History: The Problem of Symbol from *Richard II* and *Henry V*." *Pacific Coast Studies in Shakespeare*. Ed. Walso F. McNeir and Thelma N. Greenfield. Engene: U of Oregon P, 1966. 68–88.

Lanham, Richard. *The Motives of Eloquence: Literary Rhetoric in the Renaissance*. New Haven: Yale UP, 1976.

Leggatt, Alexander. *Shakespeare's Comedy of Love*. London: Methuen, 1973.

Leidholdt, Dorchen, and Janice G. Raymond, eds. *The Sexual Liberals and the Attack on Feminism*. New York: Pergamon, 1990.

Lentricchia, Frank, and Thomas McLaughlin, eds. *Critical Terms for Literary Study*. Chicago: U of Chicago P, 1990.

Lenz, Carolyn Ruth, Gayle Greene, and Carol Thomas Neely, eds. *The Woman's Part: Feminist Criticism of Shakespeare*. Urbana: U of Illinois P, 1980.

Lévi-Strauss, Claude. *Structural Anthropology*. New York: Basic, 1963.

Levin, Harry. "Literature as a Social Institution." *Accent* 26 (1946): 159–68.

Levin, Richard. *The Multiple Plot in English Renaissance Drama*. Chicago: U of Chicago P, 1971.

———. *New Readings vs. Old Plays: Recent Trends in the Reinterpretation of English Renaissance Drama*. Chicago: U of Chicago P, 1979.

———. "Feminist Thematics and Shakespearean Tragedy." *PMLA* 103 (1988): 125–38.

———. "Leaking Relativism." *Essays in Criticism* 38 (1988): 267–76.

———. "Bashing the Bourgeois Subject." *Textual Practice* 3 (1989): 76–86.

———. Forum Reply. *PMLA* 104 (1989): 78–79.

———. "The Problem of 'Context' in Interpretation." *Shakespeare and the Dramatic Tradition: Essays in Honor of S. F. Johnson*. Ed. W. R. Elton and William B. Long. Newark: U of Delaware P, 1989. 88–106.

———. "It's a Panic." *Textual Practice* 4 (1990): 101–102.

———. "The Poetics and Politics of Bardicide." *PMLA* 105 (1990): 491–504.

———. "The Cultural Materialist Attack on Aristic Unity and the Problem of Ideological Criticism." *Professing Shakespeare Now: From Theory into Practice*. Ed. Robert Merrix and Nicholas Ranson. Lewiston, NY: Mellen, forthcoming.

Lichtheim, George. *The Concept of Ideology and Other Essays*. New York: Random, 1967.

Lipking, Lawrence. "Competitive Reading." *New Republic* 2 Oct. 1989: 28–35.

Livingston, Paisley. *Literary Knowledge: Humanistic Inquiry and the Philosophy of Science*. Ithaca: Cornell UP, 1988.

MacCallum, M. W. *Shakespeare's Roman Plays and Their Background*. London: Macmillan, 1925.

Macherey, Pierre. *A Theory of Literary Production*. London: Routledge; Boston: Henley, 1978.

Mannheim, Karl. *Ideology and Utopia: An Introduction to the Sociology of Knowledge*. Trans. Louis Wirth and Edward Shils. 1936. New York: Harcourt, n.d.

Marcus, Leah. "Justice for Margery Evans: A 'Local' Reading of *Comus*." *Milton and the Idea of Woman*. Ed. Julia Walker. Urbana: U of Illinois P, 1988. 66–85.

Marx, Karl. *The Eighteenth Brumaire of Louis Bonaparte*. New York: International, 1963.

———. *Critique of Hegel's Philosophy of Right*. In *The Marx-Engels Reader*. Ed. Robert C. Tucker. New York: Norton, 1972.

———. *The German Ideology*. In *The Marx-Engels Reader*. Ed. Robert C. Tucker. New York: Norton, 1972.

Matthews, Honor. *Character and Symbol in Shakespeare's Plays*. Cambridge: Cambridge UP, 1962; New York: Shocken, 1969.

McLaughlin, M. M. "Survivors and Surrogates: Children and Parents from the Ninth to the Thirteenth Centuries." *The History of Childhood*. Ed. Lloyd De Mause. New York: Psychohistory P, 1974.

McLuskie, Kathleen, "The Patriarchal Bard: Feminist Criticism and Shakespeare: *King Lear* and *Measure for Measure*." Dollimore and Sinfield, eds. 88–108.

———. *Renaissance Dramatists*. Hemel Hempstead: Harvester Wheatsheaf, 1989.

Melchiori Giorgio. "The Rhetoric of Character Construction: *Othello*." *Shakespeare Survey* 34 (1981): 61–72.

Miles, Gary B. "How Roman Are Shakespeare's Romans?" *Shakespeare Quarterly* 40 (1989): 257–83.

Milton, John. *Milton: Complete Poems and Major Prose*. Ed. Merritt Y. Hughes. New York: Odyssey, 1957.

Miola, Robert S. *Shakespeare's Rome*. Cambridge: Cambridge UP, 1983.

Moi, Toril. "Sexual / Textual Politics." *The Politics of Theory*. Ed. Francis Barker et al. Colchester: U of Essex P, 1983, 1–14.

Montrose, Louis. "The Purpose of Playing: Reflections on a Shakespearean Anthropology." *Helios*, ns 7 (1980): 53–76.

———. " 'Shaping Fantasies': Figurations of Gender and Power in Elizabethan Culture." 1983. Greenblatt, ed. 31–64.

Morgann, Maurice. *Morgann's Essay on the Dramatic Character of Sir John Falstaff*. Ed. William Arthur Gill. 1912. Freeport: Books for Libraries, 1970.

———. *An Essay on the Dramatic Character of Sir John Falstaff* (1777). *Shakespeare Criticism*. Ed. Daniel A. Fineman. Oxford: Clarendon, 1972. 141–215.

Mueller, Martin. "Yellow Stripes and Dead Armadillos." *Profession 89*. New York: MLA, 1989. 23–31.

Muir, Kenneth. *Shakespeare's Comic Sequence*. Liverpool: Liverpool UP, 1979.

———. "Shakespeare's Open Secret." *Shakespeare Survey* 34 (1981): 1–9.

Mullaney, Steven. *The Place of the Stage: License, Play, and Power*. Chicago: U of Chicago P, 1988.

Musil, Robert. *The Man Without Qualities*. Trans. Eithne Wilkins and Ernst Kaiser. New York: Capricorn Books, 1965.

Naunton, Robert. *Fragmenta Regalia*. Ed. John C. Ceroviski. Washington, DC: Folger Shakespeare Library, 1985.

Neely, Carol Thomas. *Broken Nuptials in Shakespeare's Plays*. New Haven: Yale UP, 1985.

———. "Constructing the Subject: Feminist Practice and the New Renaissance Discourses." *English Literary Renaissance* 18 (1988): 5–18.

Newman, Karen. " 'And Wash the Ethiop White': Femininity and the Monstrous in *Othello*." Howard and O'Connor 143–62.

Novy, Marianne. *Love's Argument: Gender Relations in Shakespeare*. Chapel Hill: U of North Carolina P, 1984.

Nussbaum, Martha. "Undemocratic Vistas." *New York Review of Books* 5 Nov. 1987: 20–26.

Nuttall, A. D. "Realistic Convention and Conventional Realism in Shakespeare." *Shakespeare Survey* 34 (1981): 33–37.

Ornstein, Robert. *A Kingdom for a Stage: The Achievement of Shakespeare's History Plays*. Cambridge: Harvard UP, 1972.

Overbury, Sir Thomas. *The Overburian Characters*. 1614. Ed. W. J. Paylor. Oxford: Blackwell, 1936.

Palmer, John L. *Comic Characters of Shakespeare*. London: Macmillan, 1946.

———. *Political Characters of Shakespeare*. London: Macmillan, 1945.

———. *Political Characters of Shakespeare*. London: Macmillan, 1948.

Parker, G. F. *Johnson's Shakespeare*. Oxford: Clarendon, 1989.

Parker, Patricia. *Literary Fat Ladies: Rhetoric, Gender, Property*. New York: Methuen, 1987.

Parker, Patricia and Geoffrey Hartman, eds. *Shakespeare and the Question of Theory*. London: Methuen, 1985.

Paster, Gail Kern. " 'In the Spirit of Men There Is No Blood': Blood as Trope of Gender in *Julius Caesar*." *Shakespeare Quarterly* 40 (1989): 284–98.

Patterson, Annabel. *Shakespeare and the Popular Voice*. Cambridge: Basil Blackwell, 1989.

Patterson, Lee. *Negotiating the Past: The Historical Understanding of Medieval Literature*. Madison: U of Wisconsin P, 1987.

Pearson, D'Orsay. " 'Unless I Be Reliev'd by Prayer': *The Tempest* in Perspective." *Shakespeare Studies* 7 (1974): 253–82.

Pechter, Edward. "Teaching Differences." *Shakespeare Quarterly* 41 (1990): 160–73.

Perry, John, ed. *Personal Identity*. Berkeley: U California P, 1975.

Pinciss, Gerald M. *Literary Creations: Conventional Characters in the Drama of Shakespeare and His Contemporaries*. Wolfeboro, NH: Brewer, 1988.

Plato, *The Collected Dialogues of Plato, Including the Letters*. Ed. Edith Hamilton and Huntington Cairns. With an Introduction and Prefatory Notes. New York: Bollingen, 1961.

Plutarch. *Shakespeare's Plutarch*. Trans. Sir Thomas North. 1579. Ed. T. J. B. Spencer. Harmondsworth: Penguin, 1968.

Popper, Sir Karl. *Conjectures and Refutations: The Growth of Scientific Knowledge*. 4th ed. London: Routledge, 1972.

Porter, Joseph A. *The Drama of Speech Acts: Shakespeare's Lancastrian Tetralogy*. Berkeley: U California P, 1979.

———. *Shakespeare's Mercutio: His History and Drama*. Chapel Hill: U of North Carolina P, 1988.

Prior, Moody A. "The Elizabethan Audience and the Plays of Shakespeare." *Modern Philology* (Nov. 1951): 101–23.

Purdy, Dwight H. Forum. *PMLA* 104: 357.

Puttenham, George. *The Art of English Poesie*. London: 1589.

Pye, Christopher. *The Regal Phantasm: Shakespeare and the Politics of Spectacle*. London: Routledge, 1989.

Rabkin, Norman. *Shakespeare and the Problem of Meaning*. Chicago: U of Chicago P, 1981.

Rice, Julian. "Desdemona Unpinned: Universal Guilt in *Othello*." *Shakespeare Studies* 7 (1974): 209–26.

Richardson, William. *Philosophical Analyses and Illustrations of Some of Shakespeare's Remarkable Characters*. London: 1774.

Richmond, Hugh. *Shakespeare's Sexual Comedy: A Mirror for Lovers*. Indianapolis: Bobbs, 1971.

Ripley, John. Julius Caesar *on Stage in England and America, 1599–1973*. Cambridge: Cambridge UP, 1980.

Roesen, Bobbyann [Anne Barton]. "*Love's Labor's Lost*." *Shakespeare Quarterly* 4 (1953): 411–26.

Rooney, Ellen. *Seductive Reasoning: Pluralism as the Problematic of Contemporary Literary Theory*. Ithaca: Cornell UP, 1989.

Rorty, Amélie Oksenberg. *The Identities of Persons* (*Topics in Philosophy* 3), Berkeley: U California P, 1976.

Rorty, Richard. *Philosophy and the Mirror of Nature*. Princeton: Princeton UP, 1979.

———. *Consequences of Pragmatism* (*Essays 1972–1980*). Minneapolis: U of Minnesota P, 1982.

———. *Contingency, Irony, Solidarity*. Cambridge: Cambridge UP, 1989.

Rose, Jacqueline. "Sexuality in the Reading of Shakespeare: *Hamlet* and *Measure for Measure*." Drakakis 95–118.

Salingar, Leo. "Shakespeare and the Ventriloquists." *Shakespeare Survey* 34 (1981): 51–59.

Schanzer, Ernest. *The Problem Plays of Shakespeare: A Study of* Julius Caesar, Measure for Measure, Antony and Cleopatra. London: Routledge, 1963.

Scholes, Robert. *Structuralism in Literature*. New Haven: Yale UP, 1974.

Schücking, Levin L. *Character Problems in Shakespeare's Plays: A Guide to the Better Understanding of the Dramatist*. London: Harrap, 1922.

Scott, Sir Walter, ed. *The Secret History of the Court of James the First*. Edinburgh: J. Ballantyne, 1811.

Scullard, H. H. *From the Gracchi to Nero: A History of Rome from 133 BC to AD 68*. 5th ed. London: Methuen, 1982.

Sedgwick, Eve Kosofsky. "Pedagogy in the Context of an Antihomophobic Project," *The Politics of Education*. Ed. Darryl J. Gless and Barbara Herrnstein Smith. Special Issue of the *South Atlantic Quarterly* 89 (1990): 139–56.

Segar, William. *Honor, Military and Ciuill, contained in foure Bookes*. London: 1602.

Sewell, Arthur. *Character and Society in Shakespeare*. Oxford: Oxford UP, 1951.

*Shakespeare Quarterly 40: Annotated World Bibliography for 1988* (1990): 521–962.

*Shakespeare Survey 34: Characterization in Shakespeare*. Cambridge: Cambridge UP, 1981.

Shakespeare, William. *Hamlet*. Ed. Harold Jenkins. London: Methuen (The Arden Shakespeare), 1982.

———. *1 Henry IV*. Ed. A. R. Humphreys. London and New York: Methuen (The Arden Shakespeare), 1985.

———. *2 Henry IV*. Ed. A. R. Humphreys. London and New York: Methuen (The Arden Shakespeare), 1980.

———. *Henry V*. Ed. J. H. Walter. London and New York: Methuen (The Arden Shakespeare), 1985.

———. *Julius Caesar*. Ed. Arthur Humphreys. Oxford: Clarendon, 1984.

———. *Love's Labor's Lost*. Ed. Richard David. London: Methuen (The Arden Shakespeare), 1951.

———. *The Merchant of Venice*. Ed. John Russell Brown. London: Methuen (The Arden Shakespeare), 1976.

———. *Richard II*. Ed. Stanley Wells. New Penguin Shakespeare. Harmondsworth: Penguin, 1969.

———. *Richard II*. Ed. Petter Ure. London and New York: Methuen (The Arden Shakespeare), 1983.

———. *The Complete Works*. Ed. Hardin Craig and David Bevington. Glenview, IL: Scott, 1973.

———. *The Complete Works of William Shakespeare*. Ed. David Bevington. Glenview, IL: Scott, Foresman, 1980.

Shuger, Debora K. *Sacred Rhetoric: The Christian Grand Style in the English Renaissance*. Princeton: Princeton UP, 1988.

Sidney, Philip. *Miscellaneous Prose of Sir Philip Sidney*. Ed. Katherine Duncan-Jones and J. A. Van Dorsten. Oxford: Clarendon, 1973.

Skura, Meredith. "Shakespeare's Psychology: Characterization in Shakespeare." *William Shakespeare: His World, His Work, His Influence*. Ed. John F. Andrews. Vol 2. New York: Scribner's, 1985. 571–87. 3 vols.

Smith, Barbara Hernstein. *Contingencies of Value: Alternative Perspectives for Critical Theory*. Cambridge: Harvard UP, 1989.

Smith, Gordon Ross. "Shakespeare's *Henry V*: Another Part of the Critical Forest." *Journal of the History of Ideas* 37 (1976): 3–26.

Smith, Paul. *Discerning the Subject*. Minneapolis: U of Minnesota P, 1988.

Sorge, Thomas. "The Failure of Orthodoxy in *Coriolanus*." Howard and O'Connor 225–41.

Sowernam, Ester [pseud.]. *Ester hath hang'd Haman; or, An Answere To a lewd Pamphlet, entituled, The Arraignment of Women. With the arraignment of lewd, idle, froward, and vnconstant men, and Hvsbands*. 1617. STC 22974.

Speght, Rachel. A *Mouzell for Melastomvs, The cynicall Bayter of, and foule mouthed Barker against Evahs Sex; or, An Apologeticall Answere to that Irreligious and Illiterate Pamphlet made by Io. Sw. and by him Intituled "The Arraignment of Women."* 1617. STC 23058.

Spencer, Hazelton. *The Art and Life of William Shakespeare*. New York: Harcourt, 1940.

Spivak, Gayatri Chakravorty. "Displacement and the Discourse of Woman." *Displacement: Derrida and After*. Ed. Mark Krupnick. Bloomington: Indiana UP, 1983. 169–95.

———. "Feminism and Deconstruction, Again: Negotiating with Unacknowledged Masculinism." Brennan 206–23.

Sprinker, Michael. *Imaginary Relations: Aesthetics and Ideology in the Theory of Historical Materialism*. London: Verso, 1987.

———. "Knowing, Believing, Doing—Or, How Can We Study and Why Should We Anyway?" *ADE Bulletin* (Spring 1991): 46–55.

Stallybrass, Peter. "*Macbeth* and Witchcraft." Brown, ed. *Focus* 189–209.

———. "Rethinking Text and History." *LTP: Journal of Literature Teaching Politics* 2 (1983): 97–107.

States, Bert O. *Great Reckonings in Little Rooms: On the Phenomenology of the Theater*. Berkeley: U of California P, 1985.

Stewart, J. I. M. *Characters and Motive in Shakespeare*. London: Longman's, 1949.

Stirling, Brents. *Unity in Shakespearean Tragedy: The Interplay of Theme and Character*. New York: Gordian, 1956.

Stone, Lawrence. "The Educational Revolution in England 1560–1640." *Past and Present* 28 (1964): 41–80.

———. *The Crisis of the Aristocracy 1558–1641*. Abridged ed. London: Oxford UP, 1967.

———. *The Family, Sex and Marriage 1500–1800*. Abridged ed. Harmondsworth: Penguin, 1979.

———. "Interpersonal Violence in English Society 1300–1800." *Past and Present* 101 (1983): 22–33.

Strawson, P. F. *Individuals: An Essay in Descriptive Metaphysics*. London: Methuen, 1959.

Swetnam, Joseph. *The Arraignment of Lewde, idle, froward, and vnconstant women: Or the vanitie of them, choose you whether*. 1615. STC 23533.

"Swetnam the Woman-hater Arraigned by Women." *Swetnam the Woman-hater: The Controversy and the Play*. Ed. Coryl Crandall. Lafayette: Purdue U Studies, 1969.

Taylor, Lily Ross. *Party Politics in the Age of Caesar*. 1949. Berkeley: U of California P, 1971.

Tennenhouse, Leonard. *Power on Display: The Politics of Shakespeare's Genres*. New York: Methuen, 1986.

Thompson, Anne. " 'The Warrant of Womanhood': Shakespeare and Feminist Criticism." Holderness, ed. 74–88.

Thompson, John B. *Studies in the Theory of Ideology*. Berkeley: U of California P, 1984.

Tillyard, E. M. W. *Shakespeare's History Plays*. London: Chatto, 1948.

Toren, John. *New Republic* Aug. 28 1989: 6, 41.

Traversi, Derek A. *Shakespeare from* Richard II *to* Henry V. Stanford: Stanford UP, 1957.

Van Doren, Mark. *Shakespeare*. New York: Holt, 1939.

Veeser, H. Aram, ed. *The New Historicism*. New York: Routledge, 1989.

Velz, John W. "*Orator* and *Imperator* in *Julius Caesar*: Style and the Process of Roman History." *Shakespeare Studies* 15 (1982): 55–75.

Vickers, Brian. "The Emergence of Character Criticism, 1774–1800." *Shakespeare Survey* 34 (1981): 11–21.

Voloshinov, V. "Discourse in Life and Discourse in Poetry: Questions of Sociological Poetics." Trans. John Richmond. *Russian Poetics in Translation*. Ed. Ann Shukman and L. M. O'Toole. Oxford: RPT Publications, 1983. 5–29.

Wales, Julia G. *Character and Action in Shakespeare*. Madison: U Wisconsin P, 1923.

Walter, J. H. "Introduction." *Henry* V. London: Methuen (The Arden Shakespeare), 1983. xi–xlii.

Waswo, Richard. *Language and Meaning in the Renaissance*. Princeton: Princeton: UP, 1987.

Wayne, Don. "Power, Politics and the Shakespearean Text." Howard and O'Connor 47–67.

Wayne, Valerie, ed. *The Matter of Difference: Materialist Feminist Criticism of Shakespeare*. Hemel Hempstead: Harvester Wheatsheaf, 1990.

Weil, Herbert S., Jr. "On Expectation and Surprise: Shakespeare's Construction of Character." *Shakespeare Survey* 34 (1981): 39–50.

Weimann, Robert. *Shakespeare and the Popular Tradition in the Theater*. Ed. Robert Schwartz. Baltimore: The Johns Hopkins UP, 1978.

———. "Society and the Individual in Shakespeare's Conception of Character." *Shakespeare Survey* 34 (1981): 23–31.

———. "Mimesis in *Hamlet*." Parker and Hartman 275–91.

———. "Toward a Literary Theory of Ideology." Howard and O'Connor 265–72.

Weitzman, Arthur J. Forum, *PMLA* 104 (1989): 357.

Wells, Stanley, ed. *Richard II*, by William Shakespeare. Harmondsworth: Penguin, 1973.

Wentersdorf, Karl P. "The Conspiracy of Silence in *Henry* V." *Shakespeare Quarterly* 27 (1976): 264–87.

Whateley, Thomas. *Remarks on Some of the Characters of Shakespeare*. London: 1785.

Wheeler, Richard P. *Shakespeare's Development and the Problem Comedies: Turn and Counter-Turn*. Berkeley: U of California P, 1981.

———. *The Whole Journey: Shakespeare's Power of Development*. Berkeley: U of California P, 1986.

Wiles, David. *Shakespeare's Clowns*. Cambridge: Cambridge UP, 1987.

Williams, Raymond, *Marxism and Literature*. London: Oxford UP, 1977.

———. *Writing in Society*. London: Verso, 1984.

———. *Keywords: A Vocabulary of Culture and Society*. Rev. ed. New York: Oxford UP, 1985.

Williamson, Marilyn. *The Patriarchy of Shakespeare's Comedies: The Plays in History*. Detroit: Wayne State UP, 1986.

Wilson, Elkin Calhoun. *England's Eliza*. Cambridge: Harvard UP, 1939.

Wilson, John Dover. *The Fortunes of Falstaff*. Cambridge: Cambridge UP; New York: Macmillan, 1944.

——— and T. C. Worsley. *Shakespeare's Histories at Stratford, 1951*. London: Max Reinhardt, 1952.

Wofford, Susanne. "The Choice of Achilles: Action and Figure in Epic Narrative." Diss. Yale U, 1982.

Wolterstorff, Nicholas. "Characters and their Names." *Poetics* 8 (1979): 101–27.

Woodbridge, Linda. *Women and the English Renaissance: Literature and the Nature of Womankind, 1540–1620*. Urbana: U of Illinois P, 1984.

Yates, Frances A. *Astraea: The Imperial Theme in the Sixteenth Century*. London: Routledge, 1975.

Young, David. *The Action to the Word; Structure and Style in Shakespearean Tragedy*. New Haven: Yale UP, 1990.

Žižek, Slavoj. *The Sublilme Object of Ideology*. London: Verso, 1989.

# Index


Abercrombie, Nicholas 145n. 25
Abrams, M. H 92–93, 94n. 3
Adelman, Janet 2, 24, 52, 75n. 4, 152, 155, 161, 165n. 3, 166n. 6
Alter, Robert 80–83, 94n. 1
Althusser, Louis 5–6, 7–8, 11, 23, 40, 51, 85, 95n. 5, 97n. 12, 119, 121, 142n. 3, 147
Aristotle 140
Armstrong, Paul B. 186
Augustine, St. 190
Austen, Jane 112n. 6
Austin, J. L. 110, 209

Bacon, Sir Francis 191
Bakhtin, Mikhail 247, 256
Balch, Stephen H. 32
Bamber, Linda 61, 62, 68–70, 72, 75n. 4, 75–76n. 7, 76n. 10, 167–69, 176, 183n. 2, 221n. 1
Barber, C. L. 33, 240n. 8, 257n. 5
Barker, Francis 11n. 3, 20nn. 1, 2, 21nn. 5, 6; 58n. 2, 83–85, 86–87, 92, 95n. 3
Barroll, J. Leeds 141, 145n. 23
Barth, Hans 35
Barthes, Roland 17, 18, 20n. 3, 67, 68, 81, 99, 239
Barton, Anne 84, 191, 195
Battenhouse, Roy 60n. 15, 275n. 1
Baxter, John 240n. 6
Bayley, John 144n. 12
Beaumann, Sally 237–38, 240n. 9
Becher, William 165n. 4
Bell, Daniel 34, 35, 88
Belsey, Catherine 16, 18, 20nn. 1, 3, 21n. 6, 23, 58n. 2, 75n. 2, 81, 86, 87, 95n. 5, 108–109, 143n. 3, 148, 169, 181, 183n. 3, 275n. 4
Bennett, William 31–32
Berger, Harry, Jr. 4, 94n. 3, 105, 132, 143nn. 4, 5; 280
Berger, Thomas L. 145n. 24
Bevington, David 12n. 12, 240n. 4
Bhaskar, Roy 122, 128n. 1
Biggins, Dennis 160
Birnbaum, Milton 29, 68
Blake, Howard 262, 275n. 3
Blake, William 107
Blanpied, John W. 240nn. 5, 6
Blessed, Brian 260
Bloom, Allan 4, 31, 127, 187–90, 192, 201–202, 202n. 1, 203n. 9, 279
Blumenfeld-Kosinski, Renate 163
Bodin, Jean 254
Booth, Stephen 132
Booth, Wayne C. 202
Booty, John E. 198
Bourdieu, Pierre 40–41
Braden, Gordon 135, 144n. 11
Bradford, William C., Jr. 145n. 24
Bradley, A. C. 135, 138, 139, 140, 275n. 1
Branagh, Kenneth 4, 259–61, 267–74, 281
Brecht, Berthold 39, 43, 102

Breight, Curt 94–95n. 3
Brennan, Teresa 74n. 1
Breton, Nicholas 243, 248
Bristol, Michael D. 4, 6, 7, 9, 11nn. 3, 9; 15, 21n. 5, 32, 39, 45–46, 47–51, 52, 53, 54, 56, 58nn. 2, 3; 79, 87, 88, 90–91, 117, 132–33, 143n. 3, 147, 149, 150, 203n. 8
Brown, John Russell 259
Brown, Norman O. 241, 282, 283
Brown, Paul 21n. 6
Burckhardt, Jacob 135, 144n. 11, 211
Burckhardt, Sigurd 222n. 9, 231–32, 240n. 5
Burger, Peter 35, 38
Burke, Kenneth 86
Bynam, Caroline E 165n. 3

Cairns, David 257n. 3
Calderwood, James 206, 240nn. 5, 6, 7, 8
Callaghan, Dympna 154, 162
Camden, William 214, 222–23n. 10
Campbell, Lily B. 257n. 1
Carroll, William 206–207, 209
Castiglione, Baldassare 208, 222n. 7
Cave Terence 222n. 12
Cavell, Stanley 58n. 3, 143n. 8
Charles I 181
Chase, Cynthia 73, 77n. 12
Chidley 181
Chodorow, Nancy 53–54, 57
Chomsky, Noam 8–9
Cicero 194, 200
Cixous, Hélène 23
Clarke, Mary Cowden 145n. 25
Clover, Carol 158
Cohen, Derek 133, 143n. 7
Cohen, Walter 11n. 4, 38, 58n. 2, 75n. 3, 165n. 5, 295
Coleridge, Samuel T. 4, 139–40
Cook, Carol 3, 4, 12n. 9, 76n. 11, 115–16, 286, 287, 293
Coursen, Herbert 240nn. 1, 8
Coward, Rosalind 23, 108
Cox, John 258n. 11
Craig, Hardin 33
Crane, R. S. 103, 112n. 4
Crews, Frederick 112n. 5
Culler, Jonathan 92, 93, 145n. 21
Curtis, Mark H. 222n. 5
Cutts, John 94n. 3

Danson, Lawrence 192
Darcie, Abraham 165n. 4
Dash, Irene 61, 62, 75n. 4, 76n. 11, 105
Dekker, Thomas 243
Delany, Paul 59n. 8
de Man, Paul 107
Derrida, Jacques 69, 76n. 8, 107, 112n. 5, 140, 143n. 9, 252
Dollimore, Jonathan 6, 11n. 3, 12n. 10, 20n. 2, 58n. 2, 66, 96n. 11, 143n. 3, 164, 232, 275n. 1
Donald, James 147, 148
Donne, John 86
Donoghue, Denis 112–13n. 6
Drakakis, John 11n. 2, 21n. 5
Dryden, John 135
Durkheim, Emile 36, 38–39
Dusinberre, Juliet 61, 62, 169, 181, 183n. 3

Eagleton, Terry 11n. 1, 19, 20n. 2, 21n. 5, 58n. 2, 81, 85, 87, 95n. 6, 113n. 9
Earl, Donald 190
Easton, Richard 260
Elam, Keir 206–207, 221n. 2, 222n. 8
Eliot, T. S. 112n. 2
Elizabeth I 153, 241, 243, 246, 248, 249, 251, 254, 257n. 1
Ellis, John 23, 59n. 12, 108, 112n. 5
Emerson, Ralph. W. 38
Engels, F. 37, 38, 119
Erasmus 203n. 6

Erickson, Peter 221n. 1
Evans, Edith 192
Evans, Malcolm 20nn. 1, 2, 21n. 5, 58n. 2

Felperin, Howard 95n. 3, 145n. 24
Ferguson, Margaret 12n. 14, 28
Ferry, Anne 222n. 8
Feyerabend, Paul 122
Fineman, Daniel 144n. 16
Fineman, Joel 135, 142n. 12, 144n. 12, 145n. 21
Fish, Stanley 18, 87, 95–96nn. 7, 9; 97n. 13, 121, 128n. 1
Fitter, Chris 4, 281–82
Florio, John 247
Forset, Edward 249
Foucault, Michel 17, 20n. 3, 67, 99, 140
Fox-Genovese, Elizabeth 164
Fraser, Russell 132
French, Marilyn 61, 62, 75n. 4
French, Peter 145n. 25
Freud, Sigmund 75n. 4
Fuller, Thomas 244
Frye, Northrop 33, 45, 140
Furness, Horace Howard 133
Fuss, Diana 76nn. 8–9, 77n. 13

Gadamer, Hans-Georg 42
Gallie, W. B. 88
Gallop, Jane 62, 70, 71–72
Garrett, John 278
Gayley, Charles Mills 33
Gibson, Anthony 165n. 4
Gilbert, Felix 222n. 7
Gless, Darryl J. 4, 5, 279, 281
Goddard, Harold C. 275n. 1
Godshalk, William L. 143n. 4
Gohlke, Madelon (Sprengnether), 65, 75n. 4, 105, 166n. 6
Goldberg, Jonathan 62, 63, 68–74, 76nn. 9, 10; 77n. 12, 95n. 6, 143n. 9, 144n. 14, 145n. 24, 164, 165n. 5
Goldman, Michael 141
Gombrich, E. H. 186, 188, 203n. 4
Gonne, Maude 112n. 6
Gosynhyll, Edward 165n. 4
Gould, Gerald 275n. 1
Graff, Gerald 4, 7, 8, 18, 21n. 4, 59n. 12, 116, 121, 293
Gramsci, Antonio 23, 37, 119
Granville-Barker, Harley 206, 280
Greenblatt, Stephen 4, 58n. 3, 84, 166n. 5, 211, 245–46, 250, 275n. 1
Greene, Gayle 3, 4, 7, 11n. 9, 12n. 11, 15, 45–46, 51–58, 58n. 1, 59nn. 8, 10; 61, 62–63, 76n. 11, 79–80, 85, 86, 88, 90, 94, 105, 108–110, 117, 123, 143n. 3, 190, 191, 194, 195, 203n. 8, 287, 293–94
Greene, Thomas 223n. 17
Guess, Raymond 35
Gurr, Andrew 149
Gurr, T. R. 153

Habermas, Jürgen 42
Hall, Joseph 145n. 20, 248
Hall, Peter 273
Hall, Stuart 95n. 4, 147, 148
Hawkins, Harriet 34, 41
Hawkins, Michael 149, 150
Hazlitt, William 4, 138, 139, 275n. 1
Heilbrun, Carolyn 62, 73
Helms, Jesse 6, 125, 281
Henry VII 153
Henry VIII 254
Hesse, Mary 113n. 9
Hexter, J. H. 222n. 5
Hibbard, G. R. 240n. 6
Hill, Christopher 180–81
Hill, Stephen 145n. 25
Hobbes, Thomas 209, 254, 255, 257n. 8
Holderness, Graham 5, 12n. 10, 20n. 2, 21nn. 5, 6; 58n. 2, 174, 183n. 5, 275n. 4, 279–80
Holinshed, Raphael 150, 252

Holland, Peter 145n. 24
Horwitz, Howard 97n. 13
Howard, Jean 20nn. 1, 2, 28, 75n. 2, 143n. 3
Howe, Irving 112n. 1
Hulme, Peter 11n. 3, 20n. 2, 21nn. 5, 6; 58n. 2, 83–85, 86–87, 92, 95n. 3
Humphreys, Arthur 193, 202
Hunt, Marvin 32

Irigaray, Luce 62, 68, 70, 76n. 9

Jacobi, Derek 94n. 3, 270
Jaffa, Harry V. 187
James I 151, 153, 249, 254–55, 257n. 10
Jameson, Fredric 58n. 2, 59–60n. 14, 95n. 6
Jardine, Lisa 74n. 2, 76n. 11, 169, 183n. 3
Jay, Martin 95n. 5
Johnson, Samuel 4, 135–36, 137, 144n. 16

Kahn, Coppélia 61, 62, 66, 75n. 4, 105, 166n. 6, 167–69, 173, 183nn. 2, 3; 205–206, 221n. 1
Kahn, Victoria 4, 7, 9, 11n. 9, 89, 113n. 7, 116, 203n. 8
Kastan, David Scott 4, 257n. 8, 282
Kavanagh, James H. 95n. 5
Kermode, Frank 84, 94n. 2, 138–39, 144n. 18
Kernan, Alvin B. 8, 10, 11n. 1, 240n. 8
Kerrigan, William 135, 144n. 11
Kimball, Roger 127
Kimbrough, Robert 105
Kirschbaum, Leo 145n. 20
Kittredge, George Lyman 33, 133
Knapp, Robert S. 144n. 14
Knight, G. Wilson 132
Knights, L. C. 139, 140
Kolodny, Annette 25
Kozintsev, Grigori 273
Kramer, Hilton 112n. 2
Kuhn, T. S. 90, 122

Lacan, Jacques 40, 66, 68, 69, 75n. 4, 76n. 8, 77n. 12, 255, 257n. 9
Laclau, Ernesto 147
La Guardia, Eric 240n. 8
Lanham, Richard 96n. 9
Leggatt, Alexander 222n. 11
Lenin, V. I. 35, 119
Lenz, Carolyn Ruth 61, 76n. 11
Lévi-Strauss, Claude 223n. 15
Levin, Richard 2–4, 6–7, 9, 11nn. 5, 6, 9; 12nn. 9, 11 20n. 2, 23–29, 33–35, 41–43, 45–46, 55, 59nn. 8, 11; 60n. 15, 61–68, 69, 74, 75n. 6, 79–80, 82–83, 88, 90, 92, 96n. 10, 99–111, 112nn. 3, 4; 113nn. 7, 8; 115–17, 121–27, 132, 169, 185–86, 187, 202, 277–79, 282, 285–86, 287, 290–95, 296nn. 1, 2, 3, 4; 297nn. 6, 7, 8, 10; 298n. 11
Lichtheim, George 35
Lincoln, Abraham 187
Lipking, Lawrence 112n. 2
Livingston, Paisley 96n. 12
Lodowick, Lloyd 165n. 4
London, Herbert 32
Lysenko 59n. 9

Macherey, Pierre 147–48
Mack, Maynard 145n. 20
MacCullum, M. W. 192, 201
Mannheim, Karl 86, 89
Marcus, Leah 96n. 10
Marlowe, Christopher 132
Marx, Karl 5, 34, 36–37, 38, 43, 89, 119, 121, 142n. 3, 147
Mary (Queen) 254
Matthews, Honor 145n. 20, 275n. 1
Maus, Katharine Eisaman 5, 280
McDiarmid, Ian 264
McLaughlin, M. M. 165n. 3

McLuskie, Kathleen 20n. 1, 21n. 6, 28, 61, 62, 75n. 2, 169, 183nn. 2, 3
Melchiori, Giorgio 141
Miles, Gary B. 200
Milton, John 95n. 6, 96n. 10, 107, 296
Miola, Robert S. 203n. 5
Moi, Toril 20n. 3, 21n. 4; 58nn. 1, 2
Montaigne, Michel de 6, 191
Montrose, Louis A. 66, 75n. 2, 257n. 6
Morgann, Maurice 4, 80, 135, 136–39, 139, 140, 144nn. 13, 16, 17
Mueller, Martin 59n. 12
Muir, Kenneth 141, 223n. 11
Mullaney, Steven 257n. 6
Munda, Constantia 165n. 4
Musil, Robert 144n. 12

Naunton, Sir Robert 246
Neely, Carol Thomas 61, 76n. 11, 183n. 1, 221n. 1
Newman, Karen 75n. 2
Noble, Adrian 260, 261–67, 269, 272
Novy, Marianne 65, 221n. 1
Nussbaum, Martha 187
Nuttall, A. D. 141

O'Connor, Marion F. 28, 143n. 3
Ohmann, Richard 119
Olivier, Sir Lawrence 259
Ornstein, Robert 240nn. 1, 2
Overbury, Sir Thomas 145n. 20
Ovid 96n. 9
Ozick, Cynthia 112n. 2

Palmer, John 145n. 20, 193, 275n. 1
Parker, G. F. 136
Parker, Patricia 221, 222n. 13
Paster, Gail Kern 201, 203n. 6
Patterson, Annabel 12n. 10, 139, 257n. 7
Patterson, Lee 148
Pearson, D'Orsay 94n. 3
Pechter, Edward 4, 7, 11n. 9, 12n. 11, 80, 93–94, 123, 128n. 1, 145n. 18, 279
Perry, John 145n. 25
Pinciss, Gerald M. 145n. 24
Plato 89, 96n. 9, 187, 206
Plutarch 157–58, 165n. 4, 195, 199
Polanski, Roman 271
Pope, Alexander 135
Popper, Karl 34
Porter, Joseph A. 4, 144n. 13, 240n. 8, 280
Potter, Nick 12n. 10, 174, 183n. 5
Prior, Moody A. 112n. 3
Purdy, Dwight H. 68
Puttenham, George 256
Pye, Christopher 250, 257n. 8

Quayle, Anthony 233–34, 237, 239

Rabkin, Norman 240n. 4, 275n. 1, 282
Ravenscroft, Christopher 260
Redgrave, Michael 237
Rice, Julian 60n. 15
Richards, Shaun 257n. 3
Richmond, Hugh 60n. 15
Ripley, John 192
Roesen, Bobbyann [Anne Barton] 222n. 11
Rooney, Ellen 21n. 5
Rorty, Amélie 145n. 25
Rorty, Richard 91, 92, 93, 96n. 9, 97nn. 12, 13, 121
Rose, Jacqueline 11n. 3, 201

Salingar, Leo 141
Schanzer, Ernest 197
Scholes, Robert 25
Schücking, Levin L. 145n. 20
Scott, Sir Walter 257n. 10
Scullard, H. H. 189, 203n. 3
Sedgwick, Eve Kosofsky 203n. 9
Segar, William 255
Sewell, Arthur 140

Shakespeare, William
- *As You Like It* 182, 221n. 1
- *Coriolanus* 5, 148, 149–50, 152, 154, 155–59, 163, 164–65, 280–81
- *Cymbeline* 220
- *Hamlet* 91, 132, 228, 247, 264, 274
- *Henriad* (*1 Henry IV*, *2 Henry IV*, *Henry V*) 4, 225–40
- *1 Henry IV* 4, 172, 180, 241–58, 282
- *2 Henry IV* 231, 236, 255–56
- *Henry V* 4, 226, 228, 230–31, 234, 236, 237, 238, 251, 259–75, 281–82
- *Henry VI* 172
- *Julius Caesar* 4, 5, 9, 71, 187–203, 228, 279
- *King Lear* 172, 273
- *Love's Labor's Lost* 5, 206–23, 280
- *Macbeth* 5, 102, 107, 148, 149, 150–53, 154, 159–65, 271
- *Measure for Measure* 220
- *The Merchant of Venice* 71, 76n. 9, 172, 221n. 1, 263
- *A Midsummer Night's Dream* 220, 273
- *Much Ado About Nothing* 220
- *Richard II* 5, 167–83, 229–30, 234, 237, 238, 256, 279–80
- *The Taming of the Shrew* 205, 221n. 1, 295
- *Two Gentlemen of Verona* 220
- *Troilus and Cressida* 91
- *Twelfth Night* 134, 221n. 1

Shelley, Percy Bysshe 107
Shuger, Debora K. 195
Sidney, Sir Philip 247, 248, 251
Sinfield, Alan 11n. 3, 58n. 2, 66, 96n. 11, 232, 275n. 1
Skura, Meredith 143n. 8, 145n. 20
Smith, Barbara Herrnstein 96n. 9
Smith, Gordon Ross 275n. 1
Smith, Paul 95nn. 4, 5, 96–97n. 12
Snow, Edward 105
Sorge, Thomas 149
Speght, Rachel 285
Spencer, Hazelton 275n. 1
Spenser, Edmund 172
Spivak, Gayatri 63, 68, 77n. 13
Sprinker, Michael 4, 6, 11n. 6, 12n. 9, 128n. 1, 147, 292
Stalin, Joseph 59n. 7
Stallybrass, Peter 20n. 2, 152
States, Bert O. 132, 143n. 6
Stewart, J. I. M. 140, 193
Stirling, Brents 145n. 20
Stone, Lawrence 153–54, 180–81, 222n. 5
Strauss, Leo 187
Strawson, P. F. 145n. 25
Swetnam, Joseph 285, 286, 297n. 10

Tate, Nahum 165n. 4
Taylor, Lily Ross 190, 203n. 3
Tennenhouse, Leonard 165–66n. 5, 232–33, 257n. 5
Theobald, Lewis 135
Thompson, Anne 183n. 1
Thompson, John B. 40
Thorndike, Sybil 192
Tillyard, E. M. W. 226, 240nn. 1, 8
Toren, John 112n. 1
Tracy, Destutt de 89
Traversi, D. A. 226, 240n. 6
Turner, Bryan S. 145n. 25
Turner, John 12n. 10, 174, 183n. 5
Tuvil, Daniel 165n. 4

Uehling, Theodore E., Jr. 145n. 25

Van Doren, Mark 275n. 1
Velz, John W. 190
Vergil 96n. 9
Vickers, Brian 141, 144n. 13
Voloshinov, V. 6

Wales, Julia G. 145n. 20
Walter, J. H. 259–60

Wayne, Don 38
Wayne, Valerie 183n. 3
Wettstein, Howard K. 145n. 25
Weil, Herbert S. 141
Weimann, Robert 37, 141, 145n. 24, 247
Weitzman, Arthur J. 29, 67–68
Weldon, Sir Anthony 257n. 10
Wells, Stanley 183n. 4
Wentersdorf, Karl P. 275n. 1
Whateley, Thomas 144n. 13
Wheeler, Richard P. 240n. 6
Wiles, David 258n. 11
Williams, Raymond 37, 88, 92–93, 142–43n. 3, 145n. 20, 256
Williamson, Marilyn L. 5, 164, 280–81
Wilson, Elkin Calhoun 257n. 4
Wilson, J. Dover 145n. 20, 233–34
Woffington, Peg 192
Wofford, Susanne 40
Wolterstorff, Nicholas 145n. 24
Woodbridge, Linda 11n 6, 75n. 2, 201, 203n. 6
Worsley, T. S. 233–34

Yates, Frances A. 257n. 4
Yeats, William B. 112n. 6
Young, David 132, 143n. 6

Žižek, Slavoj 257n. 9

# Contributors

**Harry Berger, Jr.**, is Professor of Literature and Art History at the University of California, Santa Cruz. *Second World and Green World*, *Revisionary Play*, and *Imaginary Audition* are among his recent publications. He is currently completing books on Shakespearean discourses, the second tetralogy, Rembrandt's self-portraits, and Plato's dialogues.

**Michael D. Bristol** is Professor of English at McGill University in Montreal. His most recent book is entitled *Shakespeare's America, America's Shakespeare*. His next book will be a study of temporality in Shakespeare.

**Carol Cook** is Assistant Professor of English at Princeton University. Her essays on Shakespeare have appeared in *PMLA*, *Theatre Journal*, and she has an essay forthcoming in *Shakespearean Tragedy and Gender*, eds. Shirley Garner and Madelon Sprengnether. Her current book-length project addresses subjectivity and gender in Shakespeare.

**Lawrence Danson** is Professor of English at Princeton University. His work on Shakespeare and Renaissance drama includes *Tragic Alphabet: Shakespeare's Drama of Language* and *The Harmonies of* The Merchant of Venice. He is currently editing Oscar Wilde's essays for the Oxford English Texts edition of Wilde's complete works, and co-editing (with Ivo Kamps) Thomas Middleton's *The Phoenix*.

**Chris Fitter** gained his degrees from St. John's College, Oxford, receiving his D.Phil. in 1989. He has published articles on Milton and Henry Vaughan and several book reviews on Shakespeare. He is currently finishing an interdisciplinary book entitled *Landscape in Poetry from Homer to Milton*. He is Assistant Professor of English at the University of Mississippi.

**Darryl J. Gless** is Associate Professor of English and Associate Dean of General Education at the University of North Carolina, Chapel Hill. He is the author of *"Measure for Measure," the Law, and the Convent*, and he has recently completed a book titled *Dogmatic Mutability: Reformed Theology and Spenser's "Faerie Queene."*

**Gerald Graff** is George M. Pullman Professor of English and Education at the University of Chicago. His publications include *Professing Literature: An Institutional History*. He is currently finishing a book on the conflicts over the curriculum.

**Gayle Greene** is Professor of English and Women's Studies at Scripps College and has published widely on Shakespeare, women writers, and feminist literary theory. She co-edited *The Woman's Part: Feminist Criticism of Shakespeare* and *Making a Difference: Feminist Fiction and the Tradition*. Her book *Breaking the Circle: Feminist Fiction and the Tradition*, a study of women writers of the 1960s, 1970s, and 1980s, will be published by Indiana University Press in 1991.

**Graham Holderness** is Head of Drama at the Roehampton Institute, London. His books include *Shakespeare's History*, and a Penguin critical study of *Richard II*. He is co-author of *Shakespeare: The Play of History*. He is currently working on a book concerned with the cultural production of narrative.

**Victoria Kahn** is Associate Professor of English at Princeton University. She is the author of *Rhetoric, Prudence and Skepticism in the Renaissance*. Currently she is working on a book on conflict and consensus in Renaissance humanism.

**Ivo Kamps**, an Assistant Professor of English at the University of Mississippi, received his Ph.D. from Princeton University in 1990. He is currently finishing a book on Renaissance historiography and the Stuart historical drama, and co-editing *The Phoenix* for the Oxford complete works of Thomas Middleton.

**David Scott Kastan** is Professor of English and Comparative Literature at Columbia University. He is the author of *Shakespeare and the Shapes of Time* and the forthcoming *Proud Majesty Made a Subject: Representation and Authority in the Drama of Early Modern England*. He just finished co-editing (with Peter Stallybrass) *Staging the Renaissance: Essays on Elizabethan and Jacobean Drama* (Routledge, 1991).

## *Contributors*

**Richard Levin,** Professor of English at the State University of New York, Stony Brook, is the author of *The Multiple Plot in English Renaissance Drama* and *New Readings vs. Old Plays: Recent Trends in the Reinterpretation of English Renaissance Drama*. The paper and essay published here are part of a larger project devoted to a systematic critique of the new approaches to Renaissance drama.

**Katharine Eisaman Maus,** Associate Professor of English at the University of Virginia, is the author of *Ben Jonson and the Roman Frame of Mind,* and co-editor of *Soliciting Interpretations: Literary Theory and English Seventeenth-Century Poetry*. She is writing a book on interiority and spectatorship in the English Renaissance.

**Edward Pechter,** Professor of English at Concordia University in Montreal, has written *Dryden's Classical Theory of Literature* and essays about Renaissance plays and current criticism, including "In Defense of Jargon," forthcoming in *Textual Practice*.

**Joseph A. Porter,** Associate Professor of English at Duke University, is the author of *Shakespeare's Mercutio: His History and Drama* and *The Drama of Speech Acts: Shakespeare's Lancastrian Tetralogy*. Character and ideology have concerned him in this and other studies of Shakespeare published and in process.

**Michael Sprinker** is Professor of English and Comparative Literature at the State University of New York, Stony Brook. He is co-editor with Mike Davis of the Haymarket series from Verso. His current labors include a book on Proust and the Third Republic.

**Marilyn L. Williamson** is Distinguished Professor of English and Deputy Provost at Wayne State University. Her most recent publication is *Raising Their Voices: British Women Writers 1650–1750*.

**Linda Woodbridge** is Professor of English at the University of Alberta. She is the author of *Women and the Renaissance*. She is also co-editor (with Edward Berry) of a forthcoming collection on Shakespeare and ritual, and she is nearing completion of a book on Shakespeare and magical thinking.